Churchill & Son

Also by Josh Ireland

The Traitors

Churchill & Son

JOSH IRELAND

JOHN MURRAY

First published in Great Britain in 2021 by John Murray (Publishers)
An Hachette UK company

I

Copyright © Josh Ireland 2021
Published by arrangement with Dutton, an imprint of Penguin
Publishing Group, a division of Penguin Random House
LLC. First published in the United States in 2021.

A CIP catalogue record for this title is available from the British Library

Hardback ISBN 978-1-529-33775-4
Trade Paperback ISBN 978-1-529-33776-1
eBook ISBN 978-1-529-33777-8

Typeset in Bembo MT by Hewer Text UK Ltd, Edinburgh
Printed and bound in Great Britain by Clays Ltd, Elcograf S.p.A.

John Murray policy is to use papers that are natural, renewable and
recyclable products and made from wood grown in sustainable forests.
The logging and manufacturing processes are expected to conform
to the environmental regulations of the country of origin.

John Murray (Publishers)
Carmelite House
50 Victoria Embankment
London EC4Y oDZ

www.johnmurraypress.co.uk

For Ivy and Victoria

Contents

Prologue

WINSTON CHURCHILL'S HANDS were very white, delicate and slender, so slender that the triple-banded signet ring he liked to wear would sometimes slip from his fingers. One person who met him during the Second World War was surprised that a pair of such soft hands was holding off the Nazis so forcefully.

He was not alone. Many people, when meeting Churchill for the first time, were confounded by his hands' beauty, especially as he grew older and the rest of his body became coarse and bloated. Winston knew this and was proud of it. He could laugh off most insults but was hurt by a *Punch* cartoon in which his hands appeared podgy and shapeless: 'Look at my hands,' he complained to his doctor, Lord Moran, 'I have beautiful hands.'

Another thing people noticed was his hands' constant motion: the way he held his cigar – between the first finger and thumb – and rolled it untiringly around the rim of his coffee cup without seeming to have any idea what he was doing; or his habit of breaking matches.

Small, restless hands was a feature he shared with his only son, Randolph, who resembled him in so many ways. When Winston looked at Randolph, he knew that he had given him, or encouraged within him, the best elements of his own personality: kindness, originality, eccentricity, heedless bravery and a flamboyant disregard for anybody else's opinion. He would also have seen colossal faults: arrogance, recklessness, an uncontrollable temper and a perplexing weakness for self-sabotage.

There were other people about whom Winston Churchill felt as tenderly as he did for his son and there were other people who provoked in him insensate rage, but Randolph was the only person in his life to elicit both emotions.

He could draw from his father thoughts that read almost like love letters ('I have been very remiss in writing to you, but that is not because you are not constantly in my thoughts . . . I have so many things to tell you that I hardly know where to begin'), and yet he was also capable of making him so angry that those watching worried Winston would have a heart attack.

Randolph got under his father's skin, and in doing so, he left him exposed and raw, prey to gusts of emotion that he could not control. It was Randolph in whom his father confided his fears, plans and secrets. Whether they were friends or enemies (they could sometimes be both during the course of a single dinner), Winston was never more himself than in Randolph's company.

Randolph was glorious in his own way: a giver and devourer of pleasure, the kind of man who exploded into rooms, trailing whisky tumblers and mischief. He was born beautiful, blessed with eloquence, energy and a photographic memory that allowed him to recite verbatim whole passages of classic literature and history.

When Randolph was young, his father encouraged him, praised him, told him that the future was his to seize. Winston was determined that his son would not suffer the same neglect that had blighted his own childhood. He was also determined that between them they would build a dynasty to equal any in history. Winston was obsessed with his son, but he was also consumed by his own sense of destiny, his belief that fate had singled him out for a higher purpose. Everything and everyone were secondary to this. Randolph, whose loyalty to his father was so extreme that it came to hinder almost every aspect of his existence, would learn this to his cost.

This book is the story of their lives together, and how Winston built and broke his son.

I

Do Try to Get Papa to Come,
He Has Never Been

ONE NIGHT IN November 1947, Winston Churchill was sitting in the long dining room at Chartwell with Randolph and his daughter, Sarah. There was a gap in the conversation, which Randolph filled by 'suddenly' pointing to an empty chair and asking his father: 'If you had the power to put someone in that chair to join us now, whom would you choose?'

Randolph and Sarah sat back, expecting Winston to say Julius Caesar or Napoleon. Instead, he thought for a moment and then, 'very simply', said, 'Oh, my father, of course.'

Winston followed this by telling them a story. On a foggy winter evening he had been copying a portrait of his father, Lord Randolph Churchill, when just as he was trying to capture the twirl of his moustache, he realised that he had materialised before him, looking 'as I had read about him in his brief year of triumph'. Father and son talked about the ways in which the world had changed since the elder man's death, and the great events that had taken place, until the apparition suddenly said, 'I was not going to talk politics with a boy like you. Bottom of the school! Never passed any exams, except into the Cavalry! Wrote me stilted letters. I could not see how you would make your living on the little I could leave you and Jack [Winston's younger brother] . . . But then of course you were very young, and I loved you dearly. Old people are always very impatient with young ones. Fathers always expect their sons to have their virtues without their faults.'

As the conversation progressed, it became clear that Lord Randolph assumed his son had lived an undistinguished life as a mid-ranking army officer. You should have gone into politics, he told Winston, 'You might even have made a name for yourself.' With that the apparition lit a cigarette. As the match flared, he vanished.

Neither Randolph nor Sarah was sure at that moment whether Winston was recalling a particular dream or 'elaborating on some fanciful idea that had struck him earlier', although in the months before, he had complained of endless nightmares in which Lord Randolph had appeared to him.

But the story, which his family called 'The Dream' and which Winston referred to only by its original heading, 'Private Article', left both brother and sister hugely excited, and they urged their father to commit it to paper. Over the next few months, he worked obsessively at drafting and redrafting it. Then, for reasons he never disclosed, Winston locked it away in a private box for ten years. It only emerged, Randolph wrote, just before Winston's death, when he scribbled some final changes on the manuscript.

That Lord Randolph was on his mind even as his own life came to a close is not surprising. Winston never stopped thinking about the man he had hero-worshipped ever since he was a boy. He was, Winston would later say, 'the greatest and most powerful influence in my early life', a fearless, dynamic politician who died at the age of just forty-six. Winston learned his father's speeches by heart; took his 'politics unquestioningly from him'; and every step in his own career was accompanied by an insistent voice wondering whether Lord Randolph would have approved of the decisions he made.

The problem was that while he was alive, Lord Randolph barely spared his son a second glance.

Lord Randolph cut an unforgettable figure. His head was large, his body short and frail, his walrus moustache was extravagant and he was 'addicted to dressing loudly', but what struck those who met him most deeply was the pair of bulging eyes that gazed uncompromisingly back at them. He suffered from exophthalmos, which caused his eyeballs to protrude and made him seem as if looking at the world in a supercilious, offensive fashion. Which, in truth, he generally was. When he wanted, he could be charming and funny, but more often, especially when confronted by those he did not know, or disapproved of, he slipped into a glacial aristocratic hauteur.

The second son of the Duke of Marlborough, Lord Randolph had struggled at Eton and began his time at Oxford badly. He drank, broke windows and chased women. 'I don't like ladies at all,' he said. 'I like rough women who dance and sing and drink – the rougher the better.'

And yet he also possessed certain gifts. His memory was extraordinary. He could read a page from, say, Gibbon, and then repeat it verbatim. He was clever, quick and witty. These gifts were sufficient to gain him a respectable degree, which was considered so unusual for the son of a duke that it was immediately predicted that he would go on to achieve great things. (His position in society meant that an arrest for drunkenness and assault was something that could be overlooked.)

For a while it seemed that he would live a life governed by his worst qualities. A Grand Tour was followed by a brief period as an idler and a carouser. He was also afflicted by melancholy and bad nerves, and for a time these forced him to withdraw almost entirely from society. Instead, he read French novels and smoked Turkish cigarettes 'until his tongue was sore'.

But then he stood for his father's seat of Woodstock in 1874. In the same year, he made an impulsive marriage to Jennie Jerome, an American heiress, daughter of the financier Leonard Jerome. Dark, vivacious and magnificent, Jennie had an irresistible feline quality.

Winston's parents, Jennie and Lord Randolph. Their neglect would do much to shape his personality.

Margot Asquith wrote, 'She had a forehead like a panther's and great wild eyes that looked through you.' Viscount D'Abernon was another who compared her to a panther, but also noted 'a cultivated intelligence unknown to the jungle'.

The young couple were popular and sociable, and neither the arrival of their first son, Winston, in November 1874, nor their shallow pockets (Disraeli observed to Queen Victoria that Lord Randolph's father was 'not rich for a duke'; Leonard Jerome, his wife would one day claim, did not himself know how many millions he had made or lost) prevented them from entering fashionable society.

They set up home on Charles Street with a combined income of £3,000 (the average wage at the time was around £50 a year) and then spent all the money they had. Lord Randolph, like most of his ancestors, liked to gamble – he played cards, bet on horses and was a familiar presence in all the casinos around the coast of France – and Jennie knew her way around a Paris couturier.

Before long, they were negotiating loans and had been forced to put their home on the market. None of this stopped their fun.

'We seemed to live in a whirl of gaieties and excitement,' Jennie later recalled. 'Many were the delightful balls I went to, which, unlike those of the present day, lasted till five o'clock in the morning.' On those rare occasions when they did not have a party to go to, they hosted exclusive dinner parties that they could not really afford to put on. The Prince of Wales was an occasional guest.

Lord Randolph ignored his political career, and both he and Jennie ignored their child. As Randolph noted in his biography of Winston: 'The neglect and lack of interest in him shown by his parents were remarkable, even judged by the standards of late Victorian and Edwardian days.' Whereas most of their aristocratic peers established arrangements (often somewhat grudging) that meant they saw their children at set times, Lord Randolph and Jennie's hedonism meant that they avoided even this.

The couple became famous for their love of good living, and Lord Randolph became famous for his stunning insolence. At a dinner at Lord Salisbury's, he was overheard complaining, within earshot of Lady Salisbury, about the 'bad dinner, cold plates, beastly wine'. On another occasion, when cornered by a bore at a club, he rang the bell for a member of staff and said, 'Waiter – please listen to the end of Colonel B.'s story.'

It was this insolence that brought their gilded existence to an abrupt end in 1876. Lord Randolph's behaviour in the furore provoked by his brother's affair with Lady Aylesford so offended the Prince of Wales that he refused to see not only the Churchills but anybody who had received them. Socially they ceased to exist.

The situation was temporarily resolved when Disraeli prevailed upon Lord Randolph's father to become Lord Lieutenant of Ireland and to take his son with him. When they returned from their chastening exile four years later, Lord Randolph had changed. Although Lord Randolph realised he had gone too far, he could not, Winston later wrote, forgive the way so many former friends had turned their backs on him. His formerly 'genial and gay' nature 'contracted a stern and bitter quality, a harsh contempt for what is called "Society", and an abiding antagonism to rank and authority'.

Now began his astonishing rise. Returning to politics, he began working at breakneck speed. He and a small group of sympathetic Tories known as the Fourth Party made an endless stream of brutal attacks on both the Liberal government and those sitting in opposition on the Conservative front bench. There were days when his actions so outraged the House of Commons that barely a member would address him, and yet he 'continued along his sensational path with cold indifference'.

Lord Randolph was brazen and impulsive but possessed a charisma and energy that set him apart from almost everyone else. Equal parts music-hall performer and guttersnipe, he was a showman who mocked his enemies in the political establishment, flailing his arms to make points and riding a bicycle across the House of Commons terrace.

As the standard-bearer for a progressive vein of conservatism that became known as 'Tory Democracy' ('Trust the people, and the people will trust you!') he supercharged the electoral fortunes of a Conservative Party that had looked tired and listless, and gained an almost unrivalled celebrity: workmen smiled at his moustache and doffed their caps when his carriage passed by, and at meetings, people would greet him with shouts of 'Yahoo Randy!' and 'Give it to 'em hot!' William Gladstone called him the greatest Conservative since William Pitt.

After the election of 1886, another campaign in which his efforts were central to the Conservative Party's victory, he was made Chancellor of the Exchequer, the youngest man to hold the position since William Pitt, although it was plain that his ambition did not stop there. 'There is only one place,' Lord Randolph said, 'that is Prime Minister. I like to be boss. I like to hold the reins.' It seemed inevitable that he would get his wish sooner rather than later.

It was about this time that Lord Randolph's freckled, pug-nosed eldest son, who had talked incessantly since the moment he learned his first words and was incapable of sitting still for a minute at a time, developed a precocious interest in politics. He read newspapers avidly (alongside more conventional schoolboy passions such as collecting stamps, autographs and goldfish), hoovering up accounts of the Belgian conquest of the Congo, the Haymarket riot in Chicago, the death of Chinese Gordon, the erection of the Statue of Liberty and Gottlieb Daimler's invention of the first practical automobile.

But the stories he followed most closely concerned his brilliant, reckless father. Winston read every word of Lord Randolph's speeches. He bought a scrapbook and pasted into it the cartoons in which 'Randy' was depicted. Winston was a feverish advocate for his father and his father's party, passing on pieces of news that he felt sure would please him. 'I have been out riding', Winston informed Lord Randolph in April 1885, 'with a gentleman who thinks Gladstone is a brute and thinks that "the one with the curly moustache ought to be Premier" . . . Every body wants your Autograph but I can only say I will try, and I should like you to sign your name in full at the end of your letter. I only want a scribble as I know that you are very busy indeed.' On another occasion, when he was taken to the pantomime, where an actor playing his father was hissed, Winston burst into tears and turned in a rage upon another member of the audience, shouting, 'Stop that row, you snub-nosed radical.'

His adoration was not returned. Lord Randolph barely seemed to notice his son; he did not even know how old he was. When he did take time to speak to him, it was to upbraid him for his faults. One of

Jennie's sisters noted that when Lord Randolph was forced to visit his boys during 'the children's hour' he treated them like a general reviewing his troops.

Jennie, who once confided to friends that she ignored her son until he grew up and became 'interesting', offered little more affection or attention. In 1882, when he was seven, Winston had been sent to St George's School in Ascot – a prep school designed to get boys ready for Eton. Close as Ascot was to their home in Mayfair (a short hansom ride, an even quicker train), neither Jennie nor Randolph could find the time to see their son, who wrote them heartrending letters.

'come and see me soon'

'Come & see me soon dear Mama.'

'I am wondering when you are coming to see me?'

'You must send someone to see me.'

Sometimes they replied, more often they did not. Much of the work of looking after Winston was handed off to a spinster called Mrs Elizabeth Everest, whom he knew as 'Woom' (the result of a failed attempt to say 'woman'). Winston would forever be grateful for the immense love and care he received from her. 'My nurse was my confidante,' he wrote. 'It was to her I poured out my many troubles.' Her portrait hung in his room until he died. When in later life he wrote about the love Mrs Everest showed him, it was with a kind of wonder, as if he was surprised that anybody could have thought him worthy of such affection.

And yet this almost comically detached method of care from his parents did nothing to interrupt the veneration he felt for Jennie and Lord Randolph. Of his mother he wrote, famously, 'She shone for me like the Evening Star. I loved her dearly – but at a distance.' He considered her to be like 'a fairy princess: a radiant being possessed of limitless riches and power', and his father was accorded similar myth-ical status: it appeared to Winston that his father owned 'the key to everything or almost everything worth having'.

The bewilderment and distress he felt was not directed at his parents but transformed into behaviour that appalled both masters and his priggish colleagues. A school report noted, 'He cannot be trusted to behave himself anywhere.' He was flogged for taking sugar from the pantry. In response he stole the headmaster's 'sacred straw hat' and kicked it to pieces. His dancing master remembered 'a small, red-haired pupil, the naughtiest boy in the class; I used to think he was the naughtiest small boy in the world.'

There had always been doubts about Lord Randolph's unreliability and lack of judgement. At the beginning of his career, these had been confined to hushed whispers in the Smoking Room of the House, but as he leapt higher and higher, his opponents began to be more vocal about their concerns.

Lord Rosebery, who was a friend, complained that he displayed 'certain defects of brain and character which are inconsistent with the highest statesmanship'. Queen Victoria noted in her diary that 'he is so mad and off and also he has bad health.' It is possible that these critics knew that in 1875, just a year after his marriage, he had sought treatment from Dr Oscar Clayton, a specialist in the treatment of syphilis. (Winston always believed his father had contracted the condition, but medical opinion these days tends to favour a rare and incurable brain disease that, at least superficially, shared many of syphilis's symptoms.) Perhaps they were simply alarmed by his astonishing lack of decorum. Either way, he would soon give them something else to talk about.

When Lord Randolph encountered Cabinet resistance to the budget he put forward in December 1886, which included severe cuts to spending on the army and navy, he resigned, expecting that this gesture would be followed by the Cabinet's surrender and his restoration on terms of his own choosing. The Prime Minister, Lord Salisbury, having tired of his chancellor's serial disloyalty, accepted the resignation.

Winston called it the 'greatest sacrifice of any Minister in modern times'. Almost everybody else saw it as a foolish blunder. Either way, Lord Randolph's career was over. He was just thirty-seven. Before long, he had abandoned even the back benches for the racecourses, where he was often seen betting heavily.

The previous year, when Winston was ten, his father's mysterious condition had entered a new phase. In August and then November, Lord Randolph was forced to retreat to his bed. Sessions in the House put him under immense strain, he told Lord Dufferin, 'and the

constant necessity of trying to say something new makes one a drivel-
ling idiot.'

His doctors acknowledged that they were powerless to help. His
horrified friends could do little more than record his tragic decline in
diaries and the letters they exchanged between them. Although they
had become estranged in the summer of 1886, Jennie tried to nurse
her husband while pretending that nothing was wrong, especially to
the boys, who saw him so irregularly anyway that most of what they
knew of him came either from the papers or their mother. If perhaps
those letters they did receive from him seemed more intemperate
than usual, then this was not so strange; there had always been a wildness in the scrawled notes he fired at them.

Lord Randolph may have had more time to spare now that his
great gamble in Parliament had failed, but he was no more inclined
than before to spend it with his sons. Winston could tell his father, 'I
want you to come down on some fine day and see me', and yet it was
unlikely to happen, even when Lord Randolph was actually in the
same town as his son.

On one day in November 1886, just before his dramatic fall from
grace, Lord Randolph had a meeting in Brighton, which was only a
short walk from the Brunswick School in Hove, to which Winston
had been transferred in 1884, and yet he did not consider going to see
him. Winston found out: 'I hope you are quite well. The weather is
very wet today. You never came to see me on Sunday when you were
in Brighton. We went to the Museum on Saturday.'

The same thing happened again a little while later, prompting
another letter from his son. 'I cannot think why you did not come to
see me, while you were in in Brighton, I was very disappointed but I
suppose you were too busy.' What is hardest to read in these letters is
not Winston's palpable hurt, but his attempts to explain his pain away.
It was as if he was trying to inoculate himself against disappointment.

The following year Winston made elaborate plans for Christmas,
and only discovered at the last minute that his parents had decided to
go on a seven-week tour of Russia instead. On another occasion, he
had to abandon an attempt to write to his mother because he did not
have her address; he did not know which country she was in.

Even after Winston began to show signs of promise at Harrow, where he had been sent in 1888, his father's indifference persisted. Winston made the swimming team, led the school's rifle corps, starred in boxing and became, first, the Harrow fencing champion and then fencing champion of all the English public schools.* Ahead of speech day, in 1890, when he was to be honoured for the feat of memory he displayed in memorising Macaulay's *Lays*, he wrote to try to persuade his father to come and witness his moment of triumph: 'If you take the 11.7 from Baker Street you will get to Harrow at 11.37. I shall meet you at the station with a fly, if I can get one . . . You have never been to see me & and so everything will be new to you.' He attempted to enlist Jennie's support too: 'Do try to get Papa to come. He has never been.'

Lord Randolph refused. As far as he was concerned, he deserved a child he could be proud of, and who he felt would be capable of building on his achievements. Winston had shown little sign of being this boy.

In August 1893, Lord Randolph wrote to his mother about his disappointment in his eldest son: 'I have told you often & you would never believe me that he has little [claim] to cleverness, to knowledge or any capacity for settled work. He has great talent for show off exaggeration & make believe.'

As 1893 wore on, Lord Randolph's deterioration accelerated, although he remained largely oblivious to the severity of his decline and to the anguish it prompted in friends and family. Those who cared for him were so horrified and saddened that they could no longer endure to watch his increasingly erratic appearances in Parliament. Lord Rosebery summed up the remorseless depletion of his friend's dignity: 'There was no curtain, no retirement. He died by inches in public.'

Lord Randolph's brain and spinal cord rotted, which left him prey to tremors in his face, lips and tongue, crushing headaches, delusions, depression and dementia. His vision was impaired, his pupils liable to change abruptly and sometimes it could seem as if his memory had been annihilated or that he was no longer capable of coherent

---

* Winston's failures as a schoolboy have been overstated, most forcefully by Winston himself.

conversation. When he did speak, his voice was woolly and stuttering, almost unintelligible. As he showed his friend Wilfrid Scawen Blunt to the door one day he said, almost in tears: 'I know what I want to say, but damn it, I can't say it.'

In his late forties, he had become an old man. His skin was leaden grey and hung in folds. He was aged by his thick beard, and he had heavy bags under eyes that, in one friend's recollection, gleamed with 'hate, anger and fear . . . the dreadful fear of those who have learned how close madness is'.

And still there was nothing Winston could do to please his father. Even his entrance to Sandhurst, for most the source of congratulation, was a prompt for Lord Randolph to issue a majestic condemnation of his son's flaws.

'There are two ways of winning an examination,' he wrote, 'one creditable the other the reverse. You have unfortunately chosen the latter method, and appear to be much pleased with your success.' He continued:

With all the advantages you had, with all the abilities which you foolishly think yourself to possess & which some of your relations claim for you, with all the efforts that have been made to make your life easy & agreeable & your work neither oppressive or distasteful, this is the grand result that you come up among the 2nd rate & 3rd rate class who are only good for commissions to a cavalry regiment . . . you need not trouble to write any answer to this part of my letter, because I no longer attach the slightest weight to anything you may say about your own acquirements & exploits.

If, he told his son, he intended to carry on in the same disappointing fashion, then he should be assured

that my responsibility for you is over . . . I am certain that if you cannot prevent yourself from leading the idle useless unprofitable life you have had during your schooldays & later months, you will become a mere social wastrel one of the hundreds of the public school failures, and you will degenerate into a shabby unhappy & futile existence.

Lord Randolph's archives preserve an ink-smudged response from his son: 'Thank you very much for writing to me. I am very sorry indeed that I have done so badly.'

For the moment, Winston remained innocent of the true extent of his father's condition. He never witnessed a seizure, and Jennie persisted in treating her husband's behaviour as ordinary. In 1894, when Jennie told Winston that Lord Randolph's doctors had recommended a long sea voyage, he was solicitous but not alarmed. It was only after Winston spoke to his father's doctors that he finally understood how grave the situation was. 'I never saw him again,' he said, 'except as a swiftly fading shadow.'

Lord Randolph's last letter to Winston, written while he was on his long, tragic journey around the world, was biting and dismissive.

> You write stupidly on what you call the 'subject of finance'. 'Since I had my allowance you have given me a little extra without which I should have been terribly hard up (elegant). If therefore (logical!) you could make a <u>deposit!</u> Of <u>say</u> (commercial & banking expression) £15 which I was to draw upon (rather frail security) & which I was to account to you for as I drew it out (perhaps you would, you have to send your letter 10,000 miles) it would make things so much easier.' Would it? Perhaps. I do not comment on this letter so delicately expressed except to observe that Jack would have cut off his fingers rather than write such a very free-spoken letter to his father . . . Finally if you are going to write letters to me when I am travelling, type-written & so ridiculously expressed I would rather not receive them.

Lord Randolph died, owing the Rothschilds £66,000, on 24 January 1895, in the middle of a winter so cruel that the Thames almost froze over. Winston was left prostrate with grief.

By the time Winston entered the House of Commons, in February 1901, Lord Randolph had been cold in his grave for six years, and yet his ghost maintained a hold over his son. As month followed month, its power only seemed to increase. When Winston set up in his first London residence, on Mount Street, it was in a flat surrounded by memories of his father: not just his writing table, bronze inkstand and carved oak chair, but also his papers and a photograph of Lord Randolph's most successful racing horse, L'Abbesse de Jouarre, resplendent in the Churchill racing colours.

The literary and political careers he launched from this shrine to Lord Randolph were both, in their own ways, a homage to him. He had long since committed his father's speeches to heart (and used to reread them when he was feeling low). As a young MP, he championed his father's causes. Echoing the 'Tory Democracy' Lord Randolph had invented, then attempted to promote, the irredeemably aristocratic Winston claimed, 'I believe in the Tory working classes.' He was as eager to rein in naval and military expenditure as his father had been, and even adopted the same tactics in Parliament. Winston's attitude to his father's political views was similar to that of a Puritan's reverence for the Bible. He treated them as articles of faith, to be pursued for as long as he had means to do so.

Years before, at Harrow, he had spent hours before a mirror trying to imitate Lord Randolph's style and delivery; now he aped his father's clothes as well as his manner.* He copied his father's practice of using pauses as he spoke, deliberately fumbling in his pocket for a note he neither wanted nor needed to help focus his audience's attention. One journalist recorded how,

> When the young member for Oldham addresses the House, with hands on hips, head bent forward, right hand stretched forth, memories of days that are no more flood the brain. Like the father is the son in his habit of independent views on current topics, the unexpectedness of his conclusions, his disregard for authority, his contempt for conventions, and his perfect phrasing of disagreeable remarks.

Of course, no matter how well turned his insults, he could not avoid making enemies, but then perhaps that was the point. He wanted to avenge himself on the Tory establishment whom he blamed for his father's downfall.

---

* Although he was never hirsute enough to be able to grow a moustache similar to the one that had been so much part of his father's appeal.

Winston sought out those men who had been Lord Randolph's friends. In the House he sat, surrounded by the shades of the Fourth Party, in the corner seat from which his father had delivered his last speech. He made those men who had opposed Lord Randolph his enemies, and, just as his father had done before him, sought to seize the limelight by attacking established political figures.

Winston and the rest of the 'Hughligans', his own version of Lord Randolph's 'Fourth Party', launched venomous assaults on St John Brodrick, the secretary of state for war, Joseph Chamberlain, and Arthur Balfour, whom he accused of 'gross, unpardonable ignorance'.

So strong was the strain of filial piety in the speeches Winston made as a Tory backbencher that, before long, an irreparable gap had opened between him and the Conservative Party's leadership.

It was around this time that Winston began writing his father's biography. He immersed himself in the project, but also spent time with Lord Randolph's influential friends. Winston would call on figures such as Lord Rosebery, who had been close to his father, and encourage them to speak about the man that he had hardly known. The resulting book had many qualities, none of which included the detachment of a professional historian. 'Few fathers have done less for their sons,' observed Winston's cousin Ivor Guest of the biography. 'Few sons have done more for their fathers.'

Although Winston understood the central achievement of Lord Randolph – the rallying of newly enfranchised working-class voters to Tories, and how miraculous this must have seemed – the biography was more justification than assessment. It was also a dialogue between Winston and his father's ghost. Winston finished the book in 1905, a year after he had crossed the floor and joined the Liberal Party. Although Lord Randolph had once said, 'No power on earth would make me join the other side', it was essential for Winston that he could persuade himself that his father would have approved of his action.

He argued that Lord Randolph had saved the Tories and they had repaid him by casting him aside: 'would he, under the many riddles the future had reserved for such as he, have snapped the tie of sentiment that bound him to his party, resolved at last to "shake the yoke of inauspicious stars" . . .?'

The answer, Winston concluded, was yes: in the new century, his father would have become a progressive. Winston's biography was a reminder of the extent to which Lord Randolph's phantom continued to exert a preternatural sway over him. It helped determine the decisions he made, the opinions he expressed, the clothes he wore, even the way he moved his body. And yet it was also evidence of how far Winston's febrile imagination had reached into the past and wrought changes of its own, remaking the icy, cutting, distant figure who had been so dismissive of his son into a partner, even a friend.

It meant that thirty years after Lord Randolph's death he could write: 'All my dreams of comradeship with him, of entering Parliament at his side and in his support, were ended. There remained for me only to pursue his aims and vindicate his memory.' All of this was an illusion, but it was a potent one. And one thing was undeniably true: the best thing Lord Randolph ever did for Winston was to die young.

Clementine and Winston (watched by his mother) Churchill. She devoted her life to her husband; he repaid his wife with almost complete dependence.

In 1908, at the age of thirty-four, Winston married a woman who had also been scarred by a sad, loveless childhood, and in whose loneliness he recognised his own.

His new wife, Clementine Hozier, had grown up fearing her father, and never quite being able to believe she had a secure place in her mother's affections. Sir Henry Hozier was a 'born autocrat' with an 'excessive love of power' and a damaged reputation at Lloyd's. Angry and strange, he mentioned neither his wife nor his children in his entry in *Who's Who*. Clementine's grandfather dismissed him as a 'bounder', and Clementine's own earliest memory was of being carried downstairs and placed at the foot of her parents' bed. Although her mother held out her arms to her, Clementine did not move because 'on the other side of the bed was my Father's sleeping form. Even then I was afraid of him.'

As she grew older, Clementine started to wonder whether she really was her father's child. Clementine's actual father may have been – based on her mother Blanche's inconsistent recollections to friends – her uncle, the dashing, blue-eyed Baron Redesdale (paternal grandfather of the famous Mitford sisters). But she knew from an early age, and with a far greater certainty, that her parents had probably never enjoyed any true happiness.

Blanche was witty, daring, capricious and unconventional. She was friends with Jennie Churchill and dined with Henry James and Wilfrid Scawen Blunt. She was also 'an impenitent gambler' who borrowed shamelessly from any friend or relation who happened to stay with her and was reputed to juggle ten lovers at once – something she was happy to advertise widely. The scandalous, racy life she pursued meant she was often snubbed, and yet she carried on undaunted.*

In 1891, Hozier sued for divorce, and Clementine and her sister became pawns in a bitter custody battle. After a brief, unhappy period in the care of their father, the children were eventually forced into a peripatetic existence on the Continent with Lady Blanche, who

---

* As a young girl, Blanche went to the dentist accompanied by her maid. When the maid heard a scream, she ran in to the dentist's room, where she found the dentist trying to fend off Blanche's advances.

could never help losing money she did not have in the Dieppe casinos.

Clementine's childhood was full of bewildering moves, at least one of which was decided on the toss of a coin. With no real home or father, and a mother who was capable of being gentle one moment and full of violent temper the next, she was a timorous child. She was overshadowed by her boisterous, impudent elder sister, Kitty, for whom her mother showed a 'violent, indeed ungovernable partiality'. 'Strangely enough,' Clementine noted in an unpublished memoir, 'I did not mind this very much, but thought it quite natural. I looked up to her, dazzled by her prettiness, gaiety and impudence.'

The bitter drudgery of Clementine's existence was occasionally broken up by ugly encounters with her father – he once tried to kidnap her; and he would die in Panama a year before her wedding to Winston – and bleak tragedy: when Clementine was fourteen her sister died of typhoid fever, just days short of her seventeenth birthday.

More often, though, she was simply anxious about what her highly sexed mother might do next. At a very early age she had developed a contempt for Blanche's inability to control herself; and her response to the chaos of her mother's life was to try to be a perfectionist in her own.

Clementine wanted to go to university, but Blanche, who did not want a bluestocking for a daughter, did her best to sabotage these ambitions.* So instead, Clementine, desperate to escape what she would later call a 'very difficult childhood', entered into and then broke off two early engagements, one of which had been to a prosperous civil servant who was twice her age.

Winston offered her the stability and affection she had desired. She, in turn, gave herself entirely to her husband, deciding in her marriage's first days that she would 'live for him' alone.

The man who, in 1940, would save his country had been a frail, lisping child. His head was ponderous, his belly plump, his chest puny and his skin so sensitive that he would suffer rashes if he did not sleep

---

* Clementine used to sneak away to read in graveyards.

in silk sheets and wear silk underwear. He was the victim of bullies who beat him, ridiculed him and pelted him with cricket balls.

'I am cursed with so feeble a body', he once wrote to his mother, 'that I can hardly support the fatigues of the day.' In response he set out to transform himself. He became the brave, impulsive personality guided by the 'zigzag streak of lightning' in his brain who had crashed – giddy with cigars, champagne and the unimprovable delight of being Winston Churchill – into the fervid politics of the new century.

He was impish, disdainful and ruthless, strangely innocent and hungry for the world and everything it contained. His delicate pink skin was still soft; his hair still red; and his figure, swaddled in clothes that were already old-fashioned, slight. And yet by 1908, he was the veteran of exploits in far-flung wars, a man for whom danger was a source of energy and excitement. Even the vividness of his language was a reminder that he lived life at a different pitch from most people.

At the age of just thirty-three he had joined the Cabinet as president of the Board of Trade. Within two years he had become home secretary, one of the great offices of state, and it was clear there was no limit to his ambition. When asked about his future, he gleamed as if a light had been switched on inside him. He talked guilelessly about having been chosen by fate 'for a purpose far beyond our simple reasoning'.

This, at least, was what people saw. His ebullience was undercut by darker thoughts. There was his conviction that, like Lord Randolph, he would not live long. 'I am not a good life,' he said. 'My father died too young. I must try to accomplish whatever I can by the time I am forty.'

And he was predisposed to melancholy. 'I don't like standing near the edge of a platform when an express train is passing through,' he once confided to his doctor. 'I like to stand back and if possible to get a pillar between me and the train. I don't like to stand by the side of a ship and look down into the water. A second's action would end everything . . . I've no desire to quit this world, but thoughts, desperate thoughts, come into the head.'

This is why he sought out people to entertain him, and why he lived his life in a blizzard of frenetic activity. If he relaxed, he told Violet Asquith, if he allowed himself to stop, he would be consumed by 'dark moments of impatience and frustration'. Painting, friends, drink, bricklaying, could all help kennel what he called the black dog, but what he needed more than anything else was a purpose, a way of implicating himself in an existential drama.

At his most vulnerable, Winston could be afflicted by a feeling of worthlessness that was perhaps his father's most enduring legacy. 'Alas,' he said to Clementine, 'I have no good opinion of myself. At times I think I could conquer everything – and then again I know that I am only a weak fool.'

Winston once told a friend that whenever he had tried to begin a serious conversation with Lord Randolph, he was snubbed pitilessly: 'He wouldn't listen to me or consider anything I said. There was no companionship with him possible and I tried so hard and so often. He was so self-centred no one else existed for him.'

'You didn't like him?' the friend asked Winston.

'How could I? . . . He treated me as if I had been a fool; barked at me whenever I questioned him.'

Winston's sense of specialness – the burning conviction that he had been singled out by the gods for some great purpose – was a fantasy necessary to prove that he did not deserve his parents' neglect (and existed side by side with his belief that had Lord Randolph lived longer, the two men would have become comrades). He would be driven for the rest of his life by a powerful desire to prove that his father had been wrong to repeatedly reject and insult him. This came in tandem with another conviction: when he had a son of his own, he would be treated very differently.

2

The Meteor Beast

WINSTON WAS SO excited by Randolph's birth that, perhaps not knowing what to do with all the emotion that had descended upon him, he dashed off to Richmond Park to ride his horse and 'to cogitate & dream about his son'.

Randolph was born on 28 May 1911, at 33 Eccleston Square. He would later claim, dubiously, that this made him a cockney. His enthralled parents called him the Chumbolly, after a beautiful flower that grows in north-west India; it is also a word used in Farsi to describe a healthy, chubby newborn (so it is likely that Winston brought the name back with him from his days as a young subaltern in the subcontinent). They exchanged ecstatic letters in which they gloated over the family's new arrival. In early June, Winston, who was at Blenheim Camp with his fellow officers of the Yeomanry, wrote:

> Many congratulations are offered me upon the son. With that lack of jealousy wh ennobles my nature, I lay them all at your feet.
>
> My precious pussy cat, I do trust & hope that you are being good, & not sitting up or fussing yourself. Just get well & strong & enjoy the richness wh this new event will I know have brought into your life. The Chumbolly must do his duty and help you with your milk. You are to tell him so from me. At his age greediness & even swinishness at table are virtues.

In her reply, Clementine, who always worried that Winston's bounds into the world outside their marriage would one day take him away from her, introduced a slightly wistful note:

Blenheim sounds gay & entrancing, & I long to be there sharing all the fun & glitter. But I am very happy here, contemplating the beautiful Chumbolly who grows more darling & handsome every hour, & puts on weight with every meal; so that he will be a little round ball of fat.

Just now I was kissing him, when catching sight of my nose he suddenly fastened upon it & began to suck it, no doubt thinking it was another part of my person!

Randolph was immediately given more attention than his elder sister, two-year-old Diana – Clementine even breastfed him. Although Winston liked to show off both his children and see them praised, it was obvious that he was entranced by the blond, vivacious Randolph. Little red-haired Diana, the first 'Puppy-Kitten', may have been delightful and sweet; and yet she was not, like her brother, going to carry the family's name forward.

Winston and the infant Randolph.

Winston adored being a father. He was unusually determined to involve himself in day-to-day family life. He kept a jealous watch on what happened in the nursery, and his letters are full of delight at his babies' growth, and in noting their mannerisms. On at least one occasion, he gave Diana a bath.

But he also loved hunting and playing polo, country-house weekends and dining with his friends. Most of all, of course, he loved politics. His life was too full of excitement, novelty and delight, and he was too full of energy and ambition, for him to ever confine himself to the family home. When Winston was actually in the nursery, he was a vivid, active presence – his appearances the source of great excitement to Randolph and Diana – but there were always a thousand other pulls on his time and attention. This meant that for the first few years of Randolph's life, even when they were under the same roof, he and his father existed in almost completely separate worlds.

Randolph's birth had arrived in the same year as another landmark in Winston's life: in October 1911, he was made First Lord of the Admiralty. At the age of just thirty-six, he became head of the greatest fighting service of the greatest empire in the world. The job was entirely suited to his boyish enthusiasm and imagination. He was exhilarated by the great responsibility that had been thrust onto his shoulders – with tensions across Europe rising, it was more important than ever that the fleet should be prepared for war – and the splendour that came with the role. As First Lord, he had use of a yacht, the *Enchantress* (in the three years leading up to the Great War, he spent a total of eight months aboard it), and the plush majesty of Admiralty House meant that, when in London, he could entertain on a generous scale.

That he was himself short of money did not mean anything was stinted. He kept himself afloat by constantly increasing his overdraft limit and making full use of the unlimited credit that men of his class expected to have offered them. His cigars came from J. Grunebaum & Sons, and although Winston smoked about a dozen a day, he had not paid a bill for five years. He enjoyed a similar arrangement with his wine merchants, Randolph Payne & Sons.

When, a few years earlier, the minister's private secretary had asked whether he should pay any of the overdue private bills that had stacked up for his horses, membership of various exclusive clubs and his fine leather boots, Winston replied nonchalantly, 'They may as well wait a little longer, having already waited so long.'

Winston was not entirely comfortable about his unsteady financial situation. As he confided to his brother Jack, 'Extravagant tastes, an expensive style of living – small and diminished resources – these are fertile sources of trouble.' And yet these concerns were not sufficient to make him stop. He did not believe that a Churchill should lead a cramped life. Oblivious to either expense or convenience, Winston would telephone ahead to tell Clementine he was bringing his luminous, charismatic friends home and that it would be nice to have some lobster and roast duck.

Winston had omnivorous social appetites. He liked extravagant, racy company, such as the Canadian press lord Max Beaverbrook and the brilliant lawyer and Conservative MP F. E. Smith. He also liked radicals, such as the Chancellor of the Exchequer, David Lloyd George, who exerted an uncanny hold over his mind. For a while the Welshman's influence over Winston was so strong that it was as if he had almost become the father Lord Randolph had never been. The two young men, the 'heavenly twins', glowing with latent power, stood in stark contrast to the portly Victorians who sat around them in Parliament.

In truth, he was happy to dine in a high style with anybody, provided they amused him. Some saw him as a class traitor who had crossed the floor before becoming one of the reforming Liberal government's most impassioned members: he had been banned from some of the grander houses, and old acquaintances had started to cut him in the street. ('They said that I beat Clemmie and that you could hear her crying as you passed our house,' he would later say of this time. 'They said that I was drugged, and if you rolled up my sleeve, my arm was a mass of piqures. We were cut by people we had known well and had looked on as friends.') But he was still a man much in demand.

His 'slightly hunched shoulders from which his head jutted forward like the muzzle of a gun about to fire' were a regular sight at the salons of Liberal hostesses, at long weekends spent in labyrinthine country houses and in the dark, smoky, entirely masculine environment of London's exclusive gentlemen's clubs.

He was a fierce, witty presence in the House of Commons, and a whirl of driving energy in the baroque corridors of the Admiralty. Here, just metres from his son, although it might as well have been miles, he woke each morning to a substantial breakfast, then would sit up working, framed by the historic Admiralty bed's gilded dolphins, the counterpane covered with official memoranda and dispatches.

This was his world.

Randolph led a far more circumscribed life. There was the nursery; walks with nurses around Green Park; and trips to the sort of dowdy seaside resort that held little attraction to a man like Winston. Randolph expressed his boredom by behaving badly. From a very early age, it was clear that his main aim in life was teasing and baiting others. While the family were at Admiralty House, he threw one nursery maid's wrist-watch out of the window from a great height – it shattered – and pushed another nanny into a full bath. He and Diana drove out nannies that they disliked. When finally the poor women broke, the young Churchills would serenade them by bumping their bags down the staircases and crying in shrill voices: 'Nanny's going, Nanny's going. Hurrah! Hurrah!'

Winston's son had no figure like Mrs Everest in his life, someone who could provide firm but loving discipline. Instead, Randolph realised that the easiest way to secure attention was to be naughty. When he did so, the nursemaids had to call Clementine to intervene. The worse he was, the quicker they quit.

Sometimes, elements of the excitements Winston pursued away from the family home erupted violently into the existence of his son. One morning just before the Great War, during their 'daily morning airing in the Green Park', a group of suffragists tried to drag Randolph out of his pram. A nursery maid fought the women off, and from then on, a detective followed them at a discreet distance.

And then, there was the Great War. At the end of July 1914, as Europe marched towards catastrophe, the Churchills took a small house, Pear Tree Cottage, at Overstrand in Norfolk (Jack and his wife, Goonie, were across the lawn, in Beehive Cottage). Clementine, who was expecting a third child in October, would look back fondly on those 'wonderful' opening weeks of the war 'when we were so happy'. 'I wondered how long we should continue to tread on air.'

Winston managed to spend three hours playing with his children on the beach before the other world dragged him back. Randolph was gripped by an excitement he could not, at the age of just three, quite understand. He remembered looking out to sea, expecting to see German ships. But nothing happened, except that his father did not come back from London: 'We children were all disappointed – no Germans and no Papa.'

In the course of the following months, Randolph would see two very different versions of his father's personality. At a stroke, the war had made Winston one of the three most powerful men in the country. He was overflowing with energy and excitement, and able somehow to locate joy amid one of history's great catastrophes.

The conflict offered him the constant exhilaration that was so important to his well-being. In the terrible moments after the expiry of Britain's ultimatum to Germany on 4 August, as the prime minister sat with 'darkened face and dropped jowl', and the foreign secretary, Edward Grey, his countenance worn haggard by the strain of the last days, cupped his head in his hands, the oppressive silence was broken when Winston flung open the doors to the Cabinet room and burst in, radiant, cigar crammed in his mouth, his face a picture of satisfaction, 'one word pouring out on another'. 'You could see', said Lloyd George, 'he was a really happy man.'

'I am interested, geared up & happy,' Winston told Clementine. 'Is it not horrible to be built like that?' He was euphoric because he knew that the work he had done in the years before the war, and the decisions he had taken in the days immediately before it, had helped keep the fleet, and therefore the country, safe.

And yet even this did not appear enough to quell his desire for sensation. Unable to expend his dynamism by merely leading the Admiralty, Winston appeared in constant search of ever greater excitements. In mid-September, on his way to inspect naval installations in the Highlands, he led a raid upon a house suspected of harbouring German spies. (It was not.) The following month, he offered to resign from the Cabinet so he could organise the defence of Antwerp. Winston's colleagues refused (having greeted his request with unrestrained laughter), but he went to Belgium anyway. An Italian witness there was struck by the strange, bold figure the First Lord cut.

He was still young, and was enveloped in a cloak, and on his head wore a yachtsman's cap. He was tranquilly smoking a large cigar and looking at the progress of the battle under a rain of shrapnel, which I can only call fearful.

The operation was a failure: Antwerp fell, fifteen hundred members of the Naval Division were captured, and another thousand were reported as missing in action. More than this, there was something deeply undignified and irresponsible about the way he had abandoned the Admiralty and its pressing demands to make a reckless excursion to the front line. It was evidence of an irreducible element in his character that in years to come – when he was well into his sixties – led to his watching the Blitz from London's rooftops, or begging to be allowed to observe D-Day from the Channel.

At a dinner at Walmer Castle in January 1915, Winston found himself sitting next to Margot Asquith. He could barely restrain his enthusiasm for the turn his life had taken. 'My God!' he exclaimed to her. 'This is living History. Everything we are doing and saying is thrilling. It will be read by 1000 generations – think of that!! Why, I would not be out of this glorious, delicious war for anything the world could give me.' Margot was struck by the way his eyes glowed as he spoke, but also how this was accompanied by a sudden anxiety. Evidently, he had realised that he might have gone too far. 'I say,' he said quickly, 'don't repeat that I said the word "delicious" – you know what I mean.'

By April that year, however, as the ambitious scheme he had authored to force the Dardanelles Strait began to unravel, this exhilaration turned into distress. Winston believed that a decisive blow against the Ottoman Empire would help knock the Turks, who had allied themselves with Germany and Austria-Hungary, out of the war and at a stroke relieve the stalemate on the Western Front. 'I shall be the biggest man in Europe, if this comes off,' he told Lloyd George, barely able to disguise his excitement.

His success at overmastering initial scepticism from his colleagues on the War Council and in both the army and the navy about the idea ('He always out-argues me,' wailed the First Sea Lord Jacky Fisher) led only to a botched plan of attack and the unnecessary deaths of thousands of men.

At around the same time, a series of crises and scandals, of which Gallipoli was only one, pushed the prime minister H. H. Asquith into coalition with the Tories; one of the conditions was that Winston should be removed from his post, the party's revenge for what they regarded as a decade's worth of treachery. Asquith and Lloyd George could have protected him but chose not to. They were, like many of their colleagues, exhausted and exasperated by his relentless egotism, his abrasive way of forcing his arguments onto others, and his inability to resist meddling in everybody else's business. (As Lloyd George's mistress Frances Stevenson observed, it was 'strange that Churchill should have been in politics all these years, and yet not won the confidence of a single party in this country, or a single colleague in the Cabinet'.) A new government was formed, without Winston as First Lord. Winston, who had remained oblivious to the hostility his conduct had inspired, felt betrayed by men he thought were friends.

On 16 May, Winston was made chancellor of the Duchy of Lancaster. Although he still had the right to attend Cabinet, it was essentially a ceremonial post; his only serious duties were appointing county magistrates and managing the king's private estate, work which occupied less than one day a week.

Those who visited Admiralty House in the days that followed found Clementine in tears and Winston aged, as if overnight. His eyes were withdrawn, haunted, and he always seemed to be looking away or down. His shoulders drooped and his hands, when they were not occupied, were held in tight fists. Winston would be uncharacteristically withdrawn over dinner, except when, almost without warning, he launched into vehement defences of the expedition and the lost opportunity it represented. With obsessive force he delivered to a handful of dinner guests the speeches he wished he could have made to Parliament.

People who knew him as somebody who talked when he played golf, or bathed or climbed rocks, who could not keep quiet during games of bezique and bridge, were terrified by his silence. Some went further and drew parallels with the tragic case of Lord Randolph, who was a similar age to his son when he exploded his career.

Clementine later remembered that there was nothing in her and

Winston's life as agonising as the drama of the Dardanelles, or as bleak as its aftermath. She told Martin Gilbert: 'I thought he would die of grief.'

But she too was showing signs of cracking up. A clearly unsympathetic Margot Asquith recorded reports that Clementine 'was behaving like a lunatic & crying daily over Winston being turned out of the Admiralty'. Clementine said that her dying wish was to dance on Asquith's grave.

Sitting high and discrete at the top of Admiralty House, the nursery could sometimes seem like a self-contained world, and yet the anxiety that had become such a feature of Winston and Clementine's lives surged up there too. For a long time, Randolph had associated the word 'Dardanelles' only with troops glimpsed from an upstairs window at Admiralty House. Then there came an addition to his nightly prayers: 'God bless Mummy and Papa. God bless the Dardanelles and make me a good boy. Amen.' Although Randolph and Diana (Sarah was still a babe in arms) could not understand the precise meaning of the fragments of their parents' conversation that they heard at the dinner table or while playing on the drawing-room floor, they knew that something was terribly wrong.

Finally, there was no escape. This was the natural consequence of Winston's outsize personality. When things went well for him, his energy and well-being radiated all around him. When things went badly, everybody would be consumed by the blackness that enveloped his life. There was another consequence too: just as Winston had before him, Randolph grew up nursing a grievance against a Tory party that he believed had conspired to scuttle his father's career.

Winston's fall from grace had worrying practical implications. His salary dropped from £4,500 to £2,000 a year, a catastrophe for a man with expensive habits, a great many financial commitments and no private income. Things looked up when the government decided to pool ministerial salaries and distribute them on an almost equal basis, restoring Winston's income to close to what it had been before, but there was no guarantee that this would last. In addition to this, Winston's departure from the Admiralty meant that they had to find a new family home.

After perching briefly in a large house next to the Ritz belonging to Winston's aunt Cornelia and son Ivor Guest, in mid-June the family moved in with Jack and Goonie at 41 Cromwell Road.

Clementine took the drawing-room floor and Goonie inhabited the bedroom floor. The two nurseries were merged into one, on the top floor, supervised by Goonie's nurse (supported by three under-nurses) who attempted, with only intermittent success, to keep control of her charges.

Randolph, Diana and Sarah joined their cousins Johnny and Peregrine and soon discovered that there were compensations for the unwonted eviction from Admiralty House. The Natural History Museum was across the street, and it was fun to skate and slide among its dinosaur skeletons, or to play hide-and-seek in its corridors. And there was the commingled terror and excitement of being carried down to the cellar during Zeppelin raids – where their parents drank champagne as the children tried to sleep in wine racks that had been converted into bunks.

Most of their time, however, was spent in the nursery. It was a place of astonishing noise and constant upheaval, and little of what took place there was noticed by the adults living on the floors below. This meant that a 'most sadistic nurse' who filled the children's mouths with mustard to stop them biting their nails could operate unchecked, but also that Randolph could express freely his capacity for mischief.

When he was taken for walks in the streets around their new home, he would often make rude remarks and pull faces at policemen. One day a nurse who had been pushed to the very limits of her patience persuaded a bobby to 'arrest' her young charge, who raised hell when he thought he was going to be taken to prison. Yet no punishment could suppress his naughtiness for long. He would walk into his uncle Jack's study, pick up the telephone and call the Foreign Office, telling the bewildered secretary on the other end of the line that it was 'Mr Churchill speaking'.

Randolph also had a gift for mimicry and used to 'take-off' their eminent guests to amuse his cousins. He was once caught by Winston standing on a chair in the dining room, halfway through his impression of Lloyd George. His impudence left Winston puce with rage.

Thrown into the political wilderness, Winston had time he could have devoted to Randolph. But for the moment, his mind was elsewhere. Throughout the autumn of 1915, he continued to hope for the one crushing victory in the Dardanelles that would lead to the capture of Constantinople and vindicate his strategy. It did not come.

Winston had swapped the huge administrative apparatus and power of the Admiralty for small rooms in the Treasury, populated only by his secretary, Edward Marsh, and shorthand writer, Henry Beckenham. There were no more daily conferences with Cabinet ministers, no more floods of notes, minutes, intercepted German messages and intrigue from neutral capitals that had kept him in hourly contact with the inner secrets of war policy. He no longer had any opportunities to scrutinise the plans submitted daily by experts or to experience the rush of adrenaline that had raced through his system ahead of parliamentary questions or important speeches.

Undaunted, he sent a stream of memoranda about the strength of the Royal Navy, the futility of 'frantic and sterile efforts to pierce the German lines', and, always, the Dardanelles. Nobody listened.

Eventually, in November, his frustration drove him to resign from the government. Within days he was supervising the packing of cigars, port, vermouth, whisky and camping equipment ahead of his departure for France. Once again it must have seemed to Randolph as if his father had stepped out of his life.

In the mud and horror of the Western Front, Winston reacquainted himself with danger. He led nerve-shredding expeditions into no-man's-land. As the soldiers picked their way cautiously forward, they would suddenly hear their commanding officer's unmistakeable lisping voice issuing unnecessarily loud instructions: 'You go that way, I will go this . . . Come here, I have found a gap in the German wire. Come over here at once!' One of his men remembered him as being like 'a baby elephant out in no-man's-land at night'.

Crouching in his frail sandbagged shelter (his dugout was destroyed by direct hits more than once while he was elsewhere on the line), he discussed ideas for breaking the trench deadlock, such as a bulletproof raincoat; collective shields supported by caterpillar tracks, to protect troops as they advanced across no-man's-land; using gas flames to cut through barbed wire; anything that offered an alternative to attack by 'the bare breasts of men'.

Most of all, Winston thought endlessly of political events back home, and how he might clear his name: 'some day I shd like the truth to be known,' he wrote to Clementine, on whom he relied to keep him in touch with developments in London. In January 1916, his mind turned to his father, who had died twenty-one years before. I wondered, he wrote to his mother, 'what he would think of it all. I am sure I am doing right.' And he thought too of his son, the boy who – he said in a letter he had written for Clementine to find were the worst to happen – would 'carry on the lamp'.

His first surviving letter to Randolph dates from later that month. 'I am living here in a farm,' he wrote in capitals (with a lovely squiggle of a cat sitting at the bottom of the page):

It is not so pretty as Hoe Farm,* and there are no nice flowers and no pond or tree to play gorilla but there are three large fat dirty pigs. Like the ones we saw in the wood. The Germans are a long way off and cannot shoot at us here. It is too far. So we are quite safe as long as we stay here. But we can hear the cannons booming in the distance and at night when it is all dark we can see their flashes twinkling in the sky. Soon we are going to go close up to the Germans and then we shall shoot back at them and try to kill them. This is because they have done wrong and caused all this war and sorrow.

Winston's return to England for ten days' leave in March 1916 electrified his children. Suddenly, Cromwell Road felt infinitely more alive. It was not just Winston's presence. He brought with him, as if in his slipstream, a series of exciting, mysterious visitors, including Asquith and Lloyd George.

His nephew Peregrine remembered how, after months of solemn, tragic silence, 'the house was . . . full of people going in and out'. Instantly the social round continued; it seemed as if there was neither time nor space to give expression to the feelings of bitterness and betrayal that had built up over the last months. Within days of his return, Winston was back speaking in the Commons, making a disastrous intervention in a naval debate. In minutes he exploded whatever goodwill he might have established during his time in the trenches. Edward Marsh watched from the Strangers' Gallery, tears streaming

---

* A house in Surrey the family had rented the previous summer. It was here that a grief-stricken Winston started to paint.

down his face. Some began to question Winston's sanity. Violet Asquith asked herself if he might be 'deranged'. Had he inherited a strain of madness from his father that would destroy his career too?

Alongside all of this, he somehow had time to buy an enormous box of Meccano. Enlisting the help of the children, he erected a model of the Forth Bridge in the very large hall of Cromwell Road.

But just as soon as he was back, he was gone again.

It was not until July 1917, when David Lloyd George, who had succeeded Asquith as prime minister in October 1916, made him minister of munitions, that Winston's political exile came to an end.

Winston was rejuvenated. Able at last to find an outlet for the frustration that had been growing inside him (months earlier, he had slammed his hand into the arm of his chair: 'What fools they are. They could get more out of me now in two years of war than in a hundred afterwards'), he threw himself into frenzied activity. Clementine started calling him 'a Mustard Gas fiend, a Tank juggernaut and a Flying terror'.

There were hundreds of pressing tasks that demanded his attention: labour unrest, the need to reorganise his department, meetings to further the cooperation with Allies in the design and manufacture of new weapons, securing supplies of vital goods such as nitrates from neutral governments like Chile (and also making sure they would not be sold to enemies). His work eventually became so exacting that he lived in the Ministry of Munitions building on Northumberland Avenue, which, conveniently, was the commandeered Hotel Metropole. Doing this allowed him to carry on looking at his papers right up until the last moment before dinner, and to pick them up again as soon as he came back after the meal.

In the war's closing months, Winston made more and more frequent trips to France where, just miles from the front line, he would lunch in rooms still stained with German blood, occasionally stuffing his handkerchief into his mouth to ward off the effects of a mustard gas attack.

On those weekends when he was not in France, he would take his work to Lullenden, a handsome Tudor grey-stone with seven bedrooms and a long history, near East Grinstead, which he had purchased earlier that year with a substantial mortgage in Clementine's name.

What began as a holiday home swiftly became something more permanent. German air raids made the safety of rural England appealing, and once the adjoining barn was converted, the elder children lived there almost all the time.

There were many weeks when Randolph and his siblings and cousins barely saw an adult. With Jack away at war, Goonie socialising in the capital, Winston wrapped up in his return to politics and Clementine concerned but always distant, the children were looked after, for the most part, by barely trained local teenagers.

When their parents were there at weekends, they did not often leave the Tudor manor. The children camped out in the converted barn and lived a bucolic, unchecked existence. They were little savages pursuing almost completely separate lives from the civilised parents over at the big house. There was nobody to stop them from roaming across the farmlands, drinking water from the pond or untreated milk straight from the cows.

Randolph – whom his parents called 'the Rabbit', a misleadingly gentle nickname – was free to terrorise his siblings and cousins. If the children lived in a different world from their parents, it was Randolph who ruled it. He baited Johnny into urinating out of a bedroom window onto the heads of his father and David Lloyd George. When Johnny hesitated, Randolph agreed to join in. The two adults thought it was a sudden rainstorm, and the boys might have got away with their prank had they not been seen by a maid.

On another occasion, he pushed the elfin, sickly Sarah and Peregrine (aged three and four respectively) inside a model caravan the size of a piano, which he had been given by his godfather, Lord Riddell, and sent it careening down a steep hill. The caravan somersaulted a couple of times before smashing to pieces, but somehow its two passengers escaped unscathed.

Jack's son Johnny could almost laugh off Randolph's behaviour,*

---

* Johnny would grow into as unusual a character as any of his relatives. James Lees-Milne remembered that 'he was totally detached from the present, and lived in an idealistic Valhalla of his own creation. All worldly concerns were dismissed by him with amused contempt. He was drawn equally to painting and music; talented in both and disciplined in neither. He had abundant good nature, outrageous animal spirits and great physical strength and courage.' It was not unusual to see him walking

but Diana struggled to cope. Doll-like and timid, the 'gold-cream' kitten had eyes cast downwards under astonishingly white eyelashes, and she became ever more withdrawn as Randolph grew more boisterous. Nursery maids did what they could to contain Randolph, but he neither feared nor respected them. It was as if he could not stop himself. If Johnny dared him to eat live daddy longlegs, the creatures would be in Randolph's mouth almost before his cousin had finished speaking.

Slapping him made no difference; he even used to confess to crimes he had not committed so he could show that nothing the maids could do would affect him. This endeared him to the other children but was yet another challenge to the adults charged with looking after them. There was something about his indifference to punishment, his disregard of consequence, that went beyond high spirits and landed somewhere less innocent.

When Winston did descend on the farm, inevitably trailed by guards, secretaries, chauffeurs and important guests, everything suddenly seemed charged and more infused with excitement.

He was an extravagant builder of sandcastles who had always delighted in playing with his children: here at Lullenden, he was able to shrug off the cares and worries of adult life and plunge into games such as gorilla – where he would drop out of trees onto unsuspecting youngsters – or bear, where a growling Winston chased them through woods or a tunnel made from paintings propped up against a wall.

The games lasted only as long as he wanted them to. All too soon he would disappear back into an adult world that Randolph knew was unreachable. Somebody else would always have to deal with the overexcited, disappointed infants he left in his wake.

Randolph more than any other child idolised Winston. He could barely contain the pride he felt at having such a man as his father. This feeling of Winston's specialness – of his being set apart from other men – was affirmed even in what might otherwise have been

---

on the parapet of a roof on his hands, standing on a chimney stack on one leg. And he once held up traffic in Cheltenham clad in a flowing Wagnerian cape and tricorne hat.

uncomfortable situations. At Lullenden, Randolph tried to make friends with a local boy at the little nursery school where he and the older children went for half a day at a time. The boy refused: 'Your father murdered my father.'

'What do you mean?'

'At the Dardanelles.'

As soon as Randolph got home, he upset Clementine, for whom the memories were still livid, by asking what the boy had meant. The explanation left Randolph feeling an even greater admiration for his father: 'I am sorry to say it made me feel immensely proud for I realised my father was a boss man who could order other fathers about.' The experience would be repeated for Randolph and his siblings throughout their childhood: again and again they encountered other men who could not forgive Winston for his involvement in the Dardanelles or the General Strike. Sometimes this animosity was extended to the children, who became unwitting proxies for their father's sins.

Winston appeared largely untroubled by this hostility. Instead, he continued to single out his son for particular attention, indulgently feeding Randolph with oysters at the dinner table and announcing proudly that 'Randolph promises much. He has a noble air, and shows spirit and originality.' It was around this time that he encouraged him to learn 'Ye Mariners of England', an old broadside ballad by Thomas Campbell. The verse they both liked most began, 'The meteor flag of England / Shall yet terrific burn; / Till danger's troubled night depart / And the star of peace return.'

On those weekends when Winston, Clementine and their important friends came down, Randolph would be summoned to stand upon a stool and recite it to their guests. Somewhere along the line, the poem's billowing patriotic sentiments got tangled with the complex feelings Randolph had about the father who exploded into his life at irregular intervals, then returned to a place that remained stubbornly beyond his grasp. He began calling Winston the 'meteor beast'.

3

Winston is a Pasha

WHEN WINSTON WALKED through the Chartwell door, he clapped his hands. If no servant responded, he would immediately call for his valet (the man who dressed him, even pulling on his socks, and warmed his brandy snifter with a neatly trimmed candle).

At home, Clementine once said, 'Winston is a pasha.' Chartwell – the extraordinary combination of private residence, grand hotel and government department that was, as one of his closest aides once said, where he lived his 'real life' – was the one place, at least until he became prime minister, where the world really did revolve around him, 'a sort of tiny principality where Churchill could truly be himself'.

Winston was forty-seven when he first saw the property, and would be ninety when for the very last time he looked across its lakes and woodland. He loved it on midsummer mornings when the weald was submerged in mist, and he loved it on cool, dew-drenched spring evenings. He loved the constant sound of 'dripping splashing water', and the fact that an echo meant that when he walked around its grounds, his voice could be heard a quarter of a mile away. He loved the view of the South Downs – the grandest in the whole of the country, he liked to say – and the waves of scent from its roses.

In its eccentricity, industriousness and sociability, it was a living embodiment of the way he had chosen to arrange his existence. At Chartwell the steady rhythms of upper-class life played themselves out in parallel to the noise and heat created by Winston's political embroilments, as well as his industrial production of books and articles. Chartwell was a home that was also an arena for political planning and scheming – with lunches that lasted to four o'clock and dinners that carried on until dawn.

It was purchased after the family had been battered by a wave of tragedies. The first blow had arrived in April 1921 when Clementine's brother, the debonair, handsome Bill Hozier, shot himself in a hotel bedroom in Paris. He was just thirty-four. After the war he had retired from the navy and gone into business. But a weakness for gambling saw him fall into financial difficulties. Winston, who took a close interest in the lives of his extended family, had made him promise never to gamble again.* Perplexingly, it seemed as if Bill had kept this promise, and had in fact just paid 10,000 francs into his own account. Nevertheless, Winston, who had convinced himself he was somehow responsible, was stricken with remorse. He would use the elegant gold-topped malacca cane Bill bequeathed him for the rest of his life.

In June the same year, Jennie Churchill died. A broken ankle had led to gangrene, which in turn led to the amputation of most of her left leg. There were complications and an artery in her thigh haemorrhaged. When Winston heard, he ran crying through the streets in his dressing gown to be with his mother before she bled out. He described the loss of Jennie as an 'amputation' which had made his life 'seem lonely & its duration fleeting'.

Two months later, in August, while Winston was in London and Clementine was staying with the Duke and Duchess of Westminster, their youngest daughter Marigold, who had been born in November 1918, was killed by a cough that developed first into a bacterial infection and then septicaemia of the throat. She was still short of her third birthday. Years later, Winston told his daughter Mary that on learning of the news, 'Clementine gave a succession of wild shrieks like an animal in mortal pain.' Winston was rendered speechless by despair. Randolph passes over the death of his sister entirely in his autobiography; in fact, he makes no mention at all of her existence. Yet the letters he and his siblings wrote around this time are edged with a half knowledge of the bewildering pain their parents were experiencing. This quality of knowing and not knowing was exacerbated by the way Winston and Clementine removed themselves from the presence of their surviving children in order to grieve, one

---

* He also helped support his sister-in-law, Nellie Romilly, who had a severely war-wounded husband, two small children and very little money, when she was trying to set up a hat shop.

presumes, alone. Randolph, Diana and Sarah may not have seen their parents' agony – in the years to come, any mention of Marigold's existence was forbidden by Clementine, who would forever be haunted by the idea that she was away when her daughter died – and yet they clearly sensed it.

Then, the following year, at the November 1922 election, Winston lost his seat in Dundee. After two decades at the centre of power, he found himself thrust almost to its farthest edges. He had been home secretary, First Lord of the Admiralty, minister of munitions, secretary of state for war, and colonial secretary. He had helped reform the prison system, prepared the Royal Navy for its victories in the Great War, established a new empire in the Middle East and made a significant contribution to the pacification of Ireland, and his contribution in inaugurating social welfare was second only to that of David Lloyd George. But, with the exception of Lloyd George, there was perhaps no politician who was less trusted. Gallipoli still hung like an albatross around his neck, and his fevered promotion of a foolish, controversial and ultimately humiliating military intervention in Bolshevik Russia only served to harden existing prejudices about his temperament and judgement. His defeat was celebrated by men from every party, including his own.

His political future looked bleak ('What use is a W.C. without a seat?' went the family joke). Even his closest friends, such as Lloyd George and F. E. Smith, believed that his greatness would be established as a writer rather than a politician. Although Winston claimed to be feeling resilient and upbeat, his demeanour at a dinner he attended before leaving for a four-month holiday in the Mediterranean revealed his true state of mind. One of the guests recalled that 'Winston was so down in the dumps, he could scarcely speak the whole evening. He thought his world had come to an end – at least his political world. I thought his career was over.'

Only one thing promised a change of fortune. The death in a train accident of Winston's first cousin once removed, a bachelor called Lord Herbert Vane-Tempest, brought Winston, for the first time in his life, a private income: £4,000 a year, as well as £20,000 in the bank. It promised an unprecedented level of financial security and independence. Clementine, in particular, was excited: 'I can't describe the blessed feeling of relief that we need never be worried about money again. (Except thro' our own fault of course!) It is like floating in a bath of cream.'

Clementine, who was thirty-seven, and about to give birth for the fifth and final time, wanted a 'little country home within our means'. Winston wanted somewhere fit for the grandson of a duke. As so often in their marriage, the husband's desires prevailed over the wife's concerns. In September 1922, the same week that their youngest child, Mary, was born, Winston made an offer on Chartwell without bothering to consult Clementine.

The home he created at Chartwell was an 'independent kingdom, with its own laws, its own customs, even its own language'. Here, Winston could behave completely as he wished. Every atom of the house was imbued with its owner's personality. Very often, of course, as in the case of the crenellated raw-liver-red brick walls that girdled his water gardens, it had literally been created by him.

It was a testament to Winston's unruly mania for transformation – his relentless desire to force the world into a shape that suited him better. Just as he could not resist meddling in his children's lives and, when in government, could not help himself from intervening in areas for which he could not claim any responsibility, there was always something more that needed to be done.

He was fond, too fond for Clementine's liking, of the rumble of a bulldozer as it wrestled with natural obstacles. One of his valets tells of a morning when Winston looked out of his study window: 'Norman,' he announced, indicating with a lavish sweep of his arm, 'I think that little hill would look better over there.'

A few days later a bulldozer arrived, and the hill was slowly shifted. Winston watched enraptured as trees crashed and mountains of earth were moved. Clementine suspected that the reason he had petitioned to be allowed to build a swimming pool was because he had been craving a concrete-making machine for so long. She watched his efforts with a mixture of pleasure and alarm. She knew that 'Mr Pug [her affectionate name for him] is in his element with troops of workmen', but also that his excesses of energy were not always matched with equivalent levels of expertise, and that he could be cavalier with details.

Not everything turned out perfectly, but this was less a problem than it was an excuse to rip it up and have another go. Guests often woke up after a late night of talk and brandy to see their host in dungarees and high Wellington boots supervising several navvies building a dam. Over time he built new ponds and waterworks (in the course of creating these, he frequently, like the children whose aid he enlisted, got so wet that he was forced to stand dripping outside the house while maids hurried to put newspapers on the floor), a tall wall around the kitchen garden and a vast woodshed for which he took particular pleasure in cutting down and uprooting trees.

His hatred of discomfort meant that his bedroom had to be heated to 74 degrees Fahrenheit.* His hatred of fresh air and noise, particularly whistling,† meant that its windows were sealed with putty. The unstained oak tables and chairs in the house were made to his specifications by Heal's, as were the ashtrays, which had been designed in imitation of a wastebasket that Winston had admired in a West End hotel. Meals were built around his tastes: there were no cream soups, for he preferred consommé (if there wasn't clear soup or a pint of champagne – it was his rule to drink a pint every night – he did not think it was really dinner); plain foods such as rare roast beef with Yorkshire pudding, Irish stew and steak and kidney pudding were served instead of anything too decorative; cheddar was preferred to any French cheeses.‡

Even time had to be bent to Winston's will.§ The day was arranged

---

* Clementine thought his underclothes of pale pink finely woven silk, which 'cost the eyes out of his head', were an extravagance. 'It is essential to my well-being,' he argued, 'I have a very delicate and sensitive cuticle which demands the finest covering.'
† Within a few weeks of becoming prime minister, he issued a directive forbidding whistling in the Downing Street corridors.
‡ Winston's peculiar culinary preferences were most evident at breakfast. He was very particular about this meal: he wanted something different each day, and always insisted on something hot and something cold, like bacon and eggs and a slice of ham, or a leftover from the previous night, such as a cutlet or leg of chicken that had been put aside for him. He detested marmalade and loved jam – especially black cherry. Whatever else was on his plate, he would not start eating until jam had been brought.
§ As Clementine wrote in a letter to Lord Citrine, 'Winston is the most unpunctual person in the world. No, that is not the way to put it. He has no sense of time at all. He says to me, "You know, my dear, I can dress in fifteen minutes," and I reply: "No, you can't. It takes you twenty-one minutes and even then we have to hurry."'

His unpunctuality meant that for much of his life he was continually missing trains, ships, planes. At no point did his timekeeping ever improve, but what did change was that after May 1940, he had become so exalted that trains, ships and planes began to wait for him.

to help accommodate his desire to fit as much activity into twenty-four hours as humanly possible. For this reason, he loved anything that saved time – in later life most of his shoes had zip fasteners.

And yet Clementine was sometimes forced to resort to trying to trick her husband into coming to luncheon on time. Although she actually intended the meal to be served at 1.45 p.m., Winston's valet was told to inform him that he was expected at 1.00 p.m. When the message was passed on, Winston would smile in a knowing way and, by ostentatiously reading a newspaper or walking leisurely around the grounds, show that he was determined to be late for the meal, whatever anybody else wanted. On other occasions, Clementine crept into Winston's bedroom when he was not there and put his clock forward, a plan stymied by the two watches he carried with him.

Guests were forced to play by their host's whimsical rules. When birds started dive-bombing his fishpond, Winston fired at them with a pellet gun. All was well until a stray pellet hit his cat, Mr Singer Cat, in the tail. Grief-stricken, Winston called an 'enormous ambulance', and though the bleeding was stopped, part of the tail had to be amputated.

Anyone who arrived after this accident was told by Winston to pretend they had not noticed Mr Singer Cat's disfigurement; otherwise, the cat would be embarrassed. If Clementine was away, he sometimes asked the butler to lay a place for Mr Singer Cat at the dinner table.

It was a house where, every day, every meal, something exciting was happening.

Extraordinary people would arrive. Powerful men, former leaders of the country, were frequent guests – Chartwell was where people like Diana Mitford, Randolph's cousin, whose icy beauty and fascist sympathies would make her one of the following decade's most conspicuous figures, first got a sense of the fascination of politics (she was also enraptured by having a bathroom of her own and seeing chateau-bottled claret on the table). Alongside them were Winston's close friends such as F. E. Smith, Brendan Bracken and, most of all, the brilliant, scornful physicist, Frederick Lindemann, better known as the Prof.* Winston

---

* He was by far Chartwell's most regular visitor, signing the visitors' book 112 times between 1925 and 1939.

trusted the Prof's great scientific expertise, ignored his essentially cranky political opinions* and cheerfully accepted his 'canine devotion'. There were few occasions, Sarah said, when the Prof was not present. This may have been because this curious, ascetic figure (a lifelong bachelor, he subsisted largely on egg whites, which meant that during shortages in the war, he was forced into spells of semi-starvation; when he played tennis he wore long sleeves and a shirt buttoned to the neck because he did not want women to look at him as a 'sex object') was one of the handful of Winston's friends that Clementine approved of.

Glamour was provided by figures such as Lawrence of Arabia – who arrived on his motorcycle as Aircraftman Shaw and came down to dinner in the robes of an Arabian prince – and a galaxy of Hollywood stars, including Charlie Chaplin, Tilly Loesch and Ethel Barrymore. Winston's nephew Peregrine said that he found the stream of visitors 'exhilarating'. 'One came away from Chartwell transformed.'

And yet Winston remained the most interesting, unusual, uninhibited person in the room. He presided over the dining room beaming, benevolent, ringed by puffs of cigar smoke, his soft white hands grasping a tumbler of brandy. He talked brilliantly, in his 'curious insistent' manner, and almost never stopped, except to feed scraps to, or engage in loving conversation with, a favoured pet. One guest remembered, 'Winston used to say such funny things that I would run upstairs and write them down. His voice was very interesting, like a lighthouse. It would have a constant, sombre tone and all of a sudden he would shoot out a ray of light that knocked everyone over.'

Another guest recalled, 'Until the end of dinner I listened to him spellbound. I can remember thinking: This is what people mean when they talk of "seeing stars" – this is what I am doing now. I do not to this day know who was on my other side. Good manners, social obligation, duty – all had gone with the wind. I was transfixed, transported into a new element.'

Mealtimes were the main event at Chartwell. There was seldom much small talk. Winston liked to dive straight into the big questions: politics, history, art and literature, with the Prof called upon for

---

* Although Winston worried about the impact his friend's right-wing ideas would have on his impressionable son.

scientific problems.* He would speak of Henry VIII, Walter Raleigh and James I as if they were his contemporaries. Sometimes he might give a short lecture on, for instance, the various invaders of Russia, with a particular emphasis on the personality of Charles XII. On other occasions, there would be a barrage of questions: What is the strength of Soviet industry? What do you know of Radclyffe Hall?

James Lees-Milne, one of Randolph's school friends, was a witness to Winston in full flow.

> One evening we remained at that round table till after midnight. The table cloth had long ago been removed. Mr Churchill spent a blissful two hours demonstrating with decanters and wine glasses how the Battle of Jutland was fought. It was a thrilling experience. He was fascinating. He got worked up like a schoolboy, making barking noises in imitation of gunfire and blowing cigar smoke across the battle scene in imitation of gun smoke.

Argument was encouraged. Randolph, Diana, Sarah and Mary would watch enthralled as their father launched into battle against men like the cultured, companionable, and occasionally choleric Duff Cooper, one of the few Conservatives during the 1930s who, like Winston and Randolph, realised that war with Germany was inevitable. Keeping score, the children would sometimes even make an interjection of their own. (The best times were when Duff lost his temper: he would redden, the veins on his forehead pulsing so violently it looked as if they were trying to escape his skull.) Whatever direction the conversation took, it usually ended in gales of laughter. One guest remembered Clementine's full-throated laugh as 'a sound of real joy'. She would 'cackle like a hen. It was very contagious.'

During the school holidays, the children would have lunch with their parents at the round table; as they grew older, they were allowed to stay up for dinner. Each of them learned that it was essential to be able to talk well, no matter who was present. The family used to have

* This included producing a slide rule to calculate how much champagne Winston had drunk in his lifetime (Winston was disappointed to learn that it was only enough to fill a railway carriage).

competitions to see who could carry on reciting the longest the great reams of poetry and prose Winston encouraged them to store in their memories (What would you do, he asked them, if you found yourself without a book? Or in a boring or uncomfortable situation?).

Randolph was always the best at this; just as he excelled from an early age at being able to talk originally and fluently, consistently showing himself able to turn any conversation to his advantage. This delighted his father, who encouraged him to express his opinions and to challenge those of others. As Randolph entered his teens, Sarah remembered, 'glorious rows' would shake the room: with the swell of loud voices interrupted by a laughing Winston shouting, 'Randolph, do stop interrupting me while I'm interrupting you.'

This is what Winston loved, and Randolph learned to love too: the pugnacious back and forth of good conversation; using words to dominate the room; watching how they could change its atmosphere; knowing that argument could be a source of pleasure.* And this is what Randolph and Sarah both said they remembered most about the early years they spent at Chartwell: 'the fun and laughter, the equality and sharing, the humour and electricity of life, even when politics were not going their father's way'.

The environment was not to everybody's taste. Their cousin Peregrine, who was sensitive and sensible (when Winston asked him what he wanted to be when he grew up, he replied 'a retired banker'), remembered the house far less fondly.

> I found Chartwell living hell, disordered, crazy, inconvenient. My uncle was a great man but a frightful bully. So was my cousin Randolph. All those overpowering egos! All that endless talk on politics! After a certain age I felt the need to get away from all those Churchills. Otherwise they would have squashed me.

The exhilaration Peregrine had found to begin with eventually gave way to exhaustion. There was something more ambiguous, more

---

* Sarah found the eminent men Winston assembled at Chartwell boring and instead would run off to sit in corners with her cousin Anita Leslie and make plans to escape onto the stage.

potentially damaging about the energy in this home than many were willing to acknowledge. Nor was it only visitors who were disturbed by it. The family called Diana 'Chatterbox' because she never stopped talking. But anybody watching her closely would have realised that talk was just a way of concealing her deep shyness.

Most uncomfortable of all was Clementine. Johnny Churchill once drove back to London with her after a weekend at Chartwell: 'I just can't stand it any longer,' she told him. 'I just can't stand it any longer.'

When Clementine married Winston, she would later tell her daughter-in-law Pamela, she had to decide whether to be the sort of woman, like Diana Cooper, who had her own friends and her own life apart from Duff, or one who would stay home and 'give her life totally' to Winston. She chose the second option. For Clementine, Pamela recalled, 'Winston came first in every respect.'*

Winston repaid her with almost complete dependence. He could be pathetically grateful for everything she did for him, especially when he felt vulnerable and lonely. Sometimes when she was away, he climbed into her unmade bed. 'You are a rock & I depend on you & rest on you,' he would write to her when they were separated. 'Come back to me therefore as soon as you can.'

And yet – particularly when his spirits surged – he could also act as if he had no idea how severe or unreasonable were the demands he placed on her, or how hard it was to deal with him when he behaved like a petulant child.

She wanted to feel needed, and indeed had been entirely complicit in creating a marriage in which it was understood quite explicitly that her life was to be devoted to her husband and his ambitions, but the extent to which her husband relied on her drained her already limited resources.

Winston, Clementine once told Mary, was able to do so much because he 'never did anything he didn't want to do, and left someone else to clear up the mess'. 'He prides himself on keeping his temper and he makes my head ache with his arguments. I tell him the reason why he can keep his temper is because he always gets his own way.'

---

* Even years later, Pamela never felt she could explain Clementine. She had been 'wonderfully kind' to her, but at the same time she still thought her a 'strange woman'.

Three decades later, a nurse brought to look after an ageing Winston would report:

It did not take long to realise the loyalty he inspired, yet his personality was, at times, completely overwhelming. He drained the
people around him of every last drop of energy and there was never
a day when I came off duty without feeling completely all in. Apart
from the physical strain, the mental wear and tear were tremendous. For he inspired a curious love–hate relationship in those
under him, so that one loved him part of the time, hated him part
of the time, yet liked him all of the time.

All his life, people had taken care of him: Mrs Everest, manservants,
batmen, secretaries, footmen, acolytes and Clementine. It was not
exactly that he asked for this sort of support; he simply expected it.

Aside from the basic duties of running his house, raising his children and answering his gargantuan emotional needs, she had substantial political responsibilities. She was a constant presence by her
husband's side during his tours and visits, and shouldered much
constituency work, opening bazaars, visiting schools on speech days
and attending Conservative women's meetings, which involved
repressing her almost atavistic hostility to the Tories.

This all left little or no space for herself, or anything she might
have wished to do.

Clementine impressed upon all of her children that they were
expected to show the same loyalty to Winston as she had. His career
was all-important, and disruptive intrusions could not be tolerated.

As Randolph would later put it, 'DUTY was all.'

Each of the children understood from an early age that their mother's
unyielding devotion to Winston meant that they would always occupy
a peripheral role in her life. The idea that anybody's needs might be put
before those of their father was as unimaginable as if someone had told
them that the next day the sun would not come up. 'We admired and
loved our parents,' Mary said, 'and perfectly accepted that our father's life
demanded the cream of our mother's time and energy.'

It was not just that in emptying herself to serve her husband she
had less space for her children. The loving nicknames she and Winston

bestowed on them – Randolph was 'the Rabbit', Diana the 'Gold-Cream Kitten', Sarah the 'Bumble-bee', Mary the 'Mouse' – obscured the difficulty she had bonding with them. Clementine had loved her babies with a 'fierce physical relish' and was rarely happier than when surrounded in her room by playing toddlers as she dressed or ran the household. And yet as she grew older, there re-emerged the awkward formality and reserve that marked her struggle to form intimate friendships, and she realised that, without wishing to, she had created a barrier between her children and herself. She was never easy or spontaneous. She could not understand how children thought or felt, nor could she ever let go of her perfectionism, whether over manners and morals or garden clothes.*

Clementine was by nature withholding and cautious, qualities exacerbated by the fact that she was forced to spend large tracts of her life in the company of men whom she did not trust. Her reserve was a mechanism for shielding her insecurities from public view, but at some point it stopped being a means of defending herself and became instead her way of being.

A case in point was the huge treehouse at Chartwell – two storeys high and twenty feet above ground – that Winston built in an old lime tree by the front drive while Clementine was away at a tennis tournament in Cromer. The treehouse was adored by the children, and building it offered them the chance of hours of relaxed compan-ionship in their father's company, just as they had when working with him on the brick walls and dams that dotted the Chartwell grounds. (As Mary noted of her easy, natural relationship with Winston, 'it just seemed to happen'.)

But Clementine worried about their safety, which left her feeling excluded from the fun the rest of the family was having. Consumed by anxiety, she could not surrender enough of herself to join in with her husband and children, and was left watching them, her clothes

---

* Nancy Mitford's waspish take on her own upbringing is a reminder that Clementine was not unique: 'So what did my mother do all day? She says now, when cross-examined, that she lived for us. Perhaps she did, but nobody could say that she lived with us. It was not the custom then. I think that nothing in my life has changed more than the relationship between mothers and young children. In those days a distance was always kept.'

immaculate, her hair neat, the distance between them growing all the time.

Both her family and staff were often stung by her unrelenting desire for perfection. She could lose her temper over tiny setbacks such as cold soup or late deliveries, and she was merciless if any of her children did not meet her high standards. The special treatment Randolph received from his father left him feeling able, from an early age, to shrug this criticism off, or at least to give a good impression of being unbothered by it, but Sarah, who described her mother as 'formidable', and Diana were in awe of Clementine and kept their distance.

And yet perhaps she was harshest on herself. She was pitiless about what she saw as her own failings and was often conscience-stricken: happiness would always be hard for her to grasp.

By the age of thirty-seven, Clementine had suffered an annihilating series of losses: a sister, a brother and a daughter. This was compounded by the shame and disorder of her early life. The surprise is not that she was brittle, subject to nervous breakdowns, or that she could be uncompromising towards her children; it was that she was able to carry on at all. Clementine's life was an exercise in trying to avoid breaking to pieces. She succeeded, but there was a price to pay.

Although Clementine appeared to many as full of vitality, this was undercut by a lack of stamina. She was always left exhausted and low by the births of her children. And even when she was young, she needed to rest during the afternoon if she was to be equal to the evening's activities.

She always had a sense that things were falling apart, and was prey to intense bouts of nervous exhaustion: 'I am a poor wrecked ship,' she wrote to Winston after he had become First Lord of the Admiralty and she had fallen so ill that she feared she might become a permanent invalid; 'You must take me in hand as if I were one of your battleships.'

The only way she could cope was to absent herself for long periods. Even by comparison with her contemporaries, she was away from the family home a great deal. Some of this was because she was accompanying Winston on his bustling round of social and political commitments. But a lot of the time she travelled by herself, to play in tennis tournaments in Cromer, or to recover in a spa in France, or to go on long cruises to the other side of the world, which meant she could put thousands of miles between herself and the draining chaos of Chartwell.

Clementine may not always have been happy at Chartwell, but her children were, more often than not. Mary, writing years later, remembered 'the spaciousness of our life' at Chartwell. For her, 'that disproportioned, irregular, inconvenient heavenly house' was an idyll: in winter, it was a warm, scented home full of crackling log fires; in summer, it was a place of flowers, happy voices from the tennis court and long hours by the swimming pool.

Winston's offspring treated him with uncomplex adoration. In turn, he loved to have children around: 'Come to luncheon,' he used to say. 'You'll find us all bunged up with brats.' And because Clementine was so assiduous in ensuring the children were fed, clothed, washed and disciplined, he could concentrate entirely – when he had time to do so – on amusing them. Winston knew how to make children laugh and his own commitment to indulging himself meant that he had an instinctive understanding of what sorts of things would surprise and delight them. He was, Randolph recalled, 'wonderfully spontaneous, resourceful and unexpected in arranging treats for us'. In his hands, said Sarah, a lamb chop would become a feast, a glass of champagne a party.

Some evenings, when he was at home, Winston would invite his children into his bedroom and read aloud to them for an hour or so, making them late for bed and himself late for dinner. He might even help them with their essays. But no matter how fond Winston was of his children, he rarely spent anything other than very short bursts of time with them. He would feel cooped up after a handful of days and become consumed by restlessness.

It meant that all of the children were engaged in a constant attempt to please and keep up with their father, and to make a claim on his attention – always a limited resource. They wanted to be seen and valued as important parts of his life. (It is perhaps telling that he never hit his children; banishment from his presence was considered a far crueller punishment.)

Diana, Randolph, Sarah and Mary lived for those moments when they knew they had pleased him and could bask in his gaze, which was 'as warm as the summer sunshine'. Sarah remembers how from the age of fourteen, 'I wanted to be in the league of people who, if they could not help, at least understood where he was trying to go with an idea. I tried to train myself to think; not the things he thought, but the way he thought.'

It was an unfair competition. Winston loved his children fiercely, and yet there was always something different about the way he treated Randolph. If Winston was king at Chartwell, Randolph was its crown prince.

Winston wanted to ensure that Randolph's childhood would be as different from his own as he could make it. His son, he said, would be given 'every advantage'. Winston wanted to create the kind of intimate bond that he had always fantasised about having with Lord Randolph.

Because he knew the agony of feeling abandoned and alone at school, he made a point of visiting Randolph at his schools as often as he could – first at his prep school, Sandroyd (where he was sent at the age of nine, later than other boys; he might have been kept at home longer, but by this point neither governesses nor nursery maids could control him, and he had stopped listening when Clementine told him off) and then at Eton.

For instance, while Clementine was away at Saint-Jean-Cap-Ferrat in February 1921, Winston made a couple of visits to Sandroyd where, he reported to Clementine, he found Randolph in 'sprightly' form. 'The headmaster', he wrote, 'described him as very combative and said that on any pretext or excuse he mixes himself up in fights and quarrels; but they seem quite pleased with him all the same.'

Most parents would have been anxious to find that their child was so unruly; Winston seemed proud. This was, after all, exactly how he had behaved as a young boy. It was welcome evidence that the Churchill blood still ran hot, although it did little for his son's chances of learning any sort of discipline.

Winston was also far more protective of his son than Lord Randolph had ever been of him. (His letters to Clementine fretting that Randolph was not wearing enough underclothes are testament to this.) When Randolph was ten, a young assistant master called him into his room on an unconvincing pretext. As soon as Randolph arrived, he was instructed to sit down beside the master on the bed.

Next, the young Randolph, who had no clear understanding of what he was experiencing, watched as the older man undid his trousers and then 'caused me to manipulate his organ'.

Randolph was more surprised than he was disturbed. It was only when he saw the master's guilty reaction when a housemaid came in without knocking that he realised something was wrong and made a quick escape. He avoided the master for a while after this.

His next summer holidays were spent at Rugby School, where Winston had taken the headmaster's house so he could play polo with his cousin, Ivor Guest, at Ashby St Ledgers.

In between learning to swim, Randolph told Diana about his strange experience. Their conversation was overheard by a nanny, who went straight to Clementine, who then told Winston. The next morning, Randolph was summoned to his father's room, where he found Winston in bed eating breakfast.

Winston asked his son what 'the truth of the matter' was, and Randolph, who always felt compelled to be honest with his father, told him what had happened. Randolph had never seen his father as angry before. Writing four decades after the event, he struggled to remember ever having seen him as angry since. Winston charged out of his bed, ordered his car and sped off to Eton. He returned late that night, having made a round trip of some two hundred miles. It was futile; the master had already been sacked on other grounds.

Aware perhaps that there was little he could do now, Winston settled on giving some advice: 'Never let anyone do that to you again.'

The incident left Winston racked by anger and anxiety. Randolph, for his part, seems to have been completely untroubled.

When guests came to Chartwell, Winston pushed Randolph forward and introduced him before he introduced his wife. This habit left Clementine 'jealous as hell'. Her anger was only increased by the way the men sat at the table for hours after the women had left. According to Johnny Churchill, Clementine hated the fact she was no longer the centre of attention. While Winston was presenting his son at the table as an equal, she was sent upstairs to have a boiled egg on a tray on her own. Winston did not appear troubled by her pique. He was preparing his son to be prime minister one day, and that was all that mattered; it was not a woman's place to interfere.

Nor did Winston appear to be bothered by the contradiction that lay at the heart of his treatment of his son. The idea that great men were the product of a lonely childhood was a theme that ran through his books. In 1898, writing of the Mahdi, he had talked of how 'solitary trees, if they grow at all, grow strong; and a boy deprived of a father's care often develops, if he escapes the perils of youth, an independence and vigour of thought which may restore in after life the heavy loss of early days.'

Thirty years later, in his biography of the Duke of Marlborough, he was making a similar argument: 'famous men are usually the product of an unhappy childhood. The stern compression of circumstances, the twinges of adversity, the spur of slights and taunts in early years, are needed to evoke that ruthless fixity of purpose and tenacious mother wit without which great actions are seldom accomplished.'

And yet his approach to raising Randolph was completely different. If Winston was aware of this wrinkle in his intentions, he gave little sign of it.

For the moment, Randolph and his father would sit up in Winston's study, talking deep into the night. It was here that Winston filled his son's head with stories about his past, and that of their ancestors. In the process he colonised his imagination, transmitting to Randolph all his obsessions, ideas and prejudices.

Winston was a man who had strong opinions about everything, from the changes in military tactics and strategy since 1795 and the correct architecture for sandwiches (the bread must be wafer-thin, 'nothing more than a vehicle to convey the filling to the stomach'), to the fact that the Tory party had always betrayed England (his own experiences and the Tories' treatment of his and Randolph's ancestor the Duke of Marlborough were cited as evidence). Randolph absorbed all of them; in a draft of his memoir he later discarded, he wrote that he learned more from his father than he ever did at school.

Winston praised his son and told him how lucky he was to bear such a hallowed name. When an American journalist asked Randolph whether he regretted his father turning down a dukedom, he replied, 'No. To be born a Churchill, the son of Winston, is a heritage no title in the peerage can match.'

This was partly a routine aristocratic sense of superiority, and partly something particular to a man who lived as if rules were invented for other people. Randolph's father was someone who, if caught in a traffic jam, would steer his car onto the pavement and barge his way to the front of the queue: 'I hold a police pass,' he claimed to his bodyguard, 'which entitles me to break any line of traffic to get where I want to go.' What Winston was teaching his son was the same tearing disdain for the opinions of others that his own father had shown throughout his short, violent career.

Winston was obsessed with the pursuit and exercise of political power 'and the thought of this power magically passing from certain fathers to their son'. Again and again he talked to Randolph about his plans to create a dynasty, and how it would be the younger Churchill's responsibility not only to continue it but to add glory to it. This dynastic imperative would become so tightly woven into Randolph's being that even in the sixties, ahead of a journey to South America, he refused to travel in the same plane as his son. He would not risk two generations of the family being wiped out in one accident.

It must have been intoxicating for Randolph to be petted and praised by such a strange and enthralling man. A man whose overpowering charisma could, as Sarah recalled, 'imbue everybody with a sense of excitement', but which could also be deployed to dominate people, treating them almost as a ventriloquist might his puppets. A man so dedicated to his own plans and pleasures that he never did a single thing he did not want to do, who was so self-centred that he could sometimes give the impression that he was barely aware other people existed.

One night during the twenties, at the end of the school holidays, Randolph and his father stayed up once more, talking through the night. Randolph recalled that they had been discussing 'every subject', and then at 1.30 a.m., Winston turned to his son and, in a voice tinged with sadness, said, 'You know, my dear boy, I think I have talked to you more in these holidays than my father talked to me in the whole of his life.'

4

It's Only a Game, Father

IN SEPTEMBER 1924, with a general election on the horizon, Winston made a speech at Edinburgh that announced his return to full-time politics. Shortly afterwards, he was invited by the local Conservative associations to stand in the safe seat of Epping as a Constitutionalist and Anti-Socialist candidate. While Winston rampaged around the country, sounding 'alarm bells' about the threat of socialism, Clementine and the rest of the family supervised the campaign nearer to home. On 30 October 1924, a little less than two years after his unceremonious defeat in Dundee, Winston was back in the House of Commons, with a majority of just under ten thousand.

A few days later, Winston was summoned to see the new prime minister, Stanley Baldwin, who asked him if he was willing to serve as chancellor. Remembering his miserable spell as chancellor of the Duchy of Lancaster during the Great War, Winston tried to establish what exactly he was being offered. 'Of the Duchy?'

'No, of the Exchequer.'

Winston's first thought was to say, 'Will the bloody duck swim?' Instead, he opted for something more dignified: 'This fulfils my ambition. I still have my father's robes as Chancellor. I shall be proud to serve you in this splendid office.'

It was a bigger, better job than Winston could have hoped for. It was also one with great emotional significance. Lord Randolph's last post before his fatal miscalculation had been Chancellor of the Exchequer.

As chancellor, Winston believed that he could act as a reforming and moderating influence on his new colleagues. He wanted to expand the provision of compulsory and contributory insurance, make a progressive reduction to income tax and encourage the development of cheap housing. This would all be funded by checks on government expenditure elsewhere, notably the naval budget. Lord Randolph's hand was, it appeared, still guiding every step his son took.

In March 1925, after a masterful performance from Baldwin had foiled a Private Members' Bill designed to weaken the power of the Trades Unions, Winston wrote to his wife:

> A strong Conservative Party with an overwhelming majority and a moderate and even progressive leadership is a combination which has never been tested before. It might well be the fulfilment of all that Dizzy [Benjamin Disraeli] and my father aimed at in their political work.

Winston's excitement at being able to pick up the flag Lord Randolph had been forced to lay down was not sufficient to disguise the fact that the Treasury was uncongenial to him, largely because 'he had only a minimal interest in the problems of high finance'.

Like his father (who famously said of the decimals in his budget 'I could never make out what those damned dots meant'), Winston was not temperamentally suited to the post. Although he was ultimately responsible for the country's catastrophic return to the gold standard ('The biggest blunder of my life,' he would later say), it was a decision he had been pressured into making. This would not have happened in a role where he was happier or more confident. He once said to Bob Boothby, after a conference of senior Treasury officials, bankers and economists: 'I wish they were admirals and generals. I speak their language, and can beat them. But after a while these fellows start talking Persian. And then I am sunk.'

Still, the day of his first budget was an occasion of immense pride. On 28 April 1925, he had emerged from 11 Downing Street 'as happy as a sandboy, his top hat extra glossy', before going on to the House where, watched by Clementine, Randolph and Diana in the Strangers' Gallery above him, he completed what his father had been robbed of doing thirty-nine years previously.

★

Winston's return to Parliament came a month after Randolph had passed a milestone of his own. He went to Eton.

Winston had pleased the twelve-year-old Randolph by giving him the choice between going to his alma mater, Harrow, or to Eton: 'I thought', he wrote, 'it was very civilised of him to give me the option.'

After they had been to inspect both schools, Randolph opted for Eton because 'there were fewer rules and much less discipline'. To begin with, at least, Eton did offer Randolph the freedom he had been looking for. This soon palled, and what had looked like liberation began to feel more like constriction.

Lord Randolph had given the impression of barely remembering his son's existence. By contrast, Winston was passionately interested in both the formation of Randolph's mind and his well-being. He took steps to ensure the latter by asking F. E. Smith to see that Smith's son Freddie looked after Randolph, which essentially meant ensuring he was not beaten.* Randolph's addiction to provocation rendered this a near-impossible task. Winston also took a strong interest in the physical programme his son would follow: 'I do not think much of rowing as a pastime,' he wrote to Eton's headmaster. 'If boys are not good at it they only loaf; if they are good they only exhaust themselves and very likely strain their hearts. At the best it seems a monotonous form of recreation and one which leads to nothing in after life.'

Randolph was induced to share his exam papers with Winston so that they could discuss his responses in depth. Winston gave his thoughts in letters full of energy and advice. In December 1925, having looked through one of Randolph's essays, he wrote to his son, 'I have read the paper and your answers to it. I do not think you have done badly but it would have been very easy to do better.'

After a flood of imperious judgements about the identity of the best Roman general, and why Fabius had been wrong to be so

---

* A couple of years later, though by this time he had been presented with numerous examples of bad behaviour from his son, he would write to the school to ask them to spare Randolph the cane. He is halfway to seventeen, 'it would be a mistake if he were to be caned in the House without any serious cause . . . As boys begin to grow up an incident of this kind, without just and good cause, might well have an embittering effect upon a mind rapidly forming and in some respects startlingly mature.'

cautious, he concluded by asking: 'When will it be known what is to be the subject for next year? You ought certainly to go in for it next time, and if we can get the books early we can read it up together.'

As far as Winston was concerned, his son's education was a joint enterprise. Which made it all the more disappointing that Randolph was so little interested in making the most of the opportunities he had been presented. Some of this was due to the indolence that had already become a habit with Randolph. He had early learned that he could get on by doing just enough. One master noted, 'He has plenty of ability but he prefers to be thoroughly idle . . . His chief aim in school is to promote discussions which shall be as far removed as possible from the work in hand.' And the headmaster Robert Birley, writing in 1928 just before Randolph left Eton, said: 'His real trouble is facility. He finds it a great deal too easy to do moderately well.'* His cleverness and confidence supplied what effort did not.

Part of the problem was simply a question of high spirits. As his headmaster at Sandroyd, W. M. Hornby, had observed in a letter to Winston: 'He ought to do uncommonly well if he will stick to things and not run too wild. Of all the boys who are leaving I shall miss him by far the most. He is so splendidly full of life and the enjoyment of it in a nice sporting way.'

But increasingly, it was simply that Randolph had become desperate to leave. He later recalled, 'I did not enjoy Eton very much. I was lazy and unsuccessful both at work and at games. I did not conform to the general pattern and was an unpopular boy.'

He presented an image of himself as a misfit, one who eschewed the conventional paths to schoolboy popularity, such as sport. Instead, he spent time reading Keats and Shelley on a private island in the Thames that had once been owned by an eccentric master called Luxmoore and was known by Tom Mitford as Jardin de Luxe.

---

* The report continued, prophetically: 'There is no need for him merely to do this. He has a first-rate brain. But he must be prepared to do some hard thinking for himself and not to take an easy course. His easy course will not be a dull one, in fact it will be an amusing and interesting one. But it will be second-rate for all that."

Like his father, he could claim to be a rebel and a loner, and perhaps in the process exaggerated the degree to which he was shunned. The problem was aggravated by the fact that as he grew up, Randolph was steadily exposed to more and more of the glamorous adult world occupied by his father. The Prof began to pick him up at Eton and speed him across to Oxford to dine and drink port at Christ Church's high table. He gave him presents, petted him and took him on motor car holidays, before sending him back to school clutching big boxes of chocolates.

Randolph, told constantly by Winston how clever and talented he was, and given a stage on which he could demonstrate his gifts, did not hold back. When Randolph returned to Chartwell for the holidays, he ran wild during the day before coming back in time to interrupt guests at dinner.

Winston could not resist showing off his garrulous, quick-witted son. Randolph found himself sitting across from men like David Lloyd George, F. E. Smith and Max Beaverbrook. Winston would listen enraptured as Randolph held forth at the table, waving his cigar to ensure his son was given the attention he felt was his due. After Randolph went back to Eton, he found that having become accustomed to talking on equal terms with great men, it was hard to talk to other boys or focus on his work. Why bother reading about politics and history when you had been talking with the men who controlled one and had made the other?

When a tutor was hired to coach him, he knew that all he had to do to avoid being told things he had no interest in learning was to run away and hide. Winston would laugh and fuss over his son when he turned up later in the day. His enjoyment was only increased by the sight of the poor tutor's misery and Clementine's rage.

If Clementine made a rule and Randolph broke it, there was little she could do to punish him. If she tried, Randolph would go straight to Winston's study, where he would instantly be forgiven. Winston might sometimes threaten to make Randolph's life less agreeable if he did not mend his ways, but the threat was rarely followed by any sort of substantial action. Diana Mitford remembered that 'Winston never backed Clementine up. It would have been better if he had bashed Randolph, but he always let him rip.'

Winston generally dismissed the many criticisms in his son's school reports, using them as the starting point for stories of his own experiences with foolish or incompetent masters. He even encouraged him to greater impudence towards the men charged with his education. Winston had decided he would never make his son apologise to older people, so Randolph simply made a habit of being rude. To him, it appeared clever.

On those occasions when Winston's anger was provoked, his son was skilful at inventing the 'sorts of excuses, subterfuges, and palliatives' that helped to divert attention from his academic failures. And when gentle deception proved insufficient, Randolph could always just talk back. It was easy to point to Winston's own failings at school. It was riskier to make the case that he had become Chancellor of the Exchequer even though, in Randolph's view, he knew about as much about mathematics as Randolph did. But this did not daunt Randolph. He knew that the ability to argue that day was night, and down was up, was a quality his father admired.

There were rows between them – as Mary noted, 'Randolph would pick an argument with a chair' – but the moment would always come when Winston came to his son to kiss him and tell him that he had not meant to be unkind.

Clementine was less forgiving. Randolph believed that his mother hated him, and always had. It was one of the first things he told Pamela Digby when they met in the autumn of 1939. Pamela was sceptical to begin with; she thought, having 'come from a normal English family', that the claim was 'exaggerated and ridiculous'.

'No,' Randolph insisted, 'I know that she hates me, and I knew it when I was eight years old. The first time she came down to take me out at prep school she slapped me on the face in front of all the other boys, and I knew that she hated me from that moment on.'

Over the next few months, Pamela would learn that what her fiancé had told her was true. Or, at least, it was a faithful reflection of the way Randolph felt his mother felt about him. (Another witness, John Julius Norwich, also believed that Clementine really did 'hate' her son and that Randolph felt the same about her: 'I remember [Randolph's] passionate admiration for his father ... He never mentioned his mother at all.' Randolph's cousin Peregrine put it more succinctly: 'Clemmie really hated her son.')

He told other people variations of the same story. In one version, the assault came at Eton. In another, he was on his way to his father's study when he was stopped by Clementine, who told him that Winston was not to be disturbed. Determined to see his father, Randolph tried to wriggle past. But his mother struck him on the cheek, a slap so hard that it sent him tumbling down the stairs.

Randolph thought that Clemmie was a cold, distant parent whose obsessive focus on attending to his father's demands meant that she had little energy or affection left over for her children. He would complain about this for the rest of his life. 'To me she was not a real person,' Randolph would later tell his sister Mary. 'She made a marvellous public image, & then often acted it in her private life.' Once Clementine reprimanded Randolph for taking a fancy to an older woman. He shot back, 'I don't care, I need her. She's maternal and you're not.'

Randolph's cousin Anita Leslie believed that Clementine's inability, or unwillingness, to give him the love that he so plainly wanted from her left him with a feeling of rejection that he would never quite lose. Her coldness and reserve left him eternally craving affection, particularly from women.

Clementine, for her part, resented the indulgence shown to Randolph by her husband. She had spent almost two decades emptying herself to please Winston, and yet now he seemed interested only in spoiling their son.

Deprived of his mother's affection, Randolph baited her, just as he baited his cousins. Knowing that she loved tennis, he was deliberately bad at it, laughing as he flunked out of the competitions she entered him into. As he got older, he began simply to ignore her. From the age of about thirteen, Randolph centred all of his 'interests & affections' on his father.* Talking to Mary many years later, he said how much that hurt their mother. 'She felt this.'

---

* Later in life, whenever he wanted to be rude about a woman (and as an unabashed chauvinist, he often did), he would say, 'You are just like my mother.'

From time to time over the years, when the senselessness of their feud bore down on them, Randolph and his mother made attempts at reconciliation. Randolph would write affectionate letters to his mother from Eton ('I cannot tell you how much I am pining to see you. It seems such ages since last I saw you'), or Clementine would cross the Atlantic to see her son while he toured the United States ('I am thrilled about the whole adventure and I am counting the days now until I see you'). These rarely lasted. But although their relationship was disintegrating, it did not seem at first as if Winston noticed.

He was too busy encouraging in his son the same taste for luxury that had always been such a source of frustration to Clementine. He took him away boar hunting in France and on long trips to the Mediterranean, where they visited Pompeii and the newly discovered ruins at Herculaneum (although Randolph was not allowed to see its erotic frescoes) as well as having audiences with both the Pope and Benito Mussolini. Randolph was thrilled by it, and Winston exulted in his son's company.

Randolph and Winston hunting in Dieppe, 1924, with Sir Warden Chilcott.

When Randolph was sixteen, Winston taught him to gamble which was guaranteed to anger Clementine. Randolph revelled in it because it upset his mother.*

There were warning signs that something within Randolph meant he could not control his desires and that he was not bound by the set of gentlemanly obligations that were so important to his father. One day when Winston was teaching Randolph to play cards, they began a game of vingt-et-un. As they went on, and the stakes got higher with each hand, Winston became tetchy. When he called Randolph's bluff and found he had nothing, he was furious.

'How dare you gamble when you haven't got the money to pay your debts.'

'It's only a game, father, it was your idea. You wanted to have some fun, and we played.'

'You must never gamble like that. You are gambling in a dishonest way.'

Their rage at each other reached such peaks that they almost came to blows; it was only Clementine's entrance into the room that prevented matters getting out of hand.

On another occasion, when Randolph was seventeen, father and son went to stay with the Duke of Westminster, at Mimizan, near Biarritz, where he had a small hunting lodge. On the way back to Paris, the two Churchills, along with the duke and duchess, Bendor and Loelia, ate dinner in the first-class restaurant. After they had all eaten and drunk well, Randolph ordered another brandy.

'No,' Winston told him, 'you have had enough.'

The waiter, confused by what had suddenly become a highly charged situation, brought the glass anyway. Winston leaned across the table to snatch it from his son's hands, and in the scuffle that followed, most of the brandy ended up on his sleeve. Bendor and Loelia looked on in horror, both left silent by shock, but Winston only seemed amused.

---

* Clementine felt an almost physical horror at this sort of wasteful behaviour. Writing to Winston in 1924 after a trip to a casino with her mother and her sister Nellie, she reported, 'I was astounded at the reckless manner in which both Mother & Nellie gambled. Nellie very intelligently & dashingly, Mother in a superstitious & groping manner. It made me feel quite ill & ashamed to watch them & I went home to bed . . . It just seems to me a morbid mania.'

Winston never gave the appearance of being troubled by the almost effortless way Randolph could send his elders into paroxysms of rage. He laughed at his seventeen-year-old son's insolence to Lady Nancy Astor when she tried to shame him for smoking cigars (if you do not take care, she had told him, you will die like your grandfather of debauchery).

Diana Cooper said that Randolph once told her he did not know the feeling of shyness. He talked and talked and talked. Wagging his finger, monopolising conversations and expressing opinions about everything. There was a day when his incessant conversation became too much for the boys he was with. They threw him out of a first-floor window onto the street. Randolph landed, unharmed, and carried on talking.*

He possessed a dazzling skill with words and logic. His ability to speak on the 'unpinioned wing' was a gift that Winston would boast about with pride edged with an envy he could not quite confess to. But the bright floods of words obscured something: an inability to frame his thoughts properly. There were times when he wanted to express himself, and yet when he groped for the words he needed, they remained stubbornly out of his grasp. He would go red and tears of frustration would fill his eyes.

Randolph once tried to explain himself to his friend Frank Pakenham: 'I have an overwhelming urge to express myself,' he told him, 'but the tragedy is that I have nothing to express. I am an explosion that leaves the house still standing.'

What people saw was a young man whose self-confidence was so large it appeared it could swallow galaxies whole. They did not realise that his upbringing had left him deeply sensitive, and that he had learned early on to hide this vulnerability. In turn, Randolph never understood that other people could feel things as keenly as he did, had not made the same efforts to acquire a shield to keep their emotions safe.

★

* During the war, when he was stationed in Yugoslavia with Evelyn Waugh and Freddie Birkenhead, Randolph's friends were so worn down by his endless talk that they bet him £20 he could not read the Bible in a fortnight. 'Unhappily,' Evelyn reported to Nancy Mitford, 'it has not had the result we hoped. He has never read any of it before and is hideously excited; keeps reading quotations aloud . . . or merely slapping his side & chortling "God, isn't God a shit!"'

Randolph claimed in his memoir *Twenty-One Years* that his father had been 'overjoyed' when the Prof told him that an extra place had become available at Christ Church during the January term. This was a strange mis-memory.

His early arrival at Oxford was actually the result of an intense lobbying process in which his own desire to 'get on in life as quickly as I could' was only very slowly able to overmaster Winston's reluctance. For more than a year, Randolph nagged Winston, but his father argued that until he started making more progress at Eton, there was no question of his going to Oxford.

Randolph continued to plead his case up until Christmas 1928. His view was that since he had only one term left at Eton and had already passed the entrance exam, there was little point in going back to school for another four months. The Prof, who was staying at Chartwell, took Randolph's side in the rows that pockmarked the holiday. Even after he had returned to his college, father and son were still bickering. As always, though, Randolph's persistence, and the hold he exerted over his father's affections, meant that he got his way. By the end of January, he was at Oxford, writing to Winston: 'I am so enjoying being here, and I cannot tell you how glad I am that I did not have to return to Eton.'

Inevitably, he had arrived with a splash. This was par for the course for the Churchill children, who had grown up accustomed to this sort of attention. (Diana's first wedding, in 1932, attracted crowds so large that bride and groom were forced to leave the church by a side entrance.) Christopher Hollis describes there having been a 'great fanfare of trumpets from the London press', and talk that Randolph intended to attain the presidency of the Oxford Union in a shorter time than any other undergraduate in the university's history. This did not happen.

At Christ Church, Randolph led a leisurely, sybaritic life. It was not uncommon for him to be spotted walking across the quadrangle at 3.00 p.m., clad only in a tatty dressing gown, waving a cigar around. It soon became clear that, hard as he had fought with Winston to allow him to go up to Oxford early, he considered university as a formality he had to pass through before his gilded political career could begin. It was a place to make contacts; academic achievements were secondary. The circles he moved in believed that education came from conversation, not books, an approach that was, according to Randolph, 'far less laborious than getting up early in the morning and going to lectures'.

This education took place over the lobster Newburg, hock and countless glasses of port that were consumed at the lunches that formed almost the only regular part of his schedule. The wittiest and cleverest of the dons – such as Maurice Bowra, Lord David Cecil, Francis 'Sligger' Urquhart of Balliol College, Randolph's own tutor Roy Harrod and, inevitably, the Prof – picked out those they thought were the brightest of the undergraduates and invited them to luncheon parties. They were then invited to 'return luncheon' parties in the students' rooms, long meals lasting deep into the afternoon in which voices grew louder as bottles grew emptier and arguments about politics alternated with rowdy spells of banging on the table. Randolph himself gave four or so lunches a term and would attend three to four a week. It could seem at times as if for Randolph this ancient seat of learning was indistinguishable from a particularly well-appointed club.

He had arrived at the university to find a number of his older friends waiting for him: a group of clever, insubordinate boys with big cars and lots of money – including Freddie Birkenhead, Basil Dufferin, Seymour Berry and Christopher Sykes – who called themselves, with only a glance at irony, 'the smart bunch'.

Randolph, ecstatic finally to have left behind the confining atmosphere of Eton, saw them as 'glittering and attractive' and did not mind that, in the eyes of others, they 'preened themselves unduly'. This confidence was part of their attraction.

They were neither aesthetes nor hearties, and the group included peers, commoners and rich Americans. Most, however, had known each other since the nursery. Their lives were the sort that their friend Evelyn Waugh would describe in *Decline and Fall* or *Brideshead Revisited*. Although some, like John Betjeman and Edward James, had literary pretensions, what really bound them together was politics. An absolute conviction that the rest of the world was just waiting for them to rule it sat uneasily alongside a sense that the exuberant, fantasising hedonism they were all indulging in was an interlude before real life began.

The Prof was these boys' 'tutelary God', and Roy Harrod, closer in age and more approachable and patient than the Prof, his deputy. After Randolph fell out with his first tutor, Harrod took on the role. He noted two things about his new young charge: he did not care about rules, ignoring them as if they were not there; and he had a curious effect on other people. Something about his mere presence intensified their *joie de vivre*. As John Betjeman, who was part of this set, would later say: 'When I think of Randolph, I see him in terms of noise, light and laughter.'

Others took a different view. Osbert Lancaster, another contemporary, remembered, 'Everybody hated Randolph at Oxford – except me. I was always rather pro-Randolph. His nuisance value was unbelievable, the highest nuisance value I've ever come across – the rows he involved one in!'

As always with Randolph, beneath the surface arrogance lay a vein of sensitivity. In those moments when his mask slipped, he confided to friends that he did not feel completely accepted by the professors, or even the other first years. He would always feel as if Oxford had resisted him.

Once Randolph had gone up to Christ Church, he began spending most of his weekends at Charlton, his godfather F. E. Smith's country home outside Oxford. It was obvious, even to an eighteen-year-old Randolph, that his father's great friend had entered a vicious decline, and yet Randolph was quickly drawn into his world.

Randolph had always regarded F. E. with a kind of awe. When they were younger, Sarah noted that her brother became 'strangely nervous' when Lord Birkenhead visited. He would give his siblings instructions as to what they could and could not do, and what they could and could not say.

It is easy to see what it was in this tall, good-looking, sardonic friend of his father's that made Randolph respond with a mixture of adulation and fear. F. E. Smith, whose grandfather was a miner and his grandmother a gypsy, was impressive and terrifying in equal measure. Over the course of an uneven, controversy-studded career, he had wielded his coruscating wit as if it were a weapon, often unaware of the deep offence, even hatred, that his arrogance and sarcasm prompted in people who did not know him well. Worldly, cynical, suspicious of idealism, the epitome of 'wicked bachelor uncle', he lived life on an almost absurd scale.

F. E. and Winston had first forged their friendship in the turbulent times before the Great War, and it had survived the ups and downs of their personal fortunes in the years since. Asked about the enduring relationship, Brendan Bracken explained how 'F. E. was his closest friend. Oh, from 1910 to 1927. You never saw them together? Well, you missed a good sight. They both had tearing spirits – that is, when Winston wasn't in the dumps – a kind of daring, a dislike of a drab existence, a tremendous zest in life.'

They spent hours on end in each other's company, perspiring side by side in Turkish baths or presiding over meetings of the Other Club, the dining club they created in May 1911,* and at big family weekends at their respective country homes, even though Clementine never grew any fonder of her husband's great friend, whom she regarded as a vulgarian, and who she worried would lead him into 'strange ways'. She hated how insolent his drinking made him, and the thoughtless encouragement he gave to her increasingly turbulent son. The problem was that while Winston was always able to resist the temptations his friend put in his path, Randolph could not.

Weekends at Charlton followed a similar pattern. The other guests were all young men – mostly undergraduates – favoured by their host. F. E., who replenished his energy through activity, liked to play vigorous golf with his guests in the morning; nine or ten sets of tennis in the afternoon; and in the evening took any survivors for a ten-mile canter round a forty-acre field.

At night, up to sixteen people would cram into the small, oak-panelled dining room (designed to look like his Oxford college, Wadham), where their host would preside over a contentious, drink-sodden dinner. F. E. sat at the end of the refectory table in a red velvet dinner jacket with his cairn terrier on his knee and a cigar held, somewhat unusually, with all four fingers. There were times when he

---

* Randolph was never made a member of the dining club Winston and F. E. Smith had formed just days before he was born. Perhaps Winston wanted to preserve at least one space where he could exist undisrupted by his son's presence.

became so absorbed in what he was saying that he did not even notice the smoke from his cigar rising to his eyes and obscuring his vision.

After dinner, F. E. would make each of his guests give a speech, upon which he would make caustic comments. Randolph felt as if he was moving in an enchanted world. It resembled an expansion of the Chartwell he had known as a boy, but now he was old enough to 'savour with full relish' its cynical, witty, entirely male atmosphere.

It was here, Randolph's friends believed, while staying at F. E.'s and trying to match his drinking habits, that he acquired his taste for hard liquor. It was Lord Birkenhead who told him that it was only possible to make a good speech when you were drunk. And sitting at F. E.'s table, drinking his whisky, Randolph steadily absorbed many of his values. He tried and, by his own account, failed 'to emulate his style of polished repartee'. He imitated his majestic indolence, his disgust for political time-servers and his disregard for those institutions like Oxford, which he believed were governed by petty laws and peopled by petty men. The younger man also noted his host's cold contempt for bores – the way in which he refused to make even the smallest attempt at politeness in their presence. Instead, he would 'lie back with closed eyes, a look of unutterable weariness on his face'.*

Most damagingly of all, he would have seen F. E.'s extravagant disregard for thrift. By the end of his life, F. E. had acquired a yacht, six cars (only three of which were used with any regularity), three chauffeurs, eight horses with three grooms, a large house in London and another in Oxfordshire. He refused to attend to his income tax returns and in the process built an enormous overdraft. When people protested about his extravagance, he simply bought another car or motor launch.

* F. E. would occasionally arrange endurance contests between notable bores (who were of course unaware of the role they had to play), betting heavily with his friends on his own choice.

On one occasion, after the Duke of Marlborough complained that a guest had droned on to him for hours on the subject of reinforced concrete, and added that he was known to be the biggest bore in London, F. E. bet him he could find a bigger bore within a ten-mile radius, and produced a fox-hunting enthusiast. The two men were brought together, tactically left alone, and the competition was judged to be over when the visitor from London was observed asleep while his opponent leaned forward: 'You think I went through the gate – I didn't: I went over the stile – and now I am going to tell you why.'

Confident that he could always make more money by taking on another lucrative case, he lived as if heedless of the future.

Ultimately, F. E. showed Randolph a different path from that offered by his father. In his youth his dazzling wit and the vigour with which he pursued pleasure had perhaps obscured the serious vision of the world that lay beneath. Lord Birkenhead had worked phenomenally hard. The F. E. that Randolph came to know so intimately had already squandered his prodigious gifts. Nevertheless, Randolph began explicitly to model himself upon his father's friend.

Winston, increasingly, could not ignore the fact that his son had become an arrogant, lazy and overbearing young man in danger of throwing away all the advantages his education was supposed to be bringing him. Even though his life at Oxford was almost entirely devoted to his own gratification, it was obvious that he was bored, and had, in fact, been bored since the end of his first term at the university. His personality had changed too. Where once he had merely been cocky, now his conceit could be insupportable. At Oxford, Randolph became offensively rude. He could be devastatingly funny in the process, but it was a dangerous tool that Randolph began to use far too often.

A letter Winston sent Clementine towards the end of the twenties expressed the ambiguous feelings the expansion of his son's personality provoked in him. Randolph had got embroiled in an argument about the existence of God with James Grigg: 'he more than defended his dismal position. The logical strength of his mind, the courage of his thought, and the brutal and sometimes repulsive character of his rejoinders impressed me very forcibly. He is far more advanced than I was at his age, and quite out of common – for good or ill.'

Clementine's cautious reply came a couple of days later. 'He is certainly going to be an interest, an anxiety and an excitement in our lives. I do hope he will always care for us.'

One of Winston's most mischievous aphorisms was 'Politics is like prostitution and piano-playing. The earlier you start the better.'

Randolph claimed, 'I took [politics] in with my mother's milk. I was practically born on a political platform'; he was literally christened in the crypt of the House of Commons.

He and his siblings grew up knowing the arcane vocabulary of Parliament. They knew that 'upstairs' meant committees, 'another place' referred to the House of Lords and 'out of doors' was used to describe speeches made away from Westminster. From an early age, the Churchill children were also involved in their father's campaigns.

In March 1924, when Winston stood at the Westminster by-election, Randolph had been manning the telephone at their Sussex Square home. As the twenties wore on, Winston began to involve Randolph more and more closely in his political life. Three years later when, as a former minister of war, Winston attended a demonstration of some new armoured cars and small tanks, he took his son with him. While Winston inspected the vehicles, the teenaged Randolph walked behind him, asking intelligent questions of one of the officers.

Their letters were filled with gossip about politics and politicians. Winston showed his son his speeches and books as he was composing them, and shared his intimate thoughts and plans with him, often before telling anybody else. Writing to Randolph in 1928, for instance, after confiding in him about the derating scheme he was trying to introduce, he warned him:

> Please do not write any reference to my plans, as any mention of such topics on paper is dangerous. You will see from what I said in Birmingham that difficulties are gradually being cleared out of the way and that design is taking the place of chaos. You should read also the King's Speech, which will be published on Tuesday, with an observant eye.

Randolph grew into his role as his father's chief cheerleader. At Eton he rigged up a secret wireless set to follow the General Strike. He tried as often as he could to catch his father's bravura performances in the House of Commons, and in his letters to Winston, he began to express trenchant views about the issues of the day. 'I am so pleased about the enormous [Budget] surplus,' he wrote to his father. 'The press however do their best to belittle the achievement with such headings as "Surplus for first time in three years." "Chancellor obtains his first surplus." However I suppose this is only to be expected.'

In turn, Winston made it relentlessly clear to his son that success in the political arena was the only success that counted in life. A career spent outside the Cabinet was not worth anything. The ambitions Randolph's father imparted to him were so much a part of the fabric of his life, from such an early point in his existence, that it was inconceivable that he would want anything else. It would have been like asking a fish to imagine living out of water.

The future would be his, Winston assured him. But for the moment, it was Winston's career that was the priority. His star was plainly on the rise. Each of the performances he gave to present his five budgets was more brilliant than the last, even if the policies they contained were ingenious rather than spectacular. And it had escaped nobody's attention that the only men before Winston who had equalled this feat were Walpole, Pitt, Peel and Gladstone, who had each gone on to become prime minister.

Winston had achieved a mastery of the chamber that put him head and shoulders above any of his contemporaries and, even late in his career, was adding to his arsenal.

In a letter to Lord Irwin, Lord Winterton observed:

> The remarkable thing about him is the way he has suddenly acquired, quite late in Parliamentary life, an immense fund of tact, patience, good humour and banter on almost all occasions; no one used to 'suffer fools ungladly' more fully than Winston; now he is friendly and accessible to everyone, both in the House, and in the lobbies, with the result that he has become what he never was before the war, very popular in the House generally – a great accretion to his already very formidable Parliamentary power.

When Winston spoke, men who normally shouted things like 'Liar, coward, murderer' were seen so convulsed with mirth that they could only relieve the pressure by slapping their thighs.

In 1929, with another general election on the horizon, Winston was still, somehow, only fifty-four. His fine hair had retreated, leaving a halo of red at the back of his skull. If perhaps he was no longer as slender as he had been when he first made a name for himself, his body was still more solid than it was heavy, and his energy was such that he seemed to exist in a state of almost perpetual motion. It was hard to think of another politician who could rival his political experience, and impossible to think of another politician who possessed such a daring, fertile mind or who was so adept at communicating his excitement at the raw thrill of being alive.

And yet, although there were rumours that the increasingly ill and tired Stanley Baldwin would retire before the next election and advise the king to send for Winston, it was clear that Winston had not quite managed to dispel the fears about his egoism and impetuosity that had trailed him for so long. Nor had he been forgiven for his defection to the Liberals two decades previously.

As Baldwin himself explained: 'Winston's position is curious. Our people like him. They love listening to him in the House, look on him as a star turn and settle down in the stalls with anticipatory grins. But for the leadership, they would turn him down every time. If anything happened to me, the best men are Neville [Chamberlain] and [Douglas] Hogg.'

Randolph made a precocious cameo in the general election campaign. In April he addressed, after his father, a large audience at a hustings in Edinburgh, the first time he had stepped onto a stage and spoken.

> Today we have in our midst a disease, a veritable cancer, which is vitally and fundamentally opposed to our present civilization and constitution. The Socialist Party base themselves, and rely for their chief support, upon the dissemination of the most poisonous class-hatred, a class-hatred which was unknown in the comprehensive comradeship of the Great War, and which threatens to be destructive to life as we know it in this country.

His performance delighted Winston, who said: 'I have not had the pleasure of hearing him before, and from what I have heard I think I can say that after having fought and contested elections now for thirty years – this being my fourteenth – I can see at no great distance a moment when I shall be able to sit at home in comfortable retirement and feel the torch which falls from my exhausted hands will be carried boldly forward by another.'

At a lunch at Philip Sassoon's, which took place the following day, Thomas Jones noted: 'Winston had travelled through the night from two meetings in Scotland, and was very proud to have heard his son address an audience of about 2,000 for 20 minutes without a note, just over 17 years of age. So we all stood up and drank the health of Randolph II.'

That Randolph, at such a young age, was able to stand undaunted in front of thousands of people and speak so fluently was a mark of his promise. And yet there was something hollow about his denunciations of socialism, and his invocations of the comradeship of the Great War. It was somehow like watching an actor in a film speaking the wrong character's lines.

In an era when other young men who had the same restless temperament, who saw poverty and injustice around them and were revolted by both, turned to communism or fascism, Randolph had eschewed radical politics in favour of his father's strange brew of pre-Great War liberalism and revanchist imperialism.

Winston spent the evening of 30 May, election day, at Downing Street, watching the results come in by ticker tape with a whisky glass clasped in his slim, delicate hands.

As the news grew worse for the Conservatives, his face grew redder, his shoulders started to hunch, his language became 'unprintable' and he tore at the sheets as they emerged from the machine. To a watching civil servant, he resembled nothing so much as an angry bull. But anger was of little use to him. Although his own seat was safe, Winston was out of office for only the third time in over two decades.

5

I Love Him Vy Much

T HE TRIP WINSTON made to North America in the company of
Randolph, his brother Jack and Jack's son Johnny was a punctu-
ation mark in his story. It marked the end of one phase of his life and
the beginning of something new, what he called the locust years.

The explicit aim of the journey was to make money by lecturing – just as he had at the very beginning of his career – and to
show Randolph and Johnny more of the world. But hanging over
it all were Winston's anxious attempts to make out what his future
should look like. He had lost his role in front-line politics, the
world seemed on the verge of convulsive change, and his son – the
boy he had appointed as his heir and upon whose shoulders he had
rested so much hope and expectation – was growing up fast.
Perhaps now was the time for Winston to leave politics and make
money instead, ensuring that his family would be comfortably
provided for after the early death that he still believed was waiting
for him.

Those close to him had often noted the way he processed ideas and
problems: slowly, unconsciously – chewing away at them in one of
the back rooms of his mind – before finally producing a solution.
Randolph talked often of this, and Wing Commander Torr Anderson,
who would play a significant part in Winston's life over the next
decade, remembered how 'you would give Churchill a new idea, he
would say nothing. Two hours later, while feeding the goldfish
he would come out with the flaw in what you said. He had the power
to use the unconscious mind.'

It seems that this is what he planned to do in North America.
Being on the other side of the Atlantic would give him the time and
space he needed to plot his next step. The idea was to land at Quebec

and then make a gentle progress down through Canada and into the United States. Writing to his old friend Bernard Baruch, upon whom the party would call later on their journey, Winston captured the inquisitive, expansive tone he wanted the journey to strike: 'I want to see the country and to meet the leaders of its fortunes. I have no political mission and no axe to grind . . . I do not want to have too close an itinerary. One must have time to feel a country and nibble some of the grass.'

Even the thought of the trip was sufficient to soothe his mind. 'What fun it is to get away from England', he told Beaverbrook before he left, 'and feel one has no responsibility for her exceedingly tiresome and embarrassing affairs.'*

They left on the *Empress of Australia* – a Canadian Pacific ship whose owners had offered Winston free Atlantic passage and a private railway carriage in return for four speeches – on 3 August 1929, with Winston immediately assailed by melancholy as he watched the figures of Diana and Sarah, who had come to wave them off, gradually diminish. At lunch, Winston was so depressed that he announced he was going to leave the ship at Cherbourg and return to Chartwell. Gradually, a calm sea and a game of bezique helped soothe him, but over the next weeks he was never quite able to shed his anxiety for Clementine's well-being: he worried that she would be anxious and unhappy alone.

While Winston busied himself (including receiving regular stock market bulletins on the ship's new wireless from Jack's business partner, Cecil Vickers), Randolph lolled about on deck, unspeakably bored. He regarded the other passengers as dull and unworthy of his attention, and before many days had gone by, he was yearning to see the friends he had left behind. This restlessness meant he defied all his father's attempts to get him to go to bed at a reasonable hour or begin

---

* Winston's attempts to put distance between himself and British politics were immediately foiled by the discovery that his old Harrow sparring partner, Leo Amery, was making the same journey. In the diary Randolph kept of the trip, he recorded, 'On the train we discovered Amery a fat, squat, tubby little pig of a man . . . He has a stupid brutish face and wears pince-nez and a grey check pullover.'

any serious reading. The only excitements were provided by an iceberg, which emerged into view at 7.00 a.m. one day, and the presence on board of an attractive Canadian girl.

The diary he kept said almost nothing about the progress of the affair, but his mysterious disappearance when the ship docked at Quebec was more eloquent.* He was so thoroughly lost to view that the rest of the party had to disembark without him, even after having mounted a shipwide search for him. (An amused Winston liked to characterise Randolph's onboard schedule as follows. The first day of the voyage was spent on the prowl for girls. The second seeking an introduction to the girl of his choice. On the third day, he would do all he could to make himself agreeable to his target. And on the fourth day, he would make a pass. The fifth and sixth days were pledged to the 'consolidation of any previous gains'.)

After a short stay in Quebec, occupied by sightseeing and audiences with local dignitaries, what Winston called the 'Churchill Troupe' drove into the country. Randolph, overcome by the beauty and serenity of the lakes and forests, announced his desire to turn his back on civilisation, build a house and live a rural life. Winston suggested gently that it might be best to see more of North America before committing himself.

They had been supplied with a ninety-foot private rail car – Winston described it to Clementine as a 'land yacht' – with three bedrooms, two bathrooms, four toilets and an observation platform. There were fans in every room, a wireless set in the sitting room and fridges in the kitchen. Randolph, luxuriating in the care provided by the resident cook and waiter, wondered aloud whether it was possible to travel in any greater comfort.

As they moved from Montreal to Ottawa, Winston recorded his observations in a constant stream of letters to Clementine. Winston would always be expected to speak whenever they stopped. Sometimes, Randolph, who was sleeping for ten hours at a time, eating 'enormously' and seemed to grow a little more each day, was asked to add a few words of his own.

---

* This discretion is not too surprising; the diary was written to be read by his girlfriend at the time, who is never identified by name but was probably Davina Lytton.

Winston was delighted both by the furious pace of their tour – 'We have never ceased travelling, starting, stopping, packing, unpacking, scarcely ever two nights in one bed except the train; & eight nights running in that' – and by the reception he received: 'Never in my whole life have I been welcomed with so much genuine interest & admiration as throughout this vast country.'

They were approached in the street by people from every walk of life: workmen, ex-servicemen, farmers, even the girls who operated the elevators. He was almost overwhelmed by the freshness and energy of the country. 'They have a new machine called the "Combine",' he wrote to Clementine one day, 'which not only cuts the corn, but threshes it, pouring a stream of golden grain into an enormous container.'

Talking of Saskatchewan politics, he noted: 'What fun they have in these rising towns and fast developing provinces! All the buoyancy of an expanding world and all the keenness of the political game played out with true Eighteenth Century rigour!'

It is clear that on some not quite articulated level, Winston had begun to equate this 'rolling fertile country on wh every kind of crop & stock can be produced, and under which may lie fiery fortunes' with the energy and potency that spilled out of his son.

Randolph is growing into a vy strong man. His neck and thighs are vy noticeable: I think he will be quite big & solidly built. He speaks so well. So dextrous, cool & finished. Yesterday Meighen the ex PM in a laudatory speech – clumsily quoted my old diatribe about the Tory party. Randolph's rejoinder was excellent and greatly enjoyed by the audience. He sleeps ten & sometimes 12 hours a day – deep oblivion. I suppose it is his mind & body growing at the same time. I love him vy much.

A moment would always come on the evenings they spent by the lakes in Canada, after all their social obligations had been met and their servants had gone to busy themselves elsewhere, when the four Churchills were left alone. Against the background of a silence broken only by the chirping of crickets, and surrounded by bears and chipmunks, they would sit on the balcony, talking. Winston was marvellous, his nephew recalled, 'so giving and understanding'. And everyone was taken aback by the great streams of prose and verse Randolph produced from his memory. After a while, it would just be Winston and Randolph speaking, both striding confidently in their conversation, ranging one minute into history, the next into politics.

Randolph was already giving his father advice about what he saw as his laboured manner of speaking from a prepared text. He told Winston that if a speech seems 'absolutely spontaneous', then it will be infinitely more effective. 'I think,' he told his diary, 'Papa is gradually coming round to my point of view and is relying less and less upon notes.'

Winston had long adored his son. Now, increasingly, he found himself impressed by him. The question was, of course, where did this leave him? For the moment at least, the answer was clear. 'This evening after everyone else had gone to bed,' Randolph wrote in his diary,

> Papa announced his intention to me that once he is certain that he can never be P.M. he will sell out everything and come and conclude his life in Canada making a fortune. I very much doubt whether he would ever be happy divorced from public affairs, but I think it astonishing proof of his vitality that at the age of 55 when most men feel their lives are over, he should contemplate such an adventurous project.

Winston wrote something similar to Clementine:

> Darling, I am greatly attracted to this country. Immense developments are going forward. There are fortunes to be made in many directions. The tide is flowing strongly. I have made up my mind that if NCh [Neville Chamberlain] is made leader of the CP [Conservative Party] or anyone else of that kind, I clear out of politics & see if I cannot make you & the kittens a little more comfortable before I die. Only one goal still attracts me, & if that were barred I shd quit the dreary field for pastures new.

At other times the letters Winston sent home could read as if he was constructing a case for his son's defence. 'Randolph is behaving vy well,' he wrote after they had left Quebec. 'He "studies" for several hours daily. I keep him up to the mark & try to get him down to breakfast. However even if he goes to sleep before midnight he sleeps till 10. No harm in this.'

Lurking behind Winston's praise were the shadows of all of Clementine's reproaches: his impertinence and laziness, his wildness and lack of self-control. 'Randolph has conducted himself in a most dutiful manner and is an admirable companion. I think he has made a good impression on everybody. He is taking a most intelligent interest in everything, and is a remarkable critic and appreciator of the speeches I make and the people we meet.'

What Winston omitted from his letters were the moments when another, more unruly, version of Randolph stepped forward. When the Churchill Troupe arrived at Toronto on 16 August, Randolph, wearing an outsize carnation, caused a minor scandal by being rude to a reporter who had asked him what the first sound he heard on arrival was. Randolph refused to answer what he described as 'silly questions', and by the evening, the local papers were complaining about his insolence. 'Papa', he noted in his diary, 'was very angry with me.'

But Winston's deep affection and growing admiration for Randolph were unmistakeable. They had never spent such a long time in each other's company, and the pleasure they found was manifest. His letters to Clementine made it clear how much support he felt his son was providing.

I addressed an enormous luncheon, 700 or 800 men, the cream of Victoria, for an hour. Thanks were proposed to me by the Dean – a foolish Cleric with Socialist leanings who asked a number of cheeky questions and maundered on unduly. So I put up Randolph to reply and he, in a brief, admirably turned debating speech of five minutes completely turned the tables upon the Dean, to the delight of the audience and also to their amazement. His performance not only showed his curious facility for spinning words but gave proof of great poise, judgement and tact. He knew exactly how far to go and how to win and keep the sympathies of this audience. I could not have done it so neatly myself.

The admiration was returned. Randolph was enthralled by Winston's bravado and wit and wisdom, and the way that even thousands of miles from home he was treated with reverence. He was also struck by his ferocious capacity for hard work. On one hot day in the train, Randolph watched in amazement as his father locked himself away in his own small compartment and wrote by hand (this trip would be one of the few times in his life when Winston travelled without even a valet) a two- to three-thousand-word article for *The Strand* magazine. Decades later, the memory was strong enough for Randolph to tell Martin Gilbert: 'He did not do this so much because he needed the money; he had a sense of guilt which he felt he must expiate.

'I remember complimenting him on the article when he read it to us. "You know I hate to go to bed at night feeling I have done nothing useful in the day. It is the same feeling as if you had gone to bed without brushing your teeth."'

Winston and Randolph with Winston's brother, Jack, and his son, Johnny, during their 1929 tour of North America.

As they swept down into the Prohibitionist United States, father and son added conspiracy to their ever-closer companionship. At dinners they filled flasks with brandy, and Randolph and his cousin Johnny were entrusted with ensuring Winston's coffee cup always contained a measure of it. Both boys became quite adept at the acrobatic task of topping up Winston under the watchful gaze of bishops and other local dignitaries.

In California the pink-skinned Winston bought his first ten-gallon hat to protect himself from the sun, and they stayed at the extraordinary Hearst mansion at San Simeon, with its enormous sapphire bathing pool, ridiculous replica of a Moorish church and a park in which exotic animals like llamas, giraffes and elephants ran 'quite wild'.

Here, as Winston noted with a mixture of fondness and alarm,

Randolph enjoyed himself immensely. He got off at once with Mrs Hearst junior. Such a pretty little woman who married one of the sons [George] after an elopement from College at 18. The son is now enormously fat! Randolph & the wife – looking both pictures of youth & beauty – spent the greater part of the time in the sapphire bathing pool – occasioning some anxiety to the husband, some vigilance from Mrs H senior, & some relief to me when the young lady departed.

Anxious as ever to present a positive portrait of his son's behaviour, Winston did not tell Clementine that he had been surprised one night during the stay by Randolph climbing through the window of his bedroom. His son had lost his bearings on his way to a midnight assignation with the young Mrs Hearst.

Although Randolph liked to boast that he lost his virginity to another guest, the Viennese dancer and sometime guest at Chartwell, Tilly Loesch ('a lovely green-eyed faun'),* it seems likely that he had already leaped through this rite of passage by the time they reached California.

---

* Edward James thought the affair began much later – he claims that in the early thirties, his housekeeper surprised Randolph and Tilly 'having it off on a sofa' in his London house. This of course does not preclude an earlier encounter.

Johnny remembered that his cousin was 'astonishingly good-looking'. He also seemed to be liberated by finding himself away from the closely chaperoned girls he knew in London, who worried about what people would say if they were seen out in public together, and were bound by the promises they had made their mothers.* 'My goodness me,' Johnny would later say. 'It was just one nonstop bashing and crashing all over the place.'

Randolph would regularly disappear. His father would begin to grumble, then shout, 'Where's Randolph? Where's Randolph?' At this moment a voice would come from the top of the house, where Randolph was in his pyjamas with an actress. 'It's all right, Papa, I'm coming.'

Randolph came home before his father, catching the same boat across the Atlantic as F. E. Smith. Winston stayed a little longer in New York, where he dined on Fifth Avenue with Bernard Baruch and forty or so of the city's most eminent bankers on the night of Black Thursday – the stock market fall that precipitated the Great Crash. When one of the financiers around the table proposed Winston's health, he addressed the rest of the men as 'friends and former millionaires'. The next day, Winston saw a man, under his window, throw himself off the fifteenth storey and smash to pieces on the ground below.

Winston the congenital optimist had a long history of speculating on the stock market, with mixed success. His wide circle of friends meant that he was often given tips on what shares to buy, but his permanently queasy financial situation meant that he was often forced to sell before he could make any money. As they landed in North America, however, it looked as if things were going his way. He continued to keep a close eye on his investments right through the trip, visiting the stock exchanges in every big hotel, where one could watch the figures being marked up on slates every few minutes. He was also being advised by a stockbroker called Mr Van Antwerp,

---

* He was, evidently, able to dissolve the concerns of at least some of the girls he met. 'It is rather awful to think', one of them wrote to him, 'that it has taken Mummie 19 years to make a good, open-faced, upright, honest English girl of me, & that it only took you a few days to undo her work.'

whose powerful firm, Winston noted, watched his small interests like a cat watches a mouse. He wrote letters home gloating about the profits he had made speculating on the stock market ('Now my darling I must tell you that vy gt & extraordinary good fortune has attended me lately in finances') and the money he had coming in from the articles he had written, and the contract he had signed for a biography of his ancestor Marlborough. None of this would survive the Great Crash. He lost £10,000* overnight, the cause of financial instability that would dog Winston for a decade.

Randolph, however, had returned from North America in an exultant mood. The tour had brought him and Winston closer than ever before; being in his father's company, basking in the glow cast by his eminence, had been an exhilarating experience. Randolph had been impressed by the New World. He had been seduced by its scale and the teeming possibilities it contained, and had loved meeting prime ministers, press barons and Hollywood stars on equal terms. He had also come back even more committed to the vocation Winston so dearly wanted him to follow.

The problem was that Randolph had drawn the wrong conclusions about how he would get there. He had seen how glib, off-the-cuff remarks made after dinner could result in fawning attention from the rich and powerful; that one could gather as many column inches as one wanted if one was willing to be provocative; that it was sufficient to be charming and unruly and charismatic.

Randolph should have paid mind to other things: Winston, amidst the luxury of their 'land yacht', shutting himself away to write an article and suppress the voice that constantly demanded more from him; the hurt and anger caused by his comments in Toronto.

But he was eighteen. His father – the man he admired more than any other creature on the planet – could not stop telling him how clever and talented he was, and he had been fattened by his exposure to the excitements and novelty of a great continent: it was hard to see how, after this, Oxford could feel like anything other than a constricting, drab dead end.

---

* Approximately £500,000 in today's money.

6

But Words Are Useless

RANDOLPH RETURNED TO university, but virtually abandoned
his studies in favour of an ever more relentless pursuit of excitement: he sneaked off to the Derby in morning coat and top hat (and
was caught there by his father), drove to Bath with Brendan Bracken
to take part in a political campaign, missed his lectures, failed his
preliminary examinations and entertained famous actresses in his
rooms.

Winston's life began to unwind in a very different way. While he
was on the boat journey home, Lord Irwin (later Lord Halifax, or in
the Churchill family's argot, the 'Holy Fox'), the viceroy of India,
announced that the British government would grant the subcontinent dominion status.

Winston still saw India with the eyes of a nineteenth-century
subaltern; he saw little reason to change. When urged by Lord Irwin
to update his views on India by talking to members of the Congress,
Winston replied sharply: 'I am quite satisfied with my views on India,
and I don't want them disturbed by any bloody Indians.'

There were two strands to his opposition. One was his horror at
the dispersal of Britain's empire: 'When I think of the way in which
we poured out blood and money to take Contalmaison or to hold
Ypres,' he wrote to Lord Beaverbrook, 'I cannot understand why it is
we should now throw away our conquests and our inheritance with
both hands, through sheer helplessness and pusillanimity.'

Connected to this was his anxiety about the consequences of the
removal of British rule. 'We have only to look to China with its
horrors of civil war, anarchy and famine,' he warned, 'to see what
would be the consequences for the far weaker and less capable races
of India, after our effective control was relaxed.'

Winston's India campaign was anomalous and wrong-headed, it made little moral or strategic sense, and yet he threw everything he had into what he regarded, he told Stanley Baldwin, as the issue that, 'since the war, is probably the greatest question Englishmen have had to settle . . . I must care more about this business than anything else in public life.'

Winston's position put him at odds with the party he had only relatively recently rejoined – Stanley Baldwin had committed the shadow cabinet to supporting the move towards Indian self-government – and although his leader wrote him an emotional letter urging him to stay, both men knew that Winston could no longer play a role on the Conservative front bench. In January 1931, Baldwin dispatched Lord Hailes to ask Winston to resign from the Conservative front bench. When the reason for his visit became clear, Winston's face reddened, then went white. He went to a corner of the room, picked up his gold-tipped cane, came back and brought the cane down hard upon the table. Then he looked at Hailes, who began to fear he might be the next victim. Suddenly, his face puckered into a smile. 'So the Conservative P. wants to get rid of me, does it? All right, I'll go quietly now.'

The first months in the wilderness were a freeing, exhilarating experience for Winston. Untethered to party discipline, he found he could say what he wanted, fight the campaigns he chose. And he was sure another opportunity to return to power would present itself soon: fatally underestimating Baldwin's political gifts, he could not believe the House would be able to endure what he saw as the Tory leader's mediocrity for much longer.

But there were drawbacks too. His freedom had come at the loss of his status. Banished from both the shadow cabinet and Baldwin's inner circle, his influence had dropped dramatically, as had his salary. He also found that when he launched blows against the party, the party hit back. Alongside the normal methods a political operation can employ to harass an errant MP, the Conservatives launched a campaign designed to restore confidence in the idea of dominion status for India on one hand and to undermine Winston's sincerity on the other.

'My late colleagues', he told Bob Boothby, 'are more interested in doing me in than in any trifling questions connected with India or tariffs. I have a strong feeling they will not succeed.'

Perhaps as a reflection of this new uncertainty in his life, his mood fluctuated. One moment he might pronounce himself convinced that 'the forces of resistance to Indian nationalism are growing much stronger in this country'; the next he might be seen 'demented with fury' during a debate at the House of Commons, growing so angry that he refused to speak to anybody afterwards.

It appeared too that the constant pressure was exerting a toll on his health. Around this time, Harold Nicolson (the diarist, diplomat, aesthete, and future Labour MP, who was both husband to Vita Sackville-West and a connoisseur of Berlin's raciest gay clubs) ran into Winston at Beaverbrook's London home, Stornoway House.

> Winston Churchill slouched in. Very changed from when I had last seen him. A great round white face like a blister. Incredibly aged. Looks like pictures of Lord Holland. An elder statesman. His spirits have also declined and he sighs that he has lost his old fighting power . . . he is clearly disturbed at the effect on the country of Beaverbrook's propaganda. He feels too old to fight it. 'Thirty years ago,' he said, 'I should have welcomed such a combat: now I dread it.'

In September 1930, a personal bereavement was added to his political discomfort. F. E. Smith's gargantuan appetite for life finally caught up with him. When he broke, he broke quickly. Pneumonia, caused by cirrhosis of the liver, finished off a man who, at just fifty-eight years old, had already entered a precipitous decline.

F. E. Smith, the man who possessed a 'double dose of human nature', had been 'far and away' the closest friend of Winston's life. In a valedictory speech he gave to the Other Club he said, 'He was a rock; a man one could love, a man one could play with, and have happy jolly times . . . I do not think anyone knew him better than I did, and he was, after all, my dearest friend.' After F. E. died, Winston turned, weeping, to Clementine, saying over and over again: 'I feel so lonely.'* Right through the rest of that autumn, the sadness continued to press upon him.

Randolph's increasing fecklessness only served to heap more anxiety onto his father's shoulders. Although he wrote Winston fond letters from Oxford ('Your visit to the Union has called forth such praise in Oxford that I must write and tell you about it. Everybody was enchanted and captivated by your kindness and good humour'), the continued reports of his failure to make even the most minimal effort to work left his father feeling sour and resentful.

Four decades previously, Lord Randolph had been equally troubled by Winston's lack of application. He wrote a majestic, almost vitriolic denunciation of his son. It is unclear how consciously Winston sought to emulate his own father as he composed his letter to Randolph, but the echoes are uncanny.

> Your idle & lazy life is vy offensive to me. You appear to be leading a perfectly useless existence . . . You do not try to please me in any of the ways you know so well. Your personal appearance has already deteriorated under the untidy slothful & self-indulgent conditions in wh you choose to live. You do no work: you play no games: you take no exercise. You gossip & chatter & argue unceasingly.
>
> I have tried – perhaps prematurely – to add to our natural ties those of companionship & comradeship. But you do not do your part. You give nothing in return for the many privileges & favours you have hitherto received. I must therefore adopt a different attitude towards you for yr own good.

---

* Randolph, however, revealed to Robert Bruce Lockhart that in the years immediately before F. E. Smith died, the two men had quarrelled. The problem came about because Smith 'had just joined the board of Tate and Lyle's sugar and in front of a lot of people at Winston's house, F. E. began to pester Winston to do something for Sir Leonard Lyle, saying that he had stood down for Winston at Epping, etc. Latter statement was quite untrue, and Winston a little sore. F. E., however, went on nagging at Winston – showing quite obviously that he wanted an allocation of shares for himself, etc. In the end Winston became angry. The quarrel was made up, but relations were never quite the same.'

The similarities were so glaring that they almost obscure the more subtle, but perhaps more notable, differences. Winston cared what happened to Randolph in a way Lord Randolph never had about Winston. The brutal mix of anger and pain on display in this letter was a reminder of the outsize quantities of trust and affection Winston had invested in his son's future.

Randolph, by contrast, had the clear-sighted callousness that the young often possess. It meant that he could look at his father's love and see only weakness. A few emollient words were enough to cool his father's rage. 'I am doing as you have instructed me,' he assured Winston, 'and will have completed everything by the end of the week. I do appreciate most highly the generous manner in which you have treated me, and I assure you that I shall endeavour in the future to be more worthy of your kindness.'

And yet, although Randolph was now approaching the age Winston had been when he shrugged off his earlier indolence ('I wasted time until I was twenty-two,' he claimed) and began making his vigorous sallies into learning (when Winston approached books, he said, it was with 'a hungry, empty mind and with fairly strong jaws, and what I got I bit'), there were few signs that Randolph had any real intention of changing his ways.

Instead, later that month, Randolph forced matters to a head. The event that prompted the latest confrontation between father and son initially seemed innocuous; indeed, it should have been a cause for encouragement. Up until that point, Randolph's love of what he called 'indoor sports' had not only affected his studies; they had also hindered his performances at the Oxford Union, an arena where many politicians before and since have made an early reputation for themselves. Great things may have been expected of him, but he was never organised or driven enough to deliver. Instead of preparing for his first debate, he spent the night before playing poker. Unsurprisingly, the next day he stood up and flopped. Rather than accepting responsibility for what was effectively an act of self-sabotage, he claimed that he had been unfairly treated.

Now he had been given another chance. As Randolph reported excitedly in a letter written at the end of January 1930, Edgar Lustgarten, the president of the Oxford Union, had asked him to speak there. At Randolph's suggestion, they would be discussing Egypt – a subject that was uppermost in Winston's mind at the time.

In front of an unusually large crowd, Randolph made a good showing, growling, as if in imitation of his father, and echoing a number of Winston's own arguments. The combination of his famous name and a quiet few days of news meant that the event got more coverage than it might have otherwise. One thing led to another, and the story got picked up by the *New York Times*. Ten days after the debate, Randolph was lying in his bed at 10.30 a.m., hungover, when his American friend Stuart 'Boy' Scheftel passed by his rooms on his way to a lecture.

'You haven't opened your mail.'

'No.'

'There's one here from America, shall I open it for you?'

'Please do.'

'Good God. It's an invitation to make a lecture tour in the United States.'

'Do they pay?' Randolph asked, without much enthusiasm.

'Yes. Quite a lot of money.'

William B. Feakins Inc., the company that had brought Winston over for his first speaking tour of the United States at the turn of the century, wanted to pay his son $12,000 to do the same. Randolph was living on an allowance from Winston of £400 a year, which was average for Oxford but low for the exclusive, aristocratic Christ Church. He owed friends at least £600 and was not even close to living within his means. Feeling cramped by debt and the boredom of life at Oxford, Randolph accepted.

Randolph was, his tutor Roy Harrod thought, a boy who always went too far. He liked him and could see that he had some gifts, if not the desire to make the most of them. He believed that if Randolph could be prevailed upon to hang on into his final year, he would knuckle down – as so many talented, wilful boys had before him. In doing so, he might learn 'precision of language, accuracy of thought, citation of references for factual statements, due humility in the face of unresolved problems'.

Harrod knew that if his young charge left for America now, it would mark the end of his education. 'Randolph,' he told him, 'you will not come back to us.' No matter how hotly Randolph argued that he would return to Oxford, Harrod remained unconvinced.

Winston had not yet given up hope of dissuading his son from making another reckless leap. He invited Harrod down to Chartwell for the weekend so they could make a final plea to Randolph. After dinner, Winston stood up with his back to the chimneypiece and launched into a great oration on the merits of a university education. He rehearsed old arguments about how disadvantaged he had felt in debates with better-educated men like Arthur Balfour, and how much a handicap he felt that not having been to university had been to his political career.

Harrod, listening to the overpowering flow of his host's speech – with its improvisations that were 'flung out with almost reckless prodigality' – found himself wishing he was a Boswell who could go up to his room and write it all down. But he was also watching Randolph, who sat on a sofa along one side of the room, looking unutterably bored – as if he had heard it all before. What was also obvious from his mutinous expression was that he was determined to get his own way.

Moments after Randolph had slouched out of the room, Winston turned to Harrod with satisfaction and said, 'Well, we have got down to brass tacks.' How many other times, Harrod wondered, in how many other venues, had Winston made the same mistake of overestimating the success of his arguments? So intoxicated was he by the great power of his own words, he rarely noticed what effect, if any, they had on the other person. If he had expressed a point to his satisfaction, that was enough. His almost complete unawareness of what was happening in the heads or hearts of others meant that he could not always see when his arguments had fallen on stony ground.*

Violet Asquith had noticed this trait years before: 'I sometimes felt amazement and alarm at his own seeming unawareness of [other people's] reactions to himself. Though he had vision he appeared to lack antennae, to ignore the need to feel his way about other minds.'

---

* This lack of curiosity about the motivations and psychology of others extended to his history writing. He described, often brilliantly, what happened; rarely, however, did he ask why. While his biography of Lord Randolph may have shown some of his awkward edges, there is no attempt at explaining how they were formed.

Generally, this did not matter. Cabinet colleagues, generals, ambassadors, even prime ministers tended to melt when confronted by the white heat of Winston's desire to get his own way. Randolph, however, was different. In this case, as so often before, Winston's entreaties had little impact. In October 1930, having been given a term's leave from Oxford, his son set off for New York.

In the New World, Randolph found that there was nobody to check his behaviour or to remind him of his responsibilities. Just as significantly, although he found that his surname opened doors in the United States, it was also free of the inhibiting force it possessed in England. Wherever he went in his own country, he was always shadowed by his father and his father's reputation. In New York he was treated as a celebrity in his own right.*

Addressing audiences across the country in an Oxford accent so broad that to some Americans he may as well have been speaking French, his appetite for provocation and controversy appeared insatiable. He cheerfully upbraided his hosts for 'the barbaric, unlawful Negro lynchings in your South' and compared the 'outrageous treatment of your Red Indians whom you almost decimated' with the 'benevolence' of the British, under whom, he argued, the Indians multiplied and prospered.

His major concession to Anglo-American relations was to fall in love with the blonde, knowledgeable Kay Halle, an heiress from Ohio. Kay was fascinated by Randolph, but not blinded, and she was able to resist his sustained attempts to persuade her to marry him, largely because it was clear that he expected her to reprise his own mother's role, something she was understandably wary of. ('Do you realise what a serious step it is, dear Randolph – it is very, very serious to me – you know these things are permanent.')†

I am getting a good deal of publicity, Randolph told Winston, before continuing with what was, at best, a half-truth. 'Of course,

---

* The other curious effect of being an ocean away from Winston is that it improved Randolph's relationship with Clementine immeasurably. She sailed out to see her son midway through his trip and they got on better in those weeks than in almost any other part of their lives.

† They would, however, remain lifelong friends. Halle was instrumental in arranging for Winston to be made an honorary US citizen in 1963.

they publish the most silly remarks which one either makes thought-lessly or which they have invented. I trust that any reports that reach England will be discounted.'

Randolph had been paid a lot of money for his efforts during the tour, and yet by the time he set sail for home, it was all gone. Worse, he had borrowed $2,000 from Bernard Baruch, a debt it would take thirty years to pay off. On his return, Randolph declared that Oxford had nothing more to offer him. His mother disagreed. His father, somewhat reluctantly, relented, on the condition that Randolph find himself a job.

Randolph had a loud mouth, considerable reserves of charm (when he wished to deploy them) and boundless confidence. Winston suggested he consider reading for the bar. Randolph opted instead, as he put it himself, to take 'up the calling for which no credentials or examinations are required – journalism'.

It was all very easy for Randolph. Leaning – with far too much enthusiasm for Clementine's liking – on the power of his father's name, he wrote articles for Lords Beaverbrook and Rothermere, and earned a useful salary editing a magazine for ICI. While still short of his majority, he became 'a wealthy man about town'.

He lived with John Betjeman at their friend Edward James's Mayfair town house (replete with a superb collection of modern art, includ-ing the telephone that Dali had designed as a lobster). Here he drank into the early hours, stayed in bed until late and renewed his acquaint-ance with Tilly Loesch. (Enthralled by her broken English, he encour-aged her to call *All's Well That Ends Well* 'Finish Good – All Good' and to call escalators 'rolling the stairs down'.)

Randolph's friends were brittle, witty Bright Young Things: Basil Dufferin, Evelyn Waugh, Diana and Nancy Mitford. They lunched at the Ritz, dined at Quaglino's and went to parties where the guests got so drunk they 'could not speak, only bark and bite'.

Those who met the good version of Randolph remembered his spontaneous enthusiasm, his boundless capacity for affection and an almost childlike innocence. Just like Cecil Beaton and Oliver Messel, he was invited out by hosts who wanted to be amused. That he might throw a cocktail into a woman's face or push Diana Cooper's niece

Lady Elizabeth Paget so far that she emptied a plate of spaghetti over his head while groaning about his 'ghastly good looks' was, they reasoned, a risk worth taking.

He also found himself drawn ever further into his father's political life. More and more often, he was encountered at Winston's side at restaurants or in the homes of eminent friends such as Lord Beaverbrook. He was amusing, keen to dominate the conversation, and unafraid to twit 'his father with lack of political courage'.

In April 1930, Sir Robert Bruce Lockhart, the sybaritic former spy who edited the *Evening Standard*'s 'Londoner's Diary', met Randolph for the first time. 'He is a good-looking boy,' he recorded in his diary, 'with fair hair and distinguished features rather marred by a spotty complexion. Talks nineteen to the dozen and is a kind of gramophone to his father . . . Very egocentric and conceited and therefore very unpopular. I rather liked him.'

Lockhart recognised the opinions Randolph expressed (about the Conservative Party and David Lloyd George) as being 'pure Winston'.

Randolph also revealed that his father was still talking about giving up politics. Not that this would have been a surprise to anybody who associated with Winston, who was never a man much interested in keeping his cards close to his chest.

The political situation was increasingly bleak for him, his relations with Stanley Baldwin were, as he wrote to Randolph, 'chilly and detached', and although he was not quite ready yet to step away from the fray – especially with the Indian question still to be resolved – it was clear that he believed it was time for the next generation of his family to play its part. Writing to his son, he told him:

> It may well be that the historians of the future will record 'that within a generation of the poor silly people getting the votes they clamoured for they squandered the treasure which five centuries of wisdom and victory had amassed.' I do not know whether you will be able to do anything to stop this. I hope so indeed. But great sacrifices and efforts will be needed, and you should fit yourself constantly for a task which may perhaps you have been sent here for.

Scribbled at the bottom of the typewritten letter was a note in his own hand: 'My best love my dear Randolph. I pray you may realise all that I hope for you.'

Winston, who liked to tell people that while there had been two William Pitts, there would be three Churchills, talked about trying to find his son a constituency in which he could stand as soon as he turned twenty-one. In the meantime, he started to trust him with carrying out political missions on his behalf.

When, in 1931, Gandhi arrived in London in a blaze of publicity, Winston declined to meet him, but it was soon announced that his son would interview the Indian leader. The piece Randolph produced was unremarkable in itself, and yet at the same time, it was an indication of the way he was now considered a representative of his father.

Over lunch at the Carlton Grill in August of the same year, Oswald Mosley, who had left Labour and formed the short-lived New Party, told Harold Nicolson that Randolph had been sent by Winston to find out whether he would be interested in joining his father and the 'Tory toughs' in opposition to the newly formed National Government.

Despite Winston's helpless attraction to 'strange coalitions and odd regroupings' – his attachment to the Conservative Party remained ambiguous at best – the conversations came to nothing. At the general election two months later, the National Government secured a crushing victory, which left Winston even more isolated than he had been before. Although the Conservative Party possessed overwhelming power within the coalition that had been created with the former Labour leader, Ramsay MacDonald, as prime minister, Winston knew that he would not be invited to join it.

His position on India had become even less tenable: of 615 MPs, only twenty were members of the Indian Empire Society. By contrast, Stanley Baldwin enjoyed a 'virtually unassailable political predominance'. When Parliament reassembled on 10 November, Winston sat beneath the gangway. He felt as if he had been discarded. Others shared the opinion. When Joseph Stalin asked Nancy Astor about Winston's career, he received an emphatic response: 'Oh, he's finished!'

Those who encountered Winston during this period noted a marked increase in his drinking, which led to a perception that his powers were declining. That autumn, for instance, Lockhart noted that 'Winston is very weak these days – like a schoolboy trying to get into the team. He is nearly always slightly the worse for drink.' A couple of months later, Harold Nicolson noticed the same thing. Winston, he remarked in his diary, was 'noticeably drunk'.

Winston always portrayed himself as a relentless consumer of food, cigars and alcohol; he wanted to be remembered as a two-bottle man and assiduously helped cultivate this myth. (Field Marshal Montgomery to Winston: 'I do not drink, I do not smoke, I sleep a great deal. That is why I am 100 per cent fit.' Winston: 'I drink a great deal, I sleep a little, and I smoke cigar after cigar. That is why I am 200 per cent fit.') But although he believed Pol Roger champagne possessed outsize life-giving qualities and started the day with a Scotch and soda, his drinking was usually governed by restraint. He made the whisky he used as a throat-moistener last until lunch. It was important to him not to hurry drinks – he preferred to leave a whisky unfinished to gulping it down. He had a visceral dislike of people he considered drunks and hated the loss of control that true inebriation entailed.

That he was wobbling so publicly was a clear sign of how troubled he was by his ailing political fortunes, a discomfort that was intensified by financial anxiety. The 1929 crash had wiped him out – his losses exceeded $75,000 – and since he could no longer rely on his Cabinet salary, he was forced into ever-increasing volumes of work. In 1930 he committed to writing three books and more than forty articles. He needed to: his secretary's list of unpaid bills ran to two pages.

Winston's commitment to living in a high style, particularly the costs involved in running Chartwell – where cigars and champagne were 'unlimited' – came at a price. They employed a cook, a farm-hand, a groom for the ponies, three gardeners, a nanny, a nursery maid, an 'odd-man' responsible for the dustbins, boilers and boots, two housemaids, two kitchen maids, two more in the pantry, Clementine's lady's maid (also responsible for the family's sewing) and Winston's two secretaries.

Clementine's spending included purchases of gold kid shoes, an ermine coat, a skiing holiday and a new brown whipped-stitch driving suit, alpaca coat, with a matching cap and cockade for the chauffeur. And she was the most frugal member of the family.

Winston was an almost boundless optimist. His wife's tendency to fixate on looming threats was offset by his confidence that everything would turn out for the best. 'It may never happen,' he would tell her when she raised problems with him. However, the problem with their finances was that it *had* happened and would continue to. Winston always based his projections on an assumption that household bills would run at £500 a month, even though they almost always exceeded it. For several consecutive years during the thirties, annual spending at Chartwell ran at over £10,000. Nor did his thinking take into account his losses at casinos, or the way the high bills he incurred for author's corrections ate into his profits.

A cycle of peremptory attempts at cutting costs began that would last throughout the decade. The children were often lectured on the need to turn off lights, rebuked for long telephone conversations, and became familiar with seeing Chartwell run down to a low ebb, its ground-floor rooms swathed in dust sheets and only Winston's study left open, so he could work at weekends. The move out of 11 Downing Street meant that the family had lost their London home too. So, while their friends all seemed to be coasting through a wealthy and settled middle age, the Churchills spent three years in short lets, hotels or staying with friends. (This erratic spell would end only when they bought 11 Morpeth Mansions in 1932, a flat that occupied the upper two floors of a red-brick mansion block close to Westminster Cathedral.)

None of this was enough. Although Winston had written nonstop during the first half of 1931,[*] his outgoings still exceeded his income by £5,000. That summer, the ever-faithful Brendan Bracken, mindful of his idol's creaking finances, tried to help.

On 22 August, for instance, he wrote to Winston telling him that over lunch with Lord Rothermere and his son Esmond he had suggested that they might want a weekly article from Winston. When they expressed interest, he encouraged them to firm this up, then pushed them to increase their offer. 'You are, of course, a better judge of literary offers than I can pretend to be, & I may have done wrong by making this suggestion,' his letter continued, adopting the same

[*] He considered, but did not write, an article called 'Great Fighters in Lost Causes'.

respectful, even obsequious, tone he always used in his interactions with Winston, but this contract, combined with Bracken's plan to renegotiate Winston's arrangement with the *Sunday Pictorial*, promised a 'mighty increase in income for the next year'. It was in the postscript, however, that he revealed the extent to which Randolph's behaviour had contributed to Winston's troubles: 'These ideas occurred to me because I thought you were rather worried by the decline in your investments & the Rabbit's extravagance.'

Spending money, spending lots of it, was an addiction Randolph could never shake. The habits he had acquired from his father were supercharged by that strain of exuberance in him that meant he almost always took everything too far. He was louder and ruder and funnier than anybody else, he drank more, gambled more, ate more and slept with more women than anyone he knew. He also spent more. In fact, he spent uncontrollably. It was as if he did not believe he would ever have to pay the bills that flooded through his door. Randolph had the same impulsivity as Winston – he was just as liable to displays of reckless generosity, which were often prompted by sudden bursts of sentimentality. He arranged a lavish dinner dance for Winston's sixtieth birthday and could never resist dashing to Cartier to buy his friends gifts whenever he felt flush; his ragged accounts were filled with huge bills from florists.

He earned a lot, far more than many of his contemporaries, but it was never enough, and ultimately, it almost always seemed to fall to Winston to settle his son's debts. Winston oscillated between anger and indulgence. He was just as capable of writing out a cheque as he was of losing his temper. What grieved him most was that it looked as if Randolph was in danger of jeopardising his future. During a heart-to-heart talk in Germany, where they were travelling together (it was on this trip that Randolph almost arranged what would have been the only face-to-face encounter between Winston and Adolf Hitler: hours of painstaking efforts fell apart at the last moment*), Winston went for Randolph. 'What are you doing? When I was your age, I was reading five hours a day. You spend most of your time in

---

* Randolph's contact was Ernst Hanfstaengl, who he described as 'the court jester of the Hitler entourage until about 1937 when they quarrelled'.

night-clubs, staving off a vast army of debtors by eking out a precarious living as a hack-journalist.' This did not, of course, mean that Winston was going to stop bailing his son out.

Then, in October 1931, Randolph got himself into real trouble with a misguided bet: he had placed £400 on the National Government winning the general election with a majority of fewer than 150 seats. The higher their majority exceeded this number, the more he would lose.

It became clear almost as soon as the campaign had begun that Ramsay MacDonald and Stanley Baldwin were heading for a land-slide, so Winston called in his brother Jack to help. Jack closed off Randolph's original bet and then used £1,000 of Winston's money to put a bet in Winston's name on a high majority. After having given enough of his winnings to Randolph to reduce his liability to £85, Winston emerged with £876 profit (the eventual majority of 493 seats would have cost Randolph £600 on top of his original stake).

Winston had always been indulgent of his son's mistakes, and there was little reason to think that anything would be different this time round. Except that Randolph had himself driven to Chartwell in a Bentley that he had seen advertised in the personal column of *The Times*. It was as if he was deliberately trying to provoke his father, who, for all his own personal extravagances, at the time only ran a small, ageing Wolseley.

Winston wrote him a letter soon afterwards that almost trembled with hurt and exasperation.

> I am ready to pay £100 on account of yr gambling losses in election majorities. But as I told you, I will only do this if it is necessary for yr well-being. If you feel yrself able to keep a magnificent motor car & chauffeur at a rate wh must be £700 or 800 a year, you are surely able to pay yr debts of honour yrself. Unless & until you give proof of yr need by ridding yrself of this gross extravagance you have no right to look for aid from me: nor I to bestow it. I have many to look after whom you should not trench upon.
>
> I grieve more than is worth setting down to see you with so many gifts & so much good treatment from the world leading the

life of a selfish exploiter, borrowing & spending every shilling you can lay yr hands upon, & ever-increasing the lavish folly of yr ways.

Three days later, Randolph replied, apologising for the delay: 'I have been up in Liverpool and only returned today.' His response swings between apology – he begins by praising Winston's generosity and assuring him that he is making efforts to escape from the Bentley contract – and truculence: 'I think it is rather unfair of you to refer to me as "borrowing and spending every shilling I can lay my hands upon". With the exception of the majorities episode – which was stupidity rather than extravagance – I have, since my return from America, reduced my liabilities by about £200. Even with the car I should be living well within my income.'

This defiance was then followed by self-abasement: 'I really am ashamed that you should have to do this for me, and am more grateful than I can tell you for this renewed sign of the kindness with which you have always treated me.'

Randolph knew the contrite formulas he needed to express in order to assuage his father's anger, but it was as if he was reluctant to offer Winston a complete surrender – even if, perhaps, it would be more convenient to do so.

'No one so much as I cares for yr success & reputation,' wrote his father in reply, his anger clearly extinguished. 'No one I expect cherishes higher hopes of both. But you <u>must</u> give yourself a fair chance in the race of life. The formation of a small store of money alone gives independence, & the power to choose superior tasks.'

The great glare of Winston's adoration for Randolph could not be blotted out for long by what he was confident would be only temporary irritations. When, on 28 May 1932, Randolph turned twenty-one, Winston was determined to mark his passage into manhood in style.

He did this by commissioning a sitting with Sir Philip de László, the pricey, fashionable portrait artist who had already painted much of what was left of European royalty. It was a faithful image insomuch as it captured Randolph's good looks, which had long been the source of great pride to his father. (The writer Elizabeth Longford, four decades later, was still dazed by his 'extraordinary youthful beauty: thick golden hair, enormous blue eyes and a sugar-pink complexion . . . He looked like a Botticelli angel.') But it preserved little of the restlessness or chaos that had become so much a part of his character. It showed promise and confidence, and yet nobody looking at it could have guessed how easily its subject could bait and bait people until they were screaming with rage.

Two weeks later, Winston arranged a special dinner party at Claridge's. The theme was great men and their sons. There were press lords (Beaverbrook came with his son, 'Little Max', Lord Rothermere with Esmond Harmsworth, Lord Camrose with Seymour Berry) and politicians (Lord Hailsham came with Quintin Hogg, Lord Reading with Lord Erleigh).* The only exceptions were a handful of favoured men who were either too young to have sons grown up enough to attend, such as Bob Boothby and Oswald Mosley, or were irredeemably single, such as the Prof.

There were, however, two notable absences from the party. Stanley Baldwin's relationship with Winston had suffered over the past years. He and his son Oliver, whose radical politics had done much to discomfit the Conservative leader, declined the invitation (the press reported that while the elder Baldwin was otherwise engaged, the younger Baldwin absented himself because he 'did not possess any evening clothes – or, at any rate, refused to wear them'). It was a small sign that nevertheless showed, as forcefully as any statement in the House of Commons, that Winston's time in the political wilderness had begun in earnest.

The other important person who did not attend was Clementine. She had been around earlier to greet the guests as they arrived. Then, when young Freddie Birkenhead offered to take her into dinner, she drew herself up, said 'I have not been invited', and went up to bed.

The party was constructed on an elaborate, lavish scale, and cost money that Winston, whose finances were still in a perilous state,

---

* As it turned out, only Quintin Hogg would come close to matching his father's achievements. The rest either failed to do so or made no attempt to try. Freddie Birkenhead, for instance, explicitly decided to follow a different path from F. E.

could not really spare. With his customary attention to such matters,* Winston devised the menu (seven 'simple' courses), the decoration of the table (a mass of pink roses with a huge mirror in the centre) and the seating plan.

It was an evening for self-congratulatory speeches delivered as the rest of the guests ate duck and drank champagne. (They drank, and drank and drank, one guest remembered. In 1928, Winston had bought up every bottle of Pol Roger on the market in London; it seems that many of them were emptied that night.)

As the decanter 'pursued its amiable path' around the table, Winston, beaming with pleasure, stood to talk, speaking through cigar smoke about 'how the generation of fathers to which he belonged had witnessed the extension of an enormous Empire, and had made it secure during the war. He could not believe that the younger generation was not equal to the task of consolidation or would prove faithless in patriotic purposes.'

In speaking of Randolph's political prospects, he compared his astonishing verbal facility to a machine gun. 'Gentlemen,' he said, to mounting laughter and applause, 'let us only hope that he accumulates a large dump of ammunition, and – er – that he learns to hit the target.' He went on to speak, in almost mystical terms, of 'the torch, the flag and the lamp'.

Randolph's reply, after his friend Freddie Birkenhead had raised a toast to his health and his 'rise to fame', was an odd mixture of animation and restraint. As Winston beamed up at him, pride etched on his face, he said that he hoped he and his friends would live to be as proud of their sons as the fathers present should be of them.

Although it was only a twenty-first birthday party, it attracted interest from everyone from the *Daily Worker* (which sneered at the pretensions of the evening) to the *Sunday Graphic*. Randolph was described as 'the coming man' and praised for his 'engaging cocksureness'. One journalist wrote, 'I venture to predict that he will one day

---

* He had learned much from his mother, who was a skilled party giver. Winston always thought hard about the placement. He was also anxious that guests should behave themselves appropriately. It was not uncommon for him to berate men who ignored the women guests he had placed them next to.

equal, if he does not even surpass, in notability and usefulness, both his father and his grandfather', and the *Daily Herald* claimed that he was 'already a better speaker than his father', possessing 'a most charming manner and a confidence that was much less annoying than Winston's lisp'.

A more acerbic take on the evening came from Sir Robert Bruce Lockhart. Randolph, who liked to think he was a public relations expert, had telephoned Bruce Lockhart in advance to give him the details he would need to write a fawning piece in the next day's paper. This necessary act of flattery completed, he confided his actual thoughts to his diary.

What an amazing thing privilege and position still are in England! Here is a boy who, born in a less privileged circle, would have had to work hard and make his own way. As it is, he is lazy, lascivious, impudent and, beyond a certain rollicking bumptiousness, untalented, and everything is open to him. One thing position has given him is good looks and charm.

The guests sat there in the lavishly appointed dining room, dinner jackets and bow ties loosened, cigars hanging from their mouths, brandy glasses clasped between their fingers. They clapped for each other and laughed at each other's jokes, as waiting staff moved silently among them, and the younger men basked in the warmth that came with knowing that their lives would contain only good things: more amiable nights like this; the easy access to power and wealth their fathers had enjoyed; the secure knowledge that as guardians of a great empire, they would be able to sway the world for years to come. Most sparkling of them all was Randolph, who had stood up on his hind legs and 'crash, bang, wallop', delivered a brilliant speech. Whatever travails Winston was experiencing in his own career, Randolph's success seemed assured.

7

They Fight Like Cats

A S THE DECADE wore on, the lives of father and son grew ever more tightly entwined. They drank and dined together; holidayed and gambled together; confided in each other; their friendships overlapped and, increasingly, so did their professional lives.

Some evenings might find them at balls in which castles were lit so brightly they could be seen for miles, with little coloured lights lining their winding avenues. White-coated footmen; a carnation and a cocktail on your dressing table; a professional tennis player on site; and Winston arguing with George Bernard Shaw in the corner of the room.

They occupied a slightly curious place within this rich, aristocratic world. They were both of it and yet somehow apart. At parties, father and son stood out among the men with the kind of pink 'huntin'' faces that could be picked up only from spending days on end stalking grouse or deer, or whatever game was unfortunate enough to be in season, and the overdressed women fainting in the heat.

Winston had long been treated as an alarming, exotic presence in smart society. The fact that he had an American mother was sufficient to ensure that some sneeringly referred to him as a half-breed. Even now, his burning, unashamed thirst for power, his vivid imagination, his naked shows of emotion, were troubling, but he was also the grandson of a duke, related to half the aristocracy of Britain, so he enjoyed 'a sort of charmed invulnerability'.

He was, as Harold Nicolson wrote, 'the most interesting man in London. He is more than interesting: he is a phenomenon, an enigma. How can a man so versatile and so brilliant avoid being considered volatile and unsound?' The answer lay somewhere between 'the hostility to brilliance' which had scarred British public life for so long and

Winston's own restless, reckless nature. As he once said, 'I like things to happen, and if they don't happen I like to make them happen.'

And now here was his son. More beautiful, more combustible, seemingly more brilliant, than his father had ever been. He carried with him a whiff of sulphur – the result of a series of outrages. It was not always clear, when one invited Randolph for dinner, which version of him would turn up. His sallies into society were laced with excitement and uncertainty: as he entered the room, the atmosphere changed; there was a crackle of fear mixed with thrilled anticipation.

When Randolph got bored, he started fights. He enjoyed the detonations he could cause, realising he could transform a quiet, civilised evening into a fiasco. Randolph was not a cruel man, but he was, in the words of his friend Stuart Scheftel, 'a carelessly playful one'. As Stuart said of Randolph: you don't meet him, he just happens to you.

Reactions to what Randolph called his 'teases' ranged from icy stares to the kind of outraged roar that precedes a punch in the face. Even his apologies could sometimes be more incendiary than whatever he had said in the first place. He once made a dowager almost hysterical by telling her he was convinced that her daughters would commit adultery with the utmost discretion. His attempt to make amends, by trying to argue that it was meant only as a testimony to her parenting, did not calm her down.

In Venice he had initiated a brawl on the island of Murano that broke Diana Cooper's carefully planned fortieth-birthday celebrations into pieces. And many were still scandalised by the fallout from his affair with Lord Castlerosse's wife, Doris, which had led to an ill-disguised (the actual details were hidden, but the spite was not) and unseemly spat in the newspapers.*

Winston seemed entertained by his son's tumultuous behaviour. When Randolph's provocations ruined a dinner at the Savoy Grill hosted by Brendan Bracken, Winston responded only by sitting cheerfully at the other end of the table, lobbing pellets of bread at

---

* Randolph was completely unabashed about the affair and loved to boast to others about it. He even introduced Doris to Winston, who rebuked him for using the word 'bloody' in front of a lady. Jock Colville, Winston's private secretary, claimed in a 1985 interview (which only came to light in 2018) that Winston had also had an affair with Doris. This seems unlikely for a number of reasons.

him. He was luminously proud of Randolph: of his eloquence, his 'firmness of character and courage'. He collected accounts of his son's activities and examples of his repartee – the more 'Churchillian' the better. This was unusual: Winston – who once told a friend that his idea of a delightful evening was fine food enjoyed in the company of friends, followed by a discussion of the food and then a good discussion 'with myself as chief conversationalist' – had a famously limited interest in talking about people other than himself.

And he continued to pet Randolph and praise him and shower him with love, which was reflected back to him doubled in force. Randolph's adoration for his father seemed to pour out of him. People who dined with him at Boulestin or drank with him at Brooks's (Randolph consuming 'a large sherry, a pint of beer and four large glasses of port') would inevitably be regaled with accounts of Winston's extraordinary working methods, or his magnanimity towards Germany in 1918.

Winston and Randolph were so much in each other's company that they had even begun to walk like each other.* The *Morning Post* wrote, 'They both use a thrusting mode of progression, head and shoulders slightly bowed, jaw pushed forward, arms swinging low.' Seen from behind, with their hats worn tipped back over their ears, it was hard to tell them apart.

The two men lunched together at the Savoy Grill. Sometimes they would dine alone, sometimes in the company of friends such as Brendan Bracken, Bob Boothby and David Lloyd George. Winston, Randolph recorded in an unpublished set of reminiscences, would order chicken consommé, fried fillet of sole with tartare sauce, lamb cutlets and Welsh rarebit, and was always astounded if anyone else in their party had anything different. (The only deviation he allowed himself was cold roast beef with pickled cabbage, 'a dish', Randolph recalled, 'to which he was inordinately addicted'.)

In the evenings after big debates, they would head to Pratt's, where they were both members, perhaps collecting a couple of friendly MPs

---

* He also did a very good imitation of his father, which involved hunching his shoulders, pushing his stomach out and launching into a stream of words in which only 'bloody' was recognisable.

in the lobby on the way. Here, in what Randolph characterised as essentially a supper club for Tory MPs to go to after the House had risen at 10.00 p.m., they would dine on steak, sausages, cutlets, Stilton and Welsh rarebit (again). 'To the great delight of everyone who was there', Winston liked to take over the grill and cook the food himself.

In the summer they would invariably holiday together. Take, for example, August 1934, when they travelled (with the Prof) first from Chartwell to the Ritz in Paris – a journey that Winston noted with pleasure took exactly three hours by car and then aeroplane – before heading to Château de l'Horizon, Maxine Elliott's beautiful villa on the Côte d'Azur, where Winston was a favoured guest.

Clementine had never made a secret of her disdain for the louche company Winston kept in the south of France, and rarely joined him. She saw the places her husband stayed as luxurious cages that trapped her with people she found shallow, vulgar and boring (Clementine to Sarah: 'God, the Riviera is a ghastly place'). Randolph was a much more willing companion, and on this trip at least seemed to have been on his best behaviour. As Winston wrote to his wife: 'Randolph has been a gt success. His manners are the subject of highly favourable comment, and he has been vy nice to everyone.' He was still as determined as ever to persuade Clementine that Randolph was not a lost cause.

Winston would either paint or write for most of the day, making time to bathe, like a 'hippopotamus in a swamp', in the Mediterranean's crystal waters. But he was more cautious when it came to telling Clementine about how they passed their evenings. One of the other things the two men loved doing in each other's company was gamble. Here on the Riviera, they were dangerously close to temptation.

Unwilling to lie to Clementine, on this occasion he admitted, 'I have indeed been playing at the Casino though at chemin de fer and have lost uniformly, but not' – and here he moved swiftly to anticipate any reproach – 'on a large scale. Randolph too has lost & has stopped playing. I wrote an article today on Philip Snowden's Autobiography wh will pay expenses: & the stocks & shares have done well in my absence.'

What Winston omitted to tell his wife was that the casino had pressed Randolph to honour cheques worth £1,900. This in turn prompted Randolph to reveal that he was already £4,350 in the red

– all new debts incurred since he had been given his slice of his grandfather's trust fund a year previously.

Winston opted for a practical rather than a punitive approach and instructed his solicitors Nicholl, Manisty & Co. to pay his son's debts with money from Lord Randolph's trust. Randolph committed to pay £800 a year until he had covered the £6,000 which had now been paid to him. He was also induced to promise:

> In consideration of your having agreed to an advance being made out of the trust fund in order to meet my losses at the Palm Beach Casino, Cannes, and for the payment of my debts I wish to give you this undertaking that I will not in future play at any public gaming table or gamble for sums beyond my present means having due regard to all my obligations.

The fact that he was writing from the May Fair Hotel, W1 – where he had taken a suite as soon as he was commissioned by the *Sunday Dispatch* to write a column called 'Searchlight on Politics': not a luxury, he felt, but a necessity – and the bills he was trying to cover were for Cartier, expensive restaurants, Daimler Hire and an almost unbelievable amount of fresh flowers, said everything needed to show how far he was away from what anybody else would recognise as financial prudence.*

Within the year, Randolph had once more incurred crushing gambling debts, which were, once more, covered with money advanced from the Lord Randolph trust. This time, Randolph proclaimed himself 'definitely cured of casinoitis', but it is likely that he barely believed this himself.

Winston, who said of gambling, 'It excites me so much to play – foolish moth', was hardly in a position to criticise his son for indulging in pleasures that were so much part of his life too.† Before long,

---

* His archives contain a red 1000-franc chip from the Palm Beach Casino. There is no indication as to whether he kept it as a reminder of happy evenings spent in its recesses, or as a warning against ever making the same mistake again.

† Especially since he was also, at least in his son's estimation, a lamentably bad gambler. Randolph once told a mutual friend that there was nothing easier in the world than winning money from Winston. But Randolph wasn't much good either.

both men were back at the Riviera's gaming tables together. On one occasion in 1935 they played deep into the night. By five in the morning, Randolph was up £200, Winston £500. Walking jubilantly out of the casino, they could not find a taxi, so instead Winston suggested they should walk back along the beach: 'it's only four or five miles'.

When they returned to the Château de l'Horizon at half past six, Winston went straight to Clementine's bedroom – she was making one of her rare *actes de présence* – and showered her bed with thousand-franc notes.

Most significantly of all, their professional and political lives were more closely meshed than ever.

They made money together: in September 1934, for instance, it was announced that Winston Churchill had signed a contract with Alexander Korda's London Film Productions to edit a series of films dealing with subjects of topical interest (proposed topics included 'Will Monarchies Return?', 'The Rise of Japan', 'Marriage Laws and Customs' and 'Gold'). The main feature was to be a full-length script on George V's reign – he was about to celebrate his Silver Jubilee. Randolph was hired to help plan and research the scripts and, if a 24 September memorandum from Winston to Korda is anything to go by, as a sort of go-between: 'If you will kindly give my son, Randolph, a note confirming this agreement we may consider the matter formally concluded.' Although, in this instance, while Winston busied himself with the work in hand, Randolph confined himself to loafing around the London Films studios on Grosvenor Street, complaining that he was not being paid enough.

Even if they were not collaborating directly, Winston always seemed anxious to do what he could to shape his son's career. This might take the form of prevailing upon the historian Maurice Ashley, who had worked as Winston's research assistant, to send Randolph some notes about the South Sea Bubble. 'I thought it would be a very good subject for him,' Winston wrote in his letter of thanks to Ashley,

---

One friend remembered him as 'the worst poker player I ever saw. It was a case of "courage without cunning". His curiosity kept him in every hand, and he paid more attention to the running verbal exchanges than the hands.'

'as it enables the tale of this English company to be told in modern Stock Exchange parlance with which people are now so familiar and also I am very anxious for him to undertake a serious work. On no account put him off it.'

But it was politics to which they were both really devoted, and it was politics that consumed most of their time. When Winston gave speeches in the House, his son would be up in the gallery, his piercing china-blue eyes boring into MPs as they debated below. Behind the scenes he offered support and helped Winston compile lists of sympathetic MPs who might back him in his campaigns. He also did much to prepare him for the gruelling hearings of the India Committee.

Stanley Baldwin, writing to Ramsay MacDonald in July 1932 about the announcement of a Joint Select Committee on India, noted: 'As to Winston, he was completely knocked out. He had got with him sheets of typewritten invective against everybody and everything, and with all his stage army, including Randolph in the gallery, and the Bracken claque carefully dotted about the House.'

This complaint would become a common refrain among the Tory hierarchy. Whenever there was a parliamentary event, Randolph and the rest of Winston's 'camp followers' would be close at hand. Winston had begun to find speaking in the House increasingly difficult. Before his isolation had begun, there had always been a majority, or even a strong minority, to offer noisy encouragement when he made interventions. Now he was alone and needed acolytes who could at least help give the impression that he had some meaningful level of support.

In his journalism, which he saw as only a temporary phase before his own political career began in earnest, Randolph was an aggressive supporter of his father's views; week after week, in the pages of the *Sunday Graphic* (for whom both his father and grandfather had written before him) and the *Daily Mail*, he tried to draw attention to what he saw as the scandal of Winston's continuing exclusion from the government.

If Winston was involved in a fight, it was a racing certainty that Randolph would weigh in on his side too. In 1934, Winston tried to expose the operations of the secretary of state for India, Samuel Hoare, whom he accused of having forced the Manchester Chamber of Commerce to suppress a document they had produced that had articulated their objections to the White Paper on India. His complaints of a breach of parliamentary privilege led to a two-month inquiry.

Although Winston appeared before the committee convened to consider his accusations, he was given only restricted access to evidence: when he asked for a number of documents to the India Office to be submitted, they were never produced; he was prevented from questioning other witnesses; and some of the written evidence he was able to submit was omitted because it was ruled to have been harmful to the public interest.

As a result, his case was much weakened, and the publication in June of the report of the inquiry was a public humiliation for him that dealt a further blow to his standing in Parliament. It ruled that 'although Churchill's facts were substantially correct, there had been no breach of privilege because the committee was not a judicial body and there was nothing to prevent anybody from trying to persuade witnesses to change their evidence.' What happened could not, therefore, be described as 'wrongful pressure'.

Winston and his son were enraged. The day after the report was published, Randolph wrote a savage column.

> I wonder what would have been the attitude of the Committee of Privileges if persons who had an interest in the outcome of its report had spoken with its witnesses in the same fashion as their report finds that Sir Samuel Hoare and Lord Derby spoke with the witnesses before the Joint Select Committee.

Hoare was already smarting from Winston's accusations; Randolph's assault added insult to injury. 'I do not know which is the more offensive or mischievous, Winston or his son,' Hoare wrote. 'Rumour, however, goes that they fight like cats with each other and chiefly agree in the prodigious amount of champagne that each of them drinks each night.'

Randolph may not have realised it, but he was steadily making powerful enemies. This was of course an occupational hazard for anyone anxious to rise quickly in politics; and yet what, exactly, beyond his father's approval, did he stand to gain from upsetting influential figures like Hoare?

It was, however, a measure of his growing public profile, and he found he could continue to use both his journalism and his gift for public speaking to make sure that he could act as a loud supporter of his father's cause. The good things he had inherited from Winston – 'clarity of thought, command of the English language and a fearless courage' – were allied to something else. Many observers thought Randolph was more assured than his father on a public platform.

Randolph appeared with his father at decorous constituency events – in July 1934, Winston wrote to him, reminding him: 'We are counting on you to come here for the week-end of the 21st. The Epping Garden Party is on the Saturday afternoon and I hope you will make a short speech. Try therefore to come in time for lunch.'

But he was equally confident standing beside Winston at more rough-hewn occasions – such as addressing disgruntled Lancashire cotton workers as part of the India campaign. On Monday, 2 July, at a meeting at Imperial Mill in Burnley, he addressed four hundred workers, and over the next three weeks he spoke at more than fifty meetings and wrote twenty-eight articles, under either his own name or the dubious cover of 'Our Special Correspondent'.

He was an incandescent presence on stages across Lancashire. Before long, fellow supporters were writing admiringly to his father. 'Randolph', said one, 'has made a splendid impression on the thousands who have attended our meetings this week, on all sides there has been nothing but praise for his manliness, his utter lack of side and affectation.

'I have been amazed and delighted at the way he has won the hearts of all . . .'

Not everybody was quite as impressed. A few days after Winston had received this encouraging report, his secretary Miss Pearman sent her employer what she called an 'urgent note'.

Captain Orr-Ewing rang up to ask what he should do and although he did not like to have to say it, he thought for the sake of the Manchester campaign something should be done at once.

Mr Randolph is doing remarkably well in the North but has done two things which have rather upset people, and also rendered himself liable to be pulled up sharply. He made an attack on Sir

Herbert Samuel at Darwen the other day [accusing him of being totally incapable of providing the people of Lancashire with guidance, and privileging his liberal principles over the need to make a real fight for the county], which he had to withdraw later as it was incorrect, and yesterday he referred to the Lancashire members as 'rats' which greatly incensed a large number of people.

★

During this period, Winston made speech after speech on India – some as good as he had ever delivered. He was frequently able to persuade significant numbers of MPs to rebel (seventy, eighty), but every battle he fought ultimately ended in a demoralising defeat.

Just as the brute force of Winston's charisma meant that, in better times, his mere presence could fill his home with energy, now he created around him an atmosphere that veered between defiance and despondency, in which frustration seemed to be the one constant. Chartwell became a house permeated by vexation and defeat; it was hard for anyone who visited to escape untouched. The painter William Nicholson got so fed up with the gloom that he told Johnny Churchill it made him feel sick: 'Johnny, I'm going to leave the table on an excuse. I cannot stand it any more.'

Clementine urged her husband to sell Chartwell, accept that it was too late for a return to power and to settle for a gentle dotage writing books. His old friend Beaverbrook agreed, writing, 'I think Winston Churchill will retire from Parliament. It is really the best thing for him to do. In any case, if he continues on his present course, I would not be surprised if Baldwin put a veto on him in his constituency. And believe me, Baldwin can do it.'

There were days when the unending grind left Winston feeling so empty and depressed that he agreed with them. Returning to a theme that he had picked up on and off for years, he talked, for instance, to his old friend Bernard Baruch about the possibility of leaving politics altogether and devoting himself to making money. This came to nothing. Baruch, speaking with New World directness, told Winston he would be hopeless as a businessman.

It was the almost narcotic hold politics had over him, as well as his conviction that his country was on the brink of disaster, that drew him back to the fray. Winston was haunted by the idea of Vienna, once the capital of Central Europe, now only a grisly skeleton. If Britain, like Austria-Hungary, lost its empire, which it seemed determined to throw away, there would, he believed, 'be the most frightful crash and obliteration of life that has ever darkened human records'.

Randolph's frustration at the glacial progress of his political career mounted in tandem with Winston's own disquiet. He had already fallen well short of the ambitions he had expressed so forcefully only a few years before, when he had thought he would emulate Pitt the Younger, with whom he shared a birthday, by entering the House of Commons at the age of twenty-one and becoming prime minister at twenty-four. He had been so confident of this that, as he later told his own son, 'If anyone suggested that I would not match that record, I should not have been angry, I would have just laughed in their face!'

Now, though, he was already halfway through his twenties, and he had not even put a foot onto the first rung on the ladder. Randolph was still desperate to take what he thought was his rightful place at his father's side in the House. He could achieve so much more in Parliament than by cheering, no matter how vociferously, from the sidelines. In addition to this was the fact that the House of Commons was, to the Churchills, an almost holy place.

Winston had experienced some of the most thrilling moments of his life in that building. And yet perhaps most of all, he loved the building's more mundane pleasures: the alternate passages of boredom and excitement its sessions offered; the steady hum of committee meetings; the chance to sit and drink and smoke himself to death in an attempt to make friends and influence people; those moments in the chamber when he thumbed his nose at the men on the opposing benches, or drove them into fury and then blew them a kiss. All of this was, for the moment, denied Randolph, except as a spectator.

His problem was that his loyalty to Winston, and the causes Winston espoused, placed him at odds with the Conservative Party hierarchy. The distrust of Winston that had lingered since the turn of the century had not been dispelled by his return to the party; and his antagonism over India, and uneasy relationship with the party's leader, Stanley Baldwin, had only exacerbated it.

If Randolph wanted the Tory leadership to intervene with a local association on his behalf, he would have to, in effect, repudiate his father. Besides, progress in the Conservative Party was grindingly slow and involved the sort of deference and patience that his father had always taught him were reserved for people other than the Churchills. Randolph believed that Baldwin had come up with the idea that 'you rise by steady, obedient service' to the party. This meant that, as he wrote in a column (designed to excoriate Anthony Eden), 'the old gang will always encourage mediocrity rather than brilliance ... Real ability will always be suppressed. Hence the only chance is to be a rebel and to seek to master the old men, not to serve them.'

There was no recognisable 'Churchillite' faction within the Tory party, no minister or even MPs who relied on his patronage. Winston no longer possessed the sort of influence that might have secured his son a safe seat. More disturbingly, the skills and tactics he had used to such great effect in establishing his own career were beginning to seem outmoded in comparison with the ruthless efficiency of the Conservative Party's political machine.

Winston still believed that you erected your standard and then won others to your cause by making exhilarating speeches in the House, or at rowdy public meetings. This, after all, was what had worked for him, and his father before him. By contrast, Lyndon Johnson's father had told him that the key skill in politics was being able to enter a room and know instantly how many of the men inside it were on your side. The idea that one's cause might be promoted by compromises eked out in smoky back rooms, or advanced through the carefully calibrated delivery of threats and inducements, was thoroughly alien to Winston. He had little interest in this form of politics, nor in truth did he have the sort of mind or authority that would have allowed him to practise it. This meant that Randolph, so keen to imitate his father, was trying to make his way in twentieth-century politics using an essentially eighteenth-century approach. On the verge of the atomic age, he was still going into battle armed with a musket.

For a while, Randolph could divert his energy and frustration into campaigning on Winston's behalf. It could not last.

8

My Brother, the Bastard

RANDOLPH REVERED WINSTON, but he was not, he said, prepared to act as a glorified bag carrier to his father. Both his natural inclinations and the aspirations he had been encouraged to entertain precluded this. The plan he evolved was to chart a course in which he would 'substantially' support his father while remaining open to any opportunity that came along to establish an independent identity.

Quite how this could be achieved was another question. He might have deliberately bought bowler hats that were two sizes too large, sported 'distinctive' collars, and worn his hair 'rather long' (the source of disagreement with Winston; to cheer him up, Randolph had it trimmed the day his father left for a lecture tour), but all these things were superficial.

The fact of his name, and everything it meant, was defining, inescapable wherever he went. It was the one thing that everybody knew about him, and which conditioned the way they treated him. Sarah was confronted by a similar problem when training as a dancer. For her, going on stage was a way of trying to establish a reputation based solely on her own merits. To begin with she had gone to interviews using a pseudonym, a clever plan undermined by the fact that photographs of her had appeared regularly in the press since she was a child.

Decades later, far away from home in Korea, Randolph talked to the journalist Alan Whicker about the problem that had dogged his heels ever since he had been a young man: 'If I achieve anything they all say it's because of my father, and when I do something badly they say "What a tragedy for the Old Man!" I can never win.'

The only option Randolph had, or so he felt at least – in the future he would tell an interviewer that frustration stopped him from seeing his situation clearly – was to draw attention to himself by saying and writing 'rather reckless things'.

When he was beginning to try to make a career for himself, a lot of people went out of their way to be kind to him. The Churchill name came freighted with problems, yet it had its advantages too. No matter how isolated Winston may have been in the House of Commons, he retained the affection of great numbers of people in both politics and the press.

This goodwill could not, however, survive Randolph's repeated displays of arrogance and astonishing rudeness. Robert Bruce Lockhart, on meeting him, noted that this was a strategy: 'He is very ambitious, goes on the theory that to succeed one must be unpopular.' It was a strategy, moreover, that had been employed by both his father and grandfather before him. Lord Randolph had in a matter of months gained a reputation as one of the rudest men of the nineteenth century. In doing so, he changed the complexion of his party, forced Lord Salisbury to make him Chancellor of the Exchequer, and had he not self-destructed so extravagantly was likely to have one day led the country.

As a young MP, Winston had carried himself aggressively, picked fights with his elders and took the risk of abandoning the Tories for a Liberal Party intent on reshaping the nation. He was not a man for the long, uncomplaining climb, and ensured his name was seen in papers and heard on others' lips. It did not matter if he was being criticised. 'This is a pushing age,' he told his mother, 'and we must shove with the best.'

More than one man who knew both Randolph and Winston claimed that the young Winston had been by far the ruder (Randolph's friend James Lees-Milne thought the idea 'incredible'), but this did not prevent him from becoming a Cabinet minister by the age of thirty-three.

All the havoc Randolph had caused, all the noses he had put out of joint, earned him nothing but resentment. Reflecting on this time in his life years later, he would talk ruefully about not really having 'the ammunition or the skill to hit the target'. Randolph's impatience, and his father's eminence, had created a situation in which he was forced to grow up in public. He made his mistakes in full view of the world, and he would learn – though only when it was too late – that the consequences of these errors would dog his heels for the rest of his life.

The consequences rebounded not just on Randolph but on his father too, who worked hard to try to contain and mitigate the results of his son's rashness. Until his son turned twenty-one, Winston could still exert a measure of control over what he said, and who he said it to. In July 1929, for example, he had written to George Blake to decline, on Randolph's behalf, the chance to contribute to an edition of the *Strand* magazine on the theme of sons of famous fathers: 'It is very kind of you to wish to give my son an opportunity of this kind, but I am afraid that I could not allow him to take advantage of it, certainly not until he is 21 and independent of my authority.'

Increasingly, however, now that Randolph had come of age, his father found he was forced into awkward exchanges with men who had been offended by one of Randolph's columns or the outrageous comments he tossed like bombs into dinner-table conversation.

Winston's archives are full of letters by him in which he tries to soothe friends, family, colleagues and rivals. In one, to Lord Londonderry (in the aftermath of a gossip column written by Randolph in which he suggested that because Londonderry derived much of his income from coal-mining royalties, he would be unduly anxious about a socialist threat), he said, 'Randolph's paragraphs seem to me equally ill-informed and harmless and I do not think anyone could have read them as being any reflection upon you.'

After assuring Londonderry that no offence was intended and that none should be taken, he promised that he had 'however sent your letter to Randolph in order that he may see the trouble you have taken about these trumpery paragraphs because they were written by a kinsman of yours'.

Londonderry's gracious response was a telling summary of what made father and son so similar, and yet so different:

I am sorry that Randolph goes in for this kind of journalism. He is so like you and yet so unlike you: like you in your enterprise and courage and forcefulness, and unlike you because he does not seem to recognise what you always recognise that knowledge is the secret of power – and I remember well how you never had a spare moment but that you were not reading or studying anything which could make for yourself the position which you have established now in the political and the literary arena.

As time went on, both Brendan Bracken and the Prof warned Winston about his son's behaviour, but he continued to spoil him and encourage his high aspirations. Steadily, however, even Winston began to realise that his son had become almost uncontrollable.

Inevitably, this led to rows. Winston and Randolph had always quarrelled; verbal sparring was part of the currency of their relationship. That Randolph relished it slightly more than his father was not usually a problem.

Randolph liked to taunt his father 'as one might a bull from a safe distance'. He would express a 'monstrous opinion' or accuse his father of having unsuitable friends (essentially those Randolph did not like), then sit back and wait for 'long growls of contradiction'.

At this point, anyone sitting at the table with them would begin to nervously examine their shirtfronts. More often than not, the tension would be short-lived, and Winston could return to praising his son's 'bursting self-confidence' and 'intelligence'.

And yet by the middle of the decade, their quarrels had begun to look more and more like fights.

These two emotionally volatile men were seeing each other several times during the week and spending three out of four weekends a month in each other's company. They were also both struggling with immediate professional frustration, pressing financial worries and existential concern about the fate of the nation. Very often one, or the other, or both, would be drunk. They also shared a unique ability to get under each other's skin: as Winston pointed out, when one of them became angry, or felt insulted, it was 'infectious', and the other was almost certain to follow suit.

All it needed was for Randolph to go too far, or to be surprised by the fierceness of his father's response, and what had been a friendly tussle metastasised into an ugly argument that had the potential to disturb anybody who witnessed it.

Winston was sensitive, as his nephew Johnny recalled, in the 'most appalling way'. Life at the top of politics had never really thickened his skin. When he felt betrayed by a friend, he would say, with almost childlike surprise, 'You are not on my side.'

He cried at anything: 'the mention of gallantry in battles, the thought of "invincible knights in olden days", victims of anti-Semitism, Canadian loyalty to the empire'. But his relentless self-obsession prevented him from ever realising how easily his behaviour could wound others. Johnny, who felt that he and his uncle shared the same flaw, observed that 'we don't register when we hurt people, as much as we should.' It was another consequence of his obliviousness to the inner life of anybody other than himself.

Like his father, Randolph's capacity to register slights was matched only by his ability to unthinkingly deliver them. When told by his commander early in the Second World War that while his fellow officers found him merely unlikeable, the other ranks could not tolerate him, he burst into tears. His extreme sensitivity was especially pronounced when it came to Winston. He could seem at times like a jealous lover, constantly interrogating his partner to try to detect any sign that his affection or trust was wavering. Randolph needed to know that his place in his father's heart was unchallenged.

Once the spark came, things escalated quickly. Neither man had the capacity to control himself; and there was no means of reducing tension or taking the venom out of their exchanges.

Winston was 'prone to fits of unreasonable and apparently ungovernable bad temper'. Once worked up, he could quickly become 'violently offensive'. Randolph inherited this predisposition to rough passion. And, as was so often the case, something in Randolph's make-up, or upbringing, ensured that it expressed itself in him in a greatly exaggerated form.

When Randolph got angry, he would talk faster and faster. At a certain point, he simply surrendered control. He once confided to Kay Halle, 'If I can stop it before it reaches my knees I will be all right, but once it gets above them a black fog envelops me and I just don't care what I say.' At this point he might jump up and down in rage like a child, or stomp up and down rooms howling obscenities, or kick chairs over.

The two men would toss aside the deep love and affection they bore for each other and scream unforgivable things into each other's faces, as if they were helpless to do anything else. Only later would the regret begin.

After one of their rows, when Randolph had flown out of the room, Winston went to the mantelpiece, turned round an ornament, and in a voice more sad than it was angry, asked the Prof, who had been a helpless witness to the argument: 'Lindemann, you are a professor of biology and experimental philosophy. Tell me am I as a parent responsible for all the biological and chemical reactions in my son?'

John Julius Norwich, son of Duff and Diana Cooper, was a boy during the thirties, but even to him it was clear that Randolph was out of control. 'He was so badly behaved – Randolph would get possessed by the devil in drink* – that Clemmie couldn't handle it any more.' While Winston would be distressed by the immediate implications of a scene with Randolph, they never seemed to have a lasting impact on their relationship. Once father and son had made up, as they always did, they would carry on as if the argument had never happened. It was different for Clementine. A moment arrived when she actually began to fear her son and instructed her staff never to leave her alone with him.

Clementine was less a part of her husband's life during the thirties than at any time in their lives together.† 'She didn't come into it very much,' remembered Johnny, who was a regular guest at Chartwell. These years were a time of unsteady health for her. She struggled with mastoid disease and blood poisoning that tore weight off her at alarming speed. Alongside these, she suffered regular spells of what

---

* Jennie Churchill used to say, 'No one with Jerome blood should ever touch spirits. We're born intoxicated.'
† Randolph's first wife, Pamela, estimated that the couple spent 80 per cent of their marriage apart. By contrast, Stanley Baldwin and his wife were reputed to have spent only one night away from each other in their whole lives.

someone else would call her 'high mental fatigue'. More and more often she would take to her bed rather than face receiving guests or paying visits. She had also taken to reciting out loud a couplet from an elegy written for an overworked governess:

> Here lies a woman who was always tired,
> For she lived in a world where too much was required.

'You always seem to be on top of your life,' she would say to Mary many years later. 'I always felt life was on top of me.'

Winston, so easily and immediately moved by physical illness, found her nervous disorders far harder to understand. (He was after all a man who once told his doctor that he did not like psychiatrists, and nor did he like their 'queer ideas about what is in people's heads'.) He was genuinely puzzled by how mere daily life could flatten her. Nevertheless, he continued to take her complete devotion to him for granted, remaining oblivious to her growing detachment.

Mary witnessed acrimonious rows between her parents over Randolph that went on and on with little sign they would ever be resolved. Alarmed and disturbed by the shouting and slammed doors he brought in his wake, she also learned to keep out of the way when her brother came to Chartwell. Winston knew that Randolph was turbulent and idle, and a demon when drunk; he knew too that he had played his part in creating those extravagant flaws. But he had dreamed for too long of recreating the golden bond between father and son that he had been denied by Lord Randolph's majestic disdain. He could not let his fantasy go. Instead, he defended Randolph.

Winston had always prided himself on settling his arguments with Clementine before they went to bed – but now it looked as if their increasingly regular separations might be a prelude to something more permanent. At one point in the thirties, during a stay with Goonie, Clementine spoke of getting a divorce because of the frequent explosions between Winston and Randolph.

In Clementine's eyes, Randolph embodied the worst elements of Winston's character. He was also, she believed, liable to be a bad influence on his father. As Pamela recalled, 'She was very frightened that Randolph made trouble for Winston.' She did not trust him not to involve Winston in things that were not in his best interest. Guarding Winston's reputation was, for her, a life-long project, and she fought hard against anyone, or anything, that she thought might damage it.

Randolph was in both respects similar to the cronies such as Max Beaverbrook, who Clementine thought defiled everything he touched,* or F. E. Smith, men whose place in her husband's life and affections she could never stand. Winston always grieved that his closest friends should be so little liked by his wife.

But what Clementine could never quite accept was that there was some part of Winston that needed the company of these charismatic, energetic men. J. H. Plumb observed that Lord Randolph's fate 'bit deeply into Churchill's heart, drawing him to the odd, the flamboyant, the reckless, and nurturing a bud of hatred for the complacent, the controlled, the cautious men of self-confirmed moral rectitude'. Winston once said that without alcohol, life would not be worth living – he felt the same about these men. Just like champagne or cigars, Beaverbrook, F. E. Smith, David Lloyd George, Jacky Fisher and Randolph all helped Winston feel as if he was living a more exciting, elevated life. As he said of Beaverbrook: 'Some take drugs. I take Max.' To Fisher he wrote: 'Contact with you is like breathing ozone to me.'

He valued the sparkle and excitement these men offered and yet, just like champagne and cigars, he was willing to ignore – or perhaps did not see – that they could sometimes be bad for him.

Winston could only very reluctantly be persuaded to stop boarding the flimsy, flammable Great War-era aeroplanes with a lit cigar in his mouth; it would be still harder for Clementine to make him see the dangers of his obsession with learning to fly. By the same token, Beaverbrook gave rotten political advice, and when in government was not just a disruptive presence but actively plotted against Winston, yet this was never held against him for long.

---

* There were occasions when Winston dined with Beaverbrook without his wife when Clementine was seen pleading with him not to allow himself to be taken in by that 'microbe' – continuing to beg him even as he walked out of the door.

Winston's male friendships could be unusually intimate. Witness the crackling, almost romantic connection he had with the little simian genius Jacky Fisher. 'You are the only man in the world I really love,' Winston told the admiral before the Great War. Even their disagreements felt like a falling-out between lovers. 'I'VE DONE WITH HIM,' the admiral confided to a friend after one tiff with Churchill, 'I can't say yet whether Winston & I are going to be friends . . . of course you know we were very very intimate before.'

Eventually, Fisher's conduct over the Dardanelles helped derail Winston's career, and yet Winston seemed able to overlook any number of the outrages committed by him, and even continued to send him birthday cards.*

Violet Asquith recognised the curious nature of the two men's relationship. 'Poor darling W. – there is a naive and utterly disarming trustfulness about him. He makes his own climate and lives in it and those who love him share it. In an odd way there was something like love between him and Fisher – a kind of magnetic attraction which often went into reverse. Theirs was a curiously emotional relationship – but as in many such they could neither live with, nor without, each other.'

Something similar to this existed between Winston and Randolph, although its currents ran far deeper, and the words they exchanged had far more power to hurt. Randolph made his father feel bold, undaunted and alive. He offered Winston the praise and unconditional, unstinting love he wished his own father had given him. But to all of this was added something else: blood. Randolph was his only son, the literal incarnation of his dynastic obsession. This meant that Winston treated him differently from anybody else. Randolph's sisters knew this and resented it. Mary wrote in her diary of her bitterness at this. In her father's eyes, nothing they achieved could ever compare to anything Randolph did: 'for after all he is the eldest & only son.'

---

* Clementine felt differently. At one lunch at 41 Cromwell Road, F. E. Smith watched in amazement as she burst out to Jacky Fisher: 'Keep your hands off my husband. You have all but ruined him once. Leave him alone now!' As Fisher toyed with a knife, Clementine continued her assault: 'Yes you would perhaps like to plunge that knife into my heart! Well you may! I don't care but leave my husband alone.'

By the same token, he could hurt his father grievously, and know that whatever he said, or did, he would be forgiven.

Randolph was, after all, almost entirely his father's creation. Winston had spent twenty years forming his son's personality, and although he was alive to his many flaws, this did nothing to diminish his affection for him. The more Clementine criticised Randolph, the stronger Winston's love for him seemed to become. It was this, perhaps, more than anything else, that Clementine resented. For years she had emptied herself in support of Winston, and yet rather than giving her the devotion she deserved, he was infatuated by his glorious, golden, chaotic son. Clementine had been pushed to the margins of Winston's life; Randolph had been ushered to its centre. This was not to say, however, that Randolph had his father entirely to himself.

On a morning in the summer of 1923 a tall man with a squashed nose, pebble-thick spectacles and hair that grew on his head in tier upon tier of carroty waves strolled into Randolph's life. The twenty-two-year-old Brendan Bracken had met Winston earlier that year, at the Beaconsfield home of the *Observer* editor, J. L. Garvin. Winston had been impressed by his boldness and infectious enthusiasm – there was an uncanny similarity in their temperaments, despite their great disparity in age and experience – but what attracted him most was the younger man's willingness to put himself entirely at his service.

To begin with, nobody knew who he was, or where he had come from. Bracken was a fabulist, a master of evasion and a teller of grotesquely improbable tales who moulded his accent and the story he told about his origins to suit his circumstances.

One contemporary said of Bracken that 'everything about that man is false. Even his hair, which looks like a wig, is real.' Randolph, when he grew to know him better, was overheard in Boulestin calling him 'God's greatest liar because he does not mind being found out'.

As hard as his contemporaries worked to discover the truth about him (Beaverbrook became obsessed by his origins, and eventually sent men to Ireland to see what they could find out), it seemed that Bracken worked harder to increase the sense of mystery. He left false trails, helped start outlandish rumours. Some people thought he enjoyed being misunderstood. But misdirection was important to him; it was what allowed him to safeguard the part of him that he wanted to protect from the world's gaze.* He wore the sense of mystery, which he helped to create, like a cloak. Even those who grew close to him always felt as if there was an element of strangeness just beyond reach.

He was in fact Irish, the son of a moderately successful stonemason who had died young. He found his mother uncongenial, her next husband even less so, and after a minor scandal at his school, he was banished to Australia, where he began his myth creation in earnest.

Even as late as 1929, when he became Conservative MP for North Paddington (Lord Randolph's old constituency),† he was telling reporters that he was born in Bedfordshire, had homes in Westminster, Bedfordshire, Scotland and Ireland, and that he was an Oxford graduate. None of this was even close to true. But perhaps the secret he worked hard to disguise was his kindness and generosity, which he tried to bury beneath an avalanche of sarcasm and fierce looks.

During his wandering days in Australia, he began to read deeply; in the process he fell in love with England, and what he understood to be its way of life and political genius. Specifically, he had conceived an outsize admiration for an England that no longer existed – the England of Walpole, Fox, the Pitts and Edmund Burke, the England of the eighteenth century. Maybe, then, it was inevitable that he would become an acolyte of a man who could sometimes seem as if he had stepped out of the pages of a historical novel.

Many decades later, Randolph still remembered Bracken's entrance, and the curious impression he made.

> I was with my sisters, playing in the garden, when this odd-looking man with flaming red hair strolled along. My father was up the big lime tree, building a tree-house for us, and didn't come down at once. I shall never forget what an easy and agreeable impression Brendan made on us. He told me his name, and asked ours. Then

---

* After a lifetime of fabulation and evasion, he made sure that his existence would always remain foggy and obscure, by asking that his papers be destroyed within twenty-four hours of his death.

† During the canvassing, he drove a hired caravan emblazoned with the slogan 'Stop me and Ask one'.

he said: 'I don't like my name, Brendan, so please call me Peter.'
Eventually my father appeared. They went off and didn't reappear
for ages. We were all taken aback by the way Bracken put a familiar
arm round his shoulder and called him 'Father'. I wondered if it
was a joke.

Randolph and his siblings were asleep by the time Bracken, who
had talked the staff into making a bed for him, and his father sat down
to dinner. So they missed the final twist in this strange day: in the small
hours, Bracken stunned Winston and his guests by announcing he
would walk back to London. Then he simply strode off into the night.

One moment the Churchill family had known nothing of Bracken's
existence, and the next he was haunting Chartwell, sitting at their
dinner table and talking so much in his 'polyglot Irish-Australian-
Cockney accent' that he sometimes forgot to put food in his mouth.
Housemaids who went downstairs to plump the cushions would
discover him asleep on the drawing-room sofa with his boots off, or
scissoring press cuttings out of their scrapbook without Clementine's
permission. (Randolph, who was still trying to work out what to
make of this curious interloper, grinned his way through his mother's
attempts to upbraid Winston for the trouble Bracken caused the
Chartwell staff.)

Some people reported that Bracken's presence left them feeling
nauseated, but Clementine was not just immune to his cloying charm,
she was enraged by his unannounced raids on her home, and also by
his habit of calling her 'Clemmie', an honour extended to only a very
few intimates (Franklin Roosevelt also offended her on this count).*
She did not like his mystifying behaviour – he once promised to take
twelve-year-old Randolph to the zoo, and then never turned up.
Most of all, she resented the way he encouraged the rumours that he
was Winston's son, which had begun to swirl through London.

In one version Bracken was the son of a black girl Winston had
known in South Africa during the Boer War. In another, the mother
was an Irish girl Winston had met on his return to Britain. Bracken

---

* Randolph: 'Mummy won't call him Brendan because she's so afraid he might call
her Clemmie.'

made things worse by calling Winston 'father'. Clementine, who had never quite forgiven her mother for the cloud of sexual intrigue that hung over her family when she was younger, was peculiarly sensitive to even a hint of this sort of scandal. Bracken's sly encouragement of the rumours disgusted her.

Clementine's hostility to Bracken, whom she talked of as 'this red-haired freak', was such that another guest who witnessed the way she stared icily at him, or cut him off brutally when he talked, called her 'the coldest woman I ever met'. And yet Bracken seemed unruffled, pretending not to notice Clementine's barbed comments, or simply smiling sweetly at her when she had finished.

Winston treated him with fatherly affection and, as Bracken's career in publishing took off, came to appreciate the help he could offer. He knew little about his new friend's exotic and mysterious past, and his impervious self-obsession protected him from the desire to learn more. Unlike Clementine, he seemed to enjoy the whispers, not least because of the air of sexual potency it lent him, and encouraged the gossip to the point that even some of his own children half believed it. When Randolph asked Winston if the rumours were true, his father told him, 'I don't know. But when I arrived in Dublin for the first time in my life it was exactly nine months before Brendan was born. So it is possible.'

Eventually, Clementine became so exasperated that she demanded to know the truth about the 'reprobate'. 'I've looked the matter up,' Winston told her with a sly grin, 'and the dates don't coincide.'

Clementine had tried hard while Winston was chancellor to exclude Bracken from her husband's life, because she thought the presence of this garrulous, unknowable oddity on its fringes might harm his reputation. In response, Bracken rationed his visits to Chartwell and arranged to see Winston elsewhere. But by 1929, as an MP and proprietor of the *Banker*, he had achieved a certain amount of respectability, and gradually, as Clementine saw how unswervingly loyal Bracken was to Winston and how much practical help he offered, she began to warm to him.

Bracken became an ever more important part of Winston's life. An impudent coiner of nicknames, with a talent for producing startling imagery, he was the man who could always laugh Winston out of a bad temper, who never stopped talking except when it was Winston himself who was speaking. If he bickered constantly with Winston ('like husband and wife', remembered Harold Macmillan), he was also the only person given licence to enter Winston's meetings without knocking.

Brendan Bracken. The idiosyncratic, enigmatic Irishman
was one of Winston's most devoted followers.

Randolph was, Christopher Sykes claimed, the only person to see Bracken for the hoax that he was, but the real source of his disquiet was far simpler: he was jealous.

Randolph loved Bracken's company to begin with. When he was at Oxford, Randolph used to look forward to the irregular swoops Bracken made in his Hispano-Suiza, with its striking blue carriage lamps. It was a guarantee of a lavish meal and a handful of stories that Randolph had to decide were fabrications or not. More materially, he rarely left without pressing a crisp new banknote into the undergraduate's hand.

As Randolph grew older, he became more aware of the hold Bracken had on his father, and his curiosity curdled into a queasy mix of suspicion, dislike and affection that he would never quite manage to resolve. Bracken was often kind to him, showing an almost fatherly interest in his progress and prospects, and even tried to boss him around, but Randolph could not shake the thought that in some way Bracken was conspiring to, may indeed have already succeeded in, displacing him in Winston's affections. In his pique, Randolph would sometimes refer to Bracken as 'my brother, the bastard'.

Randolph and Bracken's trip to Venice in the summer of 1932 was a perfect example of the ambiguous nature of their relationship. Venice was a favoured destination for fashionable society during this period. It was where you would go if you wanted to see Oswald Mosley swimming Byronically in the Lido, or Duff Cooper strolling around the Lido in khaki shorts and a vest.

That August, Bracken invited a number of political colleagues to stay with him at the palazzo he claimed to have inherited from his mother, who had just died. Randolph, who was staying with friends, came over to visit. There was something about the presence of Bracken that could set off in Randolph an abrasive, provocative mood in which menace lurked beneath a relentless torrent of badinage. (He once took Bracken – a man so averse to lewdness that he ejected men from his home for telling dirty jokes – to a brothel in Monte Carlo, and on the way back to the hotel kept up a running commentary full of feigned concern about the diseases they had probably caught. Bracken was so worried that he readily agreed to Randolph's suggestion that he call a doctor.)

Randolph, who like everyone else was still ignorant of Bracken's true origins, was happy enough to believe the story of the inheritance, even though it was an apartment, not a palace. His suspicions were aroused, however, by the fact that all its books were in German. When he pressed Bracken to explain what these books said about his family's background, Bracken tried to laugh it off, but Randolph's hackles were up.

Bob Boothby, who was also there, was less bothered by Bracken's blatant fabrications, but he was surprised that two other guests, Sir Alfred and Lady Mond, could be so innocent that, captivated by the charm of the place, they made Bracken promise he would rent it to them in the future. (Six months later, Randolph noted sourly, the Monds hired the apartment. They were informed that Bracken had not paid his rent.)

A few nights later, Bracken and Randolph dined at the Lido Taverna with the Mosleys. Oswald Mosley was on the verge of launching the New Party and the table was soon engrossed in vivacious political discussion. All except Brendan, who was unusually abstracted and aloof. This was such strange behaviour for a man who usually dominated conversation that Mosley began to wonder whether he was unwell. It was at this point that Randolph broke off from what he was saying and turned unpleasantly to Bracken: 'Brendan, you have been very quiet. You are so talkative as a rule. Pray silence, everyone – and let my brother speak.'

Before anyone had time to work out what was happening, Bracken, who had gone red with fury, rose from his chair and strode towards Randolph, as if he were about to attack him. But then he stumbled and his glasses fell to the ground.

'The worst moment of all came', Mosley remembered, 'when there was a sudden crunching of broken glass. In his helpless efforts to carry on unaided and reach his persecutor, Brendan stepped on his own spectacles and accidentally ground them underfoot.'

The Mosleys, shocked at the macabre turn the evening had taken, made their excuses and left. Little would change in the years that followed. Randolph always wanted his father to himself. This desire meant that whenever anybody came along who, like Bracken, he saw as a threat to his place at Winston's side, he reacted badly. The elegant Anthony Eden, one of the Conservative Party's rising stars through the thirties, was another man who would be subject to the jagged edges of the younger Churchill's jealousy.

But Winston was not going to let Randolph's tantrums prevent him from doing exactly as he wished. He had never let his wife dictate who he could and could not see, why should things be any different with his son?

9

This is a Most Rash and Unconsidered Plunge

Two significant things happened in the winter of 1934–5. The first was that Clementine set off on a six-month cruise to the Dutch East Indies on Lord Moyne's yacht, *Rosaura*. The second was that in January 1935, the *Daily Mail* sent Randolph to cover the forthcoming by-election in Wavertree, a semi-rural seat on the outskirts of Liverpool, full of neat terraced houses, which the Conservatives had won in 1931 with a majority of 29,973. It was thought that the party's candidate, Mr John Platt, who was standing in his first election, would repeat this effort without trouble.

On 18 January Randolph went, accompanied by some of his friends from the Manchester branch of the India Defence League, to one of Platt's private meetings. At some point in the evening, they decided to liven things up by showering Platt – who was a loyal supporter of the National Government – with hostile questions about India. Their work done, they returned to Liverpool's Adelphi Hotel (where Randolph was the only member of the press corps who had taken a royal suite).

It was here, at around 4.00 a.m., that Randolph decided to stand as an Independent Conservative. The men had talked for hours: about Platt's weaknesses; about the dangers of splitting the Conservative vote; about the power of the local Tory machine; and more than anything, about the fact that Randolph knew virtually nobody in Liverpool and had no money. When Randolph's friend James Watt pledged £200, the mood shifted and, almost before they knew it, the decision had been made.

Randolph immediately ordered a car, and with two drivers taking turns at the wheel, they sprinted to London to speak to Lord Rothermere, who was easily persuaded to lend the campaign his personal support as well as the backing of his newspapers.

Next, Randolph announced his candidacy with a statement in the *Evening News*: 'The public pronouncements of Mr Platt have led me to the conclusion that he is not prepared, if he is elected to Westminster, to fight for the vital requirements of Lancashire trade.' For that reason, he continued, 'I have decided to contest Wavertree in the Conservative cause.' The giddy rush of activity continued and that afternoon he caught the 2.45 to Liverpool, where he was met at the station by a swarm of reporters.

The following day, the *Sunday Dispatch* printed an interview Randolph had given before leaving London. It presented his candidacy as both a challenge to the National Government and a rallying point for traditional Tories. More than that, the unashamedly partisan piece suggested that this was only the beginning of something even more exciting. 'Many Conservatives think Mr Churchill to be the leader long awaiting.'

Randolph was at great pains to make it clear that he had made the decision without consulting his father. 'I did not want my father to have the responsibility of advising me, as it is quite likely to be a losing fight.'

Out of nothing, Randolph had created a sensation. The entrance into the race by 'one of the most brilliant and forceful young men in the country' had, the *Sunday Dispatch* claimed, 'changed the face of politics'. The *Daily Mail* wrote that Randolph's challenge had 'electrified Liverpool in the same way as it will inspire the rest of the nation'.

Winston was at Chartwell by himself, missing Clementine terribly ('I miss you vy much & feel vy unprotected,' he wrote to her on New Year's Eve) and burying himself in work. His first reaction to Randolph's news was dismay. In a letter on 18 January to his wife, he worried that it would split the Tory vote: 'This is a most rash and unconsidered plunge.'

It is nothing like the Westminster Election where we had the local Tories split from top to bottom and where we developed quite rapidly a brilliant organisation. Randolph has no experience of electioneering and does not seem to want advice, and the whole thing is amateurish in the last degree.

To have a haroosh in the streets and publicity in the newspapers for three weeks and then to have a miserable vote and lose the election to the Socialist will do no end of harm. Now that the thing has started I hope it will be done as well as possible.

The next day, he issued a statement to the Press Association distancing himself from the decision but expressing a cautious measure of support.

My son has taken this step upon his own responsibility and without consulting me. He is of age; he is eligible; he is deeply interested in Lancashire affairs and in Imperial politics. He has strong convictions of Tory democracy. He believes it is his duty at whatever cost to himself, to rouse Lancashire to the dangers of the India Constitution Bill. This is still a free country and he is fully entitled to plead his cause, which is worthy and a vital cause, not only for the wage-earners of Lancashire, but for the life of Britain.

I know nothing of the conditions in the Wavertree division and cannot form any opinion at this moment upon the prospects of Mr Randolph Churchill's candidature; but I should be less than human if in all the circumstances of these critical times I did not wish him success.

Almost the first thing Randolph did during his campaign was to send telegrams to his sisters, demanding their help. He was depressed, he told them, he could not get hold of anybody, everything was closed, and he only had five supporters, none of whom could vote.

Sarah rather resented the interruption to her dancing classes, but she 'adored' her brother and, having jumped out of her dancing pants and thrown a few belongings into a bag, arrived on a train on Monday night. She was met at the station by a somewhat underwhelming reception committee consisting of a hatless Randolph, who was encased in a huge muffler, her cousin Peregrine Churchill, Randolph's secretary, Miss Buck, a collection of young men she had never seen before and a photographer.

She and Randolph posed together, the camera flashed twice and then Sarah hopped into Peregrine's car. They headed for the Adelphi

Hotel. Randolph's first meeting, at Wavertree Town Hall, was only an hour away. He was to be the sole speaker; there would not even be a chairman to introduce him. Everyone except Randolph was gripped with tension, and yet eventually, even he gave way to nerves and asked Sarah to telephone ahead.

'An idiotic child answered which wasn't encouraging,' Sarah said in a letter to her mother, then handed the phone to a truculent care-taker, whose voice was so muffled it was as if he were talking from under a pile of dust sheets. 'How many have arrived?' Sarah asked gaily. 'No one,' he replied, then slammed down the phone.

When she told Randolph, he went red and started cursing their failure to put up posters in advance. He knew what was at stake. If he was to stand any chance of making progress in the election, then he had to start it strongly. A sparsely attended rally would mean the end of his campaign before it had begun. Winston knew this too. Writing to Clementine, Winston stressed that the impression created by the first meeting was of paramount importance. Yet – and here it was clear that his pride in his son, and excitement about the enterprise on which he had just embarked had already overmastered Winston's initial pique – he was confident in his son's abilities. 'Of course in action of this kind he has a commanding and dominating personality, and there is great feeling that Lancashire needs someone of vigour and quality.'

Now was the time for Randolph to showcase these gifts, although no matter how forceful a performance he gave, it would be of little use if he was addressing an empty room.

With thirty minutes to go before he was due on stage, the little troupe, which included two journalists and a number of campaign workers, squeezed themselves into a taxi and set off. Sarah consoled herself with the thought that at least the passengers travelling with them would constitute a small audience.

They arrived, however, to find that crowds were spilling out onto the pavements: 'Mummy it was amazing. The hall was packed, and Randolph who thought he would be alone on the platform found hardly room to stand on it himself.'

Randolph's speech was exhilarating, brave and reckless in equal measure.

'I am not afraid of embarrassing the Government,' he announced to raucous cheers.

As soon as the Lancashire members get to London they are dazzled by the big lights. They are so impressed by meeting a few 'nobs' that they forget about the terrible conditions in Lancashire. I shall not be dazzled by the lights of London. I live there.

I am not frightened of Fascists or Communists as a menace to our constitutional liberties. What I am afraid of is the caucus and the party boss.

Our present party leaders were put in the present position by chance. They sit there like toads on the nostrils of the British lion.

Even as Randolph opened his mouth, stewards were already busy arranging an overflow meeting at the Women's Institute a little further up the road. Randolph closed his second address with a call for volunteers — 'If any of you feel like supporting me — please don't just go home — come now at once to my committee rooms and enrol' — and walked out with a hundred people marching behind him on the mile and a half to his headquarters. He had dived into a campaign that he should never have considered contesting, defying his father and his father's party along the way; but it was clear that something was happening.

As an excited Sarah wrote to her mother: 'I honestly think we stand a sporting chance of winning.'

Randolph was soon addressing five crowded meetings a day, making blazing speeches in which he attacked party bosses and the local Tories (including making the suggestion, furiously denied by the Liverpool Conservatives — who pointed out that he earned £2,000 a year — that he had been overlooked as a candidate because he was not a rich man).*

Or he was out canvassing in an astrakhan-trimmed coat (which looked strangely similar to the coat Winston had worn in his first

---

* It was estimated that Randolph held more meetings than all his opponents put together — speaking to 20,000 people in total.

attempt to enter Parliament) and mob cap. His campaign car, decorated by Sarah and Diana with ribbons and, alarmingly, a large portrait of their brother on the nose, became a familiar sight on the constituency's streets.

It seemed that he was everywhere. Watching him, Sarah was in awe of his confidence and charisma, the ease with which he dealt with hecklers or responded knowledgeably to even the most complex questions. She admired his tirelessness. Most of all, she was struck by his ability to inspire in his supporters the same exhilaration that seemed to pour out of him every minute of the day. Reporting again to Clementine, she told her, 'There can be no doubt that he has a great power of rallying people under his banner. Young men and girls literally hero-worshipped the "Fat boy of Wavertree" as the Daily Express called him!'

Everything, it appeared, came to him so easily. Diana, who had arrived once she had managed to resolve some of the details of her imminent divorce, agreed. They were both quite at home on the campaign trail, having so often participated in Winston's elections. But there was something different about this experience. Why, the girls asked each other, can't Papa be more like Randolph? Winston's black moods in the days before a speech hung like a cloud over their lives (Clementine: 'the whole household is in a turmoil for days before. It is like our having a baby'*); campaigning with Randolph felt like being part of a carnival. It was, as Sarah wrote, a joy to be 'in the thick of quite the most thrilling election I can remember'.

The only concern was that he was pushing himself too far. 'Randolph's voice is a great anxiety. He gets so excited and shouts much more than is necessary, and last night he nearly lost it. It is his most valuable asset – he does speak brilliantly at times – all the

---

* Winston prepared in minute detail for major speeches, including the pauses as he pretended to search for the *mot juste*, and leaving space for 'Cheers', 'Hear, hears', and, if he was feeling especially confident, a 'Standing ovation'.

A forty-minute speech took between six and eight hours of preparation. He would pace across his study, head down, arms clasped behind his back, firing words at whichever of his secretaries was on duty at the time.

F. E. Smith once said: 'Winston has spent the best years of his life writing impromptu speeches.'

women say he is a new F. E. Smith and sing "Randolph, hope & glory"!'

The reaction of smart society was one of amusement, at least at the beginning. It was treated as if it were a lark – the sort of high-spirited, short-lived joke one might expect from a Bright Young Thing.

Once the campaign began to gain momentum, this amusement turned to outrage. Chips Channon confided to his diary: 'The Churchill campaign at Wavertree is a boomerang; everybody is wild with Randolph, for he may easily put the Socialist in by splitting the Conservative vote; I think he has finally cooked his goose, and I hope so. I have never known so much social and public indignation.'

In the weeks that followed, Randolph would find that his gamble set him against not only the men he regarded as his enemies but also those he saw as friends. On Monday, 21 January, as he was returning to his hotel, he encountered a gaggle of photographers and a man he assumed was a potential voter. It was only as he leaned over to shake hands that he realised he had instead grabbed a writ for libel. His dismay was captured amid an explosion of flashing light bulbs.

The writ had been issued by Sir Thomas White, leader of the Conservative Party in Liverpool, in response to an article Randolph had published in the Manchester edition of the *Sunday Dispatch*, alleging that the year before, the Tories had voted for a Socialist mayor of Liverpool in return for Labour support for their proposals that 'the all-powerful Thomas White' be given the freedom of the city.

Alongside this legal action, loyal Tories began mounting a series of attacks on Randolph, calling him a playboy who looked like a 'slightly dissipated matinee-idol'; Samuel Hoare complained that people went to see Randolph in the same way as they might go to a new film.

Randolph seemed untroubled by the depth and viciousness of the attacks being made on him. Instead, he drew strength from the support he saw at his meetings, claiming on nomination day that 'I am tremendously pleased with my prospects . . . The numbers of people at my meetings have increased beyond my greatest dream. Really the enthusiasm has been tremendous.' When he was accused of disrupting the Conservative Party, his eyes flashed. No, he replied, 'I am reviving the Conservative Party!'

*Winston and Randolph, Wavertree, February 1935. Randolph
fought a brilliant, brave campaign during the by-election: for
once he, rather than his father, was in the limelight.*

He was exhilarated at having transformed what should have been a
dull, predictable and thoroughly local by-election into an event of
national interest. For the first time in his life, it was he who was
making headlines while his father cheered from the sidelines.

And, suddenly, it seemed possible that Randolph might win. Even
the left-wing *Daily Mirror* was impressed, speculating that the real
fight was now between him and the Labour candidate, a local magis-
trate named Joseph Cleary.

Every report that came out of Liverpool increased his father's optimism. What Winston had only a couple of days before called a 'rash
and unconsidered plunge', he now spoke of as 'Randolph's spirited
adventure'. Gleefully he began to imagine the discomfort Randolph's
victory would cause Stanley Baldwin and the prime minister, Ramsay
MacDonald.

On 23 January, in a radio message to Clementine, he abandoned any pretence of restraint: 'Randolph making progress. Great local enthusiasm. India Defence League decided give full support, therefore many good speakers. I go eve poll.'

In the letter to his wife that he wrote that same day, he talked proudly of Randolph's 'brilliant speech' and noted how 'even the enemy papers admitted the enthusiasm shown and the reality of the candidature'. Angry though the India Defence League were at not having been consulted, they were now, he said, 'all out' for his son. This was a significant step for the small caucus: it was the first time they had definitely opposed a government candidate at a by-election.

This show of defiance led to fears that the Conservatives might refuse some or even all of them the whip. Winston was not too troubled by the prospect. 'I do not believe they dare do that,' he wrote to Clementine. 'Anyhow all were resolved to go forth, so Randolph will have all our circus at his disposal including Lloyd, Wolmer, Roger Keyes, the D of A! and last but not least Papa.'

Other observers were quick to note how rapidly Winston's initial reluctance had been converted into an eagerness to exploit the situation. Not only did the furore in the press offer him the chance to renew his criticisms of the government, it seems he also hoped it could be used to exploit any disunity within the Conservative Party. He had long argued that there was widespread support for his position among the Tory ranks; it had simply been suppressed by Stanley Baldwin and his allies. The Wavertree election had the potential to act as a rallying point, drawing out supporters who might previously have been too shy to step forward. Any sort of overreaction from Baldwin and his supporters could well fracture party unity still further.

An almost rapturous tone entered Winston's letters to Clementine. The first half of the thirties had been as hard as any he had experienced in his career. But suddenly it appeared likely that his son was starting to justify all the extravagant hopes he had invested in him. 'How nice it would be', Winston wrote to her, 'if I could bring Randolph back to Westminster with me. Alas, such day-dreams must not deceive us. That he will emerge as a new public figure of indisputable political force is certain.'

Now that he was fully committed to the campaign, Winston began to display the energy and ingenuity familiar to anybody who knew his work as a minister. He devoted much of 24 January to firing off telegrams and letters enlisting support for his son. Eric Long, for instance, was asked to try to cajole the Carlton Club. To Lord Carson, he made an appeal to old ties of friendship and loyalty that went back a generation: 'Randolph would greatly welcome a letter from you, as his grandfather's old friend. I should be grateful. He is making a great fight.' A few days later, he was on to the Duke of Westminster. Winston asked Bendor if he could send some of his bailiffs, game-keepers, clerks and other employees to help canvass. After all, he told the duke, a good canvasser working for three or four days was worth one hundred votes.

Winston finished his laundry list of requests by suggesting that perhaps Bendor could spare some of his motor cars, and asked him to exert what remained of his feudal power: 'I hope you are going to bring your local lords to sit on the platform at the big meeting. It occurs to me that on your estate and among your friends there must be people who know some of the well to do folk in the Wavertree Division.' (According to Peregrine, Winston's exhortations were in vain: 'I remember Westminster promising all sorts of things and doing nothing.' He was too afraid of the party machine.)

Winston was also sending Randolph a stream of advice. On hearing reports that his son was looking tired, he urged him to take to his bed by eleven, and to 'pay great attention to his vocal cords'; he warned against Randolph committing himself to Beaverbrook's 'special follies'; suggested that he should hold meetings directed at local businessmen; as well as telling him which dissident MPs he should bring onto the stage with him, and how this news should be announced.

What had started as a lone adventure had become a family affair.

On 5 February, the eve of the poll, Winston reported breathlessly to Clementine that Randolph's odds had shortened from 50 to 1 to 6 to 4. He was now the bookies' favourite. Back in London, Chips Channon was more sceptical about Randolph's prospects: 'Tomorrow is the big day of the Wavertree election. Randolph Churchill's tide is running out.'

That evening over 10,000 saw Winston speak in support of his son. Sarah was struck by how proud Winston was of Randolph and everything he had achieved: tears frequently came to his eyes as he talked of his son's work on the campaign. 'This is not an election,' he declared, 'it is a national uprising', and defended him from some of the Conservative candidate's fiercest barbs.

> Mr Platt has said that Randolph has no soul. It is a terrible thing to say of any fellow mortal in the precarious and fleeting existence through which we are passing . . . I think he has lent his soul to England and his spirit to Lancashire, to the Wavertree electors, who will return it to him in abundant measure tomorrow.

In his peroration, which was greeted with huge cheers by the men and women who had crowded in to listen to him, he assured them: 'If you put him in as the Conservative candidate, not only will you make a great sensation, but you will have taken part in a decisive political event.'

On polling day, Wavertree's electors woke to brilliant sunshine, blue skies and a fresh breeze. Rumours about the contest continued to spread. One MP speculated that a good result for Randolph might lead to a Carlton Club meeting to decide the leadership of the Conservative Party and the end of the National Government – a view echoed by a number of papers. Journalists from France, the United States, Germany, Italy and Denmark looked on with interest, and observers in London remained electrified by the excitements caused by Randolph's campaign.

As the evening of 6 February drew on, and the result grew nearer, people began to look ostentatiously at their watches and ask each other how well they thought 'young Randolph' might do at Wavertree. A safe consensus began to emerge – 'not do too badly' – a prediction that had the great virtue of covering any combination of outcomes.

Chips Channon had been invited to a dinner at Emerald Cunard's. As he walked in, his attention was first drawn to 'three girls shimmering like goddesses – Isabel and Ursula Manners, daughters of Kakoo Rutland and Liz Paget, their Anglesey cousin'. But then, as his gaze travelled around the room, it settled upon 'old Winston Churchill'. Channon saw that Winston was almost bent double with anxiety about the fate of his son, his hands shaking with nerves.

There was a strange atmosphere in the room. All people wanted to do was discuss Wavertree, and yet Winston's presence – and his obvious disquiet, which he tried to cover with exaggerated courtesy – acted as an embarrassing constraint.

The tension grew as Edward Stanley entered the room. Only the night before, he and Winston had been standing on opposing platforms in Liverpool, speaking for opposing candidates. Now they stood in a dining room in one of London's grandest homes, studiously ignoring each other. Channon noted how 'they were only a few feet apart with only me between them, but there was really all of India too, all that dark, vast Continent'.

Winston, perhaps trying to relieve his own apprehension, tried to interest other guests in a bet that Randolph would finish in either first or second place. Buffles Milbanke took the bet. Channon bet Ursula Manners £5 that Randolph would not be first or second. As the clock ticked on, the party's attention drifted. An interest began to be taken in the sight of Mr Simpson, 'the husband of the Prince of Wales' lady – and a goodlooking Barber's Block, knowing no one, and painfully embarrassed'; and for a while Winston's distress receded among the growing noise of conversation.

At 11.30, most of the party left to go to a ball given by the Westminsters. They were greeted by Loelia in white and diamonds and Bendor, who was, that night, 'courteous and charming, with only a suggestion of his usual halitosis'. Once again, the Wavertree result became a subject of great interest. Guests walked around waiting to hear who had won. 'No one, I think,' noted Channon, 'wanted young Randolph to win or even do well.'

Winston had slipped away to the House of Commons, having told Bendor that he would come to the ball only if his son won. At midnight the results came.

Publicly at least, Randolph had given the impression he was convinced of victory. It was only at the count that his agent told him he stood no chance. Taking advantage of the split in the Conservative vote, the

Labour candidate, Joseph Cleary, had taken the seat. Randolph went white.

Sarah looked on, anxious to see how her brother would take the news. She need not have worried: 'he was marvellous – after that moment you wouldn't have known that he had lost.'

Any pleasure at seeing Randolph fall short was, for 'loyal' Tories like Chips Channon, overshadowed by the loss of a safe seat to Labour. 'It is monstrous,' he wrote in his diary, 'and it quite spoiled my evening. I was so enraged that I dragged poor Honor home.'

In a message to his wife the following day, Winston reported the result: 'Randolph beaten after magnificent battle. No harm done. Have you seen figures. Send him a message. Tender love from all. Wow.'

Thousands of miles away in the South Seas, Clementine, who was about to embark on the only affair of her marriage (with a suave art dealer named Terence Philip; it is not clear how far it went), made a show of sharing her husband's enthusiasm, but her focus was less on Randolph's own achievements and more on what impact the excitements of the last few weeks might have on her husband's position.

How anxious, & agonising & thrilling Wavertree must have been. I wish I had been there to help – Darling Winston – I hope it has not queered the pitch at Epping. I do think the Rabbit ought to have consulted you before rushing into the fray. However he seems to have done very well – Moppett tells me Sarah was most competent & astonished her by her 'poise'.

In a letter to Lord Willingdon on the same day, Samuel Hoare wrote: 'that little brute Randolph has done a lot of mischief. He gathered around him all the discontented elements in Wavertree, promised every section everything that they chiefly wanted, and stirred up as much trouble as he possibly could. The fact that he kept our man out will undoubtedly do both Winston and him a good deal of harm in the party. The fact, however, that he got more votes than we expected is disquieting. It shows that there is a great deal of inflammable material about and it makes me nervous of future explosions.'

Randolph came back from Liverpool the day after the count in a state of considerable exhaustion, but to applause from his father and those close to him. He would soon learn that others were less inclined to sympathy. On the evening of his return, he went to a supper party at 'Syrie Maugham's in her smiling, shimmering, all-white house'. Chips Channon was another guest and recorded the event in his diary.

> We were sitting in front of the fire, Margaret Birkenhead, Honor, Lady Colefax, 'Teenie' Cazalet and I, when in walked Randolph. There was no ovation, not even a slight sensation. I got up without speaking to him, and walked away, and his dramatic entrance was a fiasco. London is seething with indignation about Wavertree.

Just as Clementine had feared, on 8 February, Waltham Abbey Unionist Association made public a resolution criticising Winston's attitude towards the National Government. Winston issued a bland response that helped mollify them, but what neither he nor Randolph understood was that what looked like a defiant, romantic beginning to Randolph's political career was actually the end of his chances of making any sort of meaningful progress under the Conservative Party's banner.

His cousin Peregrine's assessment of the campaign was telling. 'He had nothing. Absolutely nothing,' he said, but he almost 'smashed the party machine'. Given another two weeks, Randolph might have won. And yet he fell short, handing a safe Tory seat to the opposition. 'I don't think the Conservatives ever forgave him.'

10

Everything is Black, Very Black

RANDOLPH SAW THE thirties as his and his father's joint 'finest hour'. Nobody in that decade saw more of Winston or shared more of his experiences than his son.

It was the period that excited him most when he worked on Winston's biography, and he could barely contain his eagerness to begin it. As he dictated passages for the first two volumes, he would often break off to make long digressions about the interwar years.

These were strange times for Winston and his son, bleak and exhilarating in equal measure. If they had spent most of the first part of the decade enmeshed in wasteful conflicts over India, their attention and energy were turned more and more to Europe after Adolf Hitler came to power in 1933 and swiftly gave notice of his aggressive intentions. Randolph had been quick, perhaps quicker even than his father, who was more preoccupied by Gandhi at the time, to divine the unique threat posed by the new German chancellor.

In July 1932, shortly after his twenty-first birthday, Randolph travelled to Germany as special correspondent for the *Sunday Graphic* to cover the forthcoming elections there. A mixture of persistence, chutzpah and the incantatory power of his family name secured him a place on the plane Hitler was using on the campaign trail. Observing the Nazi leader at close quarters, he wrote one of the earliest accounts in English of Nazi rallies.

There was an ambiguous, troubled tone to Randolph's report. Although clearly overwhelmed and impressed by the energy and excitement and glamour he witnessed – enough to send a congratulatory telegram to Hitler when his party emerged as the largest grouping in the Reichstag – he was also unsettled by the brutishness of the National Socialists' ambitions and the hypnotic influence this strange former corporal was already exerting over crowds.

Adolf Hitler was, he said,

> surrounded by a group of resolute, tough and vehement men who would never tolerate any backsliding from their leader. Nothing can long delay their arrival in power. Hitler will not betray them. But let us make no mistake about it.
>
> The success of the Nazi party sooner or later means war. Nearly all of Hitler's principal lieutenants fought in the last war. Most of them have two or three medals on their breasts. They burn for revenge. They are determined once more to have an army. I am sure that once they have achieved it they will not hesitate to use it.

At some point, Randolph concluded, there would be a war, and Britain would have to choose whether to fight alongside Germany or France.*

Winston liked to say that an accident of naval power had made Britain pre-eminent and that an accident of air power meant it would probably cease to exist: her impregnability had ended when Louis Blériot first flew across the Channel in 1909.

Now, under the Nazis, Germany was re-arming at a rate that terrified Winston. It was not just that their rise had profound implications for the balance of power in Europe, and also the precious freedoms that had been gained by the numerous new states that were formed in the aftermath of the Great War. He was haunted by visions of the Luftwaffe devastating defenceless British cities. One grisly estimate warned that after only a week of intensive bombing, London might suffer 30–40,000 casualties. In his eyes, the country was in more danger than it had been even in the months before the Great War, but neither the government nor the British public were willing to acknowledge the scale of the threat.

> They can't seem to understand that we live in a very wicked world. English people want to be left alone, and I daresay a great many

---

* Winston made his first major speech on rearmament in November 1932.

other people want to be left alone, too. But the world is like a tired old horse plodding down a long road. Every time it strays off and tries to graze peacefully in some nice green pasture, along comes a new master to flog it a bit further down the road. No matter how much people want to be left alone they can't escape.

And, worse, it was already perhaps too late. For Winston, 'the deadly years of our policy were 1934 and 1935. "The years that the locusts have eaten." I expect we shall experience the consequences of these years in the near future.' Stanley Baldwin, who had succeeded Ramsay MacDonald as prime minister, had done little to respond to the new challenges on the Continent; instead of action he had offered only inertia. As Randolph argued in the pages of the *Sunday Dispatch*, echoing the speeches his father made in the House of Commons, 'Apparently Mr Baldwin's idea is that he shall cling on to office, as long as he can, and go on doing nothing, or, at any rate, as little as possible.'

For Winston and his son, the idea of doing nothing was abhorrent. The phrase 'wilderness years' implies a sort of emptiness – but this belies the almost frenzied efforts Winston was making to draw attention to Germany's rearmament and the United Kingdom's pitiful response. Kathleen Hill, Winston's first resident secretary, who started at Chartwell in July 1937, recalled:

I had never been in a house like that before. It was alive, restless. When he was away it was as still as a mouse. When he was there it was vibrating. So much happened that I, with my small brain, I was bewildered by it. He could be very ruthless. He used to get impatient of delays. He was a disappointed man waiting for the call to serve his country.

These were the days in which Winston worked as hard as he ever had in government, perhaps harder. He kept a schedule that would have extinguished most other men, but, as Bill Deakin, one of his research assistants, recalled, 'The activities seemed to stimulate him. I never saw him tired. He was absolutely totally organised, almost like a clock. He knew how to husband his energy, he knew how to expend it. His routine was absolutely dictatorial. He set himself a ruthless timetable every day and would get very agitated and cross if it was broken.'

He would work through the day. Sometimes he would continue to dictate articles and letters as he laid bricks. Then, in the early evening, he might clear the mail he had dictated in the morning and sign letters or play cards with Randolph or Clementine. After dinner he would talk with guests until midnight. It was only when they left that he was able to bring his phenomenal powers of concentration to bear on whatever problem was facing him at that particular moment.

Winston's full-throttle approach made great demands both on his own formidable constitution and on the reserves of everybody around him, not least his secretaries, who were expected to work twelve to fifteen hours a day, with their tasks often spilling over into weekends.

He wrote a gargantuan number of words in densely argued letters and memos. He sat through and contributed to countless hours of debates and select committees, stood on thousands of platforms making his case until he was hoarse, and met and corresponded with experts, diplomats, exiles and soldiers across Europe.

In Winston's mind, he and the 'cabinet' he had formed of former colleagues, friends, civil servants and well-wishers were the real Opposition; the Labour people were too 'ineffectual, weak and uneducated'. He built something akin to a shadow government department – replete with secretaries, advisers, maps, filing cabinets and charts – which received and processed information on everything from an 'ANALYSIS OF CRASHES IN FIGHTER COMMAND' to reports from contacts in Austria about the grim and largely unreported consequences of the Anschluss. ('All my many friends in the city are in the depths of despair,' wrote David Hindley-Smith, who was studying in Vienna. 'It avails nothing to speak of the many sickening incidents. A family of six Jews have just shot themselves, a few houses down the street. They are well out of it. Yesterday morning I saw two well-dressed women forced to their knees to scrub out a "Heil Schuschnigg!" on the pavement. But these things seem to be all part of the Totalitarian's stock in trade.' Winston passed the note on to Geoffrey Dawson at *The Times*.)

Much of his information was gathered from a disparate network of civil servants, government officials and foreign politicians, some of whom contacted Winston in secret and at substantial risk to their careers. These included Sir Robert Vansittart, Ralph Wigram from the Foreign Office, Winston's neighbour and chief intelligence adviser, Major Desmond Morton, Wing Commander Torr Anderson of the RAF, the former German chancellor, Heinrich Brüning, and French Popular Front politicians Léon Blum and Pierre Cot.

Another source was his son, whose range of influential contacts allowed Winston to keep abreast of political gossip and warned about any backstairs manoeuvring. Randolph spent a lot of time abroad during the second half of the decade. As well as journeys abroad with Winston to see, for instance, French politicians, he reported on the Chaco War between Bolivia and Paraguay and the Spanish Civil War (where he first came under fire, an echo of Winston's experiences in Cuba). On top of all this, he was still making expeditions on Winston's behalf, such as a journey to the United States (where he was an increasingly regular visitor) in the autumn of 1936 to try to frustrate Sarah's plans to marry the entertainer Vic Oliver.

For the Churchill daughters, marriage offered an escape from their father's asphyxiating charisma, their mother's icy, awkward perfectionism and a home that while in many respects happy could also feel stifling and restrictive. Diana would later tell her daughter that her headlong rush into marriage with John Bailey – the son of Abe Bailey, an old school friend of Winston's – was a way of getting some sort of space of her own away from 'all the endless talk around the Chartwell dinner table'. She was anxious to secure a new, independent existence. So anxious that she failed to notice that, while handsome, Bailey was in love with Barbara Cartland. And that Cartland, once she discovered that Bailey had an 'impossible' drinking habit, refused to have anything to do with him.

Now Sarah was making her own bid for freedom, although it was an odd kind of liberty. Later, she would reflect ruefully on what drew her to a man so much older than herself. 'Maybe I was looking for a substitute father,' she wrote, 'indeed I have sometimes thought that I was trying to marry my father.'

For the moment, her actual father was incandescent with rage. Randolph could not help liking Vic, or wanting his sister to be happy. Winston took more persuading. 'He did not impress me with being a bad man,' he announced after his first interview with the man his daughter had fallen for, 'but common as dirt [he was in fact the son of a baron]. An Austrian citizen, a resident in US, & here on licence & an American passport: twice divorced: 36 so he says. A horrible mouth: a foul Austro-Yankee drawl. I did not offer to shake hands: but put him through a long examination.'

The two were married before the year was out.

Most pertinent to the cause to which he and his father had devoted themselves, Randolph continued to make exuberant sallies into Germany where, euphoric with whisky and shielded by the prestige of his name, he could sashay in and out of nightclubs in Berlin or, during the National Socialist Congress, perch on a column above the hundreds of thousands of people ecstatically waiting for the Führer.

He could draw on old connections, such as his cousins Tom, brother of Diana, Nancy and the rest of the infamous sisters, and Clementine Mitford, whose father Clement Mitford had been killed in the Great War. Tom and Clementine both lived in Germany for long stretches of the decade and had both passed into, and then out of, infatuation with the Nazis. Clementine, who was studying in Berlin at the Foreigner's Institute of Berlin University would translate for Randolph when he flew into the city. Tom, who was in Nuremberg, sent him intelligence and gossip on leading Nazis like Konstantin von Neurath, Hjalmar Schacht and Joachim Ribbentrop. All of this was passed on to his father.

Even when they were in different countries, the two men still felt a pressing need to talk to each other whenever they could. Randolph travelled pursued by telegrams from his father: 'How are you getting on', 'When are you returning'. On his return, after cabling 'LONGING TO SEE YOU', he would provide his father with details of the precise time of his arrival so Winston could greet him as he walked off the boat.

The American journalist Kenneth T. Downs, who was with Randolph in France, reporting on the Duke of Windsor's marriage to Wallis Simpson (Randolph, fresh from interviewing General Franco, was there as both a *Daily Mail* journalist and a guest at the ceremony), watched as Randolph telephoned his father night after night to exchange gossip and advice about the work they were both involved with. When Randolph wrote a piece about the position of the former king, based on his conversations with him, Winston suggested cutting down on the phrase 'the woman he loves'. 'That phrase is getting a little shopworn over here. You know, when the plumber is late these days, it is because of the woman he loves.' The intimate relationship between father and son was, Downs would later write, 'a thing of beauty'.

Closer to home, Randolph acted as go-between for Winston and Ivan Maisky, the Soviet ambassador, who was unabashed about his support for the anti-government opposition. He hoped that the steadily deteriorating international situation would see Winston or Anthony Eden take the place of those politicians who advocated a policy of Appeasement.

Randolph held meetings at his flat at Westminster Gardens, and helped to arrange encounters at the Soviet Embassy ('a grim Victorian mansion in Kensington Palace Gardens'), where guests were given corked sherry and 'a little wet dead trout' and watched as Maisky filled their glasses with red wine, white wine, vodka and curacao, but drank only water himself.

Maisky was part of the loose network of friends such as Bob Boothby and Brendan Bracken, sympathetic acquaintances such as Harold Nicolson, and fellow foreign politicians like Jan Masaryk, the Czech foreign minister, who orbited around Winston and Randolph. These men dined at Pratt's or the Carlton Grill. Over red meat and port, they would discuss the progress of their own campaigns. One of them might give a speech, another might join the meal halfway, full of news or bringing with them someone of particular interest.

On those occasions when it seemed as if a breakthrough was imminent, they could be elated, with those present giddy with a mix of drink and pleasure. At other times the scale of the disaster that was about to consume Europe, and their inability to do anything about it, was impossible to ignore. At one dinner, Jan Masaryk seemed, according to Harold Nicolson, like 'a man on the edge of a nervous breakdown. He says that the Czechs are prepared to make almost any sacrifice to avoid war, but will we please tell them exactly where they stand? What he means is, that they will make concessions provided that in return we guarantee their independence, and no British Government can do that.'

As the decade wore on, these dark moments became increasingly common.

In 1935 Mussolini's Italy invaded Abyssinia and the British government did nothing. The following year, the Third Reich remilitarised the Rhineland and still the British government did nothing. When Germany annexed Austria in March 1938, the British government behaved as if it were paralysed. Those who warned against Germany and the threat of war were dismissed as 'jitterbugs'.

Dissident Conservatives were persecuted in their constituencies, and *The Times* was stuffed with columns written by aged politicians who crept out of obscurity to urge negotiations with dictators who had thus far shown little or no desire to negotiate. In London, it was all too easy to run into Nazis who insinuated that England had Jewish watchdogs in all its important posts and that Winston was only anti-German because of his friendship with the American Bernard Baruch. Few people seemed to notice, or even care; MPs carried on drinking champagne and eating ice cream made of lobster at the Ribbentrops' table.

Winston and Clementine Churchill at Chartwell with Richard Law and the French socialist Léon Blum (beside Winston).

Neville Chamberlain became prime minister in May 1937, replacing the ageing Baldwin who had suffered a nervous breakdown the previous summer. Having inherited a huge majority, Chamberlain had little reason to fear Winston, and even less reason to bring him back into the fold.

Winston thought Chamberlain 'the narrowest, most ignorant, most ungenerous of men'. His antipathy was returned. Chamberlain had painful memories of the disruption Winston caused when they were last in Cabinet together and he had no interest in revisiting the experience. At the end of the previous decade he had written of his former colleague: 'There is too deep a difference between our natures for me to feel at home with him or to regard him with affection. He is a brilliant wayward child who compels admiration but who wears out his guardians with the constant strain he puts upon them.' Little had changed as far as he was concerned.

Not long after Chamberlain had entered Downing Street, the journalist Cecil Roberts visited Chartwell, where he found his host sunk in gloom. 'There's no plan of any kind for anything,' Winston said, staring at the black swans on his lake. 'It is no good. They walk in a fog. Everything is black, very black.'

As the situation in Europe grew darker, Winston's own personal political following was so reduced in size that his opponents felt he could be safely ignored. His party's whips were continually acting against him, sidelining him in the Commons. When he was allowed to speak, he often delivered speeches that were better than any he had ever made, but they were just as often addressed to a half-empty, or bored, chamber.*

Winston could still hush a packed House with a coruscating performance, but within minutes the spell would break. After the Anschluss, his intervention had reduced the members to a deep silence, but the way Harold Balfour talked about it when he joined American journalist Virginia Cowles (who had become friends with Randolph while they reported on the Spanish Civil War) for tea in the Ladies' Gallery made it clear that the performance had achieved

---

* Between November 1938 and March 1939, Conservative Central Office made a concerted attempt to deselect Winston as the Conservative candidate for Epping.

precisely nothing: 'Oh, the usual Churchillian filibuster; he likes to rattle the sabre and he does it jolly well, but you always have to take it with a grain of salt.'

Even those Conservatives who disagreed with Appeasement made an effort to avoid Winston's leadership – forming around Anthony Eden instead. The Eden Group, dismissed as the 'Glamour Boys' by the whips, worked hard to maintain their distance from Churchill, and actively discouraged cooperation. Diana's second husband, Duncan Sandys, MP for Norwood,* once asked if he could attend one of their meetings; it was quickly made clear that his presence was not welcome.

Winston took no offence at this exclusion, but it incensed his followers.

There was a turbulence about the behaviour of all the men in Winston's circle during the uncomfortable years of opposition. Bracken stormed about the House of Commons making outrageous remarks. But it was in Randolph that this violence was most pronounced.

One of Winston's great qualities was his ability to separate politics from his personal friendships. His son did not possess this. Randolph attacked Appeasement and its advocates whether the opportunity was offered or not. Winston may have been 'consumed with contempt, jealousy, indeed hatred, for Baldwin', and yet he did what he could to avoid letting it infect his relations with him. Everyone knew what Winston thought about men like Baldwin and Chamberlain. He was hardly discreet once he got into his stride. But Winston was also punctilious about preserving at least the appearance of civility. No matter how sharp their political disagreements, he still took care to send inscribed copies of all his books to Baldwin, who responded with warmth to this generosity.

Randolph either did not care or could not control himself. Even more than Winston, he saw the world in black and white. There were heroes, such as Duff Cooper, Lord Vansittart, the permanent under-secretary of state, and Harold Macmillan, and there were villains, such as Stanley Baldwin, Horace Wilson, the civil servant who did as much

---

* He won the seat at a by-election in 1935. Much to his father's disgust, Randolph had run a candidate (who was a former member of the British Union of Fascists) against him.

as anybody to advocate the policy of Appeasement, and, later, Neville Chamberlain, known in their circle as 'the Coroner'.

He attacked these villains and anybody who tried to defend them at dinner parties, country-house weekends, St James's clubs. His friend Virginia Cowles said that going out with Randolph was like going out with a time bomb. There were always explosions; he always left his victims 'pinned in a helpless and angry silence'. In the process he lost friends and, he said, 'such abilities as I had to influence people', and he exacerbated his rancid relationship with the Conservative Party which, realistically, was his only route into Parliament.

And although his assaults were in large part driven by his extreme loyalty to his father and his father's cause (the rest supplied by his love of controversy and chaos), they frequently ended up being counter-productive. It was this that forced Winston into sending his son stern letters warning, 'It would in my belief be vy injurious to me at this juncture if you publish articles attacking the motives & character of Ministers, especially Baldwin & Eden. I hope therefore you will make sure this does not happen. If not, I shall not be able to feel confidence in yr loyalty & affection for me.'

As always, Winston knew that the best way to secure his son's attention was to appeal directly to the importance he placed on their relationship. Randolph's chief topic of conversation remained his father, even if now, amidst his outpourings of affection and admiration, his friends noticed sad reflections on their increasingly frequent rows. (As well as complaints about his mother.)

Winston's few allies in Parliament, such as Bob Boothby and Brendan Bracken, made regular visits to Chartwell to discuss the progress of one campaign or another, or to establish what the small group's position should be on a particular topic. Randolph, who had strong feelings of his own about tactics and publicity, was present for many of these conversations, and more often than not would end up arguing with his father. Winston would shout, 'You can't say that!' Randolph, invariably, *would* say that, and they would either cease speaking to each other, or one of them (usually Randolph) would storm out of the room.

Some of their arguments could be resolved before the end of the evening. On one night at a gathering in the Prof's rooms, Winston upbraided his son for using 'some unprintable words of abuse' about Lord Rothermere: 'You can't talk about your employer like that. Unless you withdraw the words and apologise I shall leave the room and go to bed.'

For a few minutes Randolph held out, unmoved by the pleas of those assembled who had no wish to see the party broken up so early. He was, he pointed out, simply being 'factually accurate'. Winston was equally obstinate. In the end, Randolph gave in.

It was usually Winston, however, his spaniel eyes brimming with tears, who would come and make up, just as he had time and time again since Randolph was a boy. On those occasions when Randolph had leapt up from the breakfast table and swept out of the house, Winston would write him an emollient letter; sometimes he might send a peace token, like a signet ring from Cartier.

No matter how angry Randolph might have been, he would always be reconciled before long. There was, Bob Boothby wrote, something irresistible about Winston when he came towards you with his arms outstretched. Almost before you knew it, his charisma had overcome all your reservations.

What was more alarming was the way a simple disagreement between father and son about something trivial could spiral into something different, becoming instead the vehicle for resurrecting old grievances, or ventilating new ones; it would end with the two men bellowing at each other, oblivious to their surroundings, untroubled by who saw them or what others might think.

In December 1937, for instance, Randolph surprised his father by suggesting that what Winston described as 'the details of a private business transaction' might be included in his *Evening Standard* 'Londoner's Diary' column. Winston begged his son not to do this with what he conceded was 'excessive vehemence', and then before he knew it, he was trying to fend off accusations that 'there is no one to whom you speak so harshly as to myself and there is no one who speaks to me in such tones as you often employ. I do not know why you should reserve your greatest hostility and suspicion for your son and why I should have to accept violent explosions from none but my father. Please forgive me for writing all this, but I have often wanted to tell you how I feel. In future I will endeavour to hide my feelings and to bear your violent rebukes in silence.'

This time, Winston could soothe his son's hurt with a letter. ('Thank you for your nice letter. I know you did not mean to be unkind to me, and it was silly of me to have got upset.') On other occasions the damage appeared less easy to contain.

A few months later, in February 1938, a single joke by Randolph set off a row that lasted for weeks. At a dinner, he had ragged his father about his hypocrisy for on the one hand having recently given a 'vy small gift' to Leslie Hore-Belisha, and on the other subjecting him (in his absence) to a 'vicious onslaught'. Winston had, his son suggested, handed the present over only because he wanted to curry favour with the secretary of state for war. Randolph's remark was either clumsy, as he claimed, or very precisely calibrated, because it undermined two of the qualities of which his father was most proud: his generosity and his probity. Winston seemed to believe the latter. 'I wonder', he said later on in their argument, 'you are not even now ashamed that such a thought shd have sprung so readily to yr mind· and yr lips.' Whatever the truth, Winston was instantly hurt and in response ignored anything his son said until the end of the evening. Had there not been a stranger present, Randolph said, he would have stormed out rather than 'submit to such extraordinary treatment from my host and my father'.

In what he called an apology, but reads more like an accusation, Randolph wrote to his father acknowledging that, while his 'jocular remark' may have been 'clumsily worded', he could not understand why his father persisted in behaving as if Randolph had actually meant what he said.

Winston replied that he thought the remark 'singularly unkind, offensive & untrue' and that his son's letter had done nothing to diminish 'the pain it caused me, not only on my own account but on yours, & also on account of our relationship'. He would not, therefore, be coming to the lunch they had arranged that week: he did not want to risk being insulted in the same way again, nor did he want to see Randolph.

In response, Randolph produced another seven pages of self-justification mixed with anger. This prompted another lengthy set of recriminations from Winston: 'I do not see why at my age I shd be subjected to such taunts from a son I have tried to do my best for.'

More painful incidents and harsh words followed as February turned into March. Randolph knew his joke had gone too far. The problem was that he only realised this once it was too late, and, too stubborn to make a full apology, he had instead provoked Winston further.

In the past his father would have ended the argument by bearing down on his son, his love for Randolph bursting from every pore, assuring him that he did not mean to be unkind. Now, however, he refused to see him.

Randolph went to see his cousin Clementine Mitford, who scolded him for his behaviour. As Randolph stood looking out of the window, recounting the story, she realised he was crying, the first time she had ever seen a man weep: 'that was terrible,' she later told a friend. Clementine told Randolph that he had to find a way to apologise to his father.

The ill-feeling had still not dissipated later in the month, when they arranged to meet for supper after Winston had spoken at the House. Randolph had put off some of his own plans in order to watch the debate and was surprised to find that his father left immediately afterwards without leaving any message for him. A bout of frantic telephoning followed before, finally, son located father and hurried to join him. Winston greeted Randolph coldly, and then Randolph had to bow his head in humiliation as first Victor Warrender, the financial secretary to the War Office, and then most woundingly of all Brendan Bracken, were openly preferred to him. Still, Randolph hung around all evening ready to apologise, but Winston seemed determined to avoid giving him the chance. At some point Randolph's conduct became, as he rather coyly acknowledged when writing to his father, 'de trop'. The next day, however, he had returned to the attack.

When I was thirteen and fourteen years old you paid me the compliment of treating me as if I were a grown-up. Now that I am nearly twenty-seven you treat me as a wayward and untrustworthy child . . . Your reception of me was not very cordial and I felt that I was butting in. In the course of the evening you twice went out of your way to warn me against repeating what you said without

making any such admonition to the rest of the company . . . I find
it intolerable that you should publicly treat me with less confidence
than you show others whose love and devotion for you is scarcely
likely to equal mine.

What hurt Randolph most was not just the humiliation of having
his discretion challenged, but the fact that he had been undermined,
repeatedly, 'in front of hacks like David Margesson and Victor
Warrender and that amiable flibbertigibbet, Brendan'.

Randolph continued by reminding his father of the fact that many
times before, he had been 'deeply wounded by your attitude'. 'I think
you know the love & respect and admiration I have for you,' he told
Winston. 'But I cannot comprehend why you should crucify all these
feelings by treating me with such obvious contempt before such men
of straw.'

Although Randolph could say cruel, unforgivable things to his
father, and although he could sometimes behave as if he was determined to cause him trouble and distress, Randolph's sense of self-
worth began and ended with Winston's opinion and treatment of
him. The measures he used to judge his success in life were those that
had been handed to him by his father.

Not least of these was the idealised version of the father–son relationship Winston had pressed so eagerly upon him. When reality fell
short of this fantasy, as it inevitably did, Randolph struggled to cope.
The truth was, he had never learned how to protect himself from his
father, nor did he ever evolve a means of expressing sadness or disappointment that did not involve making a scene.

In this instance there is no record in the archives of a reply from
Winston, but within days of his last outburst, Randolph was writing
to him, offering him advice on his handling of the press, 'probably
the only subject in the world which I may claim to know more about
than you', and suggesting he consider 'the controlled release of information' (via, naturally, his *Evening Standard* column).

Anyone listening carefully to Winston's conversation at the Chartwell
dining table in the last year before the war began would have noticed
a change in tone. He was still talking volubly, he was still feeding

scraps of food to the dogs and cats, which he insisted should be treated like VIPs, and he was still issuing dire prognostications, just as he had for years, but there was a new particularity to these warnings. He would tell his guests that the first thing that would happen in a war, when (not if) it came, would be a gas attack, and he shared terrible forecasts about the casualties London could expect to suffer in the opening week of an assault by the Luftwaffe.

What had not changed was the fact that he was as far away from the levers of power as he had been at any point in the last decade. The same was true of Randolph. He had made a number of attempts to enter Parliament after Wavertree. All of which failed. He was the official Conservative candidate at Toxteth in the 1935 election, which he fought as an advocate of rearmament: the constituency fought back. Diana was attacked and had her hat ripped from her head; Clementine witnessed a riot that broke out as soon as her son appeared at an event – chairs were broken and used as weapons, women and children ran screaming from the hall; Winston and Randolph's open car was stoned; yet an undaunted Winston delivered his speech anyway. Randolph doubled the Tory vote, but this was still way short of enough. Much to Winston's chagrin, he also contested the Ross and Cromarty seat in northern Scotland a few months later. 'More stags than Tories in Cromarty,' Bracken had observed, and Randolph's defeat was no surprise. When his patron, the eccentric patriot Lady Houston, died in 1936, he set his parliamentary ambitions to one side.*

With war looming, Randolph decided it was time to put on a uniform. After briefly considering joining an auxiliary squadron of the RAF, he returned to the idea he had first expressed to Winston in a conversation three years earlier – joining his father's old regiment,

---

* Lady Houston, who had contributed £1,000 to the Wavertree campaign, was said to be so patriotic that she wore red, white and blue knickers. She was also said to have a Union Jack as her tablecloth. She supported Randolph's political endeavours during this period – with huge wads of banknotes – on the strict understanding that there would be neither blondes nor whisky on the campaign trail. During Randolph's unsuccessful tilt at Toxteth, he and Edward Stanley seized a consignment of Lady Houston's own electoral materials and flung them on a bonfire – then danced round flames 'yelling like Red Indians'. She found out, and was, naturally, furious.

the Fourth Hussars. So, in July 1938, Winston wrote to its colonel to see if Randolph could join its supplementary reserve. 'He thinks it is his duty to acquire military training and have a space marked out for himself should trouble come.'

The warm, grey, damp summer ebbed away, and tensions across Europe rose. A pall seemed to hang over Winston and Randolph's meetings with the other men who had ranged themselves against Appeasement. They were all humiliated by the weakness of Britain's stance towards the looming threat on the Continent, and as Adolf Hitler turned his attentions towards Czechoslovakia, it was hard for any of them to believe that Neville Chamberlain would do anything other than persist with his stubborn denial of reality.

On 15 September, the day the British prime minister flew to Berchtesgaden for his first meeting with the Führer to discuss the fate of the Sudetenland, the German-majority region of Czechoslovakia that Hitler wanted to incorporate into the Reich, Randolph wrote to his father, who was alone at Chartwell, working on his biography of Marlborough.

I'm just off to Aldershot – to learn the goosestep. I'm afraid the fun & zest has gone out of my military career.

Please in future emulate my deep-seated distrust of Chamberlain & all his works & colleagues. There is no infamy of which they are not capable. When they are with you they are careful to talk in honourable terms; if I have read them more truly it is because their underlings are less discreet with me.

Three days ago we were insulted; now we have the submission you have so often predicted. Bless you & please in future steer your own course uncontaminated by contact with these disreputable men.

Before he left, Randolph dined with Lord Beaverbrook at Stornoway House. Early news of Chamberlain's 'achievement' – he had decided to put pressure on the Czech premier, Edvard Beneš, to accede to Hitler's demands – was telephoned through to Beaverbrook who, after a moment's surprise, decided it was 'splendid' and made sure that the *Daily Express*'s headline the following day should be appropriately delighted.

Amid the rejoicing, Randolph slipped away to call his father. To begin with, Winston thought his son was playing a joke on him. When, finally, he had accepted the truth of what he was being told, he realised that it meant immediate surrender, which would be followed, before long, by war.

Randolph listened as his father broke down into tears of anger and misery, then returned to the drawing room, where the rest of the guests were drinking champagne.

'Well, what did old Winston say?'

'He cried.'

The artificial gaiety was broken by another, more awkward emotion. But only for a moment. A second later, conversation resumed.

Winston told friends that Chamberlain's gambit was 'the stupidest thing that has ever been done'. Harold Nicolson wrote in his diary, 'The morning begins by Baffy Dugdale ringing me up. She said she had been sick twice in the night over England's shame.' And yet men like Chips Channon were far more representative of the public mood. 'Of course a way out will be found,' he wrote on learning of the trip to Berchtesgaden. 'Neville by his imagination and practical good sense, has saved the world. I am staggered.'

In October, there was a four-day debate about the agreement Chamberlain had reached with Hitler in Munich the previous month. The Nazi regime had absorbed the Sudetenland without firing a shot and, in the process, decisively weakened Czechoslovakia.

Both father and son were swallowed up with rage at those who voted with the government after the Munich debate. They saw it as one of history's grubbiest betrayals; their opponents believed it was simply an accommodation with reality. Alan Lennox-Boyd said that from this moment on, Winston 'regarded me as a renegade'. Patrick Donner had a similar experience: 'After the debate Churchill came up to me in the corridor and abused me like a Billingsgate fishwife. I was no longer "Patrick" after ten years, and the intimacy was never recreated. It was the underlying principle for him. You must have principles. He was right in his way. It was very sad for me. I adored him.'

Randolph's reaction was, if anything, stronger than his father's. For him, it was the 'touchstone of any political figure's honour or good sense'. Years later his talk still returned obsessively to Munich, and the 'Filthy Munichois' for whom 'no obloquy was too damning'. The mere mention of the subject could render him incoherent with rage.* He once chased a former *Times* editor around his dining-room table, shaking and trembling, a carving knife in his hand, after the journalist revealed that, almost three decades before, he had helped prune some of the more offensive details from the paper's Berlin dispatches. 'Shits like you', screamed Randolph, 'should have been shot by my father in 1940.'

But, for the moment, they were powerless. Anger was all they had. On 3 October, Duff Cooper resigned his Cabinet post. Winston and Randolph both wept.

After the Munich debate, relations between Winston and Neville Chamberlain deteriorated still further. Chamberlain was more nakedly hostile to Winston than Baldwin ever had been. Winston was more isolated in Parliament than ever. In a debate on 17 November on an amendment calling for the immediate establishment of a Ministry of Supply, even the previously steadfast Duff Cooper seemed anxious to put some distance between himself and Winston. Only Brendan Bracken and Harold Macmillan followed him into the lobby.

The hurt and loneliness he felt was only slightly mitigated by the knowledge that he had attained a new popularity among the population at large. Although the Gallipoli landings and the intervention in the Soviet Union had been disastrously misjudged, and although his India campaign and his attempt to prevent Edward VIII's abdication were futile causes that had attracted little public support, he had been proved unquestionably right about Appeasement and rearmament. Never had his public meetings been in such demand, or his audiences so receptive. The press, both at home and abroad, leaped upon his every word. And, of course, there was Randolph, the source of constant, unflinching support.

★

* One day Randolph's son Winston, aged fourteen and still mystified by a word that had such a powerful effect on his father, summoned up the courage to ask, 'Father, what *was* Munich?'

Randolph went red and began shaking with rage: 'What is Munich? You ask! For years I have hired the most gifted teachers that money can buy to teach you, yet you do not know what was Munich?'

On 10 March 1939, Sir Samuel Hoare denounced as 'jitterbugs' those who were still clamouring for rearmament. 'These timid, panic-mongers', he said, 'are doing the greatest harm.'

Four days later, German tanks thundered into Prague. As the news broke, Winston was with Harold Nicolson and Lord Cecil. The men fell into an anguished discussion of its consequences. Cecil brought the conversation to a close by saying, 'Well, Winston, things are desperate. I feel twenty years older.'

Looking very serious, Winston responded: 'Yes, Bob, things are desperate. I feel twenty years younger.'

The Nazi invasion of Czechoslovakia brought many things into focus. Those who warned of imminent danger could no longer be dismissed as warmongers. Winston's popularity continued to rise and, steadily at first, people began to talk about bringing him back into government.

Perhaps wary of past missteps, Winston took great pains to ensure that he was not seen to encourage the campaign for his return to the Cabinet. Randolph was not shackled by the same concerns: he could act as an effective surrogate, using his columns to amplify the arguments Winston was making in Parliament, and also to make the sorts of arguments that helped his father but were better not actually coming from his mouth.

Randolph's *Evening Standard* diary had always mixed frivolous items of society gossip (an account of Lord Melchett being stung by fifty wasps after his horse stepped on their nest, or the Duke of Windsor's visit to a noted Austrian ear specialist) with snippets of interest about his family (promising sales of Winston's book *Great Contemporaries*, or Sarah falling off a balcony while playing Juliet for the Northampton Repertory Company). It also offered a platform he could use to dispel some of the more outlandish or damaging rumours that occasionally circulated about Winston, and to boost his friend Ivan Maisky, the Soviet ambassador to London.

In the weeks after the Nazi occupation of Czechoslovakia, the diary began to look like an unashamed cheerleader for his father's return to government. Alongside reports on the reception accorded his father at the Canada Club dinner by a 'varied assembly of judges, barristers, bankers, industrialists and grey headed chiefs of scores of

businesses' – proof that refusing to take Winston back would be tanta-
mount to 'defying public opinion' – were articles like 'Post for Mr
Churchill':

Mr Churchill is once more being 'tipped' for various Cabinet
positions.

If the decision rested with the public Mr Churchill would join
the Government at once. But the decision will be solely that of the
Prime Minister.

The Ministry of Supply, which has become peculiarly associated
with rumours of Mr Churchill's return to the Government, is not
an office which would suit him. For it is now evident that if this
office is created it will be a Ministry of War shorn of all its most
important functions.

The job where Mr Churchill would be most serviceable would
be as Lord President of the Council, now held by the absentee
Lord Runciman.

Freed from departmental duties, he would have plenty of time
to think and act. He would become what the Americans call a
'trouble shooter', the man who steps in whenever trouble arises.

Neville Chamberlain, who was exasperated by what he described
to his sister as hourly telephone calls from Winston, remained
unmoved: 'I know there are a lot of reckless people who would
plunge us into a war at once but we must resist them until it really
becomes inevitable.' Winston could have been forgiven for thinking
his chance would never come, and yet never, not for a second, no
matter how bleak the situation seemed, did Randolph's faith in his
father ever waver.

In July 1939 Virginia Cowles arrived in London to find the season in
full swing. The hotels were full of tourists, country houses were flinging their doors wide open, and there was a 'fever of entertaining': a
seemingly endless series of raucous, hedonistic parties and balls.
People continued to make plans for their summer holidays as if there
was nothing on the horizon, and Neville Chamberlain continued to
believe he had outwitted Hitler: 'One thing is I think clear namely

that Hitler has concluded that we mean business and that the time is not ripe for the major war. Therein he is fulfilling my expectations.'

A couple of weeks after Virginia touched down, and just before she left for Rome to try to secure an interview with Mussolini, Randolph took her to Chartwell. The wind blew through the grass, the sun streamed onto the flowers and glinted off the goldfish as they darted beneath the surface of the ponds. It was, she remembered, a lullingly beautiful day.

They found Randolph's father clad in a torn coat and battered hat, peering, fascinated, into the water. After tea they went into the high, oak-beamed study where he did all his writing. Winston was suddenly struck by gloom. He had realised, he said, that he would not be able to finish writing his *History of the English-Speaking Peoples* before the war began.

At this Randolph became indignant: 'You won't be living here. You'll be at No. 10 Downing Street.'

'I'm afraid I haven't got the same fanciful ideas that you have.'

'Well, at any rate, you'll be in the Cabinet.'

'Things will have to get pretty bad before that happens.'

11

Winston is Back

THE WAR, WHEN it came, was almost a relief. Ever since Munich the whole family had been gripped by an unrelenting tension which had dominated talk and thought at Chartwell. 'From the Anschluss onward,' remembered Mary, 'the kettle never came off the boil.' This release of pressure was mirrored elsewhere: in the House, even weak jokes were greeted with hilarity. Men doubled up, realising as they did so that it was the first time they had laughed in weeks.

On the day war was declared, Winston was at Morpeth Mansions, waiting in absolute silence for Chamberlain's 11.15 a.m. broadcast. The prime minister's voice had barely died away when the quiet was torn apart by the sudden screech of the air-raid sirens. 'You have to hand it to Hitler,' Winston said. 'The war is less than a half-hour old and already he has bombers over London.' Winston dawdled for a moment, looking up at the sky. Finally, Clementine and his bodyguard, Walter H. Thompson, persuaded him to head to the air-raid shelter with them, and down they went, Winston clutching a bottle of brandy under his arm.

It was a false alarm but, wary of being caught unawares again, Winston instructed his secretaries that next time the siren rang, they should take first-aid equipment to the shelter, along with whisky, ice and soda water for him, and 'sherry for the ladies'.

In the Commons that afternoon Ivan Maisky watched the prime minister's statement on the declaration of war.

A darkened emaciated face. A tearful, broken voice. Bitter, despairing gestures. A shattered, washed-up man. However, to do him justice, the prime minister did not hide the fact that catastrophe had befallen him . . . I sat, listened and thought: 'This is the leader of a great Empire on a crucial day of its existence! An old, leaked, faded umbrella! Whom can he save? If Chamberlain remains prime minister for much longer, the Empire is ruined . . .'

Afterwards, Winston was summoned to visit Chamberlain in his rooms behind the Speaker's Chair. Clementine, who had come with him, sat nervously outside in the car during the short interview. 'I hope', she said to Thompson, 'they don't give him a silly little job.' Minutes later Winston's sturdy frame clambered into the car: 'It's the Admiralty. That's a lot better than I thought.'

He did not wait for written confirmation (and would not formally get his patent from the king until 5 September); instead, he sent word to the Admiralty that he would take charge at once and that they should expect him at 6.00 p.m. The first message sent to the fleet on his appointment was short but pungent: 'WINSTON IS BACK.'

When he walked back into the building that evening, he was suddenly struck by a memory of the 'pain and sorrow' he had experienced when he had been forced out a quarter of a century before. 'Where is the octagonal table?' he asked, almost involuntarily, as if he expected that everything would be the same as it had been in 1915. Some things were. Looking round, he saw his old chair and the wooden map case he had fitted up himself in 1911. Over the course of the next few weeks he discovered that many of the furnishings he used during the Great War were still there, in store. One by one, he had them reinstated.

'It was a strange experience,' he wrote, 'like assuming a previous incarnation.' At a meeting later with senior Admiralty officials, he was clearly filled with emotion. 'Gentlemen,' he told them, as he drew matters to a close, 'to your tasks and duties.'

Winston seemed to know instinctively what steps needed to be taken to remedy the years of neglect. From the moment he returned, he began working night and day, as he had a quarter of a century before, his habit of a regular siesta allowing him 'to press a day and a half's work into one'.

Sitting at his desk at the Admiralty (which swiftly became covered with toothpicks, gold medals, special cuffs to save his coat sleeves from becoming dirty, and innumerable pills and powders), he interested himself in every element of its business. Before long Winston's 'driving power' was felt throughout the entire department, his energy and urgency radiating even to the messengers and typists.

Some saw him as 'a tremendous nuisance', and his enthusiasms could lead him off on false tracks, but, as his secretary Kathleen Hill recalled, 'When Winston was at the Admiralty the place was buzzing with atmosphere, with electricity. When he was away, on tour, it was dead, dead, dead.'

As the rich hauled their paintings and antiques to the country, and society hostesses held 'house-cooling' parties before covering everything with dust sheets and closing their London homes, the Churchills surrendered their lease on Morpeth Mansions, shuttered Chartwell (except one cottage kept open for family visits) and moved into the two top floors of Admiralty House.

Randolph had been at his flat at Westminster Gardens with a terrible hangover when Chamberlain gave his radio address. He refused to listen.

Ever since the declaration of war, his regiment had been left to kick their heels at their barracks in Tidworth. And while Randolph began the conflict being polite to his superiors, this did not last. He quickly surrendered himself to boredom and his devotion to intrigue. Neither quality made him popular. Somehow Randolph managed to be surprised that this should be the case.

His was not a nature suited to following orders, or a body much ready for stamping around the barrack square. Politics and debauchery had done little to improve his fitness: Randolph himself acknowledged that he had become, as he put it, 'portly'. He did not seem to understand that junior officers were supposed to be deferential, and that the strict military hierarchy actively discouraged humble second lieutenants from haranguing their seniors about how they should be running the war.

Randolph was also troubled by dynastic business that needed urgent attention. Almost as soon as war was declared, he started rampaging around London, saying he needed an heir because he was probably going to be killed in battle very soon. Although he was sleeping with the vaudeville actress Clare Luce, and in love with the unhappily married Laura Charteris (who had left her husband and set up home in her father's house on Oxford Square, taking her baby, her baby's nanny, her Pekinese, and a monkey),* neither woman would marry him, so he proposed to, and was rejected by, eight women in the course of a fortnight. Finally, someone said yes.

The Honourable Pamela Digby had grown up in Minterne, Dorset, which in the seventeenth century had been the home of the first Sir Winston Churchill. She had learned her first words from a chatty Australian parrot while her father the baron was serving as military secretary to the governor general. In the years since, she had had an entirely conventional upbringing, with one notable exception.

During the spring of 1937, she stayed with an impoverished aristocratic family in Munich. After hearing Hitler speak on the radio, she became determined to meet him, and so she tracked down the nearest Mitford sister (in this case Unity; naturally the families knew each other) and coaxed her into taking her to tea with the Führer. Pamela talked about the encounter later as 'a frightening experience. I remember the sort of cardboard figure. I mean, it was – it was almost like – like the caricatures that you saw later. But he really was like a caricature. It was as if he was made out of thin metal.'†

Pamela had wide, deep-blue eyes, pink flushed cheeks and auburn hair streaked with a patch of white – a legacy, she claimed, of a pony accident. Some saw her as 'a red headed bouncing little thing regarded as a joke by her contemporaries', and in most accounts she is presented as having arrived in the Churchill family as an ingénue.

Beneath the plumpness and a forced air of jollity that had made her season in London a crushing disappointment was an adamantine desire to escape her dull, provincial life in Dorset.

---

* The brown-eyed, magnetic Laura valued Randolph's friendship, felt great affection for him, and was willing to sleep with him from time to time, but she told friends that she was never in love with him; she believed that he wanted and needed a mother rather than a wife.

† Oddly enough, there is no record that she ever talked to her father-in-law about her encounter with his enemy – she was the only member of the family who ever met Hitler.

Pamela's father did not drink (he did not like the taste) or smoke, but always carried a box of Fortnum & Mason chocolates under his arm. Pamela's mother, who was also teetotal, indulged her so much that she was left with a conviction she could get away with anything. She had once confided in a friend: 'When I come out, I won't date men unless they are a prince or a duke or a millionaire.' This was later given a more sophisticated spin: 'I yearned for things I didn't know.'

By the time she met Randolph, Pamela was already adept at manipulation. She had had affairs with older men and knew how to get them to pay her bills. She had an ability to dissemble her discipline and energy, her boldness and ambition. Most of all, she had acquired one particular characteristic that would serve her well for the rest of her life: she did not care what her parents or indeed anybody else thought about her. She would live life on her own terms and anybody who objected could go to hell. Later in the war, Mary was racked with indecision about a marriage proposal of her own. Pamela took her to one side: 'Don't marry someone because <u>they</u> want to marry <u>you</u>,' she told her sister-in-law, 'but because YOU want to marry them.'

This singularity of purpose and the willingness to discount the opinions of others would be of immediate use as Randolph wooed her.

The beginning of the war found Pamela aged nineteen and earning £6 a week at the Foreign Office, translating from French and German (a job the Conservative chief whip David Margesson had helped her to get), and about to rent a flat near Buckingham Palace owned by her friends, Philip and Mary Dunne.

In mid-September, Randolph entered the Ritz just as Mary Dunne, whom he had known since they were children, was leaving. To stop her going any further, he made the swinging doors go round and round again 'at a vast speed'. Inconveniently for him, Laura Charteris had fallen in love with another man, the Earl of Dudley, and Clare Luce was out of town. He was at a loose end.

'Can you have dinner?'

When Mary demurred, he persisted: 'I have forty-eight hours' leave and no one to have dinner with on my last night.'

Mary hesitated, then, suddenly struck with inspiration, suggested a blind date.

Years later she recalled: 'I said, "If you'd like to have dinner with a beautiful redhead" . . . actually what I really said was, "If you want to have dinner with a red-headed whore, go round to my flat and you will find her waiting for me from two o'clock onwards."'

Not long before, Pamela had slept with Philip Dunne. 'She was the first person who came into my head.'

Instead of going in person, Randolph telephoned the apartment, where Mary was showing Pamela around. Mary was standing by the drinks cupboard, so Pamela answered.

'This is Randolph Churchill.'

'Do you want to speak to Mary?'

'No, I want to speak to you.'

'But you don't know me.'

Randolph was always good at overcoming minor objections like this. Almost before she knew it, Pamela had agreed to meet him for dinner at seven that evening.

'What do you look like?'

'Red-headed and rather fat, but Mummy says that puppy fat disappears.'

The conversation over, Pamela turned to her friend. 'Mary, what's all this about?'

'Oh, he's an old friend of mine. He's great fun, he's a bit too fat, but very amusing. I told him that you were taking our flat and that I couldn't dine with him but I would try and persuade you to dine with him. Please do – you'll have a very good time!'

Randolph took Pamela to Quaglino's, where they ran into Duff and Diana Cooper. Anxious to catch up with old friends, Randolph ignored his date for most of the dinner, except to periodically tell her, 'You're divine', but when he asked Pamela to meet him the following night, she said yes. She liked his unyielding conviction that Britain would win the war. Until then, she said, 'I found it all so depressing. Anytime one went to the Four Hundred whoever you were with, instead of asking Rossi the head-waiter to keep his whisky bottle until the next visit, as was the custom, would end the evening by presenting the bottle to the head-waiter and saying, "Take this, I won't be coming again – I'm going out to get killed." I was getting so terribly upset by seeing all my friends going off, as they dramatically thought, to be killed, and I thought how marvellous it was to be going out with somebody about whom I didn't give a damn.'

By the following morning, Pamela had received her first warning about Randolph, from their mutual friend Ed Stanley.

'You stood me up for dinner last night and I find you dining in a restaurant with Randolph Churchill. He's a very, very bad man and you shouldn't go out with people like that.'

'But he's one of your best friends.'

'Yes, he is one of my best friends – but he shouldn't be one of yours.'

It did not have the desired effect. In fact, she would later reflect, it probably spurred her on. Two days later, Randolph proposed.

It suited Pamela in the years to come to give the impression that she had accepted the proposal out of innocence, but she saw this marriage as an opportunity, one that, after the failure of her London season and given the way her reputation had lost some of its shine after her affairs with older men, was one worth taking. 'You were treated as a child until you got married,' she said. 'The status of being married gave you your first freedom.'

She did not really think the marriage would last. But, she told herself, so what? Randolph was equally aware of the transactional nature of the arrangement. He had told his fiancée that while he did not love her, he thought she looked healthy enough to be able to give him a son who could carry on the Churchill name before he died on the battlefield. This was what his father expected from him, and he remained as keen to gratify his wishes as ever. (As Randolph's sister Mary noted after the marriage had collapsed, there was little to be sad about: 'Randolph wanted a son – Pam wanted glitter & fun and a new milieu – both have got what they wanted & now there is an end.')

★

Randolph took Pamela to meet his parents. Most people came away from Chartwell impressed. Pamela, who was used to the grand style of Minterne, with its 1,500-acre estate, thought it modest, almost suburban. It had no art collection, no grand library, no ballroom and was too close to London.

Winston made a stronger impression. The young couple encountered him on a grassy knoll outside his painting studio. His first words to her were an example of the way past and present mingled promiscuously in his imagination.

'But the Digbys are Roman Catholic.'

Randolph interceded, quickly: 'They learned their lesson during the gunpowder plot when they had their heads cut off.'

Winston was 'very, very friendly', Pamela thought. At the same time, she understood instantly how overpowering the force of his personality could be.

Randolph's parents saw Pamela as a refreshing, naïve change from the worldly women their son had pursued previously. (She also brought a decent marriage settlement of £5,000, though her father kept some of it because of 'the uncertainty of the war'.) Writing to her sister Nellie at the end of September, Clementine described the girl her son was about to marry: 'Pamela Digby is a most attractive girl, a real "honey pot" as Mother would have said . . . It is all very breath-taking & Pamela's Mother is naturally dissatisfied with Randolph's financial position; but somehow I feel they will be very happy & that if Randolph is not killed that it will last. I pray for that. It certainly sounds rash & unconsidered.'

Clementine's doubts were less about whether Pamela was suitable for her son, but whether it was fair to inflict his drunkenness, gambling, philandering and rudeness on her.

Randolph happily dismissed his mother's concerns – what had he ever done that she did not disapprove of? – and fastened instead onto his father's happy optimism. When it was suggested to the First Lord that his son did not have enough money to marry, he replied: 'Nonsense! All you need to be married are champagne, a box of cigars and a double bed.'

On 4 October 1939, a grey, dry, breezy day, Randolph and Pamela were married at St John's, Smith Square. The church was packed, but even on his wedding day, Randolph had to accept that his father would outshine him. As Winston arrived at the church, he was greeted by an ovation – 'Wave on wave of cheering' – from a waiting crowd of three hundred people (the family had not announced the date of the wedding, to avoid this sort of attention, but somehow enough people had found out). Mary was so moved by this outpouring of affection that she almost burst into tears. Winston cried right through the service.

Because Lady Digby had no house in London, the Churchills gave the wedding party – a buffet lunch for sixty – in the state rooms of Admiralty House. Diana Cooper called it 'the most romantic house in Whitehall'.

Winston ate ice cream, drank champagne and told guests: 'We must eat. We must eat.' It was hard for those assembled not to wonder whether it might be one of the last purely joyful moments before the war began in earnest.

Randolph and Pamela in London, 1940.

When the Fourth Hussars moved to Beverley, Randolph and Pamela found 'a terrible little semi-detached villa' in Driffield, Hull, at £3 a week. With Randolph now only on half pay from the *Evening Standard*, they could just about afford it.

One of the reasons the engagement had been so short was that it was thought Randolph's regiment might be sent abroad at any minute. This did not happen and did not look like happening. The talk among the sergeants' wives was that their husbands would all be safe as long as Randolph was in the regiment. Winston, of course, was not actively protecting his son, but nor was he willing to pull strings to get him closer to combat.

Randolph had tried to get his father to use his influence to get him to the front, but Winston declined.

I am sure yr best & indeed only course is to obey with good grace, & do whatever duty is assigned to you. In this way you will win the confidence of those in whose power you lie.

I will write to General Barnes about yr grief at being detached from yr regiment for training duties; & of yr desire to accompany them to the front. Such feelings are in no way discreditable; but a good officer wd take care not to show them, while hoping for a better turn of events.

I am always on the look out for any compliment or pleasure I can give you, as you know; but so far as the service is concerned you must make yr own way. I am always thinking about yr interests & yr fortunes.

This stasis made Randolph miserable. He had little or nothing in common with his fellow officers, and the weather that winter was appalling, Europe's cruellest since 1895 (Pamela: 'There was snow and more snow. It was cold, there was ice everywhere. It really was ghastly').* And life, which with the outbreak of war had briefly looked like expanding, had closed down into a grim, restrictive knot.

---

* Down in London, Winston took more pleasure in the weather's cold turn, throwing snowballs at Mary.

Randolph began to make scenes at country houses. Pamela would be left so embarrassed that she wished she could vanish into the upholstery. Sometimes he stormed out, then returned to retrieve her. Sometimes he just disappeared. Although he would occasionally promise Pamela that he would stop drinking, his good intentions never lasted long.

The worst of his behaviour came during the regular visits the couple made to see Lord Beaverbrook, either at his home in London or at his country house, Cherkley in Surrey (described by Ann Fleming as an 'amazing mixture of bad taste and discomfort'). Winston and Randolph both adored Beaverbrook, even as they were wary of his capacity for mischief, which they knew could too easily sharpen into malice. At all costs, Randolph warned his wife, 'don't be enchanted by Beaverbrook's spell, because nothing amuses Beaverbrook more than to have complete control of people's lives, to smash them or put them together as he sees fit.'

Beaverbrook had always taken pleasure in getting people as drunk as possible in order to extract information from them. As they became more intoxicated, he poked and prodded until he got what he wanted. To this the puckish newspaper baron, who had been urging Chamberlain to make a negotiated peace right through the Phoney War, had recently added a new game. He invited ministers who had supported Appeasement to dine on the same nights as Randolph, because he knew he would always go too far in defending his father.

The other guests would sit back in awe as Randolph launched himself at men he still considered enemies. Michael Foot, who was a regular at these evenings, claimed that he 'had never seen such a spectacle as Randolph on the attack'.

Pamela, ashamed of her drunk and overbearing husband, simply kept quiet. At times he would turn his rage on her. If she tried to respond, he would tell her to shut up. Beaverbrook would defend Pamela when he thought Randolph had gone too far, but his determination to stay on good terms with Winston meant that he trod carefully.

Although Randolph's income had been reduced substantially, he continued to spend extravagantly. Don't worry about bills, he told his wife, there's a war on! The first sign of trouble arrived shortly after their marriage. When Lord Rothermere gave Pamela £100 as a wedding present, Randolph was delighted. 'A little while ago,' he said, 'I bought a bracelet for Mona Williams [one of his many lovers] from Cartier and the bill has just come in, I think we should use it for that.' There seemed to be no end to the demands that came in from tailors, wine merchants and jewellers. Some of the bills were five years old. Pamela started to panic. Surely, they were heading to the debtor's prison?

When she told her father-in-law of her distress, he simply said: 'Collect all the bills together and bring them to me, I'll pay them.' Pamela did this and enjoyed a brief feeling of relief. At least until the next month, when a whole sheaf of new but ancient bills arrived.

And yet the letters that passed between Randolph (or, as he signed himself, Randy) and Pamela in the months after they first met indicate what seems to have been a genuine, and shared, affection. 'I love you, darling. I can't stop thinking about you ever,' she wrote to him. Half a year on from their wedding, she telegrammed him to say 'THANK YOU FOR SIX MONTHS OF SUCH LOVELY HAPPINESS.'

Even later, when Randolph's reckless spending was beginning to alarm Pamela, her devotion to him did not seem to have dimmed:*

> So try & limit your expenses to £5 a week in Scotland. And darling, surely you're not ashamed of saying you're to [sic] poor to gamble . . . I simply can't be happy when I'm sick with worry all the time. Oh, my darling Randy I wouldn't worry if I didn't love you so deeply & so desperately. Thank you for making me your wife . . . It is the most wonderful thing that has happened in my life.

And it was an affection that was returned, albeit rather idiosyn-cratically. As he wrote in December 1940:

> I cannot tell you how much I loved the last fortnight. They were certainly the best days in my life. When I think what my life was 18

---

* While her love for her husband may not have been in doubt, her understanding of his capacity to resist temptation leaves much to be desired.

months ago . . . I am amazed such great happiness can be achieved in war-time . . .

. . . I don't believe that either of us would have been much good at marriage in the somnolent & 'louche' days of peace. I agree with Pushkin that war brings out the best in people. I would not have our lives any different.

This may be rather selfish because I am with such a really charming & splendid lot of friends. But please be glad for my sake & whatever may happen remember that your duty is never to let anyone think that you give a damn.

Nevertheless, month after month passed by, and Pamela had still not become pregnant. Whenever she visited Winston in London, he asked: 'Are you having a child?' When she said no, I'm afraid not, he would harrumph: 'Very disappointing.'

Then, in the early months of 1940, there was good news. Pamela was pregnant. Amid general rejoicing, it was Winston who seemed most excited. A letter Pamela wrote to Randolph captures his pleasure: 'his eyes lit up with great joy when I told him of our child. He drummed his fingers on the table & poured out another glass of port – then insisted that we should go & tell Clemmy [sic], in fact insisted on telling her himself. They were both very sweet & Winston says that he will pay all the nursing home expenses & that I must go to a good one.'

12

I Could Discipline the Bloody Business at Last

O N THE NIGHT of 9 May 1940 Randolph telephoned his father from Kettering, where his regiment was stationed. The war had not been going well. Almost everything that could have gone wrong in the short, humiliating Norway campaign did. The debate held in its aftermath quickly became a discussion about the government's conduct of the entire war. Neville Chamberlain was mauled in a succession of devastating attacks from every corner of the House. Suddenly, the prime minister whose position had seemed unassailable for so long looked vulnerable. When the government secured only a narrow majority in the subsequent vote, it was clear that he was fatally wounded. Things began to move quickly. Somehow, despite the fact that his hands were all over the debacle in Norway, Winston was barely touched by the fallout. (As Clementine reminded him years later when correcting the proofs of his war memoirs: 'Had it not been for your years of exile & repeated warnings re. the German peril, Norway might well have ruined you.') While there were many who felt visceral horror at the idea of him swaying like a rogue elephant into Downing Street, what had felt completely inconceivable only months before, now appeared, at the very least, like a possibility. Westminster was suffused with a new tension, Chamberlain's supporters suddenly felt overcome with dread, and everywhere people whispered, 'What will Winston do?'

'I may be in a big position tonight,' he told his son.

The next morning, the Western Blitzkrieg began. Winston was woken at 5.30 a.m. with the news. He spent the next hour or so trying to find out more information, then took breakfast at Admiralty House with Oliver Stanley, the secretary of state for war, and Samuel

Hoare, the Lord Privy Seal. None of them had slept much, and all were digesting the momentous, terrible developments, but Winston munched his way through a plate of eggs and smoked a large cigar, with the air, Hoare later remembered, of a man who 'had just returned from an early morning ride'.

At seven, Randolph, who was breakfasting in camp when he learned of the invasion, called his father again.

'What's happening?'

'Well, the German hordes are pouring into the Low Countries, but the British and French armies are advancing to meet them, and in a day or two there will be a head-on collision.'

'But what about what you told me last night about you becoming Prime Minister today?' Can you, asked Randolph, achieve the highest place, the thing you've wanted for thirty years?

Somewhat against the odds, given the thoughts that must have been tumbling through his mind, Winston's reply was understated: 'Oh, I don't know about that. Nothing matters now except beating the enemy.'

Events took their course. Towards the end of the day, Randolph, who was still in Kettering, was given a message telling him to telephone Admiralty House. He was answered by a private secretary who said: 'Only just to say that your father has gone to the Palace and when he comes back he will be Prime Minister.'

It was an extraordinary moment for both men. As Randolph wrote to his father a couple of days later, when they had found time to collect their thoughts: 'At last you have the power & authority out of which the caucus have cheated you & England for nine long years. I cannot tell you how proud and happy I am.'

Winston, who worked through the night assembling his first government, was conscious only of deep relief: 'I could discipline the bloody business at last. I had no feeling of personal inadequacy or anything of that sort. I went to bed at three o'clock, and in the morning I said to Clemmie, "There is only one man can turn me out and that is Hitler."'

The next morning, Winston swept into 10 Downing Street with Randolph (who had rushed down to London as soon as the accession was confirmed) and Bracken at his heels.

Instantly, the temperature at the heart of the government changed. Much of the heat was generated by Winston's constant movement: 'a mountain of energy and good-nature', he dashed in and out of the labyrinth of offices, surrounded by a host of new faces. Along with Randolph and Bracken, there was Beaverbrook, the Prof, a handful of Labour politicians, and a glaring hole where Chamberlain and his principal adviser Horace Wilson had once been. (Wilson had arrived that morning, clean-shaven, impeccably dressed and behaving as if nothing were different at all. Winston ordered him to empty his desk and leave Downing Street by 2.00 p.m. He returned from lunch to find Randolph and Bracken waiting for him in his office, Bracken at his desk, Randolph slouching like a gangster on his sofa, both smoking large cigars. His possessions were all piled up in the corridor outside. He left without a word.)

A host of new appointments followed. One by one, those who had stood by Winston as he fought his lonely battles throughout the previous decade were rewarded: Bracken, already his parliamentary private secretary, was appointed to the Privy Council and would soon become minister of information; the Prof was made his scientific adviser. Cronies like Beaverbrook, who was made air minister, were also given key roles, as were men like Anthony Eden and Duff Cooper. There was even space for former adversaries, those who had kept him out of office and belittled his policies. Randolph objected to the inclusion of David Margesson, the chief whip, who had done so much to choreograph opposition to Winston during the wilderness years. Winston replied, 'I have to think of unity, and I need all the help I can get.'

It was a time for rogues. Figures such as Winston, Beaverbrook and the Prof, who had been considered too wild, or erratic, or unreliable for peacetime, had become indispensable, but there was nothing for Randolph.

In the loose grouping that had supported Winston during the thirties, his son had been his closest lieutenant; now he was nowhere. Before the war, Randolph had had as much access to his father as he wanted. The very fact that Winston was so out of favour meant that few other people made a claim on his time and attention. There had been no formal office, no gatekeepers employed to preserve his energy or peace. When Winston had gone to see French ministers and politicians in Paris, Randolph had gone with him; when Winston met with the Russian ambassador, Randolph was in the room; when Winston sat down to formulate new strategies, Randolph was on hand to offer him advice (and, very often, criticism).

But when he became prime minister, Winston forged significant new relationships that excluded Randolph. There were the three Chiefs of Staff, whom he saw almost every day. His private secretaries were constantly at his side. They were privy to his innermost thoughts, learned how to interpret a grunt or a nod of the head, and knew where to find the documents that were essential to the functioning of his role. They became both omnipresent and indispensable in Winston's life. Randolph, suddenly, found he was neither, and had to watch appeasers like Jock Colville, who only months previously had seen his father as 'unstable' and 'a dangerous person unless kept well in control', occupying privileged positions and enjoying Winston's intimacy.

This brutal change in status was illustrated by a letter Bracken wrote in response to Randolph's own note congratulating him on his new post.

Bless you for your congratulatory epistle.

Please do not regard the rest of this letter as a pompous lecture. But you must give me leave to tell you that I believe you are even more indiscreet than I was at your age!

Bracken continued by explaining that a little while after Randolph had last seen Clare Luce, his on-off lover had gone straight to Joseph Kennedy, the American ambassador, and told him Winston hated him. Enjoying the chance to exact a measure of revenge on the man who had done so much to torment him, Bracken offered a patronising explanation of why this was a bad thing, before giving the knife a final, condescending, twist:

I have not, of course, had a word with your father about this matter. My job is to minimise his difficulties. But I do beg of you to be a good boy, and above all, to be discreet. PS. Looking at this letter it does seem pedantic. But you & I love W. – I don't think you will resent faithful tho' reluctant advice.

By June, Randolph found that he was only able to see his father for a few hours at a time. These trips still had a tonic effect. 'I cannot tell you', Randolph wrote to Winston, 'how stimulating & reassuring it was to see you again & to find you so full of courage & determination.' But some of their power came precisely from their rarity. The brute fact was that for most of his adult life, Randolph had been assured of a place at his father's side. In a dizzyingly short time, this had changed: the war had come between them.

In his book *The World Crisis*, Winston's fundamental criticism of the conduct of the Great War was that Britain had not appointed what John Maynard Keynes had called 'that supreme combination of the Warrior–King–Statesman who is apparent in the persons of the great conquerors of history' to run the show. As he settled into Downing Street, this is what he resolved to become.

'It took Armageddon to make me Prime Minister,' he told Bob Boothby. 'But now I am there I am determined that Power shall be in no other hands but mine. There will be no more Kitcheners, Fishers or Haigs.' He placed himself unequivocally at the centre of government and, in doing so, harnessed his luminous energy to its machinery. Things started with him, remembered Colonel Ian Jacob, the military assistant secretary to the War Cabinet, 'and they hummed till the end of the war. It was impossible to put into words the change that we felt. His power seemed to be turned on all the time.'

Winston's premiership was conducted on an imperial scale. Giddy with the new power that now swelled around him, he became a modern-day Louis XIV: dictating to his secretaries as he sat up in bed, making those of whom he disapproved wait upon his favour, sometimes until deep into the night.* Surrounded by a constant atmosphere of rush, he prowled the corridors of No. 10 smoking a long cigar, stroking his cat Nelson (and chatting to him as if he were

---

* While Britain's actual king, George VI, washed in five inches of water to save fuel, Winston insisted on taking two deep baths a day.

human: when Nelson flinched during an air raid, Winston urged him to be more stout-hearted), and wearing a soldier's steel helmet, a crimson dressing gown decorated with a golden dragon, and monogrammed slippers with pom-poms. Decca Romilly said that he looked 'like some extravagant peacock in his bright silk dressing gown'.

His desire to avoid another Dardanelles meant that he took an interest in everything, from grand strategy down to the minutest detail. 'Have you done justice to rabbit production,' he asked in one memo. 'They eat mostly grass . . . so what is the harm in encouraging their multiplication in captivity?'

In another: 'Is it really true that a 7-mile cross-country run is enforced in this Division from Generals to Privates? . . . A Colonel or a General ought not to exhaust himself in trying to compete with young boys in running across country 7-miles at a time.'

He could do this because his capacity for concentration was extraordinary – so much so that when he gave his attention to a problem, he became oblivious to everything else. On one occasion a private secretary noticed that ash from Winston's cigar had set fire to his bed jacket. 'You're on fire, sir. May I put you out?'

Winston did not look up. 'Yes, please do.'

His secretaries and ministers alike became accustomed to his childish petulance when his instructions were not followed. Winston, who had given orders all his life but had rarely had to execute them and thus had no conception of the practical difficulties of administrative arrangements, wanted things to be done before it was humanly possible. Men like Jock Colville would be given a task and then find, to their great surprise, that the prime minster telephoned them the moment they had returned to their desks to ask whether they had completed it.

There were some weeks when Winston worked 120 hours, but Brendan Bracken claimed that he had never seen him so fit. The new responsibilities had given him a fresh lease of life. Whatever his reservations about the ways in which combat had changed since he was a young subaltern in India (it was a shame, he said, that war had flung aside the glory of cavalry charges and colourful standards 'in its greedy, base, opportunistic march, and should turn instead to chemists in spectacles, and chauffeurs pulling the levers of aeroplanes or machine guns'),* Winston was exhilarated by his new role.

It is difficult to imagine Neville Chamberlain, for instance, capping off his day by watching captured German combat films. While fiddling with an operational model of a mine designed to be dropped into the Rhine basin, Winston turned to an aide: 'This is one of those rare and happy occasions when respectable people like you and me can enjoy pleasures normally reserved to the Irish Republican Army.' The world was in crisis, Britain in greater peril than for centuries, and yet Winston gave the impression that it was a great time to be alive.

Winston, with his youngest daughter Mary.

---

* As he stood on Xanten hilltop in 1945 watching British regiments cross the Rhine, he complained that the spectacle lacked drama. 'I should have liked', he declared, 'to have deployed my men in red coats on the plain down there and ordered them to charge.'

This was, after all, the role he believed fate had picked him out to perform. He was as happy as anybody could remember him. When asked after the war what year of his life he would relive if he could, Winston replied: 'Nineteen-forty every time, every time.' It was a 'wonderful' moment, he said. 'I used to wake up feeling that there was half a bottle of champagne inside me.'

There were bleak moments. Jack's daughter Clarissa remembers the nightmarish lunch at Downing Street with her exhausted-looking uncle as news of deaths during rearguard action around Dunkirk came in. He was nearly sick, the only occasion during the war when he could not eat.*

But although many of the prime minister's contemporaries were struck down by fatalism – on 24 May Chips Channon buried two tin boxes, one containing his diaries, the other his best bibelots, watches and Fabergé objects in the little churchyard at Kelvedon – Winston was not. Days later, at a time when German invasion looked like a serious possibility, the first plans for victory were drawn up: 'June the 6th, 1940,' he said, 'was one of the most fertile days of my life. I put down on paper everything that we should need for a successful invasion of France. I did this two days after Dunkirk. Dr Johnson said: "When a man is going to be hanged it concentrates the mind wonderfully."'

When Randolph was sent to a training camp, Pamela, by now five months pregnant, moved to the Downing Street annexe where her new family had set up home.

Looking back years later, Pamela reflected that to begin with, she had struggled to understand the Churchills' complex arrangements. Everything in the Digby family was on an even keel: her sister had not eloped to the United States with a twice-married Austrian comedian; her father's personality and desires did not overpower everything in sight; her mother did not hate her.

'I began gradually', she remembered, 'to realise that there was a deep difficulty between Clemmie and Randolph, and that in fact

---

* Alive as always to the precise meaning of words, Winston would not allow anybody to refer to the days when Britain's fate hung in the balance as 'dark'. He preferred instead that people followed him and described them as 'stern'.

Churchill worshipped his son and was trying by every possible means to give him any help or advantage he could.' This 'tremendous antagonism', in which mother and son were in constant competition for Winston's affection, was not what she had expected from her marriage.

Nevertheless, she was quick to find her feet. Soon Winston and Clementine were treating Pamela like another daughter – one who, thankfully, did not bring the same complications in her wake as Sarah and Diana. Winston made no secret of the great delight he took in her company – he even told her that she reminded him of his first love, Pamela Plowden. And of course he was enthralled by the idea that she was carrying Randolph's child, the newest member of the dynasty with which he was still so obsessed. By the same token, Pamela saw her father-in-law as 'the Idol of my religion. I believe in him more than any god.'

When Clementine was indisposed, or busy, Pamela stepped in to act as Winston's hostess. She listened to him talk and played bezique with him for hours at a time. On those occasions when Winston was depressed, or low, he found that Pamela's presence would soothe him. She sat with him, cutting his cigars, as he told her what was on his mind. 'He would come in to meals,' she remembered, 'and sometimes he put his head in his hands and hardly ate and then he would suddenly say, "this is one of the hardest times".'

Pamela was a clever interlocutor. She had an uncanny ability to sense what men wanted, and then give it to them. She let Winston set the tone of the conversation and listened attentively until he talked himself back into a good mood – she knew his spirits had lifted when he told a story or started humming a tune.

Pamela was just as adept at accommodating Clementine's 'Scottish' morality. She knew instinctively which parts of her life and personality to show her mother-in-law, and which it would be better to withhold. This would never change. Some years after the war, a younger member of the family accompanied Pamela to lunch with Clementine. As they took the lift, she watched with surprise as Pamela methodically took off her jewellery and put it in her handbag, anxious not to offend her former mother-in-law's puritanical streak.

Most weekends, Pamela went to Chequers or Cherkley. Over long walks with Clementine, Pamela confided in her mother-in-law as

Diana and Sarah never had. Mostly, it turned out, about their gargantuan debts. Sometimes she would appeal to Winston to help them out of whichever hole Randolph's excesses had hurled them into. If her husband found out, he would furiously accuse Pamela of siding with his parents against him.*

Whatever her troubles with Randolph, however, she could always rely on his parents for support. Clementine took Pamela's side in any dispute she had with him. 'Randolph', she once said, 'is treating our Pamela very badly.'

Clementine drew on her own experiences from the earliest days of her marriage to Winston. 'Darling, go away,' she would say when Pamela came to her distressed after another row. 'Don't say where you're going. Just disappear. I . . . would go off to a hotel for three days and he wouldn't hear from me.'

Diana and Sarah had a different perspective. They were both annoyed by what they saw as Pamela's muscling into their family. A friend of the sisters recalled: 'To Winston and Clementine, Pamela could do no wrong. The sisters didn't like her. They used the words "taken in".' Even Mary confessed to occasionally experiencing 'an unworthy – but very real stab of jealousy' about her father's unabashed adoration of Pamela.

As the summer of 1940 progressed, life before the war began to seem increasingly dreamlike. Mary found herself thinking more and more often of parties she had been to then, and the boys she had met, and how many of them were already lying dead.

Pamela was eaten up with impatience, waiting for her baby to come, and yet the dominant mood was happiness. The family discovered that a number of benefits followed on the heels of Winston's new eminence. His post came with an official salary of £10,750, and with Downing Street and Chequers staffed and supported by the state, he was relieved of money worries. Suddenly

---

* As May turned into June 1940, a time when Britain's freedom appeared to be hanging by a thread, and a time when one would imagine that Winston would have little energy or attention to spare for anything other than the prosecution of the war, his son asked him to help settle his debts: 'It was indeed generous of you to say that you would meet £100 of my bills. I do hope it is not very inconvenient for you to do this. I enclose the two most urgent.'

he had a huge apparatus designed to ensure his needs and pleasures alike were met.

Winston, the man who for so long had been shunned, also found himself deluged by presents from every section of society. The rich sent him oysters or rare vintages; those at the other end of the social scale sent him (equally welcome) butter, cream and eggs. And he was popular. As Sir Alan Brooke, at that time head of the Home Forces, remembered: 'Everywhere he had an astounding reception. He drove in my car between troops lining both sides of the road. All of them cheering him as he went and shouting "Good old Winnie". His popularity is quite astonishing.'

Chequers compensated for Chartwell's closure. Here, with its 'dark halls, old paintings, strange staircases', and surrounded by his family, close friends and staff, Winston could feel at ease. Ivan Maisky recalled how noisy and full of life it seemed: 'Everyone was talking, laughing, exchanging remarks. The air was full of chatter.' There were weekends when, if one closed one's eyes, one might almost be at a peacetime country-house weekend.

Chequers was used so enthusiastically by the Churchill family that the Ministry of Food had to raise the country residence's food rations to the level provided to foreign embassies. This was supplemented by pheasant and venison sent from Balmoral by George VI. According to Winston's niece Clarissa Churchill: 'The luxury was heavenly, quantities of rare foods, fires, lights, drinks etc.'

Winston was buoyed by the presence of people like his brother, the gentle, cheerful and discreet Jack Churchill. Diana, with her shy, sly wit, was a less frequent but equally welcome guest. Her children, Edwina and Julian, allowed Winston to behave like a grandfather.*

In the spaces between his work (whereas Chamberlain had only a single telephone there, Winston installed a battery), Winston could watch the others play croquet on the lawns, or cheer at the 'wild footraces' around the grounds between Mary and his private secretary Jock Colville, whose pre-war disdain for Winston had very quickly been transformed into devotion. Mary – either because Jock was being chivalrous or was just hobbled by cigarettes – would usually win.

---

* Winston was an excellent tipper to children, doling out double the going rate.

Conversation at the dinner table ranged widely. The guests discussed Bismarck, the last German who knew where to stop (Winston said that he would show the present Germans where to stop: the grave), the Italians' taste for octopus, and the love life of the duck-billed platypus. Winston might also talk enthusiastically about raids 'by 300 determined men, with blackened faces, knives between their teeth and revolvers under their tails'. When Winston was in especially high spirits, he would offer cigars around, or murmur under his breath, 'Bang, Bang, Bang goes the farmer's gun, run rabbit, run rabbit, run, run, run', or say that he and Hitler had only one thing in common: a horror of whistling.

Afterwards they would drink brandy and reminisce by the great fireplaces. Some nights ended in the early hours with Winston, dressed in a light-blue romper suit, giving a demonstration of bayonet exercises in the ancestral hall. Or he might waltz to 'The Blue Danube' alone; his right hand flat against his shirt, his left arm extended as if supporting a ghostly partner's hand.

Alan Brooke remembered one of these occasions:

He had the gramophone turned on and in his many coloured dressing gown, with a sandwich in one hand and water cress in the other, he trotted round and round the hall giving occasional little skips to the time of the gramophone. On each lap near the fireplace he stopped to release some priceless quotation or thought.

People rarely interrupted him – they understood that work was combined with play and he was probably thinking of a speech he was about to make, or one of the many problems that pressed upon him.

Randolph, however, was always capable of disturbing this carefully achieved equilibrium. He explodes like a bomb into accounts of the first summer the Churchills spent at Chequers.

The visit he made in late June came at a time of particularly bad news. It was not just that the threat of invasion was a daily concern.* A secret estimate prepared by the Prof for Winston showed that Britain's

---

* Although Hitler did not actually even order preparations for an invasion to be made until mid-July – the 'Sealion' directive.

air strength, including reserves, totalled 4,732 aircraft. The equivalent German figure stood at 11,600. Winston needed to work out what to do with the Duke of Windsor, who was in Madrid and insisting on several conditions being met before he would agree to come back to Britain. During the course of the weekend, Lord Beaverbrook made one of his periodic threats to resign, and Winston received the list of the 150 prominent people who had been arrested under Regulation 18B and interned, which included two of Clementine's cousins by marriage, Diana Mosley and George Pitt-Rivers.

It was this issue that caused the first trouble. When he was younger, Randolph had been infatuated by Diana Mitford, as she was then. He had tried to stop her first marriage to Bryan Guinness, and had been 'halted dead in his tracks' when she left Bryan for Oswald Mosley. Randolph could appear stunned in her presence. She was also the only person he could not argue about politics with. Some people, including his cousin Anita Leslie, speculated that his love for Diana was inspired by her close resemblance to his mother.*

Although since Diana's marriage to Mosley, Randolph could barely bring himself to face her, he could not bear the idea of her in prison. He expressed this discomfort in the only way he knew how: by being immensely rude to his father.

This was, it turned out, only a prelude to the main event.

Winston's private secretaries did not like Randolph. In Jock Colville's opinion, he was 'one of the most objectionable people I had ever met: noisy, self-assertive, whining and frankly unpleasant. He did not strike me as intelligent.' John Peck claimed that Randolph 'waged preventive war'. He would turn up at Chequers desperate for a fight

---

* Clementine Mitford once spotted the painting by Cecil Beaton of Randolph's on-off lover Mona Williams, which hung above the mantelpiece at his flat in Westminster Gardens. 'No wonder you think you are in love with her,' she exclaimed. 'She looks just like your mother . . . the same kind of calm beauty . . . the same wide blue eyes and marvellous features . . . she even turns her head in the same way. You must have an Oedipus complex, every woman you fall for looks like your mother.'

Randolph fell unusually silent as he turned the thought over in his head. Finally, he said, 'A very interesting theory. I'll think it over.'

Pamela had exactly the same reaction when she saw the painting for the first time.

(and not particularly picky about who it was with) and, before his target had even had a chance to open their mouths, attack them vigorously for what he thought they might say.

Randolph had little interest in observing the formalities of rank – he behaved as if he believed his position as Winston's son allowed him to transcend the military hierarchy. Winston's indulgence encouraged it. On one occasion during the war, for instance, he came home on leave unexpectedly and found his father busy presiding over a dinner for the Joint Chiefs of Staff – something at which normally nobody under lieutenant colonel (Randolph was at the time a major) was allowed to attend – and he was given a seat at the table, with the proviso that he keep quiet. He agreed, and did so, until over the soup course, during a lull in the conversation, he was seen leaning across the table and saying to one of the senior officers: 'It's not as if I'm accusing you, Field Marshal, of personal cowardice.'*

Randolph seemed incapable of assimilating the change in his father's status. Or, perhaps more accurately, he had failed to adjust to *his* new status. Ever since his son was a young boy, Winston had encouraged and rewarded his outspokenness. He had taught Randolph that as a Churchill he was the equal of, or even superior to, anybody else on the planet. He had taught him to challenge the opinions of others, no matter who they were. Randolph refused to see that none of this was wanted any more.

There may have been a time when Winston would have enjoyed watching his son launch into pompous generals or Munichois Conservative MPs. Once he became prime minister, this sort of behaviour was an embarrassment. The Churchills were no longer making a defiant, lonely stand against a spineless government, and the character traits that had been of such value before – Randolph's explosive energy; his willingness to defy anybody, irrespective of their rank or position – were hindrances now.

When one was the son of the prime minister, Randolph was beginning to learn, there were myriad responsibilities and expectations, but

---

* Some accounts have the field marshal in question as Bernard Montgomery, but Freddie Birkenhead, who claimed also to have been present at the dinner in question, maintained that it was Harold Alexander.

no official role or any sort of meaningful power. He was crown prince without any hope of succession, kept near the throne because he was still essential to maintaining his father's peace of mind.

Randolph managed to keep himself in check until dinner. At this point, he began to shout at his father about 'complacency in high places, inefficiency of the Generals, lack of equipment'. His audience – General Paget, his sisters Diana and Mary, Duncan Sandys and Jock Colville – were horrified by his treatment of Winston but unable to stop the tirade. Randolph continued, unaware of the effect his conduct exerted on the rest of the table. When his father went to bed shortly after 1.00 a.m., Randolph made a drunken attempt to discuss the threat of a fifth column with Jock Colville, who could not hide his disgust: 'Randolph was in a horrible state, gross, coarse and aggressive. I felt ashamed of him for Winston's sake.' Mary, perhaps more used to the relationship between Winston and her brother, would only note that he had been slightly 'truculent'.

Randolph was desperate to be sent somewhere on active service. If he was not going to be given some useful part to play in the political apparatus around Winston, why should he be left to rot in a provincial barracks? Winston was prime minister and he had already shown his willingness to trample over protocol; there was no practical reason why his son's wishes could not be granted.

There was, however, an argument that Winston could not see past. If Randolph were killed, he told those present that evening, he would not be able to carry on with his work.

Winston's ascension to the premiership added a new dimension to the rivalry between mother and son. Clementine was once more pre-eminent. Winston still 'lived' for his son – Pamela was sure of this – but for the moment, he needed the quieter, more steadying qualities offered by his wife, somebody who could help build a house, not burn one down.

Clementine understood how to balance discretion with carefully deployed advice, even admonishments. Kathleen Harriman, the daughter of President Roosevelt's envoy to Britain, Averell Harriman, wrote to her sister Mary about how gracious Clementine was in 'taking a backseat' to her husband. 'But don't get the idea she's mousy, not at all. She's got a mind of her own, only she's a big enough person not to use it unless he wants her to . . . everyone in the family looks upon him as God and she's rather left out, and when anyone pays attention to her she's overjoyed.' Clementine was alive to anything that might damage her husband and worked hard to ensure that, as far as possible, the family's conduct was beyond reproach. When Mary returned home late one evening, she found herself upbraided by her mother, who was worried not so much by the lateness itself as by the impression it might make. It does not matter if you come in at five, she told her daughter, 'but at six I draw the line – & what MUST the marines have thought.'

The family kept their distance from anyone in their circle who had previously expressed pro-German sentiments, and even those who had close connections to people who had advertised their German sympathies. The Mitfords were an obvious place to start, but so too was Sylvia Henley, Clementine's cousin and greatest friend, whose daughter Rosalind had married the eugenicist and Nazi apologist George Pitt-Rivers. Although the couple had separated in 1937, Sylvia still felt that Clementine had 'pushed her away'.

When Clementine learned that Jack Churchill's granddaughter Sally was about to leave Britain for the United States (part of the 'stampede from the country' Winston had talked about), she intervened. At the last moment, although Sally was actually at the point of embarkation, Clementine insisted she stay. To underline her point, she arranged for Sally's passport to be withheld.

Clementine was petrified that one of her children might do something to prejudice Winston's reputation. Mary's irreproachable (apart from the odd late night) conduct was an exemplar of what she wanted from her children. As Pamela recalled: 'Mary was the child that she adored. Mary never embarrassed Winston; she was too young, and then she was too good . . . the other children were an irritant to her . . . I mean Clemmy [sic] really didn't like her [other children] . . . because they were . . . very difficult characters.'

Randolph's outrages were another matter entirely. At Chequers he was disruptive and liable to pick fights with anyone, most often his father. This was often awkward of course, but it could be contained. Occasionally, however, his actions threatened to cause serious trouble.

One morning in August 1940, when Randolph was home on leave, the seven-months-pregnant Pamela was summoned to Clementine's Downing Street bedroom. Pamela saw that Clementine was wearing white gloves while eating breakfast from a tray on her bed. 'It was always a joke in the family that when she was angry about anything, she would put on her white gloves.'* She knew there was about to be trouble.

Clementine spoke: 'Darling, where was Randolph last night?'

Pamela burst into tears. This was a vexing question. The night had begun with a short, jolly family supper. Afterwards, Winston went to the Cabinet room to work, and Clementine went to bed. Randolph headed out, saying that he was going to drop by the Savoy to see H. R. 'Red' Knickerbocker, an American journalist he had met while reporting on the Spanish Civil War.

Pamela had not seen him again until he returned at 6.30 a.m., so drunk that she had to help undress him and put him to bed. Randolph later claimed that Knickerbocker had goaded him by saying his speech-making skills were nothing compared to his father's. Determined to prove Knickerbocker wrong, Randolph spent several hours making extemporaneous speeches, in the process finishing off one, maybe two bottles of brandy.

Clementine did not know everything, but she had already been told by W. H. Thompson, Winston's bodyguard, that Randolph had arrived at Downing Street 'dead drunk' at six that morning and, far more seriously, had left secret military maps in his car.

'What is going on?' Clementine asked again. Pamela, who was bewildered and hurt, could not answer her.

Clementine knew that if word got out about the security breach, it could lead to a scandal for Winston. Once a presumably still somewhat woozy Randolph was brought before her, she ordered him to leave the house and stay instead at his club. Perhaps mindful of the success Lord Rothermere had enjoyed in 1936 when he had wagered

---

* She had also worn white gloves when receiving Vic Oliver and Sarah at Chartwell for the first time after their marriage.

Randolph that he wouldn't touch a drop for a whole year, Winston also extracted a promise from his son (which both men probably knew could not be kept) that he would not drink again for the course of the war.

Then, suddenly, it appeared as if things were beginning to fall into place for Randolph.

At the height of his frustration, the job he had spent so much of the last decade battling hard to win fell into his lap. He was offered the Preston seat by local Tories who wanted to pay a loyal tribute to his father. Under the terms of the wartime coalition, he would not face a challenge.

On 8 October 1940, Winston beamed as Randolph made his ceremonial entry into Parliament. A uniform-clad Randolph looked grave. He was watched in the public gallery by Clementine and Pamela, who, already a week overdue, had a large box of laughing gas in case she went into labour. Jock Colville, writing later that day in his diary, noted maliciously that the cheers in the Chamber were for the father, not the son.

Two days later, Randolph's son was born in the chintzy four-poster bed in Winston's bedroom at Chequers. As the newest Churchill began his entry into the world, his father was nowhere to be seen. Randolph was miles away, in London, in bed with another man's wife.* He barely made it back in time to see the boy emerge at 4.40 a.m.

It is a tradition that those delivering their maiden speech avoid controversy. It was a tradition that Randolph would have been familiar with, and a tradition that he chose to ignore when he delivered his at the end of November. 'Looking around this House,' he began, ominously, his hand jammed into a pocket as if in imitation of his father, 'I say this with all deference – one can see a number of hon. and right hon. Gentlemen, who in a greater or lesser degree, bear some measure of responsibility for the state of our Forces and any shortage of equipment which might perhaps handicap those who plan our strategy.' He carried on in a similar vein before sitting down

---

* Diana Napier, who was married to the singer Richard Tauber.

to loud cheers. Winston had turned his back to avoid embarrassing his son but made no attempt to hide his pleasure and pride once the speech ended.

When Winston saw his grandson for the first time, he kissed him with joy. Winston was so proud of this child who would carry on the family name that he would sometimes stand and watch as Pamela nursed him.

On 1 December, three weeks after Randolph had delivered his maiden speech, and the day after Winston's sixty-sixth birthday, young Winston was christened at the Parish Church of Ellesborough by the Rev. C. N. White.*

The celebration was held after Matins, and most of the congregation stayed after the service. Pamela realised it was one of the very few occasions she had ever seen her father-in-law in a church. Winston had been emotional right through the ceremony. He could not help repeating, as tears ran down his pink cheeks, 'Poor child. What a terrible world to be born into.'

---

* Winston took time off from running the war to assert his dynastic ambitions. When in the weeks before his own grandson's birth the prime minister learned that the Duchess of Marlborough had named her son (an unplanned addition to that wing of the family) Winston Spencer Churchill, he leapt into action, forcing her to change the name, even though the boy had already been christened and officially registered.

'Pamela and Randolph expect to call their son Winston.'

'How do you know it's going to be a boy?'

'If it isn't now, it will be later. I would like to ask you to change the name.'

13

My Favourite American

THE YEAR 1941 was difficult for the Churchill family: Duncan Sandys, Diana's husband, was so seriously injured in a car crash that for a while it looked likely that his foot would have to be amputated; Sarah's marriage to Vic Oliver ended;* and, most tragically of all, Jack's wife, Goonie, succumbed to cancer.

Randolph, the source so often of trouble, left for the Middle East in February. Most people would have found it hard to torpedo their own marriage from a ship slowly making its way across the Atlantic Ocean. Randolph was not most people.

As soon as he heard that Robert Laycock was putting together a Commando unit and that many of his friends (Peter Beatty, Dermot Daly, Philip Dunne, Peter Milton, Harry Stavordale, Robin Campbell and Evelyn Waugh) had signed up, he abandoned the patience that had been urged upon him by his father and put in for an immediate transfer.†

The rank and file of 8 Commando consisted mostly of tough, efficient soldiers drawn from chic regiments: the Household Cavalry, Grenadiers, Coldstream, Scots Greys, and Irish and Welsh Guards. Their officers, however, were almost entirely recruited from the bar of White's Club. Writing home to his wife, Waugh noted that they all 'have very long hair & lap dogs & cigars & they wear whatever uniform they like . . . Officers have no scruples about seeing to their own comfort or getting all the leave they can.'

---

* Over time both Winston and Clementine had grown fond of him. He was, as Goonie once said, 'Much the most courteous member of the family, and the only one you could count on always to open a door for a lady.'
† Almost as soon as Randolph joined the Commandos, the Fourth Hussars were sent to Crete, where they were practically wiped out.

During their training they were stationed in the prosperous Scottish seaside resort of Largs, where they successfully re-created the atmosphere of a permanent country-house party. They drank heavily, played high-stakes games of cards, made endless calls to their trainers and escaped to dine in Glasgow every night.

While Evelyn spent his time 'cooking up more and more devious' plots, Randolph made constant calls to Winston to demand his unit be sent higher-quality weapons and equipment. The two friends managed to stand out amid the general atmosphere of flamboyant ineptitude. So much so that Laycock became anxious that once the fighting started, they might end up 'accidentally' shot by their own men.

'It's going to be terrible, being parted like this,' Randolph told Pamela once his posting was confirmed, 'but with you living very economically and I living off my Army pay we will at least be able to pay off some of the bills and that will be glorious.'

Just before their son was born, the couple had taken a £52-a-year lease on a small Queen Anne rectory, Ickleford House, near Hitchin, found for them by Brendan Bracken. 'Oh my darling isn't it rather thrilling,' Pamela wrote to Randolph, 'our own family life – no more living in other people's houses.' Pamela took the need to economise seriously. She went to bed at 6.30 p.m. to save on heating, and once her husband had departed for the Middle East, she invited Diana and her children to share the house at Ickleford, to keep costs down.

This left a small sum each week to feed her and young Winston. She kept herself busy by helping to run a soup kitchen that provided meals for two to three hundred people a day – mostly factory workers from nearby Hitchin.

Randolph, carrying enough luggage for a 'film star's honeymoon', began the journey across the Atlantic in high spirits. He was looking forward to finally being able to take part in active operations, and threw himself into his work as quartermaster with great relish. But tedium took over before long. There was very little for anybody to do beyond a bit of light PT and the odd written exercise for the officers.

To pass the time, Randolph grew a moustache, and Evelyn a 'particularly repulsive' beard.* Even the almost ritualised baiting of the unfortunate naval officers charged with carrying them safely to war lost its charms before long. (8 Commando's aristocratic officers saw themselves as 'boisterous, xenophobic, extravagant, imaginative, witty', while their counterparts were dismissed as 'jejune, dull, poor, self-conscious, sensitive of fancied insults, with the underdog's aptitude to harbour grievances'.)

Instead, the prime minister's son spent reckless amounts on food and wine, and gambled fiercely. He was with friends who, when they were at White's, used to bet on which of two raindrops running down a windowpane would hit the frame first. Here they raced clockwork motor cars and played Ludo. Most lethal of all were the nightly games of chemin de fer.

The stakes rose in direct proportion to the boredom of those playing. Writing to his wife at the end of February, Waugh explained that 'As the voyage goes on the commando gets more & more like the Russian cavalry of Tolstoy's *War & Peace*. At the last settling day for gambling poor Randolph was £800 down.† Poor Pamela will have to go to work.'

By the time Randolph had reached Cape Town, he was forced to write home to ask for help with the mountains of debt that he had piled up: equivalent to three years' wages. He instructed Pamela to arrange 'payments on the instalments plan of perhaps £10 per month to each of the following'.

Pamela had never been even a penny in debt until her marriage. Over the last year, she had grown used to the cavalier way in which her husband, indeed most of his family, approached their financial affairs. This, however, was too much to cope with alone. There were threats of legal action.

Pamela's first inclination would have been to turn to her father-in-law for help, but Randolph had insisted that under no circumstances

---

* Evelyn shaved this off when they reached Cape Town because in South Africa, a beard was a symbol of Nazi sympathies. He grew another beard in Egypt, then shaved this one off when he learned that his men called him the 'red-bearded dwarf' behind his back.

† News of Randolph's misfortune was greeted with 'sardonic amusement' by the rest of his unit. At the time, a private soldier earned only 14 shillings a week.

could she tell Winston what had happened. He had also repeated his earlier warnings about Lord Beaverbrook, calling him 'a dominator who liked nothing more than having people under his control'. Do not let him do you a favour, he had told her, or he will own you for ever. But Pamela was desperate. She destroyed Randolph's letter, then telephoned Beaverbrook, sobbing so hard that she could not make herself understood.

He told her to come to see him at the Office of Aircraft Production straight away. Beaverbrook was still paying Randolph a salary of £1,500 a year, so Pamela asked for an advance on her husband's wages. The idea of paying back Randolph's 'terribly rich' friends on an instalment plan was 'too sordid and too disgusting'.

The press lord refused. Instead, he gave her a cheque as a present. (It would not be his last gift to Pamela. He regularly handed her, whom he called 'My dear, good, sweet, lovely beautiful, golden girl from Cerne Abbas', money for clothes and wrote generous cheques for her son, which he claimed were to further his religious instruction.)

Next, she rented out Ickleford, placed her son at Cherkley, returned to London to take a £12-a-week job at the Ministry of Supply and sold all her wedding presents, and a large quantity of her jewellery. Pamela was eventually able to pay the debt off; she also felt she had learned a valuable lesson. 'I suddenly realised that if there was going to be any security for Baby Winston and me, it was going to be on our own.'

Her recovery from the financial disaster Randolph had thrust upon her was impressive. After a while his absence began to feel like a relief. Before long, it looked like a liberation.

Young Winston was safe, but Pamela could appear indifferent to him: she was determined to live her own life. By March 1941, she had moved into a room at the Dorchester Hotel. From here, Pamela continued her serene progress into the establishment. Succulent, amiable and unhindered by shame, she thrived. When she visited Mary's battery, the prime minister's daughter noted that Pamela was a hit with ' "les messieurs" . . . I think Pam is the most womanly woman I know. She has every feminine attribute – femme très femme.'

Pamela was backed by the prestige of the family she had married into, and to this she added her own substantial charm. Although she had no discernible sense of humour, or irony, this was something she was able to turn to her advantage: it meant she could act without embarrassment. And the fact that she made no jokes of her own did not stop her laughing, her mouth wide open, head thrown back, at the jokes of others – almost always older men, very frequently senior generals or politicians, more and more often Americans, and, soon, one American in particular.

On the morning of 18 May 1940, Randolph had been back in London on leave. He went straight to Admiralty House to find Winston.

> I went up to my father's bedroom. He was standing in front of his basin and was shaving with his old fashioned Valet razor. He had a tough beard, and as usual he was hacking away.
>
> 'Sit down, dear boy, and read the papers while I finish shaving.' I did as told. After two or three minutes of hacking away, he half turned and said: 'I think I see my way through.' He resumed his shaving. I was astounded, and said: 'Do you mean that we can avoid defeat? (which seemed credible) or beat the bastards (which seemed incredible).'
>
> He flung his Valet razor in to the basin, swung around, and said: – 'Of course I mean we can beat them.'
>
> Me: 'Well, I'm all for it, but I don't see how you can do it.'
>
> By this time he had dried and sponged his face and turning round to me, said with great intensity: – 'I shall drag the United States in.'

American support was always going to be crucial to the British hopes of holding out against the Third Reich – especially at a time when the country's needs were growing with every week of the war that went by. As Winston wrote to FDR in October 1940 in the course of a letter about American resources: 'The World Cause is in your hands.'

By the beginning of 1941 the United States had still not entered the war, but the country had stepped up its financial and practical support to Britain. As part of this process, a series of Americans was sent by Roosevelt to London. One of these was Averell Harriman, the president's top 'expediter' for Lend-Lease, who arrived in March 1941. His job was to evaluate Britain's defence needs and persuade US military leaders to sacrifice materiel to help. Roosevelt explained his role pithily: 'I want you to go over to London and recommend every-thing we can do, short of war, to keep the British Isles afloat.'

Harriman first came to Chequers on 14 March. He explained to Winston that if Lend–Lease assistance was to be expanded, he needed to know much more about Britain's war plans and prospects. With the US Army and Navy already making substantial demands on limited resources, it would be a struggle to get these allocated across the Atlantic unless a persuasive case could be made that the British would make better use of them.

Winston assured the American, 'You shall be informed. We accept you as a friend. Nothing will be kept from you', and set about persuading Harriman both of the inevitability of invasion and of the importance of the US declaring war. To help Harriman make his recommendations, Winston gave him the right to sit in on meetings of the War Cabinet (he was given the rank of minister in the British government) as well as access to classified British intelligence.

Harriman arrived at a moment during the war when American help was desperately needed. U-boats were sinking British ships at a rate two to three times faster than they could be replaced. The tonnage lost month by month was increasing rapidly: 320,000 in January, 400,000 in February and 535,000 in March. Britain imported half its food and almost all its raw materials, save coal. Without an acceler-ation of the support provided by the United States it would soon be strangled. And running in parallel to all of this came disturbing evidence of barges massing in ports of France and the Low Countries. A cross-Channel invasion still seemed more likely than not.

The man upon whose shoulders so many hopes rested was forty-nine years old, with a mid-Atlantic accent, a slight stammer, sad brown eyes and one of America's biggest fortunes. He had inherited an estate of $70 million before he had finished college, and then made even more money as a banker and businessman.

Those who liked him admired his debonair good manners; those who did not thought him a humourless cheap patrician who never carried cash, paid for cabs or picked up the tab at restaurants. What everybody agreed on was his ferocious competitive streak, which was driven by a mixture of persistence and egotism. When he took up polo, he swiftly became one of the top five players in the United States.

W. Averell Harriman, FDR's special envoy to Winston Churchill, and Pamela Churchill's lover.

Harriman seemed intent on charming not only Winston, whose vigour surprised him, but the family and friends he always had by his side: on his first visit, he brought a bag of tangerines that he had picked up in Lisbon. Winston liked him instantly. Before long, Harriman was a popular and regular guest at Chequers. When Mary was left crushed and miserable after the collapse of an engagement, it was Harriman who took her for a walk in the grounds of Chequers and was 'sweet & sensible & sympathetic' to her.

And it was at Chequers, at the end of March, that he met Pamela, who thought him the most beautiful man she had ever seen: 'He was marvellous,' she remembered years later, 'absolutely marvellous-looking with his raven-black hair. He was really stunning. Very athletic, very tan, very healthy.'[*]

---

[*] Even Harriman's looks seemed to have split opinion: other people described him as stooped and gaunt and always in rumpled suits.

Although she claimed to be unaware of his wealth, she did know that he 'was the most important American in London'. Harriman was also impressed. She was 'delicious', he said.

They first slept together at the Dorchester in mid-April, after a dinner given in honour of Fred Astaire's sister Adele. That night saw one of the worst raids on London in the war so far. People woke the next morning to a city that looked bleary-eyed and disfigured. A great gash had been taken out of the Admiralty, St James's Palace was burning, Chelsea Old Church was demolished, Jermyn Street crushed and the roads everywhere covered with glass. Many of whose who had spent the night sheltering from the Luftwaffe's onslaught came blinking into the sunshine to examine the devastation. Jock Colville thought they looked like sightseers. His attention was also drawn to another unusual sight: Pamela Churchill and Averell Harriman, arm in arm, picking their way through the wreckage.

It was a wartime romance, never a grand amour, and both parties entered it with their eyes wide open. They certainly cared for each other, but it was essentially a relationship that suited two people who liked both to be at the centre of things and to collect people they thought might be useful.

To begin with, they tried to keep the affair secret; they met late at night and maintained separate establishments. Although they often found themselves attending the same dinners, or invited to the same weekends at Chequers, Pamela's general demeanour was helpful: the fact that she was flirtatious with everyone meant that whatever attentions she may have paid her lover in public did not stand out. Pamela's friendship with Harriman's daughter from his first marriage,* Kathleen, who was in on the secret, meant nobody asked too many questions when the trio moved into a suite at the Dorchester overlooking Hyde Park.

And yet all this was only camouflage. Lord Beaverbrook and Duncan Sandys both saw the looks and gestures that passed between Pamela and Averell and divined what was going on. But whereas

---

* Harriman's first marriage had ended in divorce; he was now married to Marie Norton Whitney, who had herself once been married to Cornelius Vanderbilt Whitney – which meant he was connected to the Churchills by marriage.

Sandys opted to say and do nothing (beyond, it seems, telling Diana and Sarah), Beaverbrook immediately saw how Harriman's partiality for the prime minister's daughter-in-law might be turned to both his and the country's advantage.

Always fascinated by tangled sexual relationships, the press lord allowed the couple carte blanche to come and go at Cherkley (where young Winston was still staying). For her part, Pamela was intoxicated by Beaverbrook's almost compulsive manipulations, and she was intrigued by the hypnotic effect he could exert, sometimes even over Winston. She found it exciting to watch him tempt Averell with morsels of information, which he offered in exchange for the American's own closely guarded confidences. Pamela passed on what she gleaned from Harriman herself to Beaverbrook and Winston. In turn, Harriman extracted useful material from Pamela, who was gaining a reputation (which she did much to encourage herself) for being one of the best-informed women in London.

Quite when, and quite how much, Winston knew is unclear. Although Pamela had long made a habit of complaining about Randolph to Clementine, she said nothing of her relationship with Harriman. In fact, Pamela claims that it was only in the spring of 1942 that Winston came to her and said he was hearing quite a bit about her and Harriman. Well, she replied, some people have nothing to do except gossip. Winston agreed, and said no more. (One might also read this as a warning, with Winston objecting to the openness of the affair, not the fact of it.)

Mary thought Winston and Clementine had actually been oblivious to the relationship for a long time, and then, even when confronted by incontrovertible proof of its existence, they refused to believe it. Others argued that Randolph's parents were too naïve, and too wrapped up in their lives, to even think that an affair like this could be possible.

This view was not shared by everybody. A man who knew Pamela 'intimately' after the war was adamant that Winston had helped to engineer the whole thing.

I know Churchill put Harriman in her way so they would go to bed, so she could find things out and tell him. I am as convinced of that as anything. It was done in the seventeenth and eighteenth centuries by kings. Why not Winston Churchill? He was ruthless. She gave him information. She was living openly in the flat with Harriman. Of course Winston knew, even though his own son was away at war. Pam was useful to him.

Bob Boothby, who despite his long loyalty to Winston during the thirties claims never to have really liked him, would have been sympathetic to this suggestion. He thought Winston was too ruthless, too fond of war and power.

'I could never take the streak of cruelty in his nature,' he said. Winston would cry over the death of a cat or a swan but had little regard for human life – least of all his own. 'When he sacked or broke people, and he broke many, he never thanked and seldom saw them. He simply didn't care. And in some cases he did it with relish.'

Desmond Morton, Winston's neighbour and one of his chief sources of intelligence during the wilderness years, and who was also cast aside by the prime minister,* saw something of this when the prime minister ended General Wavell's command in the Middle East.

Wavell, who Winston believed lacked the charisma necessary to be a good commander, had made the decision to evacuate Somaliland and carried out a brilliant retreat, but the prime minister claimed he had sustained too few casualties. Wavell sent back a telegram saying only one thing: 'Butchery is not the mark of a good tactician.' This defiance did him no good.

'I think that the first time I ever deeply disliked Winston,' Morton told Boothby, 'and realised the depths of selfish brutality to which he could sink, was when he told me, not only that he was getting rid of Wavell from the Middle East, but why.'

After they had spoken about his destruction of Wavell, Morton described how Winston walked up and down his room, chin sunk into his chest, glowering and muttering, over and over again, 'I wanted to show him my power.'

---

* Morton was dropped from Winston's circle almost as soon as Winston entered No. 10. He was an uncongenial dining companion, and since Winston no longer had any need for the sort of intelligence Morton had once been able to provide, there was no longer any reason for the prime minister to see him.

Winston was certainly capable of being ruthless – one could argue that it was precisely this quality that made him such an effective war leader – and there was immense value to be gained by anything that helped improve Anglo-American relations at such a crucial point in the war. Moreover, he had always had an easy facility for convincing himself that any course of action that suited him was not just the most convenient, but also the right, thing to do.

Pamela believed that even once her parents-in-law had found out about her affair, they did not disapprove of what she had done. After all, she reasoned, they knew how appalling a husband their son had been.

There is only one recorded instance of Winston making any sort of criticism of Pamela. Talking to an old friend, the Countess of Rosslyn, he said, 'Why, I cannot understand it. I went out of my way to be kind to her.' But if he was upset, he had a strange way of showing it. As Pamela remembered, 'If anything, Winston made it easier for the two of us to see each other outside London by inviting both of us to Chequers nearly every weekend.'

Randolph, two thousand miles away in Cairo, where he was installed in the almost oppressively grand Shepheard's Hotel,* knew nothing.

He was mostly happy to be abroad, where he was finally in a position to make a meaningful contribution to the war effort. On his arrival, he had become his unit's intelligence officer, which meant he had considerable opportunity to roam, driving around in a car with a flag – a privilege that was in theory reserved for full colonels, but which Randolph evidently felt matched his own special status. He became an omnipresent irritant, like Egypt's flies, or the sand that was somehow able to get anywhere (including, to the disbelief of many men, under their foreskins), or the young pimps: 'Hi, George! You want my sister? Very nice, very clean, all pink inside like Queen Victoria.'

Tense, hot, uncomfortable, and home to a great many who wished to see the backs of the British, Cairo was also bewitching and luxurious for those who could afford it. The city's department stores like Cicurel, Chemla or Le Salon Vert were full of glass, fabrics and

---

* One visitor claimed that 'even the toilets have something monumental about them . . . you feel as if you were sitting in the central chamber inside a pyramid.'

cosmetics; its cafés were resplendent with the smells of roasting coffee and buttery pastries; its groceries were well stocked with butter, sugar and eggs; and, importantly for Randolph, Shepheard's stocks of decent hock and champagne would last until 1943.

Most of the English there were under thirty and the environment combined with the glamorous task of winning the war lent their world an unreal, playground-like quality. They drank and ate at places like Café Groppi, whose garden was illuminated with strings of little coloured light bulbs that sparkled into life as dusk fell; or the Kit Kat Club, where guests did their best to be discreet in front of the Hungarian dancing girls, who were widely held to be spies.

Randolph had arrived to find a number of familiar faces, such as Christopher Sykes and Robert Byron, and wasted little time in making new acquaintances. One of these was Maud 'Momo' Marriott, daughter of the American financier Otto Kahn, the wife of a colonel in the Scots Guards, and Cairo's leading hostess. Momo was rich and sophisticated, with long red fingernails and simple, beautifully cut clothes. She never rose before lunch but gave luncheons and dinners almost daily at the opulent house that she shared with her mother, known to most either as Mrs OK or Mother Bird. Visitors – generals, commandos and celebrities – came and went well into the night, which meant she knew pretty much everything worth knowing.

Although Momo denied it, everyone else in the city assumed, correctly, that she and Randolph, the man she called 'the problem child' to her friends, were lovers. Randolph did not, however, limit himself to one mistress. He was often seen fondling his Egyptian girl-friends in public at Madame Badia's, and caused a scandal by bringing whores through the doors of the Mohammad Ali Club ('a very swagger affair', as he described it to Pamela, 'to which all the rich Pashas belong').

When he was not with Momo, throwing badly accented bombs into Cairo's French-speaking high society or leaving a trail of purple-faced old men in his wake at the Shepheard's bar, Randolph spent increasing amounts of time at his friend Peter Stirling's flat. Its furniture was battered – with cigarette-singed sofas and doors that were covered in photographs of King George and Queen Elizabeth (an unconvincing attempt to hide from their landlord the results of indoor

revolver practice) – its bathroom was full of captured German ammunition and a pair of elephant tusks, and the profusion of girls, gramo-
phones and sleeping bags made it hard to find somewhere to sit, but
the food was excellent, the drink unlimited and the company smart.

It also offered Randolph a window into the activities of the SAS, a
marauding, daredevil unit that had been set up by David Stirling,
Peter's brother. Randolph remained desperate to prove himself in
combat, but 8 Commando had been dissolved, and the reluctance
of the commanding officers of other regiments to put Randolph in
danger in case doing so would upset the prime minister, plus
Randolph's own manifest physical unfitness, and also his inability to
stop talking, which many found insufferable, meant that nobody was
willing to take him on. In early May, when most of 8 Commando
(including Evelyn) had been sent to contribute to the doomed defence
of Crete, Randolph had, without explanation, been prevented from
going. He was reduced to hanging with pathetic zeal around the war
zones, trying to arrange danger for himself and saying longingly to
desert veterans, 'Of course you've done the real fighting.'

When he saw his cousin Anita Leslie, who was stationed in a camp
outside Cairo, he confessed how forlorn he felt. He told her that
being the son of Winston Churchill had always been a burden and
now that his father had become the greatest of all war leaders, things
had only become harder. This did not stop him from proudly reading
to his colleagues the long, hand-written letters that Winston sent to
him describing, for instance, his mid-Atlantic summit with Roosevelt.

A constant stream of messages passed between father and son,
who made unstinting use of the privileges of the diplomatic bag.
(Randolph's letters were dangerously indiscreet, revealing far too
much about his movements and activities. But uncomfortable as
handling these letters made the officers charged with doing so, the
fact that letters were for the prime minister made them reluctant to
refuse to deliver them or even to take out their censors' pens.)

Their letters were sometimes long and discursive. One from
Winston speaks of his pride in the service his daughters were giving
– 'Your sisters have chosen the roughest roads they could find' – but
also his frustrations at the difficulties he encountered in his prosecution of the war. 'Things are pretty hard here now that the asthma

season has come on and Max fights everybody and resigns every day.'
He then railed at his generals and admirals (who were too cautious)
and Britain's communists (who with some chutzpah were posing as
the only patriots in the country).

'In the midst of this I have to restrain my natural pugnacity by
sitting on my own head. How bloody!'*

At other times, the letters were short, but pregnant with affection:
'My darling, Only a line to give you all my love & to tell you how
often I think of you & how interested I have been by all yr cheery
letters . . . Your ever loving Father.'

There was a great deal of gossip, but there were also interventions
by Randolph on behalf of men who had engaged his sympathy and
imagination, such as the eccentric, brilliant commander Orde
Wingate, who was facing court martial after he had cut his own throat
from ear to ear in Shepheard's Hotel because GHQ would not listen
to his plans. In addition to this, Randolph, whose sympathy could
easily be engaged, often tried to use his influence with his father to
reverse injustices – for instance, he wrote to his father to protest at the
deportation to Mauritius of Jewish refugees from Europe, whose boat
the *Darien* had been intercepted by the Royal Navy. (In response,
Winston recommended to Lord Moyne that they be allowed to
continue their journey to Palestine.) More generally, officers stationed
in the Middle East knew that if they wanted a particular issue raised
with the prime minister, his son was often the best, most direct route.

Randolph's letters home offered a running commentary on the
personnel and organisation in Cairo: 'I am told that Corbett the
C.G.S. is a blockhead. (This view is widespread; but I have not met
him myself, so cannot judge.)' He occasionally even expanded these
into memos running to many pages of suggestions and observations:
'The training of drafts arriving in the Middle East is deplorable'; 'the
G.O.C. 8th Army ought to be a tank man.'

Winston took his son's comments seriously, so seriously, in fact,
that although Randolph was nominally a very junior figure in the

---

* A strange slip into old clothes. Though Winston was now at the centre of the
government, he still seemed to find it difficult to shed the outsider's attitude that had
been so much a part of the previous decade.

Middle Eastern hierarchy, his recommendations had an impact that far outstripped his rank. Randolph's criticisms of Wavell in the aftermath of the debacle in Greece helped speed his reassignment from the Middle East to become viceroy of India. Winston also responded to Randolph's recommendation that he should appoint a minister of state for the region who could coordinate the efforts of Britain's soldiers and diplomats. (Randolph was not the only man to push this idea: others, such as the ambassador Miles Lampson or former commander of forces in the Middle East Wavell, had also argued for it. But Winston's final decision followed hot on the heels of a telegram from his son.)

Winston appointed the astute Oliver Lyttelton as resident minister in Cairo. This had an unanticipated consequence when Lyttelton, who had a high opinion of Randolph's talents as a journalist, made him director of propaganda with responsibility for handling the press.

Promoted to major, Randolph threw himself into his new role. Horrified by the slack standards he found, almost his first action was to fire the chief Middle East censor and his assistant and rule that their successors should sleep in their office to ensure round-the-clock service. He set up new newssheets for the soldiers – first the *Desert News*, and later the *Eighth Army News* – which provided them with much-needed honest information. Too much information for some: one officer thought them so subversive that he burned copies in front of his men. Another assured Randolph that the ranks would be just as happy with old editions of *Tatler* and *Country Life*.

Writing to Pamela from General Headquarters, Cairo, Randolph glowed. 'For the first time in my life I really have plenty of interesting work to do and am busy from morning to night.'

Winston liked to find jobs for Randolph that fell outside the scope of his official responsibilities. In June 1941, he wrote to tell him that Averell Harriman was on his way to the Middle East. The prime minister emphasised the importance he attached to Harriman's mission, and asked Randolph to do everything he could to make his trip as enjoyable and fruitful as possible.

Harriman arrived in a blisteringly hot Cairo June. Over ten busy days, as they toured military installations together, Harriman making notes along the way on the shortages that afflicted them, the two men discovered that they loved being in each other's company. Randolph was ebullient and helpful, greatly impressing the man who was cuckolding him. In turn, Randolph noted an 'extraordinary maturity of judgment that is almost on a par with F. E.'s'.

Each night, once they returned to wherever they were staying, they sent enthusiastic reports home. In a telegram to Pamela at the Dorchester, Harriman announced: 'Find Randolph most delightful and stimulating travelling companion. Beginning to understand your weakness for him.'

Taking his turn to write to Pamela, Randolph described Roosevelt's representative as 'absolutely charming . . . He spoke delightfully about you, and I fear I have a serious rival.' To Winston, he talked of 'my favourite American . . . I think he is the most objective and shrewd of all those who are around you . . . I am sure you would do well to back his opinions on the situation out here to the limit.'

The trust that his father had shown in him by asking him to look after so important and powerful a figure, and the excitement that accompanied the intimacy that had grown so quickly between them, led Randolph into what he would later call an 'unforgivable' indiscretion.

One night during the trip, he chartered a dhow and gave a small party in his powerful new friend's honour. As their boat rocked gently on the moonlit waters of the Nile, Randolph, his head swimming with alcohol and affection, and still unaware of what was happening in London, leaned closer to Averell and boasted of his affair with Momo Marriott.

For years to come, he would be haunted by the thought that in speaking like this, he had unwittingly contributed to the end of his marriage, even if the affair had already been underway for a number of months.

It was less the thought of the break-up of the relationship itself that troubled him. In a sense, by producing an heir, it had already served its purpose. What stung Randolph more than anything was that his marriage's collapse set in motion a chain of consequences that would, eventually, change his bond with his father for ever.

14

R is His Blind Spot

SIX MONTHS LATER, on 6 January 1942, Randolph came back to London, the first time he had been home in nearly a year. Winston was still away in the United States, discussing with Roosevelt its entrance into the war, but a photographer from *Tatler* was on hand to capture Pamela at the airport, rushing to her husband and flinging her arms round his neck.

Perhaps still slightly shamed by the sacrifices his excesses at the beginning of 1941 had forced on his wife, Randolph had spent the autumn behaving in a far more conciliatory manner to her. Sending her a package of food, he wrote, 'It seems frightful living in this land of plenty while you are so tightly rationed at home. Darling, I am so glad that you are hearing a good account of my work. I do terribly want to do something of which you can be proud.'

And, for the moment, all seemed well. As Pamela cabled to her lover a couple of days later: 'RANDOLPH HOME FOR TEN DAYS HE HAS ALREADY FALLEN FOR KATH WE MAKE A HAPPY TRIO WISH YOU WERE HERE WITH US.' Randolph was looking, Cecil Beaton thought, handsome and sunburnt, if a little thicker and greyer than when he had left England. His manner had changed too – somehow more mature, 'less of a firework'.

Randolph had returned at a difficult moment. News from Russia was bad, the Battle of the Atlantic was still going poorly, Hong Kong had surrendered to the Japanese on Christmas Day, Singapore was under severe threat, earlier in December the ships *Repulse* and *Prince of Wales* were sunk off Malaya – one of the only two occasions during the war when Winston's sleep was affected* – and Rommel's Afrika Korps was rampaging through North Africa.

By the time Winston arrived back in Plymouth on 17 January, his leadership of the country – for the first time since May 1940 – looked under threat. The House greeted a tired, depressed-looking prime minister coolly when he appeared there for the first time in three weeks. In response, Winston called for a vote of confidence. Randolph, assuming his father needed his support, arranged to extend his stay from ten days to two months.

The first day of the confidence debate found the House packed, with members who had not been able to find a seat forced to balance precariously on the chamber's steps. A phalanx of Churchills and their allies entered at the same time as Chips Channon: Clementine statuesque, magnificent, almost completely grey-haired; Diana, Jack and Clarissa; Pamela, somehow, despite the occasion, flirtatious; the prime minister's secretaries; and then Winston himself, charging in like an angry bull, in his urgency almost toppling over a rope barrier. When he rose to speak, the cheers were subdued and yet it was immediately clear that he was in one of those invincible moods in which confidence hurried through his veins, his voice rang clearly and he seemed master of all before him.

Over the course of the ninety minutes that Winston spoke, it was almost possible, one witness noted, to feel 'the wind of the opposition dropping sentence by sentence'. Seeing that he had the whole House with him, the prime minister was unable to conceal how much he was enjoying making his speech. Harold Nicolson, watching in a haze of affection, observed the way his hands were thrust deep into his pockets, and how he turned his tummy first to the left, and then to the right, as if emphasising his pleasure.

By the time the prime minister had finished, it was clear that there was no opposition left, 'only a certain uneasiness'. Nevertheless, the debates continued the following day. Randolph had been quiet so far, but this was about to change. When the Labour MP Emmanuel Shinwell made a vicious personal attack on Winston, Randolph stood

---

* The other having been earlier that year, when Crete fell to the German parachute troops.

up, his uniform clinging tightly to his sturdy torso, to defend his father.

It was not a particularly considered speech. Looking out at the rows of black coats and white faces before him, he hurled himself into cruel attacks on the men who had abused his father. To those watching who were not the objects of his anger, it was 'amusing and brave', and at the same time curiously hard to witness. Steadily a fear mounted in those who knew Randolph that in trying as hard as he could to demonstrate his unswerving adoration for his father, he would go too far. Chips Channon remarked upon how Pamela squirmed in the Gallery, and Nicolson noted how even Winston looked 'embarrassed and shy'. At a time when his focus should have been on present challenges, Randolph could not help but return to old grievances. 'I was particularly amused', he said, warming to his theme,

> by those members of the Conservative Party who were upset at its being such a bad Government and were rather speculating whether they could strain their consciences far enough to support a Government with so many inferior people in it. When one remembers not only the willingness but the pleasure with which they supported administrations composed of incomparably inferior ministers, it really staggers one that there should be this sudden desire among them for perfection. Perhaps, as so many Members say, this is not a very good Government, but ought we not to ask ourselves, is it a very good House of Commons ... It is the Parliament of Munich, it is the Parliament which failed to rearm the country in time ...

There were catcalls and shouts of outrage from the Conservative benches and a backbencher called Sir Archibald Southby stood to make his own spiteful contribution. 'Will the Honourable and Gallant Member – I call him that because of the uniform he wears – ' he began, 'please tell me on what occasion he has been, as a soldier, in a battle where he has been shot at by the enemy at 1500 yards?' At this point the speaker shut him down.

Somehow, although he did add some 'fuel to the fires of bitterness', Randolph had managed to get his point across without burning everything down. Kathleen Harriman, writing an account of the day to her sister, said he had been 'brilliant, spontaneous and exceeding tactless . . . but the House enjoyed it immensely'.

Later, in the smoking room, Winston remarked to Harold Nicolson that 'Randolph had had a rough passage.' Years before, he had dreamed about the day when he and Randolph would stand shoulder to shoulder in the House. This, in all its ugly glory, was its fulfilment.

In the corridor afterwards Southby buttonholed the prime minister and in a clumsy attempt to apologise told him that had he been allowed to finish, he would have congratulated Randolph on his rapid promotion. In response, Winston shook his fist in Southby's face and shouted: 'Do not speak to me. You called my son a coward. You are my enemy. Do not speak to me.'

Winston wound up the third day of the debate with another dominant performance. Brimming over with magnanimity at the prospect of the victory he already knew was his, he complimented his critics on the quality of their speeches. It was only when he reached his peroration that he swapped this geniality for a more forceful manner. Crouching over the dispatch box, he struck it:

> It only remains for us to act. I offer no apologies. I offer no excuses. I make no promises. In no way have I mitigated the sense of danger and impending misfortunes that hang over us. But at the same time I avow my confidence, never stronger than at this moment, that we shall bring this conflict to an end in a manner agreeable to the interests of our country and the future of the world. I have finished.

With this he swept his arms downwards, with the palms open, as if, Harold Nicolson thought, to receive the stigmata. 'Let every man act now in accordance with what he thinks is his duty in harmony with his heart and conscience.'

There were loud cheers, before the MPs filed into the cramped hot lobby to place their votes. The prime minister's victory in the vote of confidence seemed complete: 464 to 1, with 3 ILP members, two of whom acted as tellers in the Divisions, voting against.

He left, beaming, arm in arm with Clementine. But it was clear that there were still many dark days to come. Leaving the House, Nicolson passed the tapes, which were

ticking imperturbably. It tells us the Germans claim to have entered Benghazi, and that the Japs claim to be only eighteen miles from Singapore. Grave disasters indeed. At the same time we have released the news of the sinking of the Barham. A black day for a vote of confidence.

On 15 February, Singapore fell. Winston called it the 'worst disaster' in British military history. Almost as bad as the fact of the defeats themselves were the constant whispers that the army had not fought well: there were rumours that an entire Indian division had panicked in Malaya, and that Australian troops had laid down their arms almost as soon as they had come under fire. These all added to the feeling Winston had that his generals, even his Cabinet, lacked fighting spirit. He held them responsible for the misfortunes. The distress of all this caused him to suffer even more pronounced mood swings than usual.

Winston had suffered a heart attack in Washington, and on his return home news of his health problems began to leak out, largely because he could not stop talking about them. The prime minister, whose doctor despaired that he had become 'heart-minded' and unable to focus on anything else, told Anthony Eden, for instance, that he felt 'his heart a bit' and had trouble breathing when he danced.

Mary's diary became a record of the emotional and physical toll the devastating sequence of disasters exerted on her father. More and more often she noticed how weary and sad he seemed. Then, in late February, things got worse still.

It was not just Winston who had been ground down by the extraordinary circumstances the family had found itself in; they had all suffered. There was a suffocating, relentless quality to their lives. Disturbances and obligations crowded out chances for pleasure, or much needed recuperation. There was no leave, little chance for them to escape from the endless demands of the war. And nowhere, really, that could be called a private space.

Chequers, with its croquet lawns and deckchairs in the garden, was ostensibly somewhere for the prime minister to relax, and yet even here it felt as if every possible second was being squeezed out of the day. Guests would arrive constantly, some coming for lunch, others dining and sleeping. This is even before one begins to consider the various aides, private secretaries, ministers and bodyguards who swarmed constantly around Winston. Mary joked that their weekends were divided into shifts.

The Churchill family's existence was crowded, but also lonely. All servants now had to be vetted by the security service. The presence of strangers, and even most friends, prevented the discussion of sensitive topics. This meant that the Churchills' formerly expansive social life was reduced to a small 'golden circle' of trusted colleagues, and those close relations known to be 'padlock'. Clementine found that she was forced even more often into the company of Winston's 'cronies', as well as her children and their spouses.

The family could not risk entrusting sensitive information to letters (as Pamela wrote to a friend, 'it is better to be dull than dangerous'), and even on the phone, they had to use guarded language. Clementine, especially, felt isolated by the burden imposed by the secrets confided to her by her husband. It cut her off even from the few close friends she had, and left her reliant on Mary and Sarah, the only people to whom she could talk freely. Or at least she could on those occasions – increasingly rare as the war drew on – when they were close by. With Mary and Sarah both posted away from London, Clementine was, more often, left alone.

It was a claustrophobic environment that strained nerves and threw old tensions into new relief. All the members of the Churchill family were trapped inside an ever-tightening circle; it is easy to see how raw and exposed their nerves were, and how quickly any one of them could lose their sense of perspective.

Amid all the tension and stress, Randolph was eager to resume the friendship he had begun with Harriman in Cairo. The two men exchanged telegrams in which they both proclaimed their hope that they would be able to see each other while Randolph was in England. Then, on the night Harriman arrived back in England from Washington, he was welcomed at the Dorchester by a pyjama-clad Randolph.

The Churchills during the war. Sarah stands between Winston and Clementine. Diana and her husband Duncan Sandys are on the far right.

The two men lunched together, or with Pamela. Averell even joined Randolph and Pamela in their room for Sunday breakfast on a weekend when they were all staying at Cherkley. The two lovers were cold-blooded and efficient about their deception. Randolph was oblivious.

Ten days with her husband was one thing, Pamela discovered. Two months was something else entirely. 'He was a wonderful person,' she would recall many years later. 'He was very enthusiastic. He was extremely intelligent. He was great company. But once a week was enough.' It was not just his incessant talking, or his propensity to flare up at the smallest provocation, or the way that when he drank – as he did, constantly, every day from 12.00 p.m. onwards – he could transform into a kind of monster. Although these things were all troubling in their own way.

He was almost entirely un-housetrained. Diana Cooper described the impact he made as a guest: 'He staggers into my room at about

9.30 & orders his breakfast. His coughing is like some huge dredger that brings up dreadful sea-changed things. He spews them out into his hand or into the vague – as soon as I get up & turn my back to run my bath he takes my place in my bed with his dirt encrusted feet on my sheets. Cigarette ash & butts piling up around him. He is cruelly bored & leaves his mouth open to yawn.'

Later that week: 'We still have darling Randolph with us. I've had to check him over bossing me too much. He has taken to clapping his bare thigh at 2 second intervals. He'll clap perhaps a 100 times running. He leaves the lights on in the house & drinks us dry.'

Randolph would get drunk at Beaverbrook's Sunday dinners and make a spectacle of himself in front of old sparring partners like Michael Foot and Aneurin Bevan. Pamela and Averell watched in horrified disbelief.

Husband and wife began by quarrelling behind closed doors. Before long, the violence of their arguments spilled out into the open. Pamela complained that all her good work in Preston (where she had made a series of dutiful, if unenthusiastic, visits while her husband was away) had been undone by Randolph, who fell out with the constituency chairman within forty-eight hours of his return. They argued about money, and Randolph's jealousy of his mother's closeness to Winston, but always, more than anything, Randolph criticised the way Pamela lived her life. He hated her frequent absences in London and the way young Winston had, as he saw it, been abandoned at Cherkley.

'I want you to be with my son,' Randolph yelled.

'He's my son too.'

'No. My son. I'm a Churchill.'

When Clementine was present she would try to intervene, but her obvious sympathy for Pamela, coupled with Randolph's hostility to her, only made things worse. Pamela sought solace in the company of the Harrimans; Randolph at the bar at White's.

News of the cleavage in the Churchill family spread quickly. When James Lees-Milne ran into Clarissa Churchill in the middle of March, she told him 'that Randolph's wife had no intention of sticking to him; and that Mr Churchill would be very sad if their marriage broke up'.

People who saw the couple in public noticed two things: there was a new note of rancour in their relationship, and whereas Randolph was little changed, Pamela was notably more confident and assertive. Whatever deference she had once displayed to her husband had long since washed away.

One night that spring, Evelyn Waugh and Cecil Beaton made a call on their friend and his wife. They found Randolph in an 'exuberant & vociferous' mood, whereas Pamela shut herself away in the bedroom for a long, secret conference with her father. What struck Evelyn most was that Pamela seemed to hate Randolph so much that she could not even sit in the same room as him. Once her father had left, she paced up and down the tiny hall rather than join her guests. When, finally, Evelyn persuaded her in, she refused to look at Randolph, saying over her shoulder, in acid tones, 'Ought you not to be resting?' each time he threatened to become too cheerful. 'She was looking', he said, 'very pretty & full of mischief.'

Tensions in the Churchill family were heightened still further by public criticism of Randolph's continued presence in London. He had been sent home to arrange various matters related to his branch of Middle East Intelligence. Having completed the work, he wanted to return, but his unit had not arranged for that to happen yet.

Continuing the sly theme that Sir Archibald Southby had introduced during the confidence debate, General Auchinleck, commander-in-chief of the Middle East, criticised what he regarded as Randolph's failure to return. While Winston believed that Randolph was being treated in an 'intolerable manner', he was also alive to how the situation might *look*. It was not a good time to face more hostile questions in the House.

Randolph was just as incensed by the swipes being aimed at him. But he was also anxious to remain at his father's side, and he was still eaten up by the frustration he felt at being prevented from doing what he most wanted: to be allowed to join a front-line regiment. Clementine was convinced that the situation could be resolved only by sending Randolph back to his unit. Otherwise, she feared, it would lead to trouble for her husband. Nobody was exactly in the wrong, but everyone had a strong opinion. The argument expanded and absorbed Randolph's failing marriage, and was exacerbated by his conduct since his return. Randolph had not learned any self-control in the months he had spent overseas. Ignoring the grievous pressures his father faced, he continued to launch violent attacks on his colleagues and made endless criticisms of the way the war was being run. He should have known that this conduct would enrage Winston, and yet it seemed that no force on earth could stop him from going ahead and doing it anyway. Mary wrote in her diary that although Randolph claimed he loved his father, 'he never seems <u>not</u> to say or do something because of any harm it might do to Papa'.

In the process, the family's arguments became more savage, personal and difficult to contain. Clementine rowed with Randolph. Randolph rowed with Winston. Winston rowed with Clementine. It all culminated in a major scene that left Winston so upset that Clementine feared he might have a seizure.

Mary was home for seven days' leave from her anti-aircraft unit. She, like her sisters, had complicated feelings about the unfolding drama. On the one hand she was sympathetic to her brother's predicament, on the other she felt that the longer his bulky frame remained in London, the more discomfort he was likely to cause their father.

On 23 March, her first night back, Clementine took her to see Vivien Leigh in Bernard Shaw's *The Doctor's Dilemma*: 'exquisite', Mary thought. They returned home to find that Winston, Diana and Duncan had already begun dinner. The evening started to deteriorate immediately. An exhausted, depressed Winston began sniping at Clementine. This escalated into a 'battle royal' over Randolph and the pressing need (as Clementine and Mary saw it) for him to rejoin his regiment if they were to avoid exposing Winston to the sort of public censure and resentment that was the last thing he needed at that moment.* Eventually even Diana was drawn in.

Mary, so often a divining rod for the mood of the family, hated rows; they left her feeling weak and sick. Even a comparatively modest disagreement, such as one earlier in the war with Randolph, who kept interfering when she was taking a phone call, could leave her out of sorts for the rest of the day. Mary's solution was to write Randolph

---

* It was being suggested that Winston, whose behaviour always laid him open to charges of nepotism, was guilty of trying to arrange a 'safe' staff job for his son.

a letter suggesting that he should return to Cairo as soon as he could. Her intentions were good, but it only resulted in another row. She also ran up against Winston's prodigious love for Randolph. Although only days earlier his son had been screaming in his face, Winston still took Randolph's side.

Two days later, Mary returned to the Annexe, after lunch at the Soviet Embassy, and discovered that Randolph and Pamela were about to arrive. This was almost enough to make Mary turn on her heels, but she screwed up her courage and stayed. Once Winston's guests – Bendor and the Prof – had left, Winston surprised his daughter by telling her that Randolph had shown him the letter she had written. He proceeded to upbraid her for being 'unsisterly'.

Stunned by the way Randolph had gone running to their father and feeling, she said, as if a cold hand had been laid upon her heart, Mary said only, 'Oh so he's shown it to you.' What more could she say?

To prove his point, Winston produced a pair of secret telegrams from Cairo which, he claimed, explained how justified Randolph was in remaining in London. Mary wanted to reply by explaining why it was that people would always ask questions about Randolph's staff job, and that Randolph would always make things worse by setting 'all the world by the ears', and that it would always end up reflecting badly on Winston, but she was overawed by her father and knew that no argument could ever persuade him: 'R is his blind spot.'

The problem, Mary reflected, was that Winston's view of his son was different to that taken by the rest of the world. He saw Randolph only as mistreated and misjudged, and unfairly maligned by the unfeeling Clementine and his jealous sisters. Just as he had done before the war, he retreated into the fantasy of the perfect father–son relationship he had created as a compensation for his rejection by Lord Randolph, and which stopped him from seeing Randolph as he really was. 'It might be funny,' Mary continued sadly, 'only somehow it all hurts so much.'

Randolph and Pamela walked in while Winston was still lecturing Mary, and immediately the room filled with tension. After fifteen minutes, Mary said her goodbyes – it had finally been decided that

Randolph would leave for Cairo the following day – and left for bed. Even as she did so, Winston grabbed her and, in a 'hoarse whisper', tried to get her to apologise to Randolph for having sent the letter. Mumbling vaguely, Mary promised only that she would write to him, then escaped to her room.

Writing in her diary later that night, Mary, who struggled with her faith, who copied prayers into her diaries, who castigated herself for 'my rowdiness and bawdiness', and who wanted, more than anything, to be good, tried to make sense of everything she had just experienced. I think, she wrote, 'the greatest misfortune in R.'s life is that he is Papa's son'. Mary acknowledged that Winston bore a great deal of responsibility for the current situation: he was the one who had spoiled and indulged Randolph for so long. But she also felt that the bitterness and anger her brother displayed in response to what were very definitely *his* failures were both hideously out of proportion and directed at the wrong person: 'I don't doubt he loves Papa – but he shows it in a very queer way.'

Randolph returned to Egypt, followed very quickly by a telegram from his father.

PLEASE LET ME KNOW WHAT YOUR EMPLOYMENT IS AS NATURALLY I LIKE TO FOLLOW YOUR FORTUNES STOP ACKNOWLEDGE

His reply came three days later.

AM JOINING DETACHMENT OF SPECIAL AIR SERVICES UNDER MAJOR DAVID STIRLING STOP I THINK I WILL FIND THE WORK INTERESTING AND AGREEABLE AS I WILL BE WITH A NUMBER OF FRIENDS IN NO 8 COMMANDO PRIOR TO ITS DISBANDMENT.

Clementine was appalled. She could not understand why her son could not 'quietly and sensibly' rejoin his old regiment rather than embark on something that would cause Winston 'harrowing anxiety . . . agony of mind'. Clementine wondered aloud if there was any merit in sending him an 'affectionate' cable begging him to reconsider his decision for his father's sake. 'He might listen to me,' she said, 'as though he does not care for me, I know he respects me.'

Randolph was, however, set on his course. And whatever Clementine's reservations about her son's activities, the mere fact of his absence had done much to improve the vicious atmosphere that had threatened to tear the family to pieces.

On a visit home to the Annexe after her brother's departure, Mary was summoned to see her father as he dressed for dinner. She told him that she had written to Randolph: 'O heaven,' she wrote ecstatically later on that night, 'something of that companionship has come back.'

Winston, who had started to emerge from his winter malaise and was now leaping vigorously out of bed after his afternoon sleep to stride around his room, cigar in mouth, whisky and soda at his side, calling for his socks as he berated whichever minister was unfortunate to have been summoned in to his presence, resumed sending his son cheerful updates about Harriman's health and reminding him that Pamela was 'a great treasure and a blessing to us all'.

It appeared distance was able to resolve what no amount of well-intentioned words ever could.

Manifestly unfit, and seriously overweight, Randolph did not look like an elite soldier. One witness remembers seeing him dressed in a 'Commando cover-all that fitted like a greengrocer's bag around a single onion'. As Winston pointed out, 'Of course I do not wish to hamper you in any way, but I am told that parachuting becomes much more dangerous with heavy people.'

And yet whatever his physical defects, these were amply compensated by extreme bravery and a fervent desire to see the action that, thus far, had been denied him.* Like his father, he was attracted to

---

* Randolph was becomingly modest about his courage. When asked if he had been afraid before his first parachute jump, he replied, 'Not at all. I have no imagination, so action doesn't bother me in advance. But when I was in the plane, the horrible thought occurred to me: what if I should freeze when I look down the hole? So I slipped five quid to the sergeant who was next in line behind me and told him to give me a shove if I showed the slightest hesitation. It wasn't necessary. When the time came, old Randolph hopped right out.'

those situations in which the presence of danger enhanced one's sense of being alive. It also offered a diversion from a swelling unhappiness that was obvious to anybody who encountered him.

He knew too that his increasingly complex relationship with Winston had trapped him in a paradox. His desire to be where bullets flew was guaranteed to create trouble in his family, and his death would cause devastating grief in his father. But Winston venerated courage; he loved surrounding himself with fighter aces and Victoria Cross winners (he told Jock Colville that he would have preferred to have won the VC than become prime minister). Had Randolph hidden away in a safe staff job, he would have been forever diminished in Winston's estimation. Heroics were the surest method of securing the approval he wanted so desperately from his father.

In May 1942, he was finally able to persuade David Stirling to let him take part in a long-planned raid behind enemy lines to Benghazi (in an attempt to prove his physical capability, he embarked on a three-day fitness blitz, which mostly involved a stout, hard-breathing Randolph running loops of their base camp).

The deal was that the prime minister's son would accompany them to a point just outside the Libyan city, and then wait with a rearguard while the rest of the unit swooped in. Randolph got his chance when a detonator went off by mistake and deprived one of the raiding party of his finger. The sound had barely died away, and the wound had still not been dressed, when Randolph appeared from behind a sand dune, bristling with weapons and ready to go.

An excited Randolph was even more talkative than usual. In the brief intermissions in his conversation, he 'yelped with pleasure and excitement, like a dog following a hot scent'.

The plan, he explained to Winston in a long letter he wrote to him after the raid, was to sink two ships in Benghazi so as to block the channel to the harbour. On these terms, the event was a failure. But the account Randolph gave his father delighted him all the same. Clutching Tommy guns and several handfuls of grenades, they drove into the city in a Ford utility vehicle stripped down to look like a German staff car. Randolph called it 'the most exciting half-hour of my life'. There were a number of close shaves, one of which was resolved by Fitzroy Maclean pretending to be a German officer and berating Italian sentries for their poor security. And the very idea of the prime minister's son hiding overnight in a house deep behind enemy lines, surrounded by Arabs and Italian soldiers, was, in its way, delicious.

Even a serious crash on the way back that left Randolph with crushed vertebrae (and killed another of the passengers) could not quite dampen his enthusiasm. Winston pronounced himself 'thrilled' by what his son had told him, and immediately shared it with Clementine and Pamela, who told her husband:

I lunched with Papa yesterday. He was very pleased with your letter to him and terribly proud; in fact, I have rarely seen him so excited. Having told me that I was not to mention it to a soul, he then said why hadn't I shown it to your friends and would I take a copy.

So impressed was Winston that he went out of his way to meet David Stirling. Borrowing from *Don Juan*, he described him as 'the mildest manner'd man that ever scuttled ship or cut a throat'. More significantly, he had a private word with General Harold Alexander, and shortly afterwards, the SAS became a brigade. Indirectly, Randolph played an important part in securing the future of what would become one of Britain's most storied military units.

In April 1942, not long after Randolph had returned to Cairo, the Harrimans moved out of the Dorchester into a flat on Grosvenor Square, right next to the US Embassy. Pamela, who was also now receiving a substantial weekly allowance from her lover, joined them. As her friend Sarah Norton recalled:

Living with him took it over the line. It wasn't discreet. No one had the time for a scandal, but among conversation it was considered that she was being a silly girl, living with a man who had a wife in America, who had no intention of divorcing his wife. We thought she was being very stupid and naughty.

Before long, people began to talk about Pamela's 'Americanisation'. She was the only Briton living on 'Eisenhowerplatz', most of her friends were now American and she had begun speaking English with a noticeable American accent.

When Randolph – his skin ugly and mottled, his belly so big that it strained against his uniform belt – was invalided home in July 1942, he was shocked by his wife's new celebrity. He was also deeply hurt by the way that, whenever he approached, American soldiers would say, 'Here comes Mr Pam.' Randolph had thought he would return to London as a war hero; instead, he found that when he tried to order Pamela around 'like a pasha', she kicked back. Looking on with his usual mix of malice and amusement, Evelyn Waugh noted, once more, 'She hates him so much she can't be in a room with him.'

It was at the bar of White's that Randolph first began to hear hints and gossip about Pamela's adultery. It was left to his brother-in-law, Duncan Sandys, to confirm the news. Randolph reacted furiously. He would drink too much and then lurch around London, spreading 'malicious inventions' about Pamela. The next morning, he would wake full of regrets and beg others to intercede on his behalf, testing the patience of even his most loyal friends.

Randolph was not jealous ('I have never believed', he once said, 'in men friends quarrelling about girls: after all, there are plenty to go round'), but he was furious that Harriman had taken advantage of his friendship after being recommended to him by Winston. The thing that hurt him most, he told Jock Colville, was that his parents 'had condoned adultery beneath their own roof', suppressing their own concerns because of Harriman's importance to Britain.

In his cups, Randolph could take this further: he was soon telling his friends that Winston had not just condoned the affair, he had encouraged it. As soon as the prime minister returned home from Moscow that August, Randolph began to turn up at the Annexe with, it seemed, the express purpose of provoking violent arguments with his father.

Randolph knew Winston better than anybody. He would have known that, as A. J. P. Taylor noted, 'When he was powerful his benevolence brimmed over', but threats and anger only served to make him more obstinate. Storming into Winston's home, yelling accusations at him, questioning his love: this was the worst thing he could do. Randolph's friend Alastair Forbes recalled how 'He used terrible language and created a rift that never healed. He said they must have known, and they said they didn't know.'

Fighting back, Winston and Clementine denied having known of the affair and accused Randolph of mistreating the mother of his son.* Randolph burst into tears and vowed never to speak to his father again.

Over and over again the two men let their great love for each other be overwhelmed by the anger they felt. Though they knew how easily hurt they both could be, neither could stop himself from saying words they knew would wound the other grievously.

When Randolph and Pamela met now, it was only to quarrel. Their fights became more public, their estrangement more obvious, and not long after his return, Randolph walked out.

At the end of October, Randolph was passed fit to return to active service by a medical board. As soon as he learned about Torch, the invasion of North Africa, he volunteered for the First Army. Winston helped his son to an appointment as an intelligence officer. Just as it had earlier in the year, the war offered Randolph the chance to escape his mounting domestic problems. There had never been an argument between father and son, no matter how vicious, that could not be resolved. This, however, felt different: something had shifted. It was clear that too many resentments lingered, more than any reconciliation could dispel. Nevertheless, an intervention by Beaverbrook established a fragile peace between Randolph and Winston.

In a letter to her father, sent shortly before the assault began, Sarah told him that 'I saw Randolph for a few minutes before he left. He looked so much better and calmer. He loves you very much as indeed we all do.'

---

* Winston was not a perfect husband, but he prized uxoriousness. He disliked Henry VIII because of his cruelty to his wives.

15

Every Day I Think of You

N O MATTER HOW fierce their rows, no matter how deep the pain they caused each other, one thing remained true of Winston and Randolph: anger never curdled into aversion. Harold Alexander remembered a moment during the war when, meeting at an airport, he had inadvertently seen the two men embrace 'in a moment of deep tenderness' – after a quarrel. Even years later, the depth of emotion on show had stayed with him.

Fragments from letters by Laura Charteris and Clementine hint at the pain both men felt while the conflict between them over Randolph's marriage stayed unresolved. Most of the time, Clementine could not bear her son's company; over and again, Randolph's conduct towards Winston left her white with rage, and yet she knew how important he was to her husband's well-being. She hoped now, she wrote in late 1942 after Lord Beaverbrook had stepped in to help mediate between father and son, that 'Randolph may see his Father constantly. He truly loves Winston & this estrangement has been a sorrow & has weighed on both of them.'

Laura's spring 1943 letter to Randolph, who was in North Africa at the time, speaks of the relief he felt after their reconciliation: 'how lovely for you to see your father, and feeling that you & he are close friends once more. I know how happy this must have made you.'

Randolph was a habit Winston could not kick. Senior officers in whichever theatre Randolph happened to be serving found themselves enlisted sooner rather than later in the rarely straightforward task of locating the prime minister's son, or reporting on his health, or passing on a message to him from Winston that he was convinced should be transmitted urgently.

He complained to the Foreign Office when telegrams from Randolph were not deciphered quickly enough – he could not abide any delay in hearing from his son. And missed telegrams and lost letters were, for him, the source of immense frustration.

On 26 February 1944, for example, he sent a telegram to Randolph, who was in Cairo at the time. 'How are you getting on? All well here.' It was followed less than a week later, on 4 March, by a more peremptory successor, addressed to Fitzroy Maclean, who was attached to the Yugoslav government-in-exile: 'How is Randolph? Did he get my message? I am surprised not to have heard from you more often.'

Winston also continued to call for his son's presence, as he had since hostilities had begun. He was 'never content', remembered Harold Macmillan, 'unless he could arrange for Randolph to come to meet him during his journeys'. Right from the first days of the war, Winston came up with a series of reasons – not always convincing – to explain why he needed his son by his side. He would telephone Randolph's commanding officer and say, 'I would like my son for three days', and off he would go, to London, or on a tour of the Maginot Line, or to conferences in Cairo, Casablanca and Tehran. The first request had actually come during the opening stages of the war, before Randolph had even joined up with his unit, when he was sent to join the naval destroyer bringing the Windsors back from France.

Randolph would get into trouble with his colonel, who told him he was not taking the regiment seriously, and incur even more resentment from the other soldiers; and Winston would be told off by Clementine, who worried that these impromptu jaunts might lead to charges of nepotism.

But Winston carried on summoning his son who would, as soon as he received the call, rush to do his father's bidding. As Pamela recalled, 'He was actually always doing things in the war to please his father.'

Randolph had fun at the banquets and was enthralled by the chance to mix with Roosevelt and Stalin as they made decisions that changed the course of history. He liked the fact that at the Casablanca conference in January 1943, where Winston had called him in to arrange the publicity, this proximity meant he could clamber into the American president's car and read out to him what he thought was an apposite passage from Machiavelli.

Winston and Randolph, Casablanca, January 1943.

But it was his father's company he really loved; existence away from him was insipid and colourless. Writing to him after one of their trips, he noted, 'After the fascinating & exciting three weeks I spent with you life now seems rather dull.' The journey, he said, was varied and interesting, 'But most of all I enjoyed it for the opportunity it gave of seeing so much of you after what seemed a very long separation.'

The sentiment was returned. Winston always appreciated, for instance, his daughter Mary's company. He could sustain a certain amount of interest in her 'humble affairs of the heart & of the barrack square', and yet a point always came when she feared she might be boring him. Randolph could be infuriating, enraging, irritating, staggeringly rude and obnoxious, often all at the same time. But he was never boring. Even Jock Colville admitted that Randolph could be 'bewitching' company.

He was a gifted mimic, and his audacity could help puncture the pomposity of those, like Field Marshal Montgomery, who were inclined to take themselves too seriously. (This irreverence was always likely to appeal to a man like Winston, who once referred to a general as 'a bladder with a name on it'.) Randolph's unshakeable faith in his father's abilities could act as another kind of tonic.

More than anything, though, Randolph understood his father like nobody else could. Winston was a man who, as Violet Asquith observed, 'makes his own climate and lives in it and those who love him share it'. Randolph knew this climate better than anybody.

This was partly a practical matter. Because of Winston's lisp, and because he growled so often, many found it hard to follow what he said. This issue was compounded by his picturesque, opaque way of speaking. It was not always clear to whom he was referring when he mentioned 'that moon-faced man in the Foreign Office' or 'Lord Left-leg-limps'. Randolph always knew. They had spent so many hours together, locked in conversation, that they had come to inhabit the same mental space. In their imaginations, ghosts from the past mingled suavely with the men who surrounded them now. When they talked, they ranged happily from Marlborough's generalship at Blenheim, to the personalities of those who accompanied Winston on the cavalry charge at Omdurman, through to Neville Chamberlain's betrayal of the country at Munich. They spoke as if all these events had happened only the day before.

Winston tried his staff's patience by often spending the greater part of the day half-sitting, half-lying in bed, surrounded by papers and breathing heavily, and then staying up all night. In between summoning his valet Sawyers to serve his breakfast, ringing the bell for a private secretary to bring him the news and playing endless games of cards, he would solve 'huge problems'. Men like Alan Brooke and Jock Colville found this style of living disorderly, almost unbearable. For Randolph, it was entirely natural.

Everybody else treated the prime minister as an invalid who needed handling with great care. No matter how many times he went into Clementine's room to tell her, 'I am so happy. I feel so much better', he was still told over and over again not to stay up so late, not to drink so much, that he needed to conserve his energy. Randolph was always concerned by his father's illnesses, and yet he never tried to suppress his behaviour. On long journeys across the Atlantic, or in wicker chairs on the terraces of North African villas, the two men gossiped and bickered deep into the night. They sat with heads inches away from each other, smoke from their cigars (Winston) and cigarettes (Randolph) meeting in the air above them, bawling at each other as everybody else around them fell asleep.

The sight of Randolph and Winston hunched over a table on HMS *Renown* in November 1943, playing endless rounds of bezique, horrified Winston's doctor, Lord Moran: every call of 'What about another cut of the cards?' was another assault on his attempts to protect his patient's increasingly fragile health. Winston was already struggling with a heavy cold and sore throat. Once the prime minister had finished his duties in Cairo, a sequel to the Tehran conference, he had collapsed with exhaustion. Moran said he had been 'profligate with his resources'. Still, that night, father and son went to bed at five.

This was one of the things that meant the arrival of the prime minister's son was not always welcomed by the secretaries, doctors and soldiers around Winston. Randolph brought trouble with him in the same way as others might come bearing a bunch of flowers. He was rude to generals, much too free with unsolicited advice about how the war might be won, and liable to disturb his father at times when the prime minister's energy should have been directed into more productive activities.

Winston would often get riled in Randolph's company. This was sometimes because they could not stop themselves from quarrelling about who was responsible for the situation with Pamela. Occasionally it would be an unrelated matter, such as Winston taking exception to his son's criticisms of Anthony Eden, another long-running source of contention between the two.

But just as often, it was that Randolph's presence worked on his father like a kind of stimulant. A few minutes with his son could leave him 'in a most excited mood, roaring like an excited bull'.

In December 1943, for instance, when Winston was supposed to be recovering in Tunis from the bout of pneumonia that had struck him down after the exertions in Tehran and Cairo the month before, and was now accompanied by an irregular pulse that alarmed all the doctors around him, he summoned Randolph to join him. Here, he allowed his son to work him up by feeding him 'with a lot of reports, partly founded on some foundation of fact, mostly invented' about the squabbling between various French factions – a situation that, for no particularly clear reason, Randolph, with his addiction to sticking his nose in where it was not wanted, and his love of causing mischief, had got entangled with.

What this meant in practice was that men such as the chairman of the Chiefs of Staff Committee Alan Brooke, who had a great many other priorities to deal with, had instead to cope with a situation in which 'the P.M. is beginning to ring up and telegraph from Tunis almost hourly. Randolph is stimulating him and I am sure it is bad for him. He was in such a passion on the telephone today that I thought he was going to have an apoplectic fit.'

The day after Randolph's arrival, Winston complained to Moran: 'I don't feel well. My heart is doing something funny – it feels to be bumping all over the place.' He had been hit by a heart attack, although not a severe one. Harold Macmillan noted in his diary, 'It is really too bad of the boy to worry his father. But Winston is pathetically devoted to him (as he is to all his family) and will not rebuke him as he should.'

And yet Randolph did not just bring trouble. Winston still confided in his son as he did with no other person. And the unusual nature of their relationship meant that there were some things that Randolph was able to do, or get away with, that almost nobody else could.

Anthony Eden, who had little reason to praise a man who spent so much of his life attacking him, claimed that Randolph was the only person, aside from Brendan Bracken, who could control his father during the war years and stop him 'bye-passing [sic] British constitutional practice'. An account by the American Lyman L. Lemnitzer* illustrates another way that Randolph exerted a positive influence.

He remembered how, in August 1944, Winston travelled to Italy for a month to take a closer look at the progress of General Alexander's forces, and also enjoy a few weeks of near-relaxation. He was found a small but comfortable villa on the shores of Lake Bolsena. Not long after his arrival, he was joined by Randolph, who had come from Yugoslavia, where he was stationed at the time, to 'confer with his

---

* Later Supreme Allied Commander Europe of NATO.

father'. After a much-needed shave, bath and change of clothes, as well as a few drinks (Randolph claimed he was fed up with slivovitz, so his American hosts managed to accommodate his demands for proper Scotch and brandy), he was taken to see Winston.

Almost before Randolph had greeted him, he was berating the prime minister over Allied policy towards the partisan forces in Yugoslavia, particularly the lack of material support for the men under Tito's command. His father reminded him that there were other priorities in the war, and although it was not clear Randolph was convinced, the meeting continued.

After the conversation had finished, Lemnitzer found himself talking the situation over with a handful of British officers, who told him how useful a part Randolph played in raising with Winston sensitive issues, or disagreements with specific features of Allied or government policy, that many government officials and members of the prime minister's own staff found almost impossible to express to him.

As the war turned decisively in the Allies' favour, Randolph found a new role. If he had not been given any sort of official appointment, this did not stop him from acting as if he were a kind of roving ambassador who operated outside the usual channels and reported only to his father. After the 1942 landings in North Africa, he started to ricochet around the Mediterranean, Middle East and North Africa, even going as far as the Congo, only minimally restricted by normal military duties or hierarchies. One moment he might appear in Tunis in a trailer loaded with 'liberated' champagne, the next at the Sicily landings, strolling through a hail of bullets to tell the SAS that they had done their bit and were to return to North Africa. On another occasion, in an odd sort of reversal, he found himself being captured by Oswald Mosley's son Nicholas while representing the enemy on army manoeuvres.

Randolph accompanied Winston during many of the major conferences (generally managing to behave himself, unlike Elliott Roosevelt) during the war, and undertook diplomatic missions on his father's behalf to figures like the Turkish president Inönü.

When Randolph wrote to Winston about something he had seen on his travels, it was highly likely that shortly afterwards a senior diplomat or general would receive a cable from the prime minister urging them, 'It would be worth your while to see Randolph if this can be conveniently arranged. He has sent me valuable information and holds views which are of interest.' Winston also passed whole paragraphs from his son's letters on to the Foreign Office.

Although this informal, floating role was in many ways congenial to Randolph, he remained unhappy. He still nursed a violent sense of grievance about his marriage, was pining for Laura – whom he pestered with letters and presents sent through the diplomatic bag, even after she had married again – and longed to return to the SAS.

A solution came from an old friend. When Winston made the decision to change the focus of Allied support in Yugoslavia from the royalist Chetniks, led by Draža Mihailović, to Tito's communist partisans – largely because the communists were killing more Germans – Fitzroy Maclean was charged with expanding the British mission to Tito. He returned to Peter Stirling's flat in Cairo to recruit men for his expanded mission to the partisans. One of the many who threw their hats into the ring was the prime minister's son.

Maclean knew Randolph well and felt that he would be a suitable man to send to Tito because of his 'naturally Balkan approach to life, and explosive quality, which I thought would go down well there'. He also felt that everybody would be safer and happier if Randolph was contained behind enemy lines rather than rampaging freely as he had thus far. An optimistic thought circulated that a diet of cabbage soup and the absence of whisky would probably be sufficient to keep him subdued.

Randolph landed by parachute into a puddle of melting snow in the highlands of Yugoslavia, or 'Titoland' as he and his father called it, on 26 March 1944, writing a colourful and romantic description to Winston of the guerrilla leader's secret headquarters, which were at Dvar, in Bosnia, 'an eyrie with a rocky and precipitous approach. His office is all lined with parachute silk and looks more like the nid d'amour of a luxurious courtesan than the office of a guerrilla leader.'

With the invasion of Europe looming, Winston appeared to be suffering under the burden of the ever-increasing pressure. As he had told the American president the previous year: 'I am more anxious about the campaign of 1944 than about any other in which I have been involved.'

Britain had suffered grievously from the loss of a generation of potential leaders in the killing fields of Passchendaele and the Somme. Winston knew that they could not afford for the same thing to happen on the beaches of Normandy. He fretted, constantly, about the plans: were there enough troops landing? Were there enough infantry? Would the Germans use poison gas? What about bacteriological warfare?

He was still regularly working until 3.30 a.m., still involving himself in every single aspect of the war, and his comic engine continued to chug away: it was around this time that Leslie Rowan, one of Winston's secretaries, had to leave the room because he was laughing so hard at one of his jokes.

But this energy and spirit were not sufficient to hide more worrying signs. Winston had not entered the war a well man, or a young one. His ageing body was still racked by the consequences of an accident in New York almost a decade before. For years he had suffered from chest problems, and during the conflict itself he had been plagued by heart trouble.

Over the course of the last years he had travelled 200,000 miles, often in unheated bombers (a problem exacerbated by his unwillingness to wear anything more substantial than a silk vest at night), working through his big boxes of documents, dictating, never sleeping enough, never free from tension or stress.

There were rumours that he was attending Cabinet swathed in a shawl, and that the dramatic daily changes of climate and temperature his schedule involved, his impatience as a patient, as well as a lifetime of brandy drinking and cigar smoking, was putting a strain on his body that hindered his recovery from pneumonia.

Sir Alan Brooke noted that he 'seems quite incapable of concentrating for a few minutes on end, and keeps wandering dangerously. He kept yawning and saying he felt desperately tired.'

His exhaustion was accompanied by melancholy. Mary noted in early February how the last few times she had seen him, she had been struck by his 'anxious preoccupation with the future – His uncertainty.' Winston knew that the road ahead was full of 'trouble & grief'.

He was distressed, for example, by the cynical Russian treatment of Poland, and had come to talk of the world as a 'dusty and lamentable ball . . . People act so revoltingly they don't deserve to survive.'

Steadily, the almost incredible level of pressure that had been heaped upon his shoulders appeared to be slowly crushing him. And alongside it all was the brutish and increasingly unignorable reality that compared to the Soviet Union and the United States, Britain was a diminished, second-order power: he experienced this as a profound humiliation. 'With his marvellous vitality he carried on', said Brooke, 'in a marvellous way, but it had become more difficult than ever to work with him.' The chairman of the Chiefs of Staff Committee worried that Winston would not see the end of the war.

Winston found time amid the accelerating pace of planning for Operation Overlord to arrange for all of Randolph's friends to write him letters. He also sent Randolph a set of classics (to which he had added a number of his own volumes). These gifts were followed by a succession of chatty letters in which he requested 'descriptive accounts of your life', and worried that his son did not have enough to eat.

They were humorous, affectionate, full of political gossip and teasing ('I have heard the most terrible news lately – namely that you have grown a beard'). Winston wrote fondly of young Winston, cheerfully of the progress of the war and about the bombing of London with the barely suppressed glee of a small boy:

Another good straddle was at the bottom of St James's Street, which really made a frightful mess with about three bombs. The raids are very fine to look at now because of the brilliant red flares which hang seemingly motionless in the air, and the bright showers of incendiaries . . . I have had my watch-tower put in order over the Annexe, so that there is enough overhead cover to stop the splinters while not impeding the view. Sometimes I go to Maria's battery and hear the child ordering the guns to fire.

What shone through most clearly of all was Winston's desire to be as close as he could to his son. 'I like to know details of your daily life,' he wrote, 'Every day I think of you.' The interest and affection were returned by Randolph: 'I think of you a great deal at what must be a period of anxiety & worry.'

Randolph was also on better terms with his mother. It was as if he had concluded that discussing his problems with his family was better than brooding about them or, worse, screaming at his father. In the run-up to Christmas 1943, Randolph had even begun treating his mother as a sympathetic confidante. Writing to her in late October, he thanked her for her 'sweet and charming letter. It was very kind of you to bear with me last night. I am so grateful to you for your sympathy and understanding of my problems.'

In turn, Clementine was supportive, despite the evident danger, of Randolph's decision to volunteer for the mission to Yugoslavia. Echoing Maclean, she told Mary that she thought the posting would suit him, and did what she could to ensure her son's comfort by sending him parcels of books.

These, it turned out, were much welcomed. The partisan camp was primitive, which meant that Randolph found it difficult to wash his treasured silk pillowcase, his handkerchiefs, his clothes or even his body. Although he soon made peace with the idea of being dirty – comforting himself with the idea that one did not become dirtier after the first thirty days – the immense boredom was harder to get used to.

Randolph's attempts to go on pony rides were frustrated by deep snow and his old injuries: some days he found it hard even to stand up straight. Eventually, his search for something to do led him to grow a beard and reread *War and Peace*. What he could do nothing to influence was the speed with which he was consuming the one thousand gold-tipped cigarettes President Inönü had given him earlier that year, and the extent of his isolation from British life. He hated not knowing what was going on. Although he realised that it was unlikely the mail would make it home – the postal service was so perilous that many of the packages he received were riddled with bullet holes – he wrote countless letters pleading for cigarettes and political gossip.

When, finally, the weather improved, he spent days at a time roaming the mountains around their base. Undaunted by his extremely limited Serbo-Croat, he carried a pencil and paper around with him and drew diagrams whenever he needed help.

As spring turned gloriously into summer, Winston was occasionally struck by how strange it felt to enjoy 'sunlit lawns and buttercup meadows' when somewhere far away the war raged. It was hard to 'conjure up its horrors'.

And then, as so often in war, extreme tedium was very suddenly succeeded by extreme violence. On 25 May, Tito's headquarters was assaulted by German paratroopers supported by glider-borne infantry. As bullets hissed through the trees around them, the partisans were forced into a dash for a train. In the fraught days before the invasion of Europe was launched, the prime minister's son was a hunted man.

On 1 June, Randolph was able to scribble a rushed note in pencil, informing his father that he was having 'a fascinating time'. But this was followed by complete silence until 9 June, when he was able to send back to London a typewritten report of everything he had been through.

Randolph had only had time to throw on a pair of trousers and a couple of coats over his pyjamas and snatch up his gun before he had to join the retreat. His boots were being cleaned, so he had to make do with a pair of highly battered shoes that hurt his feet when he walked. Nevertheless, he said, 'the whole affair was great fun'.

Moving at night and sleeping during the day, Randolph and the few hundred partisans, who were too big a force to hide but too small a force to mount a successful counter-attack, had a series of close escapes, before Tito, who recognised that he could not evade capture indefinitely, arranged an airlift to Bari for himself, a number of the partisans and the British and Russian missions.

At every stage, Randolph displayed notable courage. One partisan remembered how he was known as 'the incredible Englishman'. He endured cold, hunger, thirst, sore feet and German bullets without complaint. The only time he raised any sort of fuss was when a partisan barber tried to shave him without hot water.*

---

* In recognition of his bravery, Randolph would be recommended for the Military Cross, and awarded the MBE.

Neither the danger he had experienced, nor the fact that it became evident quite soon that he had been specifically targeted, did anything to dampen his enthusiasm for returning to Yugoslavia. He was convinced that important work could be achieved there and that he could help get it done. It could be uncomfortable and boring, but he was good at it. Maclean agreed, writing to the prime minister to praise his son.

Winston, who had sent a barrage of signals to General Henry Wilson demanding to know how his son was, sent yet another. Now that Randolph had arrived back safely in Bari, he wrote, it would be 'interesting and valuable' if, as long as his son could be spared, he could return to England to make his full report. Randolph was distressed at the thought of turning his back on the partisans, but he had never yet failed to obey a summons from his father. There was no reason he should change that now.

16

A Sorrow & a Mortification

IN LATE JUNE 1944, Christopher Sykes was sitting at the bar of White's when his attention was diverted by a familiar voice.

'Where's Evelyn Waugh? I've got to get hold of him! Where the devil is he?'

Christopher knew that Evelyn was training in Scotland, and also that his colonel did not know where to place him. Waugh had had to resign from the Commando Brigade in August 1943 after an argument with Lord Lovat. It was a surprise that they had tolerated him for that long: one of Waugh's superior officers had suffered a nervous breakdown after only two months of having the novelist serve under him. Robert Laycock, head of the Commando unit, had told Waugh in March 1943 that he was 'so unpopular as to be unemployable'.

As it was, he had been given six months' leave from the army, which he used to write *Brideshead Revisited*.* He had just finished the novel when Randolph bustled into White's. Randolph seemed to be in better spirits, and better condition, than he had been for some time. Harold Alexander said he had never seen him looking so well: having eaten little, smoked nothing and walked twenty to thirty miles a day over mountainous terrain during his close shave in Bosnia, he was, as he boasted to his father, 'fitter than ever before'. Now he was back in London, bubbling with energy.

Christopher decided to speak: 'I know where he is, and he can be with you here tomorrow morning.'

'You mean it?'

---

* Somewhat cruelly, Randolph had fed Evelyn anecdotes about Brendan Bracken, which he used to create the character of Rex Mottram, the novel's arriviste Canadian-born MP.

'I think I do, if you let me get to the telephone. Why do you need him?'

Randolph, who was still talking in what was now an unnecessarily loud voice, explained, 'Because my father has agreed to me taking charge of a mission to Croatia under Fitzroy Maclean, and Fitzroy and I have been hunting for Evelyn everywhere because I need him. I can't go to Croatia unless I have someone to talk to.'

The two friends met at the Dorchester, where Randolph tried to grab Evelyn's interest by talking about the religious conflict in the area between Catholics and Orthodox. Evelyn's responsibility, he suggested, would be to help heal this schism.

Evelyn Waugh, who was clear-eyed about his chances of persuading anyone other than Randolph to take him on, agreed instantly – he claimed he was as 'pleased as a boy' about the prospect – and Fitzroy approved the appointment without hesitation. As well as admiring the writer's bravery and resilience, he also thought he might be able to 'contain' Randolph.

Randolph had stepped back into his father's life at a time of extreme stress.

The D-Day landings had taken place only weeks previously, and although the invasion had gone far better than many had feared, much still hung in the balance. The Allied advance through Normandy had been stalled in the 'battle of the hedgerows', and British troops were embroiled in vicious fighting around Caen. In the Far East, the British had recently enjoyed victory, notably with the relief of the siege of Imphal, and victory at the Battle of Kohima, but the prosecution of the war there demanded an immense amount of attention. Winston was also engaged in a bitter argument with the American president about his desire to focus resources on the campaign in Italy. Closer to home, V1s were raining down on London and the south-east of England, causing great terror and horrifying losses.* More than one

---

* Pamela wrote to Averell Harriman to describe the strange experience of a V1 attack: the burst of gunfire, the eerie moment its engines cut out, then the dull thud of the explosion. It was, she said, like 'a black monster with a flaming tail', and yet somehow it was more annoying than threatening: 'It really is very bloody – not frightening, just uncanny & sadistic.'

witness saw their prime minister illuminated by a searchlight as he visited the site of a recent attack and wept amid the rubble.

On 25 June Winston had found that even the simple act of composing a memorandum to the Chiefs of Staff was capable of draining what little energy he had left. Sitting in the drawing room that night at around 6.00 p.m., he declared to Clementine, 'I am an old and weary man. I feel exhausted.'

'Think what Hitler and Mussolini feel like!'

'Ah, but at least Mussolini has had the satisfaction of murdering his son-in-law.'

Winston was so delighted with his joke that he hopped to his feet and went out for a walk. When he returned, he seemed revived, but it was clear that the great reserves of energy that he had once been able to restore almost at will were now severely depleted. A couple of days later, he would fall asleep as his valet Sawyers put drops in his ears.

Tension had started to build as soon as Randolph returned. An attempt the previous year at reconciliation with Pamela, encouraged by Winston and Clementine, had flickered briefly and then sputtered out, and his time in Yugoslavia had done nothing to assuage his grievances about the state of his marriage. While he was in the Balkans, he had been powerless to do anything. He had written long letters to his father, explaining his feelings about the matter, then torn them up, thinking that Winston already had quite enough on his mind. But something about being back in London activated the anger and resentment he had been unable to express while hidden away behind enemy lines.

Randolph hated that his parents continued to show Pamela such favour, even after she had cuckolded him so publicly. He had been incensed when he learned that Winston had settled £500 a year on Pamela, although he realised that he could not stop his father.

Pamela had, he said, declined 'in any way to be a satisfactory wife'. So why did she think it appropriate that she should enjoy all the fun of being Winston's daughter-in-law without fulfilling any of her obligations to Randolph? And, worse, why did Winston aid her in this 'undignified procedure'? He was convinced that Winston created illusions about Pamela in his mind and closed his ears to the truth.

And he hated that his parents blamed him for the breakdown of a marriage that he had entered into, in part, to please his father. He could not understand why his family had not taken *his* side. He disliked the way his son was being brought up at Chequers rather than by Pamela, who seldom came to visit young Winston. Most of all, he resented his father's constant meddling in what he considered his private affairs. Why, he complained in a letter to Laura Charteris, did Winston always think he could 'get his way by bullying and obstinacy'?

For his part, Winston was still grieved and bewildered by the breakdown of his son's marriage. Winston loved his son and loved his daughter-in-law; they had a beautiful child together. His fundamentally uncomplex emotional worldview buckled as he tried to accept the idea that they could not make things work. (Winston had ended his memoir *My Early Life* with his marriage to Clementine and the words 'and I lived happily ever after'. His usual reaction to talk of another couple divorcing was to say, 'Why can't they forget their troubles and just get on with it?') Nor is it clear whether he understood why his son was so hurt by his behaviour.

Randolph's objections to young Winston living at Chequers would have been an unwelcome surprise too. Winston adored Randolph's son, calling him 'a beautiful child', and drawing him into his own whimsical, humorous world: when the toddler caught German measles, Winston assured him that it was the fault of the Nazis. At a time when it was impossible to buy new clockwork train sets, he and Clementine 'scoured London' to find young Winston a second-hand one.

Young Winston visited his grandfather each morning, bringing with him a four-wagon train, an enormous motor lorry that carried twenty packages and a horse-drawn vehicle. The prime minister could be found on his hands and knees, dressed in siren suit and velvet monogrammed slippers, cigar gripped between his teeth, fixing tracks and derailments and telling his grandson with unholy pleasure, 'Now, let's have a crash!'

In his letters earlier in the year, Randolph had applauded the decision to move young Winston to Chequers. To complain now seemed less a matter of fatherly concern, and more a petty attempt to deprive his parents of the presence of a child he knew gave them enormous pleasure.

It was clear to people who saw Winston and Randolph in each other's company that something was not quite right. On 26 June Harold Macmillan was at Chequers with Winston, talking about various foreign policy matters, when a truculent Randolph entered the room. Macmillan could not help but notice the uneasy mix of irritation and affection his arrival provoked in Winston.

That night, Randolph arrived at Downing Street for dinner. He was drunk and had already entered that state where he no longer cared what he said. He told his parents, his sister Sarah and a number of the Chiefs of Staff, who were also present, that his wife was a whore, and then went on to name her lovers.* His bellowing was so loud that the marines stationed outside the room could hear every word.

Once he had got going, nobody escaped Randolph's furious assault. He turned on both his father and mother, and when Sarah – 'the only member of his family who ever liked him', according to Evelyn Waugh – protested, telling him that he could not worry his father at such a critical moment in the war, he hit her in the face and called her a bitch.

Winston went deathly white. He was so consumed by rage that he could no longer speak. It seemed to Clementine that he was on the verge of another heart attack. When, finally, Winston could talk once more, he called in one of the marines to eject his son. Both men swore that they would never see each other again.

The violence of this encounter left the rest of the family stunned. Randolph creating a scene was nothing new, but the emotions that they had seen unleashed distressed them all. Words had been spoken that could not be unsaid; old wounds had been opened and bloody new ones created.

News crept out. At the Carlton Grill, at the bar of White's, in the smoking room at the House, men talked. It had long been known that the prime minister had spoiled his son and that he could not entirely control him. Now they said that he was afraid of him.

★

---

* There is no record of how comprehensive Randolph's list was. To have been accurate, it would also have had to be long. Her conquests included the journalist Ed Murrow and Major General Fred Anderson, the top American bombing commander, another man whose opinions she could pass on to Winston.

Randolph's sisters had all been invested in the marriage from the very beginning. It was Sarah and Mary who had bought the fur coat that Randolph gave to Pamela as a wedding present. And it was always Sarah, along with Winston, who had tried to persuade the others to act with 'true Christianity' and forgive Randolph's indiscretions. Even after Randolph struck her, Sarah continued to urge forgiveness – insisting that one could not simply cast off a member of one's family, no matter what they had done. She wanted to bring her father and brother back together. Writing to Clementine on 1 July, she thanked her 'for your sweet letter. I was feeling very unhappy about the whole affair. It seems impossible to help him – but you know I will go on trying – meanwhile don't be too unhappy about it.'

Mary found it far harder to move on. In her diary she recorded that 'He has behaved it seems with such odious unkindness, rudeness and heartlessness to Papa & Mummie.' The youngest Churchill daughter realised that she did not love her brother any more, nor had she any wish to see him ever again.

What troubled her most were the parts of the relationship between father and son that seemed to lie beyond reasonable explanation. Why did Randolph claim 'it as his right to love Papa deeply', and yet at the same time he did 'nothing but grieve him & beat him up & treat him with <u>anything</u> but love & tenderness'?

Why was it that Randolph meant more to Winston than any of his daughters? Why was it that no matter how deeply they loved him, or how much they achieved, it would never compare to even the smallest gesture by Randolph? '"My son" – O God, what's wrong with daughters?'

On 27 June Winston wrote an icily polite letter to his son. Having been given your report on the attack on Tito's base, he told Randolph, speaking to him as if he were someone he barely knew, 'I must regard your mission as discharged. It seems to me that you should return as speedily as possible to the post which awaits you with the Croatian Armies.'

The only sign that there might ever have been a personal connection between the two men came in a discussion about Randolph's plans to take young Winston to stay with friends that weekend. Winston disapproved of the danger involved in taking the boy through

London. Furthermore, the prime minister continued, 'I do not know how petrol could be claimed for this, or on what grounds it could be claimed.' (The same Winston who in happier times would divert an entire plane to allow him to see, or pick up, his son.)

Then the brisk, impersonal tone reasserted itself. Winston assured his son that he would cover his bill at the Dorchester, before ending with the claim that 'I need not say that I wish you all success in your military duties.'

When, a week later, Randolph, who was leaving the country that day at 4.00 p.m., wanted to communicate the results of a conference he had had over lunch with Pamela (it had gone well, as Pamela reported to a friend: 'he saw my point of view & I saw his. The outcome being that we parted better friends than we've been for years'), he directed his note to Clementine.

They had agreed that Pamela would move young Winston from Chequers and see 'not too much' of his parents. Each of them was as keen as the other to 'get free', and, she reflected, 'I am sure it will be good for little W. to live a little less grandly & also to see more of me.'

After outlining the broad shape of the agreement, he thanked his parents for the care they had taken of his son at Chequers, but he said that now it was time to 'establish a home where we can both be free to visit the child, together or separately as circumstances may dictate'.

In a scrawled letter written at some point later that day – perhaps in response to a (now lost) reply from Clementine – he explained his position in more detail. In the calm, measured tone of which he was capable when sober, he told his mother:

Pamela & I reached agreement this afternoon on certain matters. One of the things we agreed upon was that in future we would settle any differences between ourselves. So my earlier letter to you was merely intended to let you know what we had agreed. I am not asking Papa to agree to anything. He knows my views. I know his. They are clearly irreconcilable. It makes me very unhappy that I cannot persuade him to leave my affairs alone. But I have no intention of worrying him with these arguments again. I do not intend to discuss such matters with him in future either verbally or by letter. It is much too painful for all of us . . .

. . . I hope you don't think me unappreciative of your position in all this disagreeable business. I know how difficult things have been for you and I do know you have tried to understand my point of view.

Twelve days later, after a brief stop-off in Algiers, where Harold Macmillan noticed that Randolph seemed far less exuberant than normal, Randolph and Evelyn set off from Bari en route to Yugoslavia. They shared their Dakota transport with the war correspondent Philip Jordan of the *News Chronicle*, an air commodore, and a group of partisans.

Night had already fallen by the time they took off. The plane's lights were extinguished once they were over the Atlantic. One by one the stars went out; there was no sign of the moon. The passengers sat for the next few hours in an eerie darkness relieved only by the summer lightning that would briefly illuminate the plane's wings, and sparks from the exhausts that flew past like tracers.

Eventually the noise of the engines told them they were descending. They could see the safety flares far below being lit on the runway. Then, without warning, they shot upwards, before hurtling back down into the ground. The men inside regained consciousness in an aircraft that seemed to be lit by thousands of candles.

Randolph, who thought he had been unconscious for a couple of minutes, had no memory of the flames, just of leading the survivors towards a door that had buckled so badly it would not open until he had hauled at it enough to make a gap big enough for them all to escape. Then, ignoring his injuries, Randolph tried to go back into the fire in a futile attempt to rescue his batman, Douglas Sowman. Randolph wept when he learned that Sowman had died.*

Evelyn had blacked out. When he came to, he recalled, 'I was walking in a cornfield by the light of the burning aeroplane talking to a strange British officer about the progress of the war in a detached fashion and . . . he was saying "You'd better sit down for a bit skipper." I had no recollection of the crash nor, at the time, any knowledge of where I was or why.'

Evelyn and Randolph were taken by ambulance to Topusko, south of Zagreb, before being flown back to Bari two days later. Of the

---

* Winston took steps to 'supplement' the pension Sowman's widow received.

nineteen passengers and crew, only nine survived, and the evening's tragedy was compounded by the fact that the wounded partisans who had been waiting patiently for evacuation were instead stranded.

Evelyn had been badly burned on his hands and legs, and his head was so heavily bandaged he resembled a mummy. What made him suffer most, however, were a boil on his neck and the proximity of his friend. Randolph was cruelly bored and tried to fill the empty hours by 'drinking, talking, making passes at the night nurse, demanding treatment, sampling everyone else's medicine and loudly dictating letters'.

A little later, the two men were sent to recuperate in Algiers, as Diana Cooper recalled in a letter to her son:

> On this day of all days Randolph staggered in looking like the man that was – grey-haired, ashen-faced, black pits harbouring dead blue eyes, emaciated, with perished thighs and bandaged knees . . . Randolph's injuries are water on knees, jolted spine and obvious shock, yet his spirits are as ebullient as ever. He lies in a hot cupboard upstairs and is carried to the sitting rooms by four Wop gorillas [Italian POWs].

Though the pain in his legs had not dispersed, after a few days Randolph found he was able to walk, albeit with some difficulty. He had already begun to consider leaving when he learned that Winston, who was travelling to see Tito in Italy, had decided to make a stop in Algiers to visit his son. Although to begin with, they were unaware of the full extent of Randolph's injuries (largely because he had himself played them down) and Clementine was unsure whether she ever wanted to see him again, Winston and Clementine reacted with concern to their son's condition.

Unlike her mother, Mary knew exactly how she felt. She was, she recorded in her diary, completely untroubled by the accident. Even were Randolph to die she would not mind. She would be saddened only by the grief it would cause Winston.

Winston arrived on the morning of 11 August. He was met at the airport by Randolph, and they then drove immediately to the embassy, where Winston stayed an hour or so before flying to Naples. Father and son started talking the moment they laid eyes on each other in the heat and dust of the runway at Algiers and did not stop. They discussed English and French politics and fell into the easy way they had of arguing about the subjects that had for so long obsessed them both. Neither man dared approach the events of the month before, or indeed anything to do with the family.

Nor did Winston tell his son that he was carrying with him a letter that Clementine had written to Randolph in an attempt to clarify her own complex feelings. The 'terrible scene' between Winston and Randolph had left her almost dazed with shock; and its impact had not diminished, instead leaving 'a permanent grief & darkness'. She had also experienced the removal of young Winston from Chequers as a 'sorrow & a mortification': it was, she believed, 'unkind – indeed cruel – & deepens & widens our existing breach'.

I did not have the heart to give it to him, Winston told his wife in a sad letter written in the air above Algiers. 'I am sure he wd have been profoundly upset & his pent up feelings wd have found a vent on me. Please forgive me for not doing as you wished. Where words are unclear silence is best.'

Usually, Winston's letters to Clementine were full of enthusiasm and excitement, with impressions of people and places tumbling over each other, but there was a flatness to this one. The desolate sight of his wounded son – he noted how lonely he had looked as they spoke – was too much for him. At the bottom of the page was a drawing of 'a sheepish pig'.

Winston did end up sending the letter on to Randolph, before they met in Rome later that month. Randolph was, in the opinion of Waugh, who was also in the city, lame but 'much calmer'.

Neither father nor son had forgotten their last argument, but for now they were pleased that a superficial peace had been restored. Before he returned to Yugoslavia, Randolph wrote to Laura Charteris to tell her how happy he was to be friends with Winston once more.

Randolph's brush with death had only sharpened Winston's anxieties about his safety, enough to alarm his staff. As Pug Ismay confided to Sir Robert Birley, 'He welcomes danger and loves getting into dangerous corners. One of these days he will get himself killed and that will finish Winston. What is going to happen to this country then?'

Winston knew he could not stop his son returning to Yugoslavia and cloaked his worry with humorous admonitions. 'Do take care not to be captured,' he told him before Randolph set off again. 'The Gestapo would try to blackmail me by sending your fingers one by one – a situation I would have to bear with fortitude.'

With others he was less successful at disguising the potent combination of pride and fear he felt. On 12 August he met Tito in Naples. Winston apologised that he was so advanced in years that he could not land by parachute, otherwise, he claimed, he would have been fighting in Yugoslavia.

'But you have sent us your son,' Tito replied.

When he looked up, he saw tears glittering in Winston's eyes.

Randolph and Evelyn eventually found their way to Topusko, their original destination, in early September. A small spa town surrounded by chestnut forests, it was Tito's Croatian headquarters and the final link in the chain that took escaped Allied POWs out of the Balkans.

Topusko's pristine new communal baths were in stark contrast to the town. Its shops were gutted, its buildings ruined and most of its population had fled. Randolph and Evelyn's quarters were on the town's outskirts. Their house was set in the middle of a farmyard, with an orchard on one side. It had four rooms, a veranda, and what they were told was the town's only indoor toilet. The whole place reeked of animal manure and woodsmoke and was infested by rats. They were looked after by a cheerful old peasant lady called Zora. Any other women they saw carried rifles.

In theory their responsibilities included promoting pro-British propaganda to a communist army that instinctively turned to Russia for aid, supervising airdrops of arms and supplies from Italy, and compiling reports on the military situation.

In practice they were left with a blank series of empty days. Writing to his wife, Laura, Evelyn complained: 'Today has lasted about a week already and it is only 4.15 pm. We are like Chekhov characters.'

Evelyn kept himself busy by going to Mass and trying to stir up the Croats' religious fervour. Randolph was just himself, which was sufficient to bring out the worst in his friend. 'Hour after hour Randolph trampled and trumpeted, talking, shouting, scratching, farting, belching and yawning; he tapped incompetently into the typewriter, bellowed into the telephone and sat "clucking over the signals like an old hen".'

Randolph, who now found it difficult to walk and was crippled by any unusual exertion, was still clearly in a great deal of physical pain after the crash. He was also distressed by the scenes with Winston in London, which had left him pathetically desperate for both affection and attention, neither of which his companion was willing to provide. Quite why Randolph thought a man whom their mutual friend James Lees-Milne called 'the nastiest tempered man in England, Catholic or Protestant', and who Hilaire Belloc believed was diabolically possessed, would provide this sort of sympathy is unclear.

Most evenings Randolph got drunk on rakia, the local brew that according to Evelyn, who could not stomach it, 'gave off a powerful stench, part sewage, part glue'. Randolph talked endlessly of his father. And when he was not talking about his father, he was arguing about him. He and Evelyn quarrelled about Winston's *Life of Marlborough*, which Evelyn had dismissed as 'the special pleading of a defence lawyer'.

In response, an agitated Randolph asked his friend: 'Have you ever noticed it is people who are most religious who become the most mean and cruel?'

'But my dear Randolph, you have no idea what I would be like if I weren't a Catholic.'

Evelyn tried to control Randolph by snubbing him. Despite his temper, Randolph, like his father, rarely held on to resentments, so, more often, he reacted to his friend's provocations like a hurt child. When Randolph begged for kinder treatment, Evelyn reported that he had been left 'unmoved'. These two short, sturdily built men pecked at each other like a pair of belligerent robins, each mired in their particular misery.

When planes came to the airfield, they would sprint out of their quarters to meet them: each flight offered the possibility of letters from home, boxes of whisky or cigars sent by Winston to his son and a variation in the monotony of their days. But more often than not, they were left wailing at the sky as they heard the planes, which could not land in the autumn fogs, roaring away back to Italy.

Freddie Birkenhead's arrival in October promised a release, although it was accompanied by the same confusion that had reigned over the whole mission (Stephen Clissold, a former teacher, arrived at the same time: Clissold was calm, amenable and spoke fluent Serbo-Croat, three qualities that were shared by precisely none of his companions). He was nominally Randolph's second-in-command, but there was doubt over when, where and by whom this had actually been decided. Robert Bruce Lockhart came away from a meeting with Brendan Bracken convinced that Birkenhead's sole purpose was looking after Randolph. Whether or not this was true, before Birkenhead set off he had been summoned for a bedside audience with a troubled Winston, who poured out to him his grief at the state of his son's marriage.

Randolph was delighted by the prospect of fresh company. The first thing Freddie and Stephen saw as they approached the farmhouse was the unmistakeable figure of the prime minister's son at the door, his arms spread out in welcome. They fell into enthusiastic conversation and a little later were joined by Evelyn.

'There he is!' bellowed Randolph, 'there's the little fellow in his camel-hair dressing gown! Look at him standing there!' Evelyn stared at him viciously, before saying with careful malice: 'You've got drunk very quickly tonight.'

In a letter to his wife, Evelyn recorded Randolph's joy at the new arrivals.

It is a pleasure to have Freddy here to take Randolph off my hands for a bit but the result of his arrival has been to undo much of the good work I had done in subduing him. He bursts out in such exuberant, spontaneous, full-hearted joy that it should be a pleasure to see him – but it is no great pleasure to me . . . The table cloth smells of rakia spilled by Randolph in his joy yesterday.

Soon, Freddie began to find Randolph unbearable too. Randolph had a habit of tuning in to the BBC Balkan service through the night, with the volume at full blast. One morning, Freddie broke, and launched himself at his friend. The quarrel that followed was so violent it woke the rest of the house. Freddie was equally wound up by the malicious stories Evelyn fabricated to keep himself entertained – for instance that Freddie was a morphine addict conducting a homosexual affair – and bored by the long-running joke about Tito's sex. In the opening years of the war Tito had been such a figure of mystery that some doubted whether he even existed, which gave rise to the only half-facetious suggestion that he was in fact a she. Evelyn found this irresistible, and kept on telling everyone that he could not wait to meet 'her'. On their first meeting, Evelyn, in his smart regimental khakis, was introduced to a handsome, powerfully built man in a pair of tight bathing shorts. 'Ask the Captain', Tito said as he shook Evelyn's hand, 'why he thinks I am a woman.' Undaunted, Evelyn had kept the gag going. So, when Birkenhead remarked upon Tito's intransigent behaviour with the Allies, Evelyn explained patiently to him, 'She has come to a rather difficult age for a woman.'

'For God's sake stop this nonsense! Everyone knows that Tito's a man and a good looking one at that.'

'Her face is pretty, but her legs are very thick.'

The squabbling and tension between the three men (Clissold appears to have maintained a dignified silence) resembled the simmering violence of the guerrilla conflict they had been parachuted into. And, like the partisans' struggle against the Germans, the tedium and squalor were occasionally interrupted by violence.

Once again, its trigger was Winston Churchill's son, whose presence in Topusko was one of the war's worst-kept secrets. A few weeks after Freddie's arrival, the British party was woken at dawn by the unmistakeable growl of a Luftwaffe raid.

Randolph tumbled out of bed, shouting at Freddie, 'Get up, you fool. The Germans are overhead and trying to get me. They've got this house pinpointed.'

Pulling on his trousers, Randolph ordered everyone to take shelter in a trench at the back of the farmhouse.

Bombs exploded all around them. Zora, the peasant cook, pulled Freddie on top of her, screeching, 'Cover me, Lord.'

Then Evelyn appeared in the bright white sheepskin coat he had started wearing once the weather turned cold. He strolled about in full view of the German planes, giving every impression of being unbothered by the chaos around him. Randolph screamed at Evelyn to take cover. Evelyn refused.

'You bloody little swine, take off that coat! TAKE OFF THAT FUCKING COAT! It's an order! It's a military order!'

Evelyn kept his coat on, and as he eased himself into the trench, he only said, quietly, 'I'll tell you what I think of your repulsive manners when the bombardment is over.'

An uncomfortable silence descended on the two friends crouching in the trench. Randolph broke first and apologised.

'My dear Randolph,' came Evelyn's reply, 'it wasn't your manners I was complaining of: it was your cowardice.'

They did not speak to each other again for another two days. At this point, Randolph and Evelyn realised that if life in Topusko was going to be anything close to bearable, then a truce was necessary. With most of Yugoslavia still swarming with Germans or collaborators – the Germans still had twenty-one divisions in Yugoslavia, only two fewer than Italy – they were doomed to staying put. They ceased any outward shows of hostility and achieved a wary peace – even if they could not bring themselves to make any real sort of conciliation until November. Freddie noted Randolph's excessive relief at having made friends again.

By the end of November, both Birkenhead and Clissold were back in Bari. A little later, Evelyn was posted to Dubrovnik. Randolph made a brief trip home at the end of October. He stayed once more at the Dorchester rather than at Downing Street and was galled to discover that his own son did not recognise him. He took young Winston for a visit to Chequers, where it appears his encounter with his parents passed off without incident, then returned to Topusko, where he remained until the British Mission was wound up in December.

Pamela had kept at least one part of her bargain with her husband, moving into a cottage of her own with young Winston in late September. But even while Randolph was back in London, Clementine continued to seek out her daughter-in-law. They went to events at

Buckingham Palace and prayed together at Westminster Abbey, all the while carefully avoiding any reference to Randolph. Clementine brought caviar to Pamela's bed after she had had her tonsils out and asked her to spend Christmas with the Churchill family.

It was this invitation that prompted the final argument of the year, one that for once did not directly involve Randolph, although it was about him, or was at least an anticipation of how he might react.

On 12 December, as a 'typical London winter of fog & cold' set in, Winston sent Pamela a handwritten note:

Dearest Pamela

I find our Christmas plans may cause friction as some of the family are worried about the effect on Randolph when he hears the news. Clemmie & I therefore with great regret suggest to you that we fix another date for you to come and bring Winston. She & I were looking forward so much to seeing you & him around the Christmas tree. But I am sure that another weekend later on will be better for all. I hope this will not cause you inconvenience.

The next day Clementine wrote too. 'What has happened is a grief to me,' she told Pamela, adding, 'I hope to see you very soon my dear and will telephone. Your loving "Mama".'

There is no record of a response to either letter, but in the weeks that followed Pamela worked hard to find out who, or what, was responsible for her rescinded invitation. The answer was a surprise: Mary.

The youngest Churchill's manoeuvring was animated by a mixture of resentment at her sister-in-law, whom she did not really like, and felt had escaped much of the blame surrounding the break-up of her marriage – 'It does irritate me when people try to make out she's a poor pathetic little lily' – and also a fear that Winston would die before he and Randolph were fully reconciled. Mary and her sisters did not believe that this could be achieved while their parents continued to see Pamela regularly. Pamela herself seemed unbothered.

'That is I think the gist of their attitude,' she confided airily to a friend. 'It is all very unimportant really.'

17

Finis

O N 8 MAY 1945, just after Big Ben struck three, Winston was able to tell the nation that the war in Europe was over. His daughters Diana and Sarah were in London. Clementine listened at the British Embassy in Moscow. Mary heard her father speak while she played bridge in the country with Jock Colville, and Randolph, who was in a plane eight thousand feet above the Dinaric Alps en route from Belgrade to Caserta, missed the broadcast altogether.

Later on, in an afternoon that had included standing ovations in the House, and struggles to get anywhere amidst thronging, grateful crowds, Winston stepped out on to a Whitehall balcony and told the people gathered below. 'This is your victory.'

The crowd yelled back: 'No, it is yours.'

The next day, though, as her dressing gown-clad father welcomed her back to the Annexe with open arms, Mary could not help noticing that in the midst of the greatest triumph of his life, he suddenly 'looked old & deflated with emotion, fatigue & a heartbreaking realisation of the struggles yet to come'.

During the last months of the war, Randolph had remained abroad, floating tubbily around the fringes of Europe. He began the year with Winston in Athens. There had been little reason for him to be there, but the twin attractions of his father and excitement (Athens was in turmoil, at risk of a communist revolution, and Britain had sent troops to try to ward off this threat: Winston was shot at by a sniper; 'Cheek!' he said as the bullet flew past) were enough for him to decide to poke his nose in. Waugh noted that Randolph added to the unrest by 'insulting everyone in sight'.

After this, Bari (for dental treatment), Belgrade, Rome, where he had an operation to remove fluid on his knee (contracted, he told his father, 'through dancing kola in Belgrade with Marshals Tito and Alexander'), followed by a few weeks of convalescence, a short trip to Malta to be by his father's side at the February Cricket Conference,* then a return to the boredom of Topusko, where, he wrote to Winston, a combination of snow and German mischief (in severing the roads) had meant that he had been effectively cut off.

The letters he wrote were gentle, amused and grateful, and seemed designed to reassure and please his father. 'Am thinking of you so much in these triumphant days,' he told him, before assuring Winston that his finances were likely to be in a better state than at any time since he had left Eton† and that he had taken to heart Winston's advice about smoking ('Already my catarrh is much reduced, the cough is much less hacking, my fingers are losing the stain of nicotine and my voice is even beginning to acquire a little of that "timbre" to which you rightly attach such importance').

With the war in Europe winding down fast, Randolph began thinking about what he might do next. He was done as a soldier. His ruined vertebrae and dodgy knees meant that no unit could claim to have any use for him, and yet still he was considering trying to find a post in the Pacific. He had joined the ranks of those who, as Pamela said, seemed to be 'scared of the peace'.

In April a single telegram from Winston told Randolph of the death of two of his oldest friends: Basil Dufferin and, most painfully, Tom Mitford. Randolph was crushed by the loss. 'How', he asked, 'did one live without such companions?'

Another, more peremptory telegram from his father came in early May, warning him that if he did not return soon, he would be leaving the field open in his constituency at the general election: 'Events are moving very fast. Show this to nobody.'

---

* Not, however, to Yalta. Randolph was angry about not being invited, but focused his rage on Anthony Eden.

† Which, presumably, meant only that he was not in mountains of debt – obviously easier to achieve in a remote field in the Balkans than the bar at White's.

It looked as if it was time to return to the old plan: making storming or witty speeches (as the situation dictated) in the House of
Commons and then, in due course, becoming prime minister. What
was not clear was how far Randolph's expectations of the future
matched those held by his father. While the war was being fought,
Winston had talked again and again of his desire to step away once
peace had been won. For most of those listening, there was no way of
knowing how sincere the prime minister's desire for a gentle retirement really was. After all, he had spent a large proportion of the
previous decade saying something very similar. Pamela thought she
knew the answer: Winston had promised at a family dinner not long
after he became prime minister that he would resign the moment
victory was won; but she knew even then that he was too attached to
power. He had waited all his life for this moment, there was no way
he would surrender it now.

Randolph's return to London was greeted, by some members of the
family at least, with trepidation. The memories of the previous
summer were still vivid. But Mary was pleasantly surprised to find
that her brother's first evening back 'passed better than might have
been expected'.

Staying once more in a hotel rather than in the family home,
Randolph began tentatively to try to work out how to build a peacetime existence. He had his seat to defend and was soon drawn into
helping advise Winston on his election strategy.

Sometimes it could feel as if normal life, or a version of it, was
returning. At the end of May, David Stirling came to lunch at 10
Downing Street with Randolph, Winston and young Winston. At
one point, young Winston hid behind a sofa and lobbed a cushion
that struck Winston full in the face as, with a lit cigar in his mouth,
he entered the room. At first he assumed Randolph's playfulness had
got out of hand again: 'How dare you throw cushions? Will you never
grow up?' until stifled giggles gave the real culprit away.

'What a wonderful aim you have for a little fellow.'

Mostly, however, the two Churchills directed their attention to the
election that would take place on 5 July. Winston was almost absurdly
uncomprehending of the people he professed to represent, which

makes it all the more striking how completely he was able to secure their affection during the nation's darkest months. As the 1945 election approached, he assumed that the mood of national exaltation of summer 1940 would last indefinitely, and he would always be in tune with the emotions of his countrymen. The next months would prove him wrong.

Winston had read a little of William Beveridge's three-hundred-page proposals for domestic policy after the war and yet he was largely resistant to its recommendations. His radicalism had always been rooted in generosity as well as a genuine, albeit paternal, concern for the less well-off. He was not interested in a radical restructuring of the country's social security system. As much as anything, he knew Britain was broke and did not, he said, want to deceive its population 'by false hopes and airy visions of Utopia and El Dorado'.

Although he did eventually tell the War Cabinet that the plan 'constitutes an essential part of any postwar scheme of national betterment', he never publicly voiced this opinion, so the British people did not know what his plans were for postwar reconstruction. He had saved the country in 1940; five years later he had nothing to offer it.

On 4 June he gave his first campaign address. He had been allotted thirty minutes by the BBC – too little, he thought – and in speaking against the clock for the first time in six years, his delivery was rushed. His words tripped over each other as he began to lay out an argument which suggested that:

> Socialism is inseparably interwoven with Totalitarianism and the abject worship of the State . . . Socialism is, in its essence, an attack not only upon British enterprise, but upon the right of the ordinary man or woman to breathe freely without having a harsh, clumsy, tyrannical hand clapped across their mouths and nostrils.

After taking time to name some of those he thought posed the greatest threat, he continued:

> I declare to you, from the bottom of my heart, that no Socialist system can be established without a political police . . . They would

have to fall back on some form of Gestapo, no doubt very humanely directed in the first instance. And this would nip opinion in the bud; it would stop criticism as it reared its head, and it would gather all the power to the supreme party and the party leaders, rising like stately pinnacles above their vast bureaucracies of civil servants, no longer servants and no longer civil.

Randolph was one of the few who had seen the speech ahead of its broadcast. Unlike Clementine, who had begged her husband to remove the 'odious and invidious reference to the Gestapo', he had seen nothing wrong. Most of the country disagreed, and the campaign never really got out of second gear.

Vita Sackville-West, writing to her husband Harold Nicolson, was typical of many:

> You know I have an admiration for Winston amounting to idolatry, so I am dreadfully distressed by the badness of his broadcast Election speeches. What has gone wrong with him? They are confused, woolly, unconstructive and so wordy that it is impossible to pick out any concrete impression from them. If I were a wobbler, they would tip me over to the other side.

Winston knew he was flailing and felt it deeply. 'He is very low, poor darling,' Clementine noted. 'He thinks he has "lost his touch" & he grieves about it.' 'The Election is very tiresome and I long for it to be over.'

By contrast, Randolph arrived in Preston to defend his seat, equipped with several cases of champagne, an impregnable self-confidence and a number of ideas about how to inject some excitement into the campaign. He had wanted to hire two elephants from Manchester zoo, so he and Julian Amery – the son of Leo Amery, and the other Tory in this double-barrelled constituency – could parade through the streets shouting slogans from atop the howdahs. Although the zoo was willing and the cost reasonable, the local Conservative association thought it was too much of a stunt. Randolph called them narrow-minded provincials: 'No imagination and no guts,' he said. They did not forgive him.

Winston's support was exciting enough. He drove from the station to the town hall – where he delivered a twenty-minute speech – in an open car lent to his son by King Peter of Yugoslavia. Julian and Randolph sat on the hood and crowds surrounded the car, shouting 'Good old Winnie' as he gave the V-sign.

Randolph believed the prediction – backed up by canvassing figures from polling day – that he and Julian would sweep home with five thousand votes to spare. None of the other candidates had seemed to create any enthusiasm. None of the other candidates had been given nicknames – he and Julian were dubbed the 'lively lads' and the 'terrible twins'. None of the other candidates had been carried on the shoulders of their supporters after their eve-of-poll meeting. None of the other candidates were greeted by barmaids offering trays of drinks, or were wished good luck by policemen on duty at polling stations. What chance did they stand?

This bullishness was shared by Winston, Eden and Beaverbrook, who thought the Conservatives would secure a majority of over eighty seats. Even the Labour leader Clement Attlee thought the best-case scenario was a Tory majority of forty.

All this meant that on the night before the results were announced, Randolph was ebullient as he set off after dinner to catch the train to Preston. 'He was very confident,' noted Mary in her diary. His high spirits were undercut by a gloomy Duncan Sandys, who had arrived later in the evening with Diana, convinced he was about to lose his seat.

That night Winston too was troubled by doubts. By the morning, he had managed to recover only a cautious optimism. He told Mary, who had woken up full of excitement, that he was suddenly feeling 'low' about the results and feared a stalemate.

The first real sign for Mary and Clementine that something had gone awry came when they went to Winston's constituency count. The prime minister's opponent – Alexander Hancock, a middle-aged farmer with a reputation for eccentricity – secured a shocking 10,488 votes. Winston held the seat with a majority of 17,000, but the two women were left unsettled.

This feeling was deepened when Clementine telephoned the private office and was told about reports that credited Labour with forty-four gains in London to one by the Tories. Clementine and Mary left the count in Woodford to come back to the Annexe, where they ran into Jock Colville, who seemed depressed. 'It's a complete debacle, like 1906.'* Inside, Winston dressed in his siren suit, stared uncomprehendingly at the wall of the map room, which had been readied to receive the results as they came in. By one o'clock, there was no question that Winston was headed for a defeat. Only one question remained: by how much?

Bad news arrived in a steady drip: Randolph, Bob Boothby, Brendan Bracken, Leo Amery, Ralph Assheton and Duncan Sandys had all lost their seats. Some of those watching tried, without much success, to hide hot, disappointed tears; everyone in the room hovered between shock and devastation. Lunch, so often for the Churchills the occasion for joy, passed in what Mary called 'Stygian gloom'.

The day crawled on. Sarah arrived, looking 'beautiful & distressed', to find staff thrust into a dazed kind of despair, Mary wandering from room to room in aimless misery, and her father sitting transfixed by the results, as if he could not quite believe the scale of the disaster that had overwhelmed him. Exhausted by her superhuman attempts to keep her composure, Clementine went upstairs to rest.

At 6.00 p.m. Winston ordered drinks and cigars for the staff and headed off to Buckingham Palace to resign. Dinner was another challenge. Mary and Sarah had tried to lift spirits by putting on their best evening dresses. To little avail. One of the guests later told journalist Virginia Cowles that 'she had never sat through a more depressing meal. Churchill's daughters were in tears and the old man himself sat immobile as though too stunned to speak.'

Afterwards Winston talked in sombre tones to some of the staff. 'Give them a chance,' he told them, 'let's see what they can do. Only this – let them try to tamper with the Constitution & we will be at their throats.'

This brief show of defiance, and a few jokes, were glimpses of the man they had worked with for the last five years. But it was impossible for many there to look at him, and at the devotion of those who

---

* The Conservatives lost more than half their seats in the 1906 election, the first that Winston fought as a Liberal after crossing the floor in May 1904.

loved him so much, and not feel an immense wash of sadness. Winston was stunned by the repudiation by voters and felt that there was 'some disgrace in the size of the majority'. He might have coped had it only been thirty or forty (it was 146). It made him think of the cool reception he had received from soldiers at the 'Winston Club' in Berlin. Although they all dutifully cheered for him, as it was obvious they had been ordered to do, it was just as clear that they had not voted for him. He was too old for a comeback.

In some ways, Friday 27 July was worse than the day before. For the first time since May 1940, Winston woke and found there were no dispatch boxes waiting for him. When Lord Moran arrived at 9.45 a.m., he thought the place seemed deserted.

The absence of activity or urgency was almost unnerving. But there were no meetings now, no telegrams, no decisions that had to be made; in their place only sweet, consoling letters, which served to make what had happened even more final.

Randolph arrived back from Preston during the morning, already on the hunt for a new seat. His energy made a contrast to the melancholy that had seeped into the house's every corner. He and Mary went for drinks at the Ritz, then lunch, before returning home to the emptiness of No. 10. Without the pressures of government, the day seemed endless. At one point, Winston turned to Mary and summed up the sense of drift that left them all feeling unmoored. 'Yesterday seems years ago.'

There was time for a last weekend at Chequers.

In Mary's opinion, Winston was not so much grieving over his loss of office as for the loss of purpose. He had lived five years under unbelievable mental and physical pressure; the prosecution of the war had nearly killed him; and yet it was also the fulfilment of a destiny that had filled his mind since he was a young man. Victory was an anticlimax. For half a decade he had been one of the handful of men who through force of will had changed the course of history. Now he was not much more than a private citizen.

'It was a shock', Mary wrote, 'amounting to a shattering and unexpected blow in the solar plexus, and that blow from a friend.' It was those things, mundane in themselves, but which acted as reminders of the fact that an entire nation had once depended on the decisions he made, that he missed most: the dispatch boxes, and the key that opened them, which for half a decade he had kept on his watch chain and never slept without; the screech made by the motorcycle that delivered his pouch as it roared to a halt on the gravel outside; the secret boxes and Ultra decrypts.

On the first night, in the company of Mary, Clementine, Jack and Jock, Winston managed to be cheerful throughout dinner. It was only later, walking downstairs after Clementine had gone to bed and the rest of the party had sat through a number of newsreels, that Mary noticed how miserable her father looked. He turned to her: 'This is where I miss the news – no work – nothing to do . . .'

In the past, he had always cheered up when someone played him Gilbert and Sullivan records. Mary tried, without success. His spirits only began to rise after she put on some French and American marches. They lifted still further after hearing 'Run Rabbit Run', so much so that he requested the theme from *The Wizard of Oz*.

Finally, his grief and agitation had been soothed enough for him to feel sleepy, and they all escorted him upstairs.

The next day Randolph, Sarah, Diana and the US ambassador, Gil Winant, arrived. They all sat together on the sunlit lawn, where Mary played with the children. At dinner, where they were joined by Bracken and Bevin, Winston appeared gay again. Afterwards, there was a film ('awful', according to Mary), and then his children played records for him again and he watched as Randolph, who had been unusually gentle and quiet all evening, waltzed with Mary and Sarah.

He could have been forgiven for believing that his father's defeat meant that the way was open for his own ambitions. So long the aide-de-camp, now was the time for Randolph to have a show of his own. He could afford to be calm, content in the knowledge that, having given so much of himself to his father's causes before the war, he could devote his energy to achieving everything Winston had once promised would be his.

Randolph may have been thinking about the future, but nobody who had gone to Chequers that weekend could have avoided being overwhelmed by memories of everything that this group had experienced and felt under its roof over this turbulent half decade. Even the visitors' book was a map that allowed one to trace the twists and turns of the conflict.

Winston was the last of the party to sign. Beneath his name he wrote one word: 'Finis'.

Days passed, and Winston was 'perching in film-starry luxury' in the penthouse suite at Claridge's. He and Clementine had bought a home at 28 Hyde Park Gate earlier in the year, but his early departure from office meant that neither it nor Chartwell was ready to occupy.

Winston's naked pain made him almost unapproachable. It was only after Mary had returned to her unit in Germany that she realised she had not dared ask her father how deeply he had been hurt. There were moments when this feeling was soothed – such as when he ventured out to a performance of *Private Lives* and the audience stood up and applauded him; or the cheers of 'Churchill for ever' and 'We want Churchill' at the opening of Parliament in August – but he still missed the work and being able to give orders. Winston had slept soundly through even the sternest passages of the war, but now he needed sleeping pills: 'What is there to stay up for after midnight?' he asked sadly.

His friends urged him to leave Parliament and devote himself to writing a history of the war. You are the world's greatest living statesman, they told him, save yourself for the Test matches, not village cricket. At the very least, resign as leader of the opposition. But I like village cricket, he replied.

Randolph was rudderless too. He had returned from the war to a broken marriage and a son who barely knew him,* and now he had lost his seat in Parliament. His conviction that great things awaited him remained, and yet it began to dawn on him that the path to that glorious future was not quite as clear as he might have hoped.

Conscious that the Conservative Party despised him, Randolph returned to an idea he had flirted with during the war: forming a centre party in the spirit of Lord Randolph's Tory Democrats, which might

---

* It was a bewildering time for young Winston, who thought that the change in prime minister meant that Clement Attlee had become his grandfather.

ultimately replace either Labour or the Tories. Talking about it was one thing, however; making something of it was another thing entirely.

In the meantime, he moved back into the Old Rectory at Ickleford, where he could lick his wounds and improve his acquaintance with his son.* Young Winston was joined by Evelyn Waugh ('a funny little fat man', the boy later remembered) and his eldest son, Auberon. It was a bleak place to start life over again, furnished as it was only with the items Pamela had not already taken. As Waugh noted: 'the house is comfortless & the telephone rings too often. Few of the doors have fastenings and the wind whistles through the house.'

Although Randolph was 'dazed by adversity', he was already hoping he might be adopted as the candidate for Bromley, whose MP had died in August. During the day he kept up a frantic correspondence by telephone and obtained a generous salary to write columns for United Features; by night he drank Armagnac and allowed himself to be hectored by Evelyn: 'I attempted to explain to Randolph that he had reached a grave climacteric in his life and must now grow up or perish. He will perish. I slept naturally and heavily.'

In truth, it was hardest for Clementine, who had been forced to swap her role at the heart of power for something far less rewarding: she was, once more, simply a housewife. She was bewildered and alarmed to discover that having achieved so much during the war – the Russian Fund, her work as chairwoman of the Maternity Hospital for the Wives of Officers, keeping Winston alive – she was now struggling to cope with her own life.

What she wanted, more than anything, was for her husband to step down. She felt she was owed a peaceful retirement. It turned out, however, that he remained as obsessed with politics and glory as he had always been. He was oblivious to Clementine, only appearing to notice her existence when he needed reassurance from her.

---

* During the war, he had tried to ensure he remained in his son's thoughts, but his methods were erratic. When young Winston was three, a large package arrived from North Africa. His excitement gave way to disappointment as he discovered it contained only a number of unappealing green objects. He was told they had been sent by someone called 'Father'. His nanny made him eat the unripe bananas, whose sour taste put him off the fruit for the rest of his life and created a strange connection in his mind with the idea of 'father'.

At the end of August, she poured her heart out to Mary, begging her to return home:

> My Darling please ask for a job at the War Office so that you can live at home in your lovely bed-sitting room at Hyde Park Gate. Because I am very unhappy & need your help with Papa. I cannot explain how it is but in our misery we seem instead of clinging to each other to be always having scenes. I'm sure it's all my fault but I'm finding life more than I can bear. He is so unhappy & that makes him very difficult. He hates his food (hardly any meat) has taken it into his head that Nana tries to thwart him at every turn. He wants to have land girls & chickens & cows here & she thinks it won't work & of course she is gruff and bearish. But look what she does for us. I can't see any future.

They were even about to lose their car. 'We are learning', Clementine concluded, 'how tough & stony the world is.'

A few weeks later, Winston and Randolph walked together in the gardens at Chartwell. The house itself had become cold, damp and badly in need of redecoration. The garden was overgrown, although this was more attractive. Winston had remarked how lovely Chartwell was when it was wild: 'like the Sleeping Beauty'.

Winston, who his son said 'felt every situation through his finger-tips', was morose and withdrawn. Randolph tried hard to cheer him. Without warning, the old man stopped, turned to his son and said quite angrily: 'It is very silly of the child to mind when his toys are taken away from him. But he does mind.'

Randolph saw then how isolated his father felt 'from the great world of power', but what he saw too over the months that followed was how quickly Winston recovered his equilibrium. He did not, aged seventy-seven, possess the same resilience and strength that had helped him perform superhuman feats in 1940, but that was not the same as saying he did not have enough of either.

18

A Walking Volcano

'WE'D ALL SORT of changed a great deal after the war,' claimed Johnny Churchill. The six years of conflict had affected the individual personalities and constitutions of the family and irreversibly altered its dynamics. No relationship was the same, but it was Winston and Randolph's that had altered most dramatically.

Randolph had expected that with Winston out of office again, they could slip back into the intimacy of the wilderness years. This did not happen. Right through the war, Winston had continued to believe in Randolph's abilities – much to the frustration of people like Mary and Clementine, who thought he had already squandered whatever talents he might have possessed. This belief no longer existed. Winston's affection and pride in Randolph was now mixed with a melancholy realisation that his son would never achieve the things that he had for so long dreamed he would. It would be hard to pinpoint a particular moment when Winston abandoned his faith in Randolph. Perhaps the change was simply the result of attrition: too many 'blood rows' over the years. Or perhaps it was caused by a shift in Winston's dynastic ambitions. He had become a figure so titanic, so glorious, that there was no need for the next generation to preserve his legacy. Either way, fervent expectation had given way to a fond but disappointed pessimism.

Sir Colin Coote remembered telling Winston that Randolph had just published a brilliant article in an evening paper. Winston flushed with pleasure, then murmured, sadly: 'I am always very glad to hear that Randolph has done anything very well.' The former prime minister did what he could to encourage his son. Randolph's personal files are full of telegrams from his father congratulating him on articles he had written, or public appearances he had made. Winston might write to him, telling him, 'I wish I knew more of how things are going w you. I think so often of you and your fortunes, in which so much of my hopes reside', and yet what he actually did was more eloquent than what he said.

By 1947 Winston was, perhaps for the first time in his life, free from money worries. The first offer for his memoirs had landed on his desk at 6.36 p.m. on the day of his resignation (from King Features, an American newspaper syndicate). When they were finally sold, it was for $1.4 million in the United States, and £555,000 in Great Britain, the biggest ever non-fiction publishing deal.* This was accompanied by vast sums offered for film rights and the rights to Winston's books published before the war.

The Chartwell Literary Trust was created to safeguard his family's future (and also to shield him as much as possible from the burden of paying too much tax). Randolph stood to benefit handsomely from the arrangement, especially since Winston had altered the first draft of the agreement: it had originally split the capital equally between the siblings; after Winston's changes, Randolph would inherit half.

What was more ominous for Randolph was the fate of Chartwell. It had always been understood that it would pass to him after Winston's death. During the thirties, Winston had even talked about the possibility of him and Clementine making way for Randolph and moving into a cottage elsewhere on the grounds.

In 1947, however, he enthusiastically agreed to what he called a 'princely plan' to make Chartwell a national possession. A consortium led by Lord Camrose bought Chartwell for £85,000 (twice what it was on the market for when Winston had tried to sell it in 1938), and handed care for the upkeep of its roof, walls, timbers, drains and outside decoration to its new owner, the National Trust, which received £35,000 of the purchase price, with Winston taking the rest.

Winston retained life tenancy and was left with the responsibility for looking after insurance, rates, gardens and internal repairs or decoration. He moved quickly to use the money he had been given to buy the neighbouring Chartwell Farm – a renewal of his agricultural ambitions – and a further purchase extended the Chartwell estate to 340 acres.

---

* Approximately $16.1 million and £16.7 million in today's money.

Randolph was ecstatic at the news, in February 1947, that Winston had acquired Chartwell Farm and that he intended to leave it to him in his will. He had always wanted to live in the country, and to be able to do so, so close to Chartwell, he told his father, with 'all its happy memories and associations, fills me with joy'.

Still, Chartwell itself would never be his. He was to be disinherited.

More wounding still was that Winston had gradually begun to seek out his son's company less and less. When they did meet, their conversations did not contain the same easy exchange of confidences as they once had. Randolph could see this, and it hurt.

Randolph still wanted desperately to please his father. As he wrote to Winston in April 1946, 'I hope that one day I shall do something worthy of the love and confidence you have shown me.' And he still adored him. His devotion to Winston remained almost religious. Chips Channon remembered a moment in the House of Commons, as Winston spoke, when he looked up to see Randolph in the Journalists' Gallery over the clock: 'the rays of the sun caught his face, and it seemed transfixed with filial pride'.

But he could no longer draw him close, as he had in the years before the war. As so often, Randolph's unhappiness manifested itself in a form that only managed to make things worse. When he came to stay at Chartwell, or saw his father elsewhere, he would try to provoke him. There was no real purpose to his antagonism, it was just, he said, that he found it impossible to sit at the table and 'prattle platitudes', even when talking about an abstract subject like politics.

Winston would tell him to 'shut up'. His appetite for argument had diminished and he no longer took the same delight in paradox, or the sort of uproarious levity Randolph claimed had once been so much a part of their relationship. When Randolph was young, Winston had taught him that these were the 'proper terms' in which to discuss politics; Randolph never saw that the years of war had changed his father for good. In the thirties, Winston had cheerfully tossed little balls of bread at his son while he had monopolised conversations and abused his elders; he had lost his patience for this sort of behaviour. He wanted peace and affection, not explosions or torrents of reproaches.

Sarah, in between making her own unsteady way in her career as an actress – moving to Rome in the process – provided her father with the easy, sympathetic company he wanted from his children now. Bearing many of her own sadnesses, she was quick to understand other people's. Writing to Winston in February 1947, after the death of his brother Jack, for instance, she told him, 'I know what it will mean for you – how suddenly terribly lonely you will feel.'

Randolph was still bitter about what he regarded as his parents' collusion with Pamela. This was only exacerbated by the fact that Clementine continued to see and sympathise with Pamela, who she felt had suffered unfairly since the war.

In addition to this, his jealousy of men like Anthony Eden, who occupied the position of political heir that Randolph felt was his by right (no matter how unrealistic the prospect really was), spilled out into vicious rants that distressed Winston. These in turn led to more painful scenes, more nights that ended with father and son bellowing at each other at two in the morning.

Neither father nor son wanted to fight, but sometimes the unfortunate coincidence of an excess of drink, or the wrong words spoken in the wrong way at the wrong time, or just a memory forcing its way to the front of their minds was enough to rip the scabs off old wounds. As always, once the anger had started, something within both of them meant that it could not be stopped.

'Every time we meet', Winston told a friend, wonderingly, as if what happened between him and his son was out of his control, 'we seem to have a bloody row.'

It was hard for Winston not to compare his actual son to his son-in-law, Captain Christopher Soames, to whom he became increasingly close after his marriage to Mary in 1947. Clementine had initially found it hard to trust Soames, but as time went on, she came to both like and rely on him. This process was accelerated by the young couple's move into the house at the newly acquired Chartwell Farm (Soames was forced to leave the army after bursting a duodenal ulcer on honeymoon), as well as by Soames's assiduous flattery in the letters he wrote to his parents-in-law. Clementine got to keep Mary close and dote on her grandchildren ('You have so much fun with your children that I now realise how I missed out'), and Winston, once he had overcome his own doubts, discovered in Soames what he had lost in Randolph.

Mary's husband played cards,* listened to Winston, made him laugh, drank with him. And, unlike Duncan Sandys, who could not, according to Moran, 'follow Churchill's moods', Soames had a natural instinct for the things that pleased him. Winston liked his ebullience and the sense that he represented a new generation in politics.

Soames admired Winston unreservedly but was not afraid to speak his mind. As Julian Amery said: 'The great thing about Christopher is that he wasn't in the least frightened by the old gentleman.' Still, unlike Randolph, he was willing to be Winston's aide-de-camp. If Soames did want to have his own show, he did a good job of hiding it.

In 1949, encouraged by Soames, who was the family expert on the subject, Winston decided to follow his father into horse racing. Clementine was horrified, fearing this new passion would do irretrievable damage to her husband's reputation, but within two months, Lord Randolph's racing colours (pink with chocolate sleeves and cap) had been re-registered and a stable of seven racehorses assembled. The stable's star was Colonist II, whose portrait was hung beside Lord Randolph's own champion, L'Abbesse de Jouarre.†

Although Randolph and Christopher were 'neutrally friendly', with the younger man especially wary of the elder's temper, Randolph resented the fact that the Soameses' occupation of Chartwell Farm indicated that the promise he would inherit it seemed to have been forgotten. More than that, just as with Eden, he was lacerated by the idea that somebody else might have superseded him in his father's affections.

---

* Even in his gambling, Soames enjoyed more luck than Randolph. A diplomat who knew him well said of him: 'Plays bridge with a lot of flair, and makes money out of it at White's by staying sober.'
† After Colonist II went to stud following his last race, a flop, Winston recounted how 'I said to Colonist, "This is your last race. From now on you will spend your life in agreeable female company." I fear his mind was not on the race.'
　On another occasion, when asked if Colonist was still racing, Winston replied: 'No, he has given up racing. He is now rogering.'

But there was little Randolph could do except seethe. Aware that launching a direct attack on Soames would only worsen his relationship with his father, he allowed his bitterness to seep out in pointed asides about the man he scornfully called 'The Master of the Horse'. 'He hasn't opened a book in his life,' he once complained to an increasingly embarrassed audience, 'but he's shrewd, very shrewd. He'll get on whatever side of the Tories predominates.'

Randolph's divorce had finally come through in 1946. Before the war, when his and Winston's lives were so tightly stitched together that it would have been difficult to see where one man's started and the other's ended, he would have found solace in his father's company. Now he was deprived of this and had few people he could turn to. There was still nobody else who meant as much to him, nobody else whose approval he desired so strongly.

Randolph, who had always craved affection and hated to be alone, was deeply unhappy living by himself, first in Dolphin Square, where he rented a flat for a while, and later in a large house on Hobart Place in Belgravia.

He drank more and more, growing fat and grey. It was difficult to believe that he was still in his thirties. Although he relied upon newspaper work to make a living, he told friends that it was 'difficult for him sometimes to reconcile his "dignity" as an Englishman and a Churchill with his reporting'.

He still talked about becoming prime minister, and yet it was obvious to everybody except him that this would require a turn in his fortunes far stranger and more profound than his father had enjoyed in May 1940. Although he affected to despise the Conservative Party establishment ('We were never Tories and we never will be!' Randolph had drunkenly bellowed at Woodrow Wyatt. 'We just make use of the Tory Party'), he was dependent upon their favour if he wanted to make any progress. He was anathema to both Labour and the ailing Liberals; and while he occasionally still fantasised about the emergence of a centre party, this was a fragile thread upon which to hang his hopes.

His life became disfigured by a sequence of angry scenes. It could seem as if he no longer wanted to talk, just quarrel. What had once been provocative had become merely tiresome. Even those, like Beaverbrook, who had once been sympathetic to Randolph, thought the way he treated Winston was outrageous.

Although pursued by a horde of financial and legal difficulties – he was still dependent on his father to bail him out when the pile of bills on his secretary's desk grew too high, and sometimes had to sell possessions* – and very often in quite severe pain in consequence of those wounds he had received during the war and which had never quite healed, he continued to live the life of a princeling. One could find him in his beige camel-hair overcoat looming massively in the doorway of the Ivy, cigarette between nicotine-stained fingers, or dining majestically at the Beefsteak. Most often, however, he would be at the bar at White's, where he played billiards for £50 a game. His son spent long empty hours waiting outside for Randolph to 'finish his drink' or dictate his latest article for the *Evening Standard* over the phone.

Young Winston learned that life with his father was like 'going around hand in hand with a walking volcano'. One moment everything was happy and serene, the next it seemed that Armageddon had broken out. He learned to recognise the changes in Randolph's demeanour that indicated if a waiter had been slow or surly, a taxi driver ignorant or a British Railways employee incompetent. This was traumatic for young Winston, who averted his eyes when his father abused those unable to answer back. (His discomfort was only slightly alleviated when he learned that Randolph was apt to heap even greater abuse on powerful figures like press barons who certainly could answer back. And although Randolph was often foul to waiters – those at the Savoy actually paid each other 'good money' not to serve him – he might later apologise to them with tears in his eyes.)†

---

* Evelyn Waugh reported splitting 'a magnum of champagne in the afternoon with Randolph who tried to sell me a £100 gold cigar case. Instead I bought a £20 edition of Pope.'

† As always, Randolph was just as capable of great, disinterested generosity. He gave generous encouragement and support to young MPs like his former partner in Preston, Julian Amery, and stood aside at the November 1945 Bromley by-election to allow Harold Macmillan to take what was then a safe Tory seat.

It never lasted long. Soon the stream of fun and stories would begin again. His cousin Nancy Mitford had a similar experience of Randolph's mercurial behaviour. After the war, he had been commissioned by a US newspaper group to write a weekly column on Paris, a job he outsourced to Nancy, who sent him chatty paragraphs on black markets, musical soirées and the pathetic situation of the writer Henry de Montherlant: 'Montherlant is hiding in Paris but nobody bothers to look for him. Rather humiliating, like when one hides for sardines & nobody comes!'

Randolph repaid her by writing 'an absolutely hateful' article about her lover Gaston Palewski in a French communist paper. Despite all this, they stayed in touch. There was always enough charm left over to win back even those who had sworn never to see him again. When his anger and bitterness receded, his friends saw once more the affectionate, impulsive, innocent boy they had first come to love.

'You see,' Nancy explained, 'he rings up, sounding like a rusty old bicycle going up a hill, & is very disarming – then one goes to see him & is subjected to an hour's bellowing roaring unpleasantness. I always say never again & always succumb.'

Randolph became ever more vulnerable to romantic fantasies about personal and political success. These alternated with his childlike losses of control when angry and his perplexing displays of bravado. In the years after the war, he travelled more and more for his work as a journalist and took on numerous speaking tours of the United States: it was as if he was afraid that staying in one place for too long would force him to examine his unhappiness.

His peregrinations were almost always attended by trouble of some sort. And, more often than not, he was its direct cause. When invited to make a speech at a Red Army parade in Moscow, he tried to give the Russians, who were bemused by how Winston had allowed himself to be deposed, a lecture on parliamentary procedure, which evolved into a critique of the USSR.* An altercation with an American

---

* On a visit to the British Embassy in Moscow ten years later, a chain-smoking, whisky-and-soda-drinking Randolph was found by a Soviet official admiring the Kremlin from a first-floor window.

plumber, who had complained that Winston Churchill was 'putting all those kings back' in Europe, made the front page of the *New York Times*.

Isaiah Berlin, whose fondness for Randolph did not preclude thinking, like Diana Cooper, that he was 'not altogether house-trained', remembered an encounter in the British Embassy in Washington just before his father's celebrated Fulton Address in 1946. Randolph flung open the door of Berlin's office and emerged into the room violently flushed, with one of his trouser legs ripped just beneath the knee and a wound under his left eye, to which he was pressing a handkerchief. Berlin asked him what had happened.

I went to see a man in the State Department, called, I believe, Braden. He seems to have occupied some kind of post in the Argentine. I believe he was American Ambassador there. I tried to interview him about Latin America. In the course of the interview he made highly offensive remarks about England and her policies. I struck him at once. I always do that to anyone who attacks my country; don't you?*

It was magnificent, in its own way, but futile. He would return from his trips 'exactly 3 times as fat as before', his pockets empty, and realise that nothing had changed in his absence.

In February 1947, alone in Salt Lake City, Randolph took stock of his life. He was travelling on another lecture tour through the United States, a country that was full of memories of a happy time when it seemed that life stood waiting for him. In the past months he had been in France, Africa, Greece and Scandinavia. Not long before, he

---

'Don't you think that is a fine view of the Kremlin?' the Russian asked.

'Yes, indeed, and, furthermore, I have a brother-in-law called Sandys who could send the whole place to kingdom-come in three hours and twenty minutes.'

Fire hoses were sent for and only an urgent intervention from the ambassador prevented an actual outbreak of hostilities.

* Nevertheless, the new world seemed to have more patience for Randolph's excesses than the old. 'Do you think I should use THE NAME?' he asked his friend Alastair Forbes before a Washington party, as if it were a nuclear weapon to be deployed.

had also been the subject of a vicious attack by the *Daily Mirror's* 'Cassandra' column, which called him a 'pale satellite of another's fame who reflects a little light and some glory from being the son of Winston Churchill. He generates no heat of his own, except the spark of controversy which only becomes dangerous when introduced by the potency of his father's name into the arsenal of public affairs.'

In the last few days, he had received a letter from his father full of advice and reflections about his future. Winston's deep concern for his welfare meant a huge amount to Randolph, as he explained: 'Though I always try & put a brave face on it to the world, & indeed to you, I must own that I am myself far from pleased with my present situation.'

Randolph was still as committed as ever to the idea of a political career. It was the only life he was interested in, he said, and one for which he believed he possessed the sorts of 'aptitudes & abilities which are granted to few'. Although he recognised he had made mistakes, including ignoring Winston's advice to become a lawyer, he was convinced that he had been the victim of bad luck. And, of course, he was still young – a few years short of forty.

There was much self-recrimination in the letter. Randolph described sloth as his 'besetting sin', acknowledged the extent of his improvidence and berated himself for his overconfidence. 'I always expected', he said, 'that political life would suddenly open up for me.'

At other times he was defiant. 'There is no other Englishman of my age who knows this country as well as I do or has so many influential American friends. There is no other Englishman of my age who can get his articles regularly printed in the American press; and there is nobody else alive of any age (except yourself) who could have had the amazing <u>oratorical</u> success I have had on this present tour . . . I promise you it is the sober truth.'

'I know', he wrote to Winston, 'how much you want me to achieve "solid" success in your lifetime. But you must realise how improbable that is; – even harder for me than for Duncan.'

As unhappy as he was with his current progress, he assured his father, 'I have confidence that I will eventually make my mark &

carry on the tradition. It's very hard however for two generations to carry the same flag simultaneously.'

More and more, the letter became a naked plea for understanding.

I know how often I have offended you by my clumsy attempts to stand on my own feet, & develop my own personality and make my own way in life . . . Please don't expect too much of me now. Believe instead, I beg you, that I have no other ambition than to be ultimately judged an honourable & faithful son. No day passes but that you are constantly in my thoughts & I am grateful that you think so often of me. Give me your confidence & I shall not fail you.

Many of his arguments with Winston in the past had been variations on a theme. Over the war, they had returned endlessly to the same subjects. But reading the letter, it does not feel inconceivable that this was the first time, amidst all the millions of words they had spoken to each other, the thousands of hours they had spent in each other's company, that Randolph had made such a naked appeal to his father.

We do not have Winston's reply.

Randolph returned home to his life of drinking, shouting and trouble, and in most other respects the years after the war were ones of stasis. On the surface, there was great activity; underneath, little really changed.

Randolph swapped his unhappy marriage with Pamela for another unhappy marriage, in 1948, to June Osbourne, the 'wide-eyed, elfin-faced and much sought-after' daughter of a colonel; she dressed elegantly and gave a good impression of quiet confidence; all this was a façade that concealed 'a mass of uncertainties. She was highly-strung, tense and given to a fretfulness that called for subtle handling and deep understanding.'*

---

* 'I do not know the young lady,' Evelyn observed when he learned of his friend's engagement, 'but she must be possessed of magnificent courage. Does the colonel, her father (also notably courageous I observe) receive you in his house?'

They fought grievously even before they had tied the knot, but this did not seem to bother Randolph. (Laura Charteris to Randolph: 'You can't seriously think of going through with it.' Randolph in answer: 'Of course I am. It's a scientific fact that couples who fight before marriage live happily ever after.')

Undaunted, the couple moved into 12 Catherine Place, a London house that Winston had arranged for the trust to buy them as a wedding present. In 1949, a daughter, Arabella, was born. Randolph and June dined with the Digbys; Winston continued to correspond cheerfully with them.

Winston, perhaps more quickly than anybody had anticipated, recovered much of his vitality. It was soon clear that he had little intention of settling into obscurity. Immediately after the 1945 election, he had returned to the coy games he had played before the war, ruminating out loud on the certainty of his retirement. On a recuperative trip to Lake Como with Sarah, he had told her as they gazed out over the water, 'I'm damned glad to be out of it. I shall paint for the rest of my days. I've never painted so well before.'

This resolution barely outlasted the trip. By the time he was back, the 'royal jelly' of politics and power had regained its old hold on him. Before long, Winston was pacing up and down as he talked to his doctor, Lord Moran, telling him about the 'very vigorous' speech he had made in the House at 2.00 a.m. the night before. Suddenly, he stopped and poked his nose close to the doctor's face: 'A short time ago I was ready to retire and die gracefully. Now I'm going to stay and have them out.' His vehemence mounted – 'I'll tear their bleeding entrails out of them. I'm in pretty good fettle' – then subsided into something more contemplative: 'It's the Jerome blood.'

19

I Love You More Than Any Man
or Woman I Have Ever Met

IN THE DAYS leading up to Winston's journey to the Conservative Party's October 1952 conference in Scarborough, his office rang Randolph twice to see what train he would be taking. Randolph's heart filled with joy.

Winston had swept back into Downing Street in the previous year's general election. Randolph was peripherally involved in the campaign, drafting some of Winston's broadcasts and sending him eccentric congratulations when he felt his father had excelled himself ('YOUR MAGNIFICENT MASTERLY MEATY SPEECH').

Randolph's efforts were, however, chiefly concentrated on securing his own return to Parliament: he was once more trying to beat his old friend Michael Foot to the Plymouth Devonport seat.*

Randolph's approach to electioneering remained quixotic. He thought politics should be fun and arranged his campaigns accordingly. He assembled three butchers, named Winston, Randolph and Randolph, to meet him, his father and his eleven-year-old son as they stepped off the sleeper on the way to support him at a rowdy, open-air meeting. He also chartered a 'colossal' funfair. Sadly, on the day it should have opened, it poured with rain.†

---

* He had contested the seat for the first time at the general election of 1950, when despite Conservative gains, Labour held on to a slim majority. To Evelyn Waugh: 'I tell you what the trouble at Devonport was, old boy. There just weren't enough Conservatives.'
† This ebullience was paired with a staggering lack of grace. Nigel Nicolson once called in to see Randolph in his office in Devonport during one of his election campaigns. As they were talking, a young man came in to ask Randolph if he could do anything to help him. He was nice, inoffensive but wearing quite a dirty mackintosh. Out of the blue, Randolph flew into a rage: 'I don't want men in dirty

For a few moments on polling day, it seemed as if his efforts had paid off. Randolph had been so nervous at the count that he left the room and returned just as they were finishing to ask the town clerk how he was getting on. 'Thirty something thousand and something,' he was told. 'Isn't that rather good?' 'Oh yes you're quite safe. We've only a few more to count and they can't affect the result.' Dazed with joy, he rushed out to tell his committee. Two minutes later, the town clerk shuffled back out: 'Oh Mr Churchill I made such a silly mistake. I gave you Mr Foot's figures.'

Insult was added to injury. Randolph was booed and wolf-whistled as his defeat was announced. 'I cannot recall any [election]', one witness remembered, 'where the mob was filled with such bitterness and hatred as that night in Devonport . . . the crowd was howling like a pack of hyenas baying for blood.'

The local police superintendent suggested that it would be safest to exit through the rear of the building to avoid the angry crowd. Randolph exploded with rage: 'I don't go out of back doors.'

Instead, over a dozen burly policemen made a path to Randolph's car through a mass of men and women who pulled at June's hair, kicked at their shins and spat on them. It was enough to move even Evelyn Waugh to sympathy: 'Nothing he has ever done', he reflected, 'deserves such punishment.'

Winston had done better. After six years, he was back in Downing Street. Stung though he was by suggestions that he was too old or somehow unsuitable to be a peacetime prime minister ('It's a big job to take on at my age, but there's no alternative. It's my duty'), in returning to office he had effaced the bitter humiliation of 1945 and could, as Clementine had urged him, retire gracefully. He said he would within a year.

---

mackintoshes hanging around this office. Get out, get out.' There were stories that he left Plymouth after the election without saying a word to any of the people who had helped canvass for him. He plainly had no idea what people were doing for him behind the scenes and took everything for granted. (This was not new. Johnny Churchill thought it was the result of growing up surrounded by great men at Chartwell: 'When you're living with those sorts of people, everything seems easy . . . If you want to do something, it's done. If you want to order something, it's ordered.')

*Winston at Chartwell in 1950. Although he was in his
seventies he remained as hungry for power as ever.*

Slowly, the seventy-seven-year-old Winston assembled the men
who had served him so well years before. Pug Ismay, his chief military
assistant during the war, who had long retired from public life, was
asleep when, late on the night of 26 October, his phone rang.

He recognised the voice at the end of the line immediately: 'Is that
you, Pug? . . . I want to see you at once. You aren't asleep are you?'

Fifteen minutes later, having splashed his face with water and rushed
to 28 Hyde Park Gate, he was Secretary of State for Commonwealth
Relations.

Jock Colville was at Newmarket races the following morning
when a Jockey Club steward tracked him down in the crowd and told
him the prime minister wanted to speak to him.

'Whatever he asks you to do, say no,' Colville's wife told him, to no
avail. Over the next four days, Anthony Eden was brought in to lead
the House and head the Foreign Office. Rab Butler was chancellor

of the exchequer; Oliver Lyttelton, colonial secretary; the Prof, paymaster general; Harold Macmillan, minister of housing; Duncan Sandys, minister of supply; and Christopher Soames became Winston's Parliamentary Private Secretary.

Randolph wrote to congratulate his father on the 'imaginative' appointments in the Cabinet, but his letter was tinged was sadness. There was nothing for Randolph, and no sign that there was space for him to reprise the informal role – part confidant, part adviser, part jester – that he had played during the war.

He did discover some compensations after his father's return to power. In the days after the election, as Winston was forming his government, Randolph took to calling his enemies in the Conservative Party at dinnertime and having them fetched to the telephone with the message that Mr Churchill wanted to talk to them. The excitement of being summoned by the new prime minister was swiftly followed by the horror of discovering a cackling Randolph at the other end of the line.

That this was no surprise was a measure of the state of his relationship with his father, and the stranded nature of his own political career. His marriage was in an appalling mess – and had in fact been in trouble almost before it began – and although he had entered his fifth decade, he was still dependent upon his parents' generosity to keep him afloat.

Randolph continued to fantasise about leading the country himself, but the chances of this happening were vanishingly small. More and more often, in conversations with friends, he would say, mournfully, that he 'could do nothing' while his father was still alive. This was true, at least in part. But it was a useful way of concealing a larger, more uncomfortable truth. The idea that once his father died, or retired, the way would be open was a comforting fiction. It was easier to blame Winston, the man on whose behalf he had expended what political capital he had ever possessed. In reality, it was already too late.

He had never really been forgiven for Wavertree. He exacerbated this situation both by failing to show any contrition for the damage he had caused and through his constant agitation on his father's behalf during the wilderness years. Beyond all this, he was too often angry, too often drunk, too often gratuitously offensive, and too unwilling to engage in the sort of patient grind upon which careers were built in the twentieth century.

But most distressing of all to him was the way in which his bond with his father had become so corroded that it was at once jagged enough to hurt both men, and fragile enough to seem as if it might crumble altogether.

Randolph did not think he had changed much in the past decade. He was certain that Winston had. The feeling that ran between the two men had not ebbed – Winston had, he said, 'a deep animal love' for his son – but its nature had changed. As time went on, Winston claimed that he liked Randolph less.*

Winston preferred to take Mary and Christopher Soames to the theatre, or sit with Mary while she played him the Gilbert and Sullivan records she had bought him during the war. He confided to her as he had once confided in his son: he talked about his fear at the prospect of another war, and his disquiet at the rising cost of living, but he also talked fondly of episodes from his childhood.

Worse, as far as Randolph was concerned, was the way in which the man who for so long had told him he was destined for glory had started to treat him as a failure. Winston was no longer able, or maybe even willing, to disguise his disappointment in front of other people. Randolph would arrive at Chartwell, determined to be emollient, and find only that the person he loved most in the world repeatedly 'disregarded & snubbed him'.

When they met now, he believed, they did so 'occasionally, formally, half-heartedly, almost as a duty & with manifest misgivings on both sides'. Randolph seldom visited his father, and when he did

---

* Winston's personal secretary Anthony Montague Browne suggests this should be treated with a pinch of salt, offering an exchange between Winston and Clementine as an example of how Winston was guilty of occasional acts of overemphasis.

In the conclusion to an argument, Clementine swept out, saying: 'Winston, I have been married to you for forty-five years, for better AND FOR WORSE.'

Winston was silent for a moment and then said solemnly to his secretary: 'I am the most unhappy of men.'

Montague Browne saw that this was so patently absurd that he laughed out loud. Winston watched, benevolently, aware he had gone too far.

so was unlikely to stay the night: long stretches of time in each other's company offered too much potential for conflict. Anthony Montague Browne, who watched the Churchill family closely, saw how hours of cheer and affection could be wiped out by a misunderstanding over whether or not Winston had consented to allow his son to read a confidential letter from Eisenhower. There was something terrible, remembered Montague Browne, about watching the way in which the two men could not meet without striking damaging sparks.

Three generations of Churchills at the coronation of Queen Elizabeth II in 1953.

Montague Browne thought that Winston's blunt rejection of his son was excessive. This was partly a function of Winston's obliviousness to the impact his behaviour could have on others. On three different occasions during the war, Winston had promised Sir Alan Brooke the supreme command of the Allied forces. And yet when it was confirmed that Eisenhower would be given the role, Winston could not understand Brooke's bitter disappointment: 'Not for one moment did he realise what this meant to me,' Brooke recalled. 'He offered no sympathy, no regrets at having had to change his mind, and dealt with the matter as if it were one of minor importance.'

The same was true here: it was as if Winston could not see the devastating effect his dismissive behaviour had upon his son. More and more often, Winston gave signs that he no longer trusted him. During one of Randolph's rare visits to Chartwell, he tried to rescue some of the house's treasures that he felt had been neglected. Randolph found a complete signed set of Mark Twain that the author had given to Winston. The books had been left in the stables at the bottom of the hill during the war, and now they lay abandoned, getting damp and eaten by mice.

Approaching his father, he told him how valuable the set was: 'If you don't want these books it would be a pity to let them rot and I should very much like them.'

'Well, my boy, I'll think about it.'

The next evening Randolph saw a mackintosh-clad Winston strolling up the hill in the rain with the books under his arm. He was on his way to hide them.

What Randolph wanted more than anything was to be admitted once more as an ally and intimate of his father, to resume the place at his side, working closely with him, that had been his before and was now occupied by his brother-in-law, Christopher Soames. This is why the call from Winston's office, which implied that he might be re-admitted to his father's inner circle, felt so exciting to him.

His happiness did not last long. When he telephoned Winston the following morning, he discovered that his presence was the last thing the prime minister seemed to want. Winston took pains to establish that Randolph was catching the 2.00 p.m. service, then told him that he would be on the train leaving an hour later. Please do not change your plans, he told Randolph, for I need to be alone to work on my speech. Winston, accompanied by Clementine and Christopher Soames, duly travelled north. Randolph did not.

In a furious scribbled note sent on 9 October, he told his father that he had discovered that Winston's reluctance to see him was not, as he had told Randolph on the telephone, because he needed privacy to write his speech but rather 'distaste for my presence in your entourage'. He was sure his father would not be surprised to learn that he would not be coming to Scarborough at all.

Randolph told his father that to disregard such an insult would be a 'supreme act of moral cowardice'. He reminded him of his loyalty and devotion and the fact that his admiration for him had grown with every passing year. 'I love you', Randolph wrote, 'more than any man or woman I have ever met', but when all this was 'scorned as worthless', it would inevitably lead to jealousy and resentment.

Two days later, Winston tried to pacify his son while at the same time sticking stubbornly to the explanation he had given earlier. The same day, over fifteen pages of the same angry scrawl he had used for his letter the week before – with words blotted out and others crammed into tight spaces between the lines, his desperation to express himself made clearer with every sentence – Randolph replied. His screed was part accusation, part howl of rage.

Randolph levelled the same charges again and again, one minute self-pitying, the next almost shivering with rage.

'I ask something now,' he wrote:

> that you should try to understand me (and not as you imagine I am & think I ought to be): that you should try once more to show me the love & trust which you brought me up to expect & value above all else in this life.

And then, at the letter's end, he declared that none of what he had said – not a word – was intended as self-justification or reproach: 'The only object of this excruciating exercise has been to explain some of the reasons for the wayward conduct & profound unhappiness of Your devoted son, Randolph.'

As so often, there is no record of a reply. Winston still knew how to assuage his son's hurt: a few kind words, a gift, anything that allowed Randolph to believe for a moment that he was still special was usually enough. It is perhaps telling that on 21 December 1952 Randolph thanked his father for a 'princely Christmas present', which filled him with an inexpressible gratitude. It was, he said, welcome not only in material terms, but 'as a renewed expression of your affection'.

There were some days when Randolph's visits were a source of joy and contentment to his parents. In February 1953 Clementine could write of one such occasion. 'Randolph & June came to luncheon to-day. They looked happy & June very pretty.' As Winston's affection for his son appeared to be waning, Clementine's own feelings for her son grew warmer. She and Randolph went house-hunting together and shopped for garden chairs. Clementine signed her letters by saying, 'I hope to see you soon my darling Boy.' Christmases could still be happy, joy-filled occasions, with Christopher playing Santa Claus and Randolph ringing sleigh bells off stage.

Randolph routinely sent his articles to Winston for his approval, and they posted each other books that they thought would touch on their respective interests and passions. They still met, playing cards in a room half in darkness, lit by a single lamp that illuminated the small card table's green baize.

And when he was calm and sober, Randolph was sensible of how much reason he had to feel grateful to them. 'It was a great surprise & help to receive the handsome cheque of £350 from the Trustees,' he wrote to Clementine in March that year. 'Thank you so much for this thoughtful act which adds so much to the security of Winston & Arabella.' Speaking cheerfully about a forthcoming visit, he mentioned how he and June 'are so much looking forward to bringing Arabella to Chequers'.

Moreover, whatever the state of their private relationship, there was never any question of Randolph's public support for his father wavering. Randolph could not allow any criticism of Winston. It seemed a matter of psychological necessity to him, and he was willing to lose friends to sustain it. Nor would he entertain the suggestion that Winston had been anything other than an ideal father. In *Twenty-One Years*, the sloppy, vague memoir Randolph wrote in 1964, a year before Winston's death, he repeatedly insists on this. He was willing to go further in person.

The psychoanalyst Rupert Strong, a distant cousin, was a close neighbour when the Churchill families lived at Lullenden. His memories were mostly bucolic: of burrowing in sand cliffs, bird-nesting, climbing trees and manipulating in mock battles the huge gun captured from the Germans that stood at the end of the drive leading to the Sussex manor house. But he obviously saw, or thought he saw, something else.

Two years before Randolph's own death, Strong encountered Randolph at a talk at Trinity College, Dublin. Strong spoke with his cousin about the time they had spent at Lullenden and also about psychoanalysis, specifically whether he would accept that some of Diana's troubles 'stemmed from childhood causes'. He later wrote to Randolph's one-time fiancée Kay Halle, 'I knew enough of the facts to be quite sure of the ground I was treading on. Perhaps I was insensitive. Perhaps I was wrong to intrude so delicate a matter on such an occasion.'

Strong was shocked at the impact of his questions. Randolph was incandescent. As he stabbed the air with his glass, Randolph asked: Who was Strong to question the upbringing of the Churchill family? He and his sisters had had a flawless relationship with their parents. 'You nonentity,' he screamed at his cousin. 'You utter nonentity. I refuse to discuss your crackpot ideas.'

At this point Strong withdrew from the room and escaped into the night.

Lord Stanley of Alderley, another cousin of the Churchills, managed to catch Strong before he had gone too far.

'I wish to apologise for Randolph's behaviour,' he said. 'When he's like that he can be a first class swine.' And then, after a moment, almost lovingly, 'But it's only the drink. I think I agree with most of what you said.'

Whatever the truth of the matter, it was the last time Strong ever saw Randolph.

Winston's second term was supposed to have been a celebration of his return to power; instead, it became a drawn-out psychodrama in which his own evident signs of ageing were used by many of those who he thought were his intimates as an argument for handing his crown on to a younger man.

James Lees-Milne noted his increasing resemblance to a 'small, fat and frail doll or baby, with a white and pink face, most unnatural in an adult, and no lines at all. There is a celluloid quality about the skin which is alarming. He shuffles . . . I suppose he does look old, or rather unreal. It is hard to detect a human being behind the mask. Everyone deferred and played up to him when he did vouchsafe a word, laughed rather too hilariously.'

When Harold Nicolson asked Bob Boothby how he had found their old friend the day after he had returned to office, Boothby answered sadly, 'Very, very old, tragically old.'

A combination of age, excess, and a stroke he had suffered eighteen months before, had robbed Winston of the vitality that had distinguished him during the war. He was increasingly deaf, his memory was less formidable than before and the arteries that fed his brain were closing up.

It was soon obvious that the demands of governing in peacetime were not as exciting to Winston as the stimulation offered by a wartime premiership. He was not interested in what Harold Macmillan called 'the vast dullness of the administrative structure'. In Winston's view, government had become more complicated: 'we have to consider intricate matters, valuations and that kind of thing, which never came before the Cabinets I can remember.' The new prime minister's priorities did not extend much beyond putting a stop to rationing and reversing as many of Clement Attlee's socialist reforms as possible.

It was not just that he was liable to lapse into dreamy states where he produced a series of unconnected sentences, or drop off to sleep mid-morning while dictating, he also started to play hooky from his prime-ministerial duties to read books, sometimes polishing them off in single eight-hour sittings. 'I get bitten by books nowadays,' he told his doctor. An increasing number of mornings were wasted feeding fish rather than attending to Cabinet business.

What he still enjoyed were foreign affairs; the feeling that things were about to happen could still prick his ears up. He loved those moments when he could stand, homburg hat and gloves in one hand, gold-tipped cane in the other, at the top of a plane's stairs as Eisenhower and his administration waved at him from the Washington tarmac.

And yet even these experiences came tinged with sadness: England, in its fallen state, could no longer address the United States as an equal. These days it had to come cap in hand to its old ally and do its bidding. The empire, he believed, had been thrown away 'by a hideous act of self-mutilation, astounding to every nation of the world'; postwar 'London was a world-centre of impotence'.

Although he felt this as a deep humiliation, he still believed he could make a difference that nobody else could. 'I don't think we've done badly in the last two years,' he would claim. 'The Government has been sensible if not brilliant. Doing nothing is often very important in the art of government. You see, I have influence and a store of experience which no one else has, and I can decide things at a meeting as well as ever I could.'

Winston had talked often during the opposition years about the tragedy of FDR, who had not left a successor. He would not make the same mistake and would hand over to Anthony Eden when he could no longer carry on himself. It was understood that 'when the Conservatives came back there must be a full partnership between himself and Anthony.'

Once he had returned to Downing Street, however, he gave no sign of wishing to give up the reins. Instead of making plans for the succession, he teased Eden, reminding him how William Gladstone had formed his last administration at the age of eighty-four. He told Jock Colville that he would not be hounded out of office just because his second-in-command wanted his job, and talked with distaste of 'Anthony's hungry eyes'.

His stroke in the summer of 1953 should have been a golden opportunity for Eden to press his case and accelerate the handover. But it took place while Eden was away in the United States having an operation on his gall bladder. When the Edens returned in July, in time for a weekend in Chequers, Winston suggested that he should hang on until autumn, explaining to Clarissa: 'Anthony must get his strength back.'

Winston's sly game continued. He would tell the people around him that he had set a date for his departure, and then almost in his next breath he would inform foreign dignitaries that he would not leave until he dropped down dead.

It led, inevitably, to bad feelings on all sides. A point came when Eden was no longer mentioned by name at Chartwell; instead, he was referred to as 'the Successor'. Randolph, who contended that Eden's supporters had been conducting a 'loud-mouthed' campaign to speed up his father's departure, did what he could to frustrate it. As always, he took Winston's cause to perverse extremes, yet in this case it was spiced by his own personal jealousy.

The languorous, elegant Anthony Eden with his wife Clarissa, Jack Churchill's daughter.

Although he might have been expected to feel some empathy for somebody else whose life was also being bent out of shape by Winston's refusal to stand aside, Randolph saw Eden, whom he called 'the Jerk', as a small man trying to wear a big man's boots, and he wanted to expose it. While his father had quickly moved on from the bitterness of the wilderness years, Randolph was still mired in it. He could not forgive Eden for the way he and his 'little fidgety, busybody faction' had kept his distance from Winston when it had been politically expedient to do so, or for the pusillanimous nature of his resignation when, belatedly (in Randolph's reckoning at least), it had come. Randolph maintained that his objections were political, not personal, but few believed him. His behaviour was so extreme that it frequently led to rows with his father.*

In the face of all this, Eden was reduced to petulant shows of exasperation. 'I cannot go on like this with the old man,' he exploded, 'I must escape somehow.'

Winston's departure from office, when it finally came in April 1955, was a relief to almost everybody except the prime minister himself.

Clementine had been ground down by the demands of the second term. She was frequently swamped by weariness and depression so pronounced that it troubled those who witnessed it. And yet time and time again, no matter how low her spirits in private, she would have to perform in public. Mary remembered how one night, ahead of a Downing Street dinner, Clementine was behaving in such a hysterical, agitated way that her daughter begged her to be allowed to tell guests that she was ill. Clementine agreed and Mary went to tell Winston.

But just as the first guest arrived, Clementine appeared, immaculate, her diamonds glittering, her hair perfect. These performances exerted a toll on Clementine, and also on those around her. She could be unbearably demanding, even on occasion becoming difficult and aggressive to Winston, who usually endured her behaviour rather than kick back at it: oblivious to so many other consequences of his single-minded obsession with power, he knew that she had never wanted this.

In the days leading up to her husband's resignation on 6 April, Clementine suffered a recurrence of the neuritis that had pursued her for so many years, which at times had caused pain so severe that she had to wear a surgical collar. Her physical discomfort matched Winston's misery. His last weeks in Downing Street were suffused with sadness that sometimes edged into bitterness, with Winston

---

* Years later, as Winston junior talked with Lord Blakenham about who he might speak to when researching his biography of Randolph, Eden's name came up in conversation. You could approach Eden, Lord Blakenham mused, but 'If you mention Randolph, I think he'll be sick.'

lashing out, imputing malign motives to everyone around him. In her diary, Mary, a regular visitor to No. 10, noted how painful the spectacle was to those who cared for him. 'Mama feels it – she said "It's the first death – & for him, a death in life."'

On the night before the handover, Winston gave a dinner for Elizabeth II. The outgoing prime minister used the occasion to toast the queen, speaking warmly of 'the wise and kindly way of life of which Your Majesty is the young and gleaming champion'.

Randolph spent the evening pursuing his increasingly obsessive campaign against his father's successor. Anthony Eden, the incoming prime minister, had been so keen to shake the queen's hand that some suggested he had jumped the queue. In retaliation the Duchess of Westminster tried to put her foot through Clarissa Eden's train. Clarissa's troubles did not end there. Randolph, who was drunk, chased Clarissa around the room, trying to read her an offensive article he had written for *Punch* about her husband. Finally, he cornered her. Looking 'huge, pale, sweating', he told her, 'I suppose you know I'm against the new regime.'

Clarissa replied that she had guessed as much, and as pleased as she was that he retained sufficient integrity to keep his distance from her while he was out attacking her husband to anybody who would listen, she was still sad that he placed their 'friendship lower than the pleasure he derived from a cheap campaign in clubs'.

It is difficult to know what Randolph thought his conduct would achieve. Perhaps he thought the conversation was a success. Clarissa did not, and their relationship never recovered.

The next morning Winston woke, threw off his bedclothes and padded over to his window to look out at Horse Guards Parade. 'I am going to bury myself at Chartwell,' he told Lord Moran. 'I shall see no one. I have to deal with an immense correspondence. I am in a good frame of mind, unjealous.' At this he grinned broadly.

'There is no doubt it does me good to be petted. I don't know what it would have been like if there had been newspapers [his resignation occurred during the middle of a printers' strike]. I might live two or three years. I have been blessed with good health. My nerves are good. I don't worry about things and I don't get upset, though occasionally I may become bad-tempered.'

He fell silent; then, after a pause, looked up.

'If it were painless, swift, unexpected . . .' He did not continue, as if he would not, or could not, finish the sentence.

Winston chaired his last Cabinet, and then went to Buckingham Palace to resign. Pamela came to lunch.

Randolph went, as usual, to White's. As he left, he saw a policeman ticketing a car on the street outside: 'The Eden terror', Randolph announced, 'has begun.'

The ebullience Winston displayed in the days immediately following his resignation was quickly followed by depression and lethargy. He seemed to become slower and sleepier with every day that passed.

Winston was bored, his mood changeable. He was unsettled by the speed and completeness with which 'letting the trappings of power fall in a heap to the ground' had changed him.

In May he told Lord Moran, 'Since I retired and relaxed I have noticed a decline in my interest in things – oh, in everything. I hate London. I don't want to see people. They don't interest me. I am bored with politics.'

The man who had dominated the conversation at every meal now sat 'all huddled up in silence'. It was suddenly clear that he could not hear a great deal of what was being said. Sometimes, when there was a gale of laughter, someone would have to explain to him what it was about.

Even the adulation he received wherever he went – when Winston left a restaurant, its orchestra would routinely play 'For He's a Jolly Good Fellow' – or his old standbys, painting and Chartwell, or even an increased interest in horse racing could do little to assuage his misery.

Randolph stayed with Winston that August and did what he could to soothe him. On the morning he headed off, he left a letter out for his father to find. Entitled 'Pensées matinales et filiales (presque lapidaires)', it assured him, 'Power must pass and vanish. Glory . . . alone remains. Your glory is enshrined for ever', and ended with a plea: 'So please try to be as happy as you have a right and (if it is not too presumptuous for a son to say it) a duty to be. And, by being happy, make those who love you happy too.'

★

Winston's resignation was not the only significant event in Randolph's life that spring. After a long search for a country property, he bought Stour, an elegant pink Georgian mansion on the border between Essex and Suffolk.

His move out of London was a way of breaking away from the heavy gambling and drinking at White's. More than that, it was an acknowledgement − even if, to begin with, it was on a subconscious level − that he would never fulfil the ambitions he had nurtured for so much of his life. The break was far from clean; he could still be tormented by visions of what might have been, and even what still might be. But he was beginning to understand that the time had come instead to divert his energies to something else.

Stour became, very soon, the centre of his universe. Much to the surprise of his cronies from White's, who could not believe that he really wanted to live in the provinces, and also of his mother, he took to country life with the relish of a convert, gardening all day and telephoning through the night.

The lawns and woodland surrounding the house, which had fallen into disarray, were reclaimed. He filled the woods with thousands of daffodils and snowdrops, the gardens with walnut, wisteria and mulberry trees, and Stour itself with roses, peonies and dahlias. Nothing excited him more than the planting of the gently sloping avenue of pleached limes, where on hot days he could walk in the shade with his black pugs at his heel.* (Even as a gardener he was boisterous. One guest remembered his host accosting a fallen elm: 'You bastard, how could you do this to me?')

He took great pleasure too in sitting beneath the arbour he had designed, on which climbing roses, honeysuckle and clematis all tangled together, and listening to Arabella reciting the poems he and Winston loved so much. On these occasions, remembered guests, he appeared suffused with joy.

---

* Before long, he was 'generously' sharing his gardening advice, with his opinions somehow finding their way into the columns of ladies' magazines. This was despite the fact that he rarely, if ever, got dirt under his fingernails (he saw his role similar to the constitutional monarch as defined by Walter Bagehot: 'to be consulted, to encourage and to warn'), and also that he relied heavily on the knowledge of Xenia Field, the *Daily Mirror*'s gardening correspondent, and a near neighbour.

As always, his thoughts turned towards his father. Randolph wanted to show off his home and the new seriousness of his life to Winston, and did everything he could to try to coax him into a visit. The letters he wrote to Clementine trying to enlist her support resemble those Winston sent to Jennie so many years previously, begging for more of his parents' time.

'Do please try and persuade Papa to come,' he wrote in September 1955. 'Of course we should be delighted for you to come to luncheon one day, but much prefer if you would spend a night or two.'

In the end, Winston made only one visit to Stour. Randolph's old school friend, Lord Blakenham, a near neighbour, was another guest that weekend. Randolph was, he recalled, being 'very naughty and drinking far too much but he was thrilled to have his father there'. Even now, though, he could not help himself. Drink always washed away his resolutions to be good. Randolph resumed his tired rants against Eden, again calling him 'the Jerk'.

It was too much for his father: 'My dear boy, Anthony is a friend of mine. Would you please not go on using this "Jerk" expression.'

Randolph continued to try to induce his father to make another trip to Stour, but somehow, without ever extinguishing Randolph's hopes, Winston found ways of keeping away. Winston had spent a lifetime avoiding doing things that displeased him; he was not going to change now.

Randolph's obsessive campaign against Eden carried on. Deprived of any meaningful political power, he was left to vent his frustration and resentment in his newspaper columns and the bar at White's, where, as Evelyn Waugh wrote in a letter to their mutual friend Christopher Sykes, he roared 'obscene gossip about Sir A. Eden'.

Then came the evening at Chartwell when Randolph tore so badly into his father's successor, and for good measure called Christopher Soames a shit, that Winston went white with rage. Just as in the worst moments during the war, those watching feared he would have a heart attack. Randolph stormed out of the room to find June, who had long sickened of the subject, already in bed.

He dragged her from the sheets: 'You have got to dress and pack. We are leaving this house forever.' June refused, and soon after, Winston, in his dressing gown, tapped on the bedroom door and entered. 'I am going to die soon,' he said. 'I cannot go to bed without composing a quarrel.' With this he kissed them both and left. Randolph grew quiet while June lay in the darkness beside him, wondering how much more she could stand.

It is unclear to what degree Randolph's parents were aware of the extent to which a chaotic kind of misery had been the dominant chord in his relationship with June almost from the outset.

They had quarrelled hideously in London, their neighbours often woken by the sound of June pitching her belongings into the street as she threatened to leave. Laura Charteris had lived for a while around the corner from the couple: more often than she cared to remember, her evenings were interrupted by an angry and distraught Randolph begging her to come over to calm June down. Laura might discover June screaming on the balcony of the flat; at other times she was refused entry altogether. Soon she realised that there was little an outsider like her could do.

On one occasion at Chartwell Mary and Christopher were sent for at 1.30 a.m. They walked through the garden to find that June had locked herself in her room after inflicting a deep wound on Randolph's face with some smashed china.

When not with her husband, June could be merry and even amusing. As soon as he appeared, she withdrew into herself. Or worse. As Mary observed: 'June, for all her languor and fragility, can become a frenzied & hysterical maniac.' There was no contentment or peace in their relationship, just periods of ceasefire, and yet they struggled on for the sake of the children.

Then came what was probably the final straw. Randolph arrived late and drunk to a dinner given by John Sutro and, within moments, accused June of being 'a paltry little middle-class bitch always eager to please and failing owing to her dismal manners'. Within a year she had left him for good. Randolph could not understand what he had done wrong, nor why he was left with only his garden and a growing awareness of all the opportunities he had missed, or scorned, or sabotaged, to keep him company.

'If you knew Randolph well,' John Julius Norwich said, 'you loved him.' Randolph would help anyone in need. If a stray Arab he had met once in the war turned up on his doorstep at Stour with a sob story, he could feel confident of leaving with £100 in his pocket. The defence Randolph made at the trial in Versailles of Pierre Flandin, a pre-war acquaintance who had served in the Vichy government, played a crucial part in securing Flandin's acquittal on the main charge of collaboration with the Nazis (even though much of Randolph's speech alternated between jokes and nasty digs at old enemies like Stanley Baldwin).

When he heard that his friend Quintin Hogg was more than usually hard up after losing his ministerial post, and the ministerial car that came with it, Randolph got ten friends to club together, each putting in £200, and they bought him a car of his own. (Admittedly this was in part because he thought it inappropriate for former ministers to be seen bicycling.)*

And he despised injustice. Landing once in Apartheid-era Johannesburg, Randolph was incensed by an immigration form asking him to state his race: 'Damned cheek!' he exclaimed, and began writing furiously, embellishing the family myth that Indian blood ran in their veins: 'Race: human. But if, as I imagine is the case, the object of this inquiry is to determine whether I have coloured blood in my veins, I am most happy to be able to inform you that I do, indeed, so have. This is derived from one of my most revered ancestors, the Indian Princess Pocahontas, of whom you may not have heard, but who was married to a Jamestown settler named John Rolfe.'

But when he drank, the demons inside him escaped. This had always been true, and only became more so in the midst of this inglorious stretch of bitterness and rage. He burned through one hundred cigarettes a day and two bottles of whisky. Those brave enough to eat with him saw the way his eyes expanded with desire as plate after plate of delicacies were brought to the table.

His attempts to wash away his anger and loneliness with drink, or to fill the gaping hole in his heart with food, did nothing to assuage his misery or improve his conduct. The impudence of his youth had been succeeded by a deplorable cruelty. There was little wit or

---

* As Christopher Sykes once pointed out in a letter to Kay Halle, the surprises with Randolph were not hidden sins, but hidden qualities.

mischief to his behaviour, just the obnoxiousness accessible only to the deeply unhappy.

Randolph staggered around London, littering his path with gratuitous insults. He ruined parties, gatecrashed private dinners, immolated friendships that had lasted for decades, and for a while it seemed that nobody was safe from him. He tossed a pot of coffee over Ann Fleming (in an attempt to atone for this outrage, he drenched her with a jug of cold water; this did not help matters); bundled the bulky frame of Rab Butler into his own fire (Julian Amery had to fish him out); and in an argument with Pamela Berry, his dark, beautiful childhood friend, he had shouted as he left: 'Look here, my girl, you'd better go home and have a shave. You've not been using the electric razor given you for Christmas.' Afterwards Randolph assumed his words had been forgotten and tried to invite himself to dinner. 'Don't come if you value your life,' Pamela replied.

There were nights when Randolph would be thrown out of three hotels before dawn. He became 'a shambling, pitiful object, much like King Lear on the heath'. The next day, he would be assailed with regret, sitting hungover at lunch: pale grey, quite silent, his bright pink eyes streaming tears as once again he asked Laura Charteris to marry him.

Gradually, however, Randolph began to grope towards something like peace.

This was in large part because he had fallen in love, with Natalie Bevan, the wife of a naval officer who lived four miles from East Bergholt. Natalie came to Stour for the first time in May 1957 to see her friend Lord Kinross, who was staying with Randolph.

As Randolph walked across the hall to greet his guest, he suddenly stopped and fell silent. For a long period of time, this man whose appearance was usually heralded by a cacophony of noise said nothing, and instead fixed Natalie with an uncanny gaze. She returned his look without speaking. Then, after what a witness to this strange moment described as 'extraordinary recognition', he stepped forward and took her by the hand. 'Come out on the terrace,' he said, 'and smell the roses.' Then, almost tearfully, 'I've been waiting for you so long. I love you.' At this point he started to kiss her.

Natalie was a beautiful and unusual woman who had had two daughters with Lance Sieveking, then married Bevan after the war. She was charming, an accomplished painter, an original dresser, and almost from the moment they met, Randolph did something that for him was almost unprecedented: instead of demanding that the object of desire change herself to suit *him*, he did what he could to change himself to suit *her*.

What he wanted more than anything was to marry her. 'Come then,' he wrote to her (sometimes he would send her six or seven telegrams during the middle of the night, when his mind was at its clearest; she would find them bunched together on her breakfast tray), 'let us act with courage, conviction and good sense . . . Whatever you decide I shall love you, now and forever. Please help me to make us both happy.'

Although Natalie went to Monte Carlo with him, spent time with his parents and managed to restrain him from foolish gambling, she also knew that abandoning her husband would hurt him too much, and that the secret to the success of her relationship with Randolph was that she could walk out of the door whenever she chose. So, despite the complexity, she told him they would have to go on as they were. Rather against the odds, Randolph accepted this.

In her diary, she wrote that 1958–9 were 'the most golden of my years'. On summer days Natalie would shimmer across the lawn at Stour in high heels, carrying a bottle of Pol Roger, her husband walking several paces behind. She and Randolph would disappear for an hour or so, leaving an unfazed, complaisant Commander Bevan to talk to a member of staff.

Natalie was the relationship Randolph had been waiting for, for decades. The happiness she provided seemed to radiate into every other part of his existence.

On 12 September 1958, Winston and Clementine celebrated their golden wedding anniversary. Randolph's orchestration of the festivities was a sign of the new ease he had found with his parents.

Randolph had originally wanted to plant an avenue of golden roses at Chartwell. Since digging could not begin until late October, Mary suggested instead they create a large illuminated book incorporating a dedication, the design of the avenue and a list of the twenty-eight roses embellished with individual paintings of the roses by artists such as Paul Maze, Duncan Grant, Vanessa Bell, Cecil Beaton, John Nash, Augustus John and Oliver Messel.

Randolph threw himself into the task, choosing beautiful roses in every possible shade of gold and yellow that could then be reproduced by the artists selected. He conducted his correspondence with them with considerable grace and (only when necessary) force. He bought brushes and watercolours for Stour to make sure no artist could excuse themselves. And so it did not matter if, for instance, Cecil Beaton was going to Greece tomorrow, the roses would not last and he would have to complete his painting overnight. Augustus John was persuaded to use watercolour for the first time in fifty years.

Gripping nine dozen real roses and the finished book – which weighed sixty-seven pounds – Randolph and Arabella flew to La Pausa, Lord Beaverbrook's villa in the south of France. The whole thing was kept as a surprise until Arabella handed the book over at a family party. Photographs from the trip show father and son smiling happily as they sit together in dappled sunlight, content despite the manifest physical decline that afflicted them both.

Writing to thank him a few days later, Clementine told Randolph, 'Your swift visit was a joy; like a meteor flashing across our sky. And it was an inspiration to bring Arabella. I look at that glorious book every day . . . Much love darling Randolph from your devoted Mama.'

20

He's Asked Me. He's Asked Me at Last

IN FEBRUARY 1932, while Winston was on a lecture tour of the United States, his son sent him a proposition.

HAVE BEEN OFFERED 450 POUNDS ADVANCE ON SUBSTANTIAL ROYALTIES FOR BIOGRAPHY OF YOU HAVE YOU ANY OBJECTION TO MY ACCEPTING IF I DO IT IT WILL NATURALLY BE UNAUTHORIZED UNOFFICIAL AND UNDOCUMENTED MY AIM WOULD BE PRESENT POLITICAL HISTORY LAST THIRTY YEARS IN LIGHT UNORTHODOX FASHION BELIEVE COULD PRODUCE AMUSING WORK WITHOUT EMBARRASSING YOU MUMMY LOOKING VERY WELL COUNTING DAYS TO YOUR RETURN LOVE R.

He received a firm reply from Indianapolis:

STRONGLY DEPRECATE PREMATURE ATTEMPT HOPE SOME DAY YOU MAKE THOUSANDS INSTEAD OF HUNDREDS OUT OF MY ARCHIVES MOST IMPROVI-DENT ANTICIPATE NOW STOP LECTURE PILGRIMAGE DRAWING WEARILY FINAL STAGE MUCH LOVE MAMA = FATHER

Winston had long been wary about the idea of anybody close to him making any revelations about him. 'You're not writing anything,' he would say to Grace Hamblin when she worked as a secretary for him. Bill Deakin absorbed the need for discretion so completely that when asked later in life to make a contribution to a volume about

Randolph, he refused, saying, 'I trained myself stubbornly not to retain in my memory any family details of the Churchills. Even under torture, I could now not recall episodes and scenes.'

This did not mean that Winston was against the idea of being the subject of a biography. Far from it. He was obsessed by the place he would occupy in history and wanted a monument to his life and career to be written; it was just that he was anxious to make sure it was the right sort of monument.

The thought that Randolph would be its author had been on Winston's mind for a long time, perhaps even before his son had been born. And Randolph fervently wanted the chance to write his father's story, just as Winston had before him. For a long time there had been an unspoken understanding that the tradition would be upheld: only a Churchill could write the authorised account of Winston's life.

But the fact that the understanding was unspoken, and that Winston had become increasingly indecisive, as well as horrified by the reports that filtered back to him about Randolph's outrages, had confused the issue. Summoning as much delicacy as he could muster, Randolph would try to probe Anthony Montague Browne about Winston's plans for his biography, asking him what more he needed to do to prove himself, always, however, stopping short of actually asking him to intervene.

Randolph's life had been characterised by uninhibited self-expression: very few thoughts entered his head that were not articulated at great volume seconds after they first appeared. And he, perhaps less than anyone in the world, was not daunted by his father's presence. Norman McGowan, who started working at the age of twenty-five as Winston's personal valet in 1950, felt that 'my Guv'nor's son was, in my opinion, his greatest friend.'

'It is indeed fair to say,' remembered McGowan, 'as it possibly cannot often be done in the case of a father and middle-aged son, that the two men were passionately fond of one another', even though 'each could easily be hurt by the other.'

In McGowan's view, their intimacy depended on their ability to hurl 'robust Anglo-Saxon words at one another'. Randolph was the only person, out of the hundreds whom he saw descend upon Chartwell, Chequers and No. 10, who did not defer to Winston. Important politicians, businessmen, foreign diplomats – even those entitled to regard him as a familiar friend – were so 'bemused by his importance' that they addressed him with utmost deference, calling him Sir Winston or Mr Churchill.

By contrast, Randolph, he said, 'would never diverge by a single inch from his own line'. On those days when Winston had seen or spoken with his son, he would often tell Norman that he felt Randolph's attitude 'was the greatest compliment that could be paid to him'.

And yet Randolph's special pride and his fear of being hurt meant that he could not bring himself to ask to be given the commission. It was the one thing he could not say to his father. Montague Browne was painfully aware that Randolph would be crushed if the job were to be awarded to somebody else. He also believed that when he did put in the requisite effort, he could be a fine writer, so he began to quietly lobby Winston on his son's behalf.

The first sign that Winston was leaning towards Randolph came in 1953, when he told Lord Camrose that his son had become a 'more serious writer'. The move to Suffolk built on this impression, which was burnished further in 1960, after Winston read proofs of Randolph's book on Lord Derby – its 618 pages were the result of six years of effort by Randolph as well as three researchers and two secretaries – and pronounced them 'remarkable'. Then, over dinner one night, Harold Macmillan told Winston how much he had enjoyed his son's book. There were other people acting on Randolph's behalf. Sylvia Henley persuaded Clementine to make the case to the Chartwell Trustees.

In May of the same year, Randolph finally broke and asked directly. He did not receive a response, at least not immediately. But a little while later, as Montague Browne and Winston sat talking together at Chartwell, Winston broke off from the conversation and said simply: 'He can do it.'

Montague Browne had long before drafted a letter confirming Randolph's appointment and, after letting what he judged to be a tactful amount of time elapse, slid it in front of Winston for him to sign.

My dear Randolph,

I have reflected carefully on what you said. I think that your biography of Derby is a remarkable work, and I should be happy that you should write my official biography when the time comes.

On the day Randolph learned that he had been appointed his father's biographer, Natalie had driven over to tea to see if a set of pottery elephants she had modelled and baked in clay would suit his dining table.

She was starting to drive away afterwards when he came chasing after her. In his eagerness, he fell over in the drive. Panting, he yelled at her: 'He's asked me. He's asked me at last.' Natalie got out of the car and embraced her lover. 'He couldn't speak,' she would later recall. 'It meant so much to him.'

The excitement persisted through the rest of the day. 'Millions!' he whispered to Arabella as she went to bed. 'It will make us millions!' Writing to his father, Randolph was exultant.

Dearest Papa,

Your letter has made me proud and happy. Since I first read your life of your father, thirty-five years ago when I was a boy of fourteen at Eton, it has always been my greatest ambition to write your life. And each year that has passed since this ambition first started in my mind, has nurtured it as your heroic career has burgeoned.

When the time comes, you may be sure that I shall lay all else aside and devote my declining years exclusively, to what will be a pious, fascinating and I suppose, a remunerative task.

Thank you again from the bottom of my heart for a decision which, apart from what I have already said, adds a good deal to my self-esteem and will, I trust, enable me to do honour in filial fashion, to your extraordinarily noble and wonderful life.

The hunched, grey and heavy-looking Randolph had by now decisively given up his personal political ambitions,* preferring instead to cheer on his friends (he was particularly pleased when Harold Macmillan had promoted his brothers-in-law Sandys and Soames in the 1960 reshuffle) and cause mischief from a distance. Throughout

---

* His last meaningful attempt to enter Parliament had come in 1959, when he expressed close interest in standing at Bournemouth, but he was not among the eight candidates shortlisted. (When asked by a member of the committee whether he planned, if successful, to live in the constituency, he answered immediately: 'No! I promise I won't do that to you.')

the fifties, he conducted an eccentric and fairly lonely campaign against what he saw as an appalling decline in the moral quality of the press as well as entangling himself in a number of complicated libel suits. He combined this with spreading outrageous gossip, such as the idea that everyone in government was having a 'Boyle's Operation', a procedure designed to prevent a man from having any sexual desire, and terrorising the local Tories.

His presence at a constituency fete, where he was liable to shout at Conservative ladies or insult dignitaries such as Enoch Powell, was a source of commingled embarrassment and fear. By the same token, the sight of Randolph plotting in Conservative Party conference corridors with Rab Butler, Harold Macmillan and the chief whip was always 'a bad sign'.

The extinction of his political ambitions meant he could devote himself to what he began to call the 'great work'. Arabella said that being given the role he had wanted desperately for so long infused his existence with new purpose. It also made him rich. The book secured a worldwide advance of £535,000, with £200,000 from the *Daily Telegraph* for serial rights and £150,000 from William Heinemann. As soon as he laid his hands on the first tranche of the advance, Randolph sped into London where, at Asprey's of New Bond Street, he bought six hugely expensive black pigskin 'dressing-cases' (containing, inter alia, silver hair and clothes brushes) and gave them to his closest and most favoured friends.*

But to Randolph, the most valuable thing of all was that in entrusting him with the task of writing his biography, Winston showed that he still had confidence in his son's abilities. He had always craved his father's validation, even more so since their relationship had cooled in the years after the war. This commission was tangible proof that he could still impress and gratify the man he had adored his entire life.

*

* More practically, it offered him relief from the local shopkeepers who would periodically queue outside his door, seeking payment for long-overdue bills. Randolph adhered stubbornly to the idea that 'gentlemen live by credit', which was even then an antiquated notion. The exception was the landlord of his local pub, who cannily refused to offer him credit. In emergencies, he had to put on a black frock coat and plead his case to the manager of Coutts on Park Lane.

Randolph on his way to New York, 1963.

Randolph's plan for the project was monumental. In addition to the main volumes of narrative, he intended to produce 'companion' volumes containing relevant or interesting documents. In his initial conception, the biography would run to fifteen or more volumes. No life of a British prime minister had been planned on a similar scale since Moneypenny and Buckle's six-volume *Life of Benjamin Disraeli*.

Randolph refused to be daunted by the size of the task. He saw himself as commander of a military operation that demanded detail and discipline and set about altering his entire way of life to help him achieve this.

Once work began, it was as if he could think of nothing else, especially once his father had relented on his original stipulation that nothing could be published until five years after his death. He cleared the top floor of Stour to provide offices for a staff of as many as five researchers, backed up by four secretaries. What had once been Arabella's old nursery was converted into a 'Book Office'. Divided into three sections, it became the enterprise's operational centre. Just as significant was the construction of a strong room with a massive Chubb safe-door. It would eventually hold over a million documents assembled from Chartwell and Blenheim, but also the Royal Archives, Admiralty, Home Office, and the papers of Asquith, Bonar Law and David Lloyd George.

The American Michael Wolff was brought in as Randolph's right-hand man and was responsible for directing the research. Wolff was supported by a research assistant who, along with an archivist, collated the material sent to the Book Office.

Randolph worked downstairs, where he was supported by his personal aides, including Barbara Twigg, his secretary, and Andrew Kerr, his indispensable research-assistant-cum-secretary-companion, who often accompanied him when he travelled abroad.

Then there were the 'Young Gentlemen', such as Tom Hartman, who had previously worked in a publisher's office, and Martin Gilbert, a young Oxford don who was recommended by Diana Cooper. Haphazardly assembled, they were usually attached to Stour on a temporary basis. Some had worked with Randolph on his biography of Derby, some were Fleet Street contacts, others came on board more recently.

Work on the book began erratically – in the middle of the morning, after lunch, before dinner, after dinner – but when things had got started, it could often acquire a singular momentum. It was not unusual for progress to continue until well after sunrise.

Once Randolph had drafted a chapter, he handed it to an assistant to read aloud from the desk that had once belonged in turn to Disraeli, Lord Randolph and Winston.* Randolph would listen enthralled, his imagination set on fire, to these unfinished passages and recently discovered documents, treating them as if they were accounts of events that had taken place the day before. Martin Gilbert would always remember Randolph's eager voice calling out to him: 'More, dear boy, read on, box on.' When a letter or story gave him particular pleasure, he would say, 'Wonderful. Lovely grub.'

---

* The desk was his greatest treasure, he wrote, when thanking his parents for the gift. 'It will inspire me to write an even better life of Papa than I had been planning.'

So much of the work he had done in the past had been dashed off while he was drunk, or waiting for an assignation, or rushing towards a deadline, but he was determined that this would not be the case for the Great Work. As the chapters-in-progress were read to him, he checked and rechecked his facts: 'We must do our prep,' he would say, leaping up to grab another reference book from the shelves.

Randolph was always delighted to learn of something clever his father had said, or of those moments when his father displayed particular acuity about a long-vanished political controversy. When, one night, an assistant read to him something Winston had written when he was eighteen, Randolph interrupted: 'Wonderful stuff. Even then he could write you and me out of the ring.'

His battered face would often be overcome with emotion. As extracts relating Jennie's cruelty to Winston's old nanny were read, he sobbed. He talked about his father as 'Winston' or 'the dear boy', and his grandmother as 'Jennie' or 'that bitch Jennie'.

Sometimes, as he sat there in a deep chair beside the fire that he kept blazing even during the height of summer, taking deep drafts on his cigarette (like a workman, Jonathan Aitken remembered), his dogs tumbling by his feet, a glass of barely diluted whisky by his side, he would inhabit Winston's voice. His uncanny ability to conjure up his father – reproducing his snarls, swoops and distinctive vocal patterns – was such that to others in the room, who minutes before might have been furtively looking at their watches or suppressing yawns, it could suddenly seem as if ghosts from long-forgotten moments in time now swarmed around them.

At Stour, Randolph had created an idiosyncratic home whose every atom, just like Chartwell, was imbued with its owner's personality. Guests – including a succession of local girlfriends; Randolph made a pass at everybody – flowed through the house like water. Randolph would talk continuously in his rich, cracked, resonant voice, a conversation that was almost unbroken by other people's contributions. It was only at the end of their visits, when he resorted to childish stratagems to delay, or even prevent, his bewildered guests' departures, that his loneliness revealed itself. Although Natalie's love, and the sense of great purpose that the Great Work had afforded him, left him happier than he had been at any point since the war, it was probably true that no amount of affection or attention would ever satisfy him.

Randolph lived in a cheerful kind of chaos, a function of the self-sabotaging streak in him that had been nurtured by alcohol. He was after all a man who owned neither raincoat nor umbrella and displayed a flamboyant disregard for conventional timekeeping: he believed trains should be given a 'sporting chance' of getting away.

The house itself was a strange mixture of opulence and mess. Books, papers and files lay everywhere, mixed – indiscriminately, it seemed – with valuable items that Randolph treated with reverence. Most precious of all to Randolph were those objects that possessed an intimate connection to his father. He had Disraeli's desk; many of his father's paintings; and, he claimed, the largest collection of Churchilliana in the world.

Guests ate well, often encountering new foods. Martin Gilbert was surprised to be served, on his first night, gulls' eggs, hare pâté and Jerusalem artichoke soup. Breakfast consisted of buttered kippers, rashers of bacon 'like the ears of a giant, kidneys that must have come from the entrails of mammoths', kedgeree, liver steaks and poached eggs. This was followed by a no less extravagant lunch that, depending on the season, might include oysters, caviar, asparagus, artichokes, great piles of strawberries and cream, egg and anchovy savouries.

For eight months of the year – as long as the weather was fine – Randolph and the other denizens of Stour would eat raucous al fresco luncheons beneath a pergola covered with clematis, wisteria and honeysuckle (Randolph drinking litres of his favourite summertime cocktail, the bullshot, a mix of consommé and vodka). All this was, of course, dependent on Randolph not having rowed with the cook. If they had walked out – a common occurrence – there would be a barbecue instead.

When he was happy, he moved around, making friendly noises (most often 'ho-ho') and calling everyone 'my dear'. Many people who saw him in this disarmingly sweet mood said that he rivalled his father: he was funny, witty and capable of producing wonderful turns of phrase.

Randolph was just as capable of behaving in a toweringly offensive manner, his temper provoked by something – like the wrong kind of salt for the gulls' eggs or the mispronunciation of a word – that most others would be able to pass over without comment. If you liked Randolph you could easily put up with his rages, which were usually over in five minutes. If you did not like him, these passing thunderstorms were harder to overlook.

The Young Gentlemen were especially subject to this erratic mode of existence. Randolph had no conception of appropriate behaviour or boundaries and operated more like a feudal lord than a twentieth-century employer. He might sack an assistant at midnight, who would then find a blank cheque waiting for him on the breakfast table the following day. Within hours he might be reinstated or banished from the property for ever. It would not always be clear what he had done to deserve his fate.

But Randolph also regarded his staff as his friends and, as such, accorded them total loyalty. Their lives, families and problems were treated almost as if they were his own. He made it his business to discover what pleased them and upset them, he asked them probing questions designed to identify their strengths and their weaknesses, and he involved himself in their private problems.

When one of Michael Wolff's children was recovering from a serious illness, Randolph demanded a daily progress report and spent hours choosing the right present for the ailing child. Instead of the more usual sweets and chocolates, he produced a 'perfect peach', carefully wrapped in cotton wool.

At times like this, it was possible to forget his bad characteristics.

Perhaps it was this side of Randolph that, in the summer of 1963, lulled Anthony Montague Browne into lobbying Winston to invite his son for a cruise on Ari Onassis's yacht, the 'last and least fortunate' such journey Winston would take.

Randolph had introduced Winston to Onassis in 1956. The former prime minister was impressed. 'Randolph brought Onassis (the man with the big yacht) to dinner last night. He made a good impression on me,' he told his wife. 'He is a vy able and masterful man & told me a lot about whales. He kissed my hand.' Predictably, Clementine was not quite so dazzled: 'Somehow I don't want to be beholden to this rich and powerful man, & for the nest to be blazoned,' she wrote to a friend.

Nevertheless, in the years since his retirement, Winston and Clementine had taken nine cruises on what he called 'the monster yacht', *Christina*, a converted British frigate complete with a small hospital, a laundry run by a Greek husband and wife, a red-and-white seaplane parked on its stern, and a mini car stowed on the lower deck. It had gold taps made in the shape of dolphins; a two-thousand-year-old Cretan mosaic dance floor that could be converted at the touch of a switch into a swimming pool; and a bar with a glass top, below which a procession of miniature vessels revolved, from fully rigged ships to triremes to Mississippi stern-wheelers, with Moses in his reed basket bringing up the rear, towed by Moby Dick.* Its salon was full of gold and silver ashtrays in the form of seashells, with, as a centrepiece, one of Winston's landscapes. Winston revelled in this luxury; Clementine loathed it. She was as suspicious of Ari Onassis as she had been of F. E. Smith, Brendan Bracken and Lord Beaverbrook before him.

Onassis treated the man he always called Sir Winston with filial reverence. There were days when it seemed as if he could not take his eyes off his new friend. Dressed in an old sweater, faded trousers and canvas tennis shoes, he scampered around Winston, fetching a glass of whisky, or a blanket to keep the chill out, or a clothes brush to deal with hairs on the collar of his coat. Sometimes when Clementine's back was turned, Onassis would sink to his knees and spoon extra caviar, which the former prime minister was capable of eating 'like toast', into Winston's mouth.

He once asked Winston what he should like to be in another existence. 'A tiger,' came the response. 'What about you?'

Onassis smiled. 'I would like to be your budgerigar, Toby.' (Toby, a green budgerigar, travelled the world with Winston, along with a supply of seed, sandpaper, spray and cuttlefish. Toby began the day by crawling across Winston's breakfast tray and then would fly around the dining room during lunch, knocking over glasses and salt cellars. Winston possessed a conviction – not shared by anybody else – that Toby could say 'Sir Winston will be pleased.' In 1961 he escaped

---

* The bar's stools were covered with the foreskins of whales killed by the Greek's whaling fleet. There was also an El Greco that only a small minority of people could tell was a fake.

through a salon door in the Hôtel de Paris, Monte Carlo, leaving Winston heartbroken.[*])

Most importantly, he was able to offer Winston comfort without inconvenience. *Christina* could be anchored offshore to protect Winston's privacy – whenever they approached land, hundreds of sightseers filled the quaysides or swarmed around the yacht in boats manned by binocular-wielding passengers. Onassis even ensured that when they passed through the Dardanelles, they did so at night, in a journey only occasionally lit up by a Turkish searchlight. He explained to Montague Browne, 'It would have been very interesting, but it might have brought on very sad thoughts and memories for the Boss.'

In return Winston invited him to dinner at Hyde Park Gate and proposed him for membership of the Other Club. When asked later why he seemed to prefer the company of a dubious Greek to his oldest friends – many of whom felt neglected by him – he retorted, 'Which of my old friends offers me his yacht?'

It suited Winston to be petted and praised amid such luxury. The last decade had been one of retreat from the world. The galaxy-sized capacity for enjoyment that had characterised him for so much of his life, had shrunk. Winston used to get so excited before entering a town that he would shove his head out of the train's window to get a better view – heedless of the danger involved. In his eighties, however, he had become increasingly withdrawn, more unwilling to open himself up to strangers. The frenetic pace he had maintained for decades had subsided. Instead he could be seen in his spotted bow tie and large cowboy hat of white felt, shuffling down the steps of Beaverbrook's villa in the south of France, or following the shafts of sunlight on the Chartwell lawn in a basket chair dragged by his nurse and a detective. At each stop, his whisky and soda would be set up at a special garden table. He sat there staring at the butterflies dancing in the air above him, or reading and smoking, ashes trickling down his front, the smell of his cigar mingling with that of freshly cut grass.

His skin had lost the pink tinge that had distinguished it for so long; now it was whitish and blotchy. His eyes were watery and dim, his voice very

---

[*] He was once overheard to saying to one of the fish at Chartwell, a particularly endearing black guppy: 'Darling, I do love you. I would make love to you if only I knew how.'

faint, and his hearing had faded almost to nothing. There were lunches when he could appear torpid and unengaged, interested only in his food and the location of the mustard. Clementine would be forced to repeat words to him, almost as if she were translating from another language.

And yet gradually he would be re-animated by the food and drink (three glasses of wine, two of port, two of brandy and two coffees), and the old Winston would step for a few moments out of the shadows.

'It was like watching a very strong lightbulb during an electrical crisis,' remembered one guest. 'First a faint reddening of the filament, then a flickering, then a glow, then a brilliant blaze of light. Finally, after being blinded by the sustained glare, again flickering, subsiding, just a red filament; then nothing.'

More often, though, he spent his days sunk in a melancholy caused by the knowledge that terrible things were happening in the world, and that the relentless deletions of his energy and will meant he could do little to influence them. Every day time took more away from him; every day was a reckoning with what he had lost. Britain's decline bore down on him with terrible clarity, and it was inextricably linked with his own. 'I have achieved a great deal,' he told Sarah once, 'to achieve nothing in the end.'

Sometimes he would try to escape the present by reminiscing about the past, but even this led inevitably to endless fretting about his position in history. How would he be judged? What would he be held responsible for? Lord Moran recalled finding his old friend 'brooding over his bed-rest'.

'Why do I get stuck down in the past?' Winston asked. 'Why do I keep going over and over those years when I know I cannot change anything? You, Charles, have spent your life puzzling how the mind works. You must know the answer.'

To some people who encountered him during the last years, he seemed already to have entered another world.*

★

* Winston was sceptical about space travel. 'Why would anyone wish to leave this planet? That would be foolish. I cannot believe that.' He was also stubbornly uninterested in popular culture. When Frank Sinatra bounded up to him in a French casino and wrung his hands, saying fervently, 'I've wanted to do that for twenty years,' Winston bellowed, 'Who the hell was that?' Anthony Montague Browne told him. He remained nonplussed.

His trips on the Onassis yacht allowed him to sit in the sun, watch dolphins and flying fish, play bezique (his host had learned the game so that he could play against him) and relax in undemanding company.

This last requirement had so far precluded asking Randolph to join him on board. It was not a question of love or affection: his eyes still lit up with pleasure when his son came into a room. But he was well aware that even the best incarnation of Randolph was not conducive to any sort of peace.

The party was originally designed to comprise Prince and Princess Radziwill, the Colvilles and young Winston. Randolph was only included 'after a tussle' between Winston and his secretary. Montague Browne intended it as a reward for the dignified silence he had maintained at not having been invited before.

Winston's son had come straight from London, where he had inserted himself into the aftermath of the Profumo scandal. When everybody else shunned the Profumos, and they were besieged by reporters who had camped outside their house, Randolph made a very public visit to them. As he forced his way through the scrum on their doorstep, he was asked what the purpose of his visit was.

At this he turned in scorn: 'I have come to visit my friends! What the hell are you doing here?'

As a young MP of only two months' standing in May 1940, John Profumo had voted against Neville Chamberlain, helping ease Winston's path to power.[*] He and Randolph had subsequently served (and caterwauled) together in North Africa. These old ties of loyalty, added to Randolph's impulsive generosity, led to what he called 'Operation Sanctuary', which essentially meant letting them shelter in secret at Stour until the furore died away.

The trip had begun well. The *Christina* had passed through Monte Carlo, and Winston, dressed in a blue jacket with white flannels, as well as his favourite yachting cap (that of an Elder Brother of Trinity House – part of his strong belief that you should dress correctly on all

---

[*] 'I can tell you this, you utterly contemptible little shit,' he had been told by David Margesson, 'on every morning that you wake up for the rest of your life you will be ashamed of what you did last night.'

occasions)* – seemed impervious to seasickness, calmly puffing on his cigar while everyone else suffered.

Even at eighty-five, his curiosity and sense of adventure could occasionally appear unimpaired: he insisted on being taken to see the most inaccessible parts of the deck; even the bridge's near vertical stairways could not put him off. However, these moments of excitement alternated with ever more sustained passages where he would appear apathetic and withdrawn.

During the first few days of the cruise, Randolph treated his father with infinite affection and respect. So much so that Winston's secretary was beginning to congratulate himself on having pushed for the invitation. And then one night at dinner, after they had gone through the Strait of Messina, and up into the Adriatic, Randolph erupted. There was no obvious cue. One minute he had been amiable, the next he fell into an inchoate rage directed at Winston, which slowly resolved itself into a series of 'violent reproaches' about his parents' encouragement of Pamela's seductions of important Americans during the war.

Ari tried to calm Randolph, or at least to divert his anger, but Anthony Montague Browne saw that the only way to stop him would be to hit him on the head with a bottle, an extreme measure he could not quite bring himself to take. Winston remained silent, staring back at his son with 'brooding rage'.

'It was one of the most painful scenes I had ever witnessed. I had previously discounted the tales I had heard of Randolph,' Montague Browne recalled. 'Now I believed them all.'

Winston went to his cabin, followed by a disturbed Montague Browne. The old man was shaking all over. Anthony feared he would suffer another stroke and sat with him for a while, both men sipping whisky and soda until the former prime minister grew calm.

Even writing years later, when father and son were both in their graves, Montague Browne did not feel he could reveal what Winston

---

* As William Manchester observed, Winston was perhaps the only man in London with more hats than his wife: 'top hats, Stetsons, seamen's caps, his hussar helmet, a privy councillor's cocked hat, homburgs, an astrakhan, an Irish "paddy hat", a white pith helmet, an Australian bush hat, a fez, the huge beplumed hat he wore as a Knight of the Garter, even the full headdress of a North American Indian chieftain'.

said to him during those minutes they spent together. All he would say is that it was clear he had to find some way of removing Randolph from the *Christina*.

Montague Browne found Onassis, who was still so dazed that to begin with he could only repeat, 'But how could we have prevented it?' His bewilderment did not, however, stop him from forming a plan.

The next morning, Randolph woke to a cable from the King of Greece's Royal Chamberlain, inviting him to interview the Greek king and his queen, Frederika, who was enjoying a brief spell of notoriety in the British press. Randolph was delighted but unsure how he would reach the palace on the eastern Greek mainland. Ari, of course, had an answer. When they put into Corfu, after a peaceful if somewhat silent dinner, an Olympic Airways aeroplane was ready to fly Randolph to Athens.

Randolph headed off, humming 'Get Me to the Church on Time' under his breath. As Montague Browne sat with him in the launch to the harbour, he noticed first that Randolph had fallen silent, then that he was weeping.

'Anthony,' he said after a while, 'you didn't think I was taken in by that plan of Ari's and yours, do you? I do so very much love that man but something always goes wrong between us.'

It was melancholy, more than anger, however, that came to dominate the final phase of their relationship. Randolph told friends that it would be better if Winston were to die. Others felt that he tried to avoid seeing him. This was not because of any sense of grievance, or because he was afraid they might fall out. Rather, he could not bear the sight of Winston's diminished state. Randolph did not want to spoil the image he carried with him of his father in his glorious, nation-saving pomp.

In the summer of 1964, Randolph and Laura went to visit his father in his room at Hyde Park Gate. Winston was like a hulk that had collapsed in on itself, sitting peaceably with an unsmoked cigar between his lips. As a young man, Winston had not been able to stop talking; the sound of his own voice had seemed to have a galvanising effect on him. In his last years, he shied away from the immense physical effort speaking demanded. On bad days, an entire meal might pass without his saying a word.

Sarah would sit with him for hours, willing time to pass.

'What time is it, Sas?'

'Twelve o'clock, Papa.'

Five minutes later, he would repeat the same question. He still hated to be alone. Occasionally, he would stretch out his hand affectionately or say, 'I'm sorry I'm not very amusing today.' Sarah believed that her father had fallen quiet because he had said and done everything he needed to 'and was only waiting with increasing courtesy and patience for the end'. As Laura and Randolph left that day, Winston spoke, offering them a momentary glimpse of his state of mind and the extraordinary strength of character that had allowed him to bend the course of history: 'The Dark Angel beckons – but I still say NO!'

On 11 January 1965, he was felled by another stroke. Clearly far from well, even more remote and silent than usual, he lay helpless in the ground-floor room that had been made for him after he broke his hip in 1962. Montague Browne called Randolph to let him know. The following morning, having spoken to both Clementine and Mary, Randolph set off for London for lunch with his family at Hyde Park Gate. He found his father sitting propped up in bed with hot soup before him on a tray, which he was taking slowly.

Just once, Winston looked straight at Randolph with his large blue eyes as if wondering what he was doing there, but it was clear to Randolph that his father did not recognise him. Later that evening he went in to watch him sleeping peacefully.

Winston's last words were spoken not to his son but to his son-in-law. When Christopher Soames offered Winston a glass of champagne, he seemed barely aware of his presence. 'I'm so bored with it all,' Winston said. With that he sighed and fell into a coma.

Lord Moran decreed that he could be given no more food or liquid; instead, his mouth was moistened with water and glycerine. He slept peacefully, the only sign of life the sound of his breathing and the gentle heave of his chest beneath the bedclothes.

Winston's softly lit, flower-filled room became the centre of the house, a contrast to its outside, which had quickly become a scrum of reporters and television cameras. His quiet form lay in the big bed, with his beautiful hands spread on the quilt and a marmalade cat curled up by his feet. Family members would gather around, trying and failing to make conversation naturally.

On 15 January, after a night in which Winston's condition deteriorated, Randolph and young Winston sat up late, holding the invalid's hand; occasionally he returned their squeezes and grips. Sometimes, there would be a flicker of more sustained activity. His hand would move as if he were making painting gestures. Witnesses chose to see this as a sign of happiness and wondered which moment from his life was crossing his mind. At other times he would move his hands as if he were smoking. Sylvia Henley tried to place an unlit cigar in his fingers, but he waved it away.

He was most alive between midnight and 2.00 a.m. One night, young Winston and Arabella became so excited by the increase in his activity that they called the nurse: 'Did he usually work late at night?'

'Yes.'

'That, then, I'm afraid is the explanation.'

Throughout this last illness, Clementine remained preternaturally calm and quiet. 'I don't know where all my tears have gone,' she said wonderingly to Mary. Each day, 'in a somewhat robot-like trance', she went for a drive or walk with Mary, or she would wander the halls of the Wallace Collection or National Gallery, all the time watched at a distance by a curious, sympathetic public.

In the evening she would always go to say goodnight and sit with her husband for a while. Sometimes she broke her sleep to go and see how Winston was.

While Clementine rested on 22 January, Randolph came to the house to say that young Winston's wife, Minnie, had given birth. Not wishing to disturb his mother, he left a note, which ended by saying, 'in the midst of death, we are in life'.

Early in the morning of 24 January, Lord Moran called by the room Randolph had taken in the Hyde Park Hotel to be close to his father in his last hours.

'It is unbelievable', the doctor told Randolph, 'that he is still breathing, he hasn't had anything to eat for ten days or anything to drink for five. What a heart he must have to keep on breathing.'

At 7.15 a.m., Randolph and young Winston headed over to 28 Hyde Park Gate. A little later, while the rest of her family were in the drawing room, Mary, who was sitting opposite Winston, noticed a change in his breath. She signalled to the nurse to fetch the others, who gathered around the bed.

Sarah, Mary and Celia Sandys, Diana's youngest daughter, knelt at its foot, Randolph and young Winston sat by Winston's pillow and Clementine, with Lord Moran standing beside her, held Winston's right hand. At the back of the room Anthony Montague Browne and two nurses had fallen to their knees.

Randolph lifted his father's left hand to his lips. Clementine watched with a blank face, as if she were in a trance. There was complete silence, then Winston gave a couple of long, long sighs.

Clementine looked at Lord Moran. 'Has he gone?'

'He has gone,' the doctor replied.

Later that morning, Randolph, clutching a copy of Winston's biography of his father, joined his mother and sisters in Clementine's sitting room. They were all silent; there was nothing they wanted to, or could, say.

'Would you believe it, he has died on the same day, and at almost the same hour that his father died.'

Randolph barely outlived Winston.

He wanted desperately to survive long enough to finish his biography of the man who still dominated his life. But his own declining health meant that he only had a tiny chance of doing so. He told Mary, who was beginning her own biography of Clementine, of his fear that he would not be able to complete the book in time and of the depression this caused in him.

By the middle of the decade, when he was still only in his fifties, he had been reduced to a shuffling wreck who could struggle out of his chair only with Natalie's assistance. Severe pneumonia in 1963 was followed by a long operation in the spring of 1964 and a mild stroke in April 1965. The next year Randolph's doctor noted that his liver had started to shrink. More alarming even than this, he told his patient that he had suffered five minor heart attacks, which were, he suspected, due to failure of the left side of his heart.

Randolph was told in the bluntest terms that if he did not want to die within months, he had to give up the whisky to which he had so long been addicted, and all other spirits. From this point on, he survived on a liquid diet of milk and Complan. The only food he could manage was his secretary Barbara Twigg's plum cake, and his drinking was restricted to the occasional Danish lager and one or two glasses of wine a day. Even this, though, was too late. He had already developed cirrhosis of the liver. Randolph had destroyed everything of himself but his brain.

After the publication of the second volume of the biography in 1967, Randolph entered a still steeper decline, broken by moments of feverish activity. Some days he could not write and instead lay in bed, too weak and depressed to talk to his staff, or to do anything except think and scatter his sheets with crumbs of chocolate.

Cecil Beaton, who encountered him in August that year, wrote in his diary:

> Randolph, looking old and grey, like a haggard hawk, has been on the brink of death for three years. The other night he told me that he was now happier than he had ever been. He was at last doing something that justified his life – his book on his father, the best thing he had ever done, his contribution to the world; the fact that he was no longer restless was balm to him. I am sure he was being sincere, but it is hard to believe. His eyes looked so abysmally sad.

In June 1968 Randolph fell gravely ill. He issued a stern command that not even his family should be with him at his end. In his last hours he learned that Robert Kennedy had been shot (a great blow, for he had become close to the entire family; he said he loved JFK 'like a brother' and had been asked by Robert to write the former president's biography). When his assistant Andrew Kerr told him the news at 11.00 p.m., Randolph said only: 'That is the most terrible news I ever heard. Do you suppose the same one that got me, got him?'

By the morning of 6 June, he had died.

★

One document in particular had affected Randolph deeply as he sifted through Winston's papers and letters in the course of his research for the biography: an unsent note to Clementine drafted by Winston in 1915 as he contemplated the prospect of an early death in the trenches. 'There is nothing that Randolph will need to be ashamed of in what I have done for my country,' he said, but if anything should happen to me, 'Randolph will carry on the lamp.'

Randolph never lived up to his father's extravagant hopes for him, he did not even come close, but as Winston's biographer, he was given a chance to create a lasting record of his love and devotion to the man he had loved more than any other person he had ever known. In the process of telling the story of his father's life, he belatedly gave meaning to his own. 'It's a monument to my father,' he said, 'and I'll have left something worthwhile, something worthy of me. I've never done that before. It's nice to leave something behind that someone will remember.'

Winston's relationship with Randolph shares a great deal with many other less famous father–son relationships. Not every son is subjected to disregard as flamboyant as that inflicted on Winston by Lord Randolph, but many men have tried to avoid repeating the mistakes made by their own fathers and succeeded only in handing down more misery to the next generation. Winston was not the first parent to invest ambitious hopes in his infant, only to be disappointed in the years that followed. There is nothing unusual about a family dispute festering for years.

Nor was Randolph's story notably different from the ways in which, throughout history, offspring of great figures have struggled. There are echoes in Randolph of the unhappiness and drama that disfigured the lives of the children of the two other members of the Second World War's 'Big Three'. All of Franklin Roosevelt's children found it hard to escape their father's gravitational pull and construct lives of their own. This left them in an eternal state of rootless confusion, and dangerously susceptible to emotional and financial troubles – between them, the American president's five children had nineteen marriages. 'How many of these marriages and lives were bent and perhaps broken by the pressures of prominence?'

asked James Roosevelt. 'Or were we merely betrayed by our own weaknesses?'

Joseph Stalin's children were even more damaged by their father's position and personality. Koba's domestic cruelties were so many-layered they were practically sedimentary. His callousness meant that he greeted his son Yakov's failed suicide attempt by exclaiming, 'Ha! He couldn't even shoot straight.' His neglect left his daughter Svetlana with 'an unappeasable emotional hunger' that would return to sabotage her throughout her life. She stumbled into a series of ill-judged relationships, none of which relieved her loneliness.

And yet at the same time, there was so much about the bond between Winston and Randolph that was particular to them. It was the product of Winston's romantic, contradictory, quixotic personality.

Randolph was shaped by his father's affection, humour, courage and generosity. He was also damaged by his egotism, his ruthlessness, his obsession with his own destiny and desires, and the strange fact that this man so capable of staggering intuitive flashes, the man of whom Violet Asquith had said, 'Demons seem to whisper things to him', could be so completely oblivious to what was going on in anybody's mind but his own. And he never saw Randolph clearly, neither when he encouraged his young son to dream that he would one day lead the country, nor when he rejected him as a troublesome failure. Winston's great imaginative facility – the 'strange capacity for making his fantasies a reality' – which was the foundation of the visionary leadership that saved his country in 1940, failed his son.

Winston was one of the most paradoxical men of his time, or any other. He was the wild risk-taker who cleaned his teeth and changed his shirt three times a day, and who was so attached to routine that he got upset if he could not have a cup of cold consommé on retiring, wherever he was, no matter how big the banquet he had just been to.

He claimed that the invention of the aeroplane was a tragedy for the British Empire, and yet he was so enthralled by the possibilities and excitements of flight that he was willing to ignore any sort of risk, as well as the entreaties of both his family and Cabinet colleagues, in order to learn how to fly.

He was a sentimentalist who wept at films and could be plunged into misery by the death of a beloved pet, but he was also quite capable of upbraiding his generals for withdrawing before they had sustained what he believed was an appropriate quantity of casualties.

It was another of these perplexing contradictions that was at the heart of his relationship with Randolph. Towards the end of his life, Randolph told his own son how, when he was twenty, his father had taken him for a walk on the lawn at Chartwell. Winston had begun talking about 'the battle of life', put his arm round Randolph, and said: 'My father died when I was exactly your age. This left the political arena clear for me. I do not know how I should have fared in politics had he lived on.'

It was at once a recognition of the difficulties he knew his son would face as he attempted to make his own way, and also a warning, a reminder that while he was alive, his own ambitions would always take priority over Randolph's, and that the world, big as it was, only had space for one Churchill.

For a while, it had seemed as if this conflict would not have to be faced. After all, Winston had spent most of his time on the planet predicting his own imminent death. And throughout the twenties and thirties, he constantly flirted with the idea of stepping away from politics to write and make money.

None of this happened. Winston, far from not being a 'good life', lived until he was ninety. And existing in direct contradiction to his frequent suggestions that he wanted to slip away into comfortable obscurity was a far more urgent conviction that ran through his existence: destiny had chosen him. In 1940 he was sixty-four and Randolph about to turn twenty-nine. At the time when Randolph had expected to enter his prime, and finally outshine his illustrious father, fate called upon Winston to save his country, and the lives of father and son were knocked forever out of balance.

Winston demanded an asphyxiating loyalty from those closest to him. This meant that Randolph was compelled to attach himself to a series of doomed, unpopular causes, and to their leading proponent, a man who had spent the best part of half a century collecting enemies. Every step Randolph took to try to set a course of his own was treated as if it were a deliberate attempt to sabotage his father. The inhibiting effect of his fidelity prevented him from ever building an identity or a career that was truly his own. At the same time, he was desperately trying to live up to the prodigious ambitions that Winston had implanted within him, a path laid out for him by his father long before he ever had a chance to ask himself whether it was what he truly wanted.

Randolph was trapped in a cage built by his father. Wherever Randolph turned, there was Winston, 'grinning and dangling his watch chain', looking 'like a plump naughty little boy dressed as a grown up'. Svetlana Stalin, whose own stunted existence was immeasurably sadder than Randolph's, had a similar experience: 'You are Stalin's daughter. Actually you are already dead. Your life is already finished. You can't live your own life. You can't live any life. You exist only in reference to a name.' For most of the time he spent on the planet, there was no story about Randolph that was not also a story about his father, nothing in his life, except his failures, that was wholly his own.

One thing remained true, right up until Winston took his last, gentle breath. No matter how often father and son ended up screaming insults at each other at two in the morning, no matter how many times Randolph stormed out of Chartwell, vowing never to talk to his father again, no matter how searing the pain of the betrayal over Pamela, 'Winston was', as Laura Charteris said, 'the only person Randolph truly loved.'

Randolph and his daughter Arabella in the garden of Stour, his home in Suffolk.

Acknowledgements

I RECEIVED VALUABLE advice and help at various stages from Andrew Roberts, Roland Philipps, Sonia Purnell and Cate Haste. Thank you all.

I am immensely grateful to Jonathan Aitken and David White for sharing their memories of Randolph Churchill with me.

This book leans heavily on the material contained within the excellent Churchill College Archives Centre in Cambridge. It was a pleasure spending so many hours reading through documents there, and every single member of staff was unfailingly helpful and knowledgeable. The same is true of my experiences at both the JFK Presidential Library in Boston and the US Library of Congress in Washington, DC. This book would not exist without the work they do.

Brent Howard at Dutton and Jon Elek at United Agents showed faith in this book from the very start. I cannot thank either of them enough for giving me the chance to write it. Brent's advice, support and careful editing was invaluable from beginning to end. It has been a huge privilege working with him. I also owe a great deal to Daniel Greenberg, who did so much to make the deal possible. Dutton's Cassidy Sachs has been incredibly helpful, efficient and cheerful. I would like to thank John Murray's Mark Richards, Joe Zigmond and Caroline Westmore for their enthusiasm and skill. Howard Davies' forensic eye for detail on the proofs saved me from myself. Thank you too to my agent, Chris Wellbelove, for keeping an eye out for me.

I feel slightly embarrassed to have dedicated books about treachery and family strife to my wife, Victoria Murray-Browne. But for the last ten years she has been the most important person in my life, so how could I *not*? In March 2020 we were joined by our beautiful daughter, Ivy. I do not want her to be prime minister, or queen, or anything like that; I only wish for her the sturdy, undramatic happiness that always remained outside Randolph's grasp.

Text and Picture Credits

Text

Writings by The Lady Soames: Reproduced with permission of Curtis Brown, London on behalf of The Beneficiaries of the Literary Estate of The Lady Soames © The Beneficiaries of the Literary Estate of The Lady Soames.

For quotes reproduced from the speeches, works and writings of Winston S. Churchill: Reproduced with permission of Curtis Brown, London on behalf of The Estate of Winston S. Churchill © The Estate of Winston S. Churchill.

Letters by Clementine Churchill: Reproduced with permission of Curtis Brown, London on behalf of The Master, Fellows and Scholars of Churchill College, Cambridge © The Master, Fellows and Scholars of Churchill College, Cambridge.

Letters by Randolph Churchill: Reproduced with permission of Curtis Brown, London on behalf of The Master, Fellows and Scholars of Churchill College, Cambridge © The Master, Fellows and Scholars of Churchill College, Cambridge.

Excerpts from the letters and diaries of Evelyn Waugh Copyright © 2021, The Estate of Evelyn Waugh, used by permission of The Wylie Agency (UK) Limited.

Pictures

Chapter 1: (Jennie Churchill) Fremantle/Alamy; (Lord Randolph Churchill) Chronicle/Alamy; (Clementine Churchill) Classic Image/ Alamy; (Winston Churchill) Fremantle/Alamy. Chapter 2: Fremantle/

Alamy. Chapter 4: Suddeutsche Zeitung/Alamy. Chapter 5: Time Life Pictures/Getty. Chapter 9: Central Press/Getty. Chapter 10: Suddeutsche Zeitung/Alamy. Chapter 11: Bettmann/Getty. Chapter 12: Fremantle/Alamy. Chapter 13: Keystone/Getty. Chapter 14: Fremantle/Alamy. Chapter 15: Fremantle/Alamy. Chapter 19: (Winston Churchill at Chartwell) Mark Kauffman/Getty Images; (Anthony Eden) Keystone Press/Alamy. Chapter 20: Randolph Churchill (Associated Newspapers/Shutterstock); Randolph and Arabella Churchill (Carl Mydans/Getty Images).

Notes

Abbreviations

CHAR: Churchill Archives, Churchill College, Cambridge

CHOH CLVL: Papers of Sir John Colville, Churchill Archives, Churchill College, Cambridge

CHUR: Churchill Archives, Churchill College, Cambridge

CSCT: Papers of Lady Soames, Churchill Archives, Churchill College, Cambridge

DIAC: Papers of Lady Diana Cooper, Churchill Archives, Churchill College, Cambridge

KH: Kay Halle Archives, John F. Kennedy Presidential Library, Boston, MA

MCHL: Papers of Lady Soames, Churchill Archives, Churchill College, Cambridge

PH Papers: Pamela Digby Churchill Hayward Harriman Papers, Library of Congress, Washington, DC

RDCH: Papers of Randolph Churchill, Churchill Archives, Churchill College, Cambridge

WA Papers: W. Averell Harriman Papers, Library of Congress, Washington, DC

WLFF: Papers of Randolph Churchill, Churchill Archives, Churchill College, Cambridge

Prologue

1 Winston Churchill's hands: MCHL 1/1/9; Montague Browne, *Long Sunset*, p. 322; Sulzberger, *Last of the Giants*, p. 302.

1 One person who met: KH 2/1 Box 47.

1 'Look at my hands': Moran, *Struggle for Survival*, p. 523.

1 Another thing people also: Gilbert, *Churchill*, vol. 4, *Stricken World*, p. 139.

1 his habit of breaking: Lockhart, *Diaries*, vol. 1, p. 155.

2 'I have been very remiss': RDCH 1/3/1.

2 He was also determined: RDCH 10/19.

Chapter 1: Do Try to Get Papa to Come, He Has Never Been

3 One night in November: PH Papers 2; Pearson, *Citadel of the Heart*, pp. 354–6.

4 Lord Randolph cut: Lovell, *The Churchills*, p. 71; Winston S. Churchill, *Lord Randolph Churchill*, pp. 15, 31–2; Pearson, *Citadel of the Heart*, p. 19; Manchester, *Last Lion: Visions of Glory*, p. 95.

6 'She had a forehead': Pearson, *Citadel of the Heart*, p. 31.

6 Leonard Jerome, his wife: Lough, *No More Champagne*, p. 14.

6 They set up home: Ibid., p. 24.

6 'We seemed to live': Manchester, *Last Lion: Visions of Glory*, p. 112.

6 'The neglect and lack': Randolph S. Churchill, *Churchill: Youth*, p. 45.

6 'bad dinner, cold plates': *The Churchills* (Television).

7 'Waiter – please listen': Bonham-Carter, *Churchill as I Knew Him*, p. 330n.

7 Although Lord Randolph realised: Winston S. Churchill, *Lord Randolph Churchill*, p. 74.

7 Now began his: Cowles, *Winston Churchill*, p. 24; Pearson, *Citadel of the Heart*, p. 33.

8 It was about this time: Cowles, *Winston Churchill*, pp. 28, 33; Randolph S. Churchill, *Churchill: Youth*, pp. 65–6, 127–8.

8 'Stop that row': Pearson, *Citadel of the Heart*, p. 44.

9 One of Jennie's sisters: Lovell, *The Churchills*, p. 73.

9 'come and see me': Manchester, *Last Lion: Visions of Glory*, p. 125.

9 'My nurse was my': Winston S. Churchill, *Roving Commission*, p. 19.

9 'She shone for me': Ibid.

9 The bewilderment and distress: Randolph S. Churchill, *Churchill: Youth*, pp. 50, 52; Manchester, *Last Lion: Visions of Glory*, p. 127.

10 'he is so mad': Pearson, *Citadel of the Heart*, p. 36.

11 'I want you to come': Randolph S. Churchill, *Churchill: Youth*, p. 83.

12 Winston made the swimming: Manchester, *Last Lion: Visions of Glory*, pp. 166, 178.

12 As 1893 wore on: Manchester, *Last Lion: Visions of Glory*, pp. 203–5; Lovell, *The Churchills*, p. 108.

12 'There was no curtain': Randolph S. Churchill, *Churchill: Youth*, p. 235.

13 'There are two ways': Ibid., pp. 196–8.

14 For the moment, Winston: Ibid., p. 235.

14 Lord Randolph died, owing: Lovell, *The Churchills*, p. 113.

14 When Winston set up: Manchester, *Last Lion: Visions of Glory*, p. 375.

16 Winston sought out those: Cowles, *Winston Churchill*, p. 85.

16 It was around this time that Winston: Cowles, *Winston Churchill*, p. 76.

16 'Few fathers have done': Kennedy and Lee, *Lives of Houses*, p. 119.

16 Although Winston understood: Taylor et al., *Churchill: Four Faces and the Man*, p. 131.

16 It was also a dialogue: Cowles, *Winston Churchill*, p. 109.

17 'All my dreams': Winston S. Churchill, *Roving Commission*, p. 76.

18 His new wife, Clementine: Purnell, *First Lady*, pp. 8–17; Soames, *Clementine Churchill*, pp. 5, 11, 16, 31.

18 Clementine's own earliest memory: MCHL 5/1/17.

18 Blanche was witty, daring: Hardwick, *Clementine Churchill*, p. 7; CSCT 3/2.

19 The bitter drudgery: Purnell, *First Lady*, pp. 19, 21.

19 Clementine wanted to go: Ibid., p. 22.

19 The man who: Manchester, *Last Lion: Visions of Glory*, pp. 17–18, 24; Taylor et al., *Churchill: Four Faces and the Man*, pp. 210–12; Moran, *Struggle for Survival*, p. 744.

20 'I am cursed with': Randolph S. Churchill, *Churchill: Youth*, p. 212.

20 'I am not a good': Bonham-Carter, *Churchill as I Knew Him*, p. 53.

21 Winston once told: Manchester, *Last Lion: Visions of Glory*, p. 188.

Chapter 2: The Meteor Beast

22 Winston was so excited: RDCH 1/3/17.

22 Randolph was born on: Winston S. Churchill, *His Father's Son*, pp. 1, 342; Randolph S. Churchill, *Twenty-One Years*, p. 11; Lovell, *The Churchills*, p. 268.

23 Randolph was immediately given: Purnell, *First Lady*, p. 57; Hardwick, *Clementine Churchill*, p. 106.

24 He was unusually determined: Brian Roberts, *Randolph*, p. 4.

24 That he was himself: Lough, *No More Champagne*, pp. 78, 91.

25 Oblivious to either expense: Colville, *The Churchillians*, p. 7.

25 For a while the Welshman's: Lloyd George, *David & Winston*, pp. 9, 32, 37.

25 'They said that I': Montague Browne, *Long Sunset*, p. 147.

25 'slightly hunched shoulders': Bonham-Carter, *Churchill as I Knew Him*, p. 55.

26 Here, just metres from: Pearson, *Citadel of the Heart*, p. 132.

26 Randolph led a far more: Randolph S. Churchill, *Twenty-One Years*, pp. 12, 14, 15.

26 And then, there was: Gilbert, *Churchill*, vol. 3, *Challenge of War*, p. 6; Randolph S. Churchill, *Twenty-One Years*, p. 15; Winston S. Churchill, *His Father's Son*, p. 11.

27 In the terrible moments: Gilbert, *Churchill*, vol. 3, *Challenge of War*, p. 31; Stevenson, *Lloyd George: A Diary*, p. 37.

27 Unable to expend his: Gilbert, *Churchill*, vol. 3, *Challenge of War*, pp. 82, 111.

28 At a dinner at Walmer: Asquith, *Great War Diary*, p. 84.

28 'I shall be the': Lloyd George, *David & Winston*, p. 120.

28 His initial success: Gilbert, *Churchill*, vol. 3, *Challenge of War*, pp. 259, 262, 304, 448, 472–82.

29 As Lloyd George's mistress: Charmley, *End of Glory*, p. 136

29 Those who visited Admiralty: Pearson, *Citadel of the Heart*, pp. 144–5; Stevenson, *Lloyd George: A Diary*, p. 253; Hardwick, *Clementine Churchill*, p. 149; Bonham-Carter, *Churchill as I Knew Him*, p. 465.

30 But she too was: Pearson, *Citadel of the Heart*, pp. 145–6.

30 Sitting high and discrete: Randolph S. Churchill, *Twenty-One Years*, p. 14; Winston S. Churchill, *His Father's Son*, p. 16; PH Papers 2; Soames, *Clementine Churchill*, pp. 136–7.

30 Winston's fall from grace: Gilbert, *Churchill*, vol. 3, *Challenge of War*, p. 493; RDCH 10/19; Sarah Churchill, *Keep on Dancing*, p. 1; Randolph S. Churchill, *Twenty-One Years*, p. 15; Leslie, *Cousin Randolph*, p. 4; Winston S. Churchill, *His Father's Son*, pp. 16, 23.

31 Throughout the autumn: Pearson, *Citadel of the Heart*, p. 146.

32 Winston had swapped: Gilbert, *Churchill*, vol. 3, *Challenge of War*, pp. 484–6, 503, 504.

32 Eventually, in November: Ibid., p. 564.

32 In the mud: Ibid., pp. 592, 625, 647.

33 And he thought too: Ibid., p. 512.

33 'It is not so': RDCH 1/3/2.

33 His nephew Peregrine remembered: Winston S. Churchill, *His Father's Son*, p. 23.

33 Within days of his return: Gilbert, *Churchill*, vol. 3, *Challenge of War*, pp. 701, 729.

34 Alongside all of this: RDCH 10/19.

34 'What fools they are': Gilbert, *Churchill*, vol. 3, *Challenge of War*, p. 816.

34 Clementine started calling him: Pearson, *Citadel of the Heart*, p. 155.

34 There were hundreds of: Gilbert, *Churchill*, vol. 4, *Stricken World*, pp. 76, 122, 124, 155.

34 On those weekends when: Ibid., p. 18; Manchester, *Last Lion: Visions of Glory*, pp. 617–20; Lough, *No More Champagne*, p. 116; Purnell, *First Lady*, pp. 107, 111, 113; Brian Roberts, *Randolph*, p. 11.

35 Randolph – whom his parents: RDCH 10/19; Brian Roberts, *Randolph*, p. 13; Winston S. Churchill, *His Father's Son*, p. 24.

35 Johnny would grow into: Lees-Milne, *Another Self*, p. 90.

36 When Winston did descend: Gilbert, *Churchill*, vol. 4, *Stricken World*, pp. 18–19.

36 Randolph more than any other: Randolph S. Churchill, *Twenty-One Years*, pp. 15, 17; Sarah Churchill, *Keep on Dancing*, p. 14.

37 'Randolph promises much': Brian Roberts, *Randolph*, p. 13; Randolph S. Churchill, *Twenty-One Years*, p. 15.

37 It was around this time: Randolph S. Churchill, *Twenty-One Years*, pp. 17–18.

Chapter 3: Winston is a Pasha

38 When Winston walked through: Moran, *Struggle for Survival*, p. 433; Manchester and Reid, *Last Lion: Defender of the Realm*, p. 7.

38 'a sort of tiny': Pearson, *Citadel of the Heart*, p. 202.

38 He loved it: MCHL 1/1/6; Soames, *Clementine Churchill*, p. 249.

39 The first blow had: Soames, *Clementine Churchill*, p. 227.

39 In June the same: Purnell, *First Lady*, p. 134.

39 Two months later: Lovell, *The Churchills*, p. 335; Soames, *A Daughter's Tale*, p. 3.

40 Then, the following year: Taylor et al., *Churchill: Four Faces and the Man*, pp. 20, 247; Brian Roberts, *Randolph*, p. 30.

40 'Winston was so down': Gilbert, *Churchill*, vol. 4, *Stricken World*, p. 892.

40 Only one thing promised: Ibid., p. 793.

41 He was fond: McGowan, *My Years with Churchill*, p. 49.

41 She watched his efforts: MCHL 5/178.

41 Guests often woke up: Jones, *Whitehall Diary*, p. 67; Cowles, *Winston Churchill*, p. 273.

42 His hatred of discomfort: Manchester, *Last Lion: Alone*, p. 5; Sarah Churchill, *Thread in the Tapestry*, p. 47; Hickman, *Churchill's Bodyguard*, p. 116.

42 Meals were built around: Stelzer, *Dinner with Churchill*, p. 166; RDCH 10/27; MCHL 5/8/52; Howells, *Simply Churchill*, p. 19.

42 Even time had to: MCHL 5/1/83; Howells, *Simply Churchill*, p. 40; Manchester, *Last Lion: Visions of Glory*, p. 193.

43 And yet Clementine was: McGowan, *My Years with Churchill*, p. 17.

43 When birds started dive-bombing: KH 2/1 Box 51.

43 It was a house: RDCH 10/19.

43 Alongside them were Winston's: Green, *Children of the Sun*, p. 84; Sarah Churchill, *Thread in the Tapestry*, p. 37; Frederick Birkenhead, *The Prof in Two Worlds*, pp. 23, 48; Soames, *Clementine Churchill*, pp. 257–9; *The Churchills* (Television).

44 He talked brilliantly: Asquith, *Great War Diary*, p. 117; KH 2/1 Box 48; Bonham-Carter, *Churchill as I Knew Him*, pp. 116–17.

44 There was seldom much: Soames, *Clementine Churchill*, pp. 259–60; Gilbert, *Churchill*, vol. 5, *Prophet of Truth*, p. 302; Stelzer, *Dinner with Churchill*, pp. 19, 22.

45 'One evening we remained': Lees-Milne, *Through Wood and Dale*, p. 3.

45 Randolph, Diana, Sarah and: Soames, *A Daughter's Tale*, p. 74; Soames, *Clementine Churchill*, p. 260; Purnell, *First Lady*, p. 159.

45 During the school holidays: Sarah Churchill, *Thread in the Tapestry*, pp. 31, 45.

46 Their cousin Peregrine: Pearson, *Citadel of the Heart*, pp. 213–14.

47 The family called Diana: Leslie, *Cousin Randolph*, p. 8.

47 Johnny once drove back: Pearson, *Citadel of the Heart*, p. 213.

47 When Clementine married Winston: RDCH 10/21.

47 'You are a rock': Purnell, *First Lady*, p. 147.

47 Winston, Clementine once told: MCHL 5/1/83; Soames, *Clementine Churchill*, p. 260.

48 'It did not take long': Howells, *Simply Churchill*, p. 19.

48 Aside from the basic: Soames, *Clementine Churchill*, pp. 239, 266.

48 Clementine impressed upon all: Brian Roberts, *Randolph*, p. 5; MCHL 5/1/306.

48 'We admired and loved': PH Papers 2.

48 The loving nicknames: Purnell, *First Lady*, p. 115; Manchester, *Last Lion: Visions of Glory*, p. 757; Soames, *Clementine Churchill*, p. 267.

48 Clementine was by nature: Purnell, *First Lady*, pp. 43, 54.

49 the huge treehouse: Ibid., p. 147.

49 'So what did my': Laura Thompson, *Life in a Cold Climate*, p. 6.

50 'it just seemed to': Soames, *A Daughter's Tale*, p. 91.

50 The special treatment Randolph: Pearson, *Citadel of the Heart*, p. 207.

50 And yet perhaps she: Ibid., pp. 383–84; PH Papers 2.

50 'I am a poor': Purnell, *First Lady*, p. 60.

51 Mary, writing years later: Soames, *Clementine Churchill*, pp. 263, 267.

51 He was, Randolph recalled: Randolph S. Churchill, *Twenty-One Years*, p. 27; PH Papers 2; MCHL 1/59; Soames, *Clementine Churchill*, p. 232.

51 It meant that all: Manchester and Reid, *Last Lion: Defender of the Realm*, p. 27; Sarah Churchill, *Thread in the Tapestry*, p. 33.

52 His son, he said: RDCH 10/19.

52 Because he knew the: Hardwick, *Clementine Churchill*, p. 163; Leslie, *Cousin Randolph*, p. 6; Lovell, *The Churchills*, p. 326; Randolph S. Churchill, *Twenty-One Years*, p. 21.

52 For instance, while Clementine: Winston S. Churchill, *His Father's Son*, p. 27.

52 When Randolph was ten: Randolph S. Churchill, *Twenty-One Years*, pp. 24–5.

53 When guests came to Chartwell: Jones, *Whitehall Diary*, p. 67; RDCH 10/19; RDCH 10/20.

54 Nor did Winston appear: Randolph S. Churchill, *Churchill: Youth*, p. 241.

54 'nothing more than a': Stelzer, *Dinner with Churchill*, p. 10; KH 2/1 Box 48.

54 Randolph absorbed all of: RDCH 1/2/46.

54 'No. To be born': KH 2/1 Box 48.

55 'I hold a police': Hickman, *Churchill's Bodyguard*, p. 65.

55 This dynastic imperative would: Winston S. Churchill, *Memories and Adventures*, p. 121.

55 A man whose overpowering: PH Papers 2.

55 'You know, my dear boy': RDCH 10/4.

Chapter 4: It's Only a Game, Father

56 In September 1924, with: Gilbert, *Churchill*, vol. 5, *Prophet of Truth*, p. 48.

56 A few days later, Winston: Manchester, *Last Lion: Visions of Glory*, pp. 784–5, 788.

56 As chancellor, Winston believed: Gilbert, *Churchill*, vol. 5, *Prophet of Truth*, pp. 62, 66, 67, 104, 112; Boothby, *Recollections of a Rebel*, p. 46; Winston S. Churchill, *His Father's Son*, p. 37.

57 'As happy as a sandboy': Hickman, *Churchill's Bodyguard*, p. 48.

58 Winston had pleased the: Randolph S. Churchill, *Twenty-One Years*, pp. 31, 42, 44–8, 64; Pearson, *Citadel of the Heart*, p. 207; Leslie, *Cousin Randolph*, p. 8; RDCH 1/3/1; Halle, *Young Unpretender*, p. 25; CHAR 1/172/64–65; CHAR 1/199/12–13; CHAR 1/178/63–65; CHAR 1/172/14; Brian Roberts, *Randolph*, pp. 23, 26.

60 The Prof began to: Green, *Children of the Sun*, p. 270; Brian Roberts, *Randolph*, p. 33; Halle, *Young Unpretender*, p. 29.

60 Randolph found himself sitting: Leslie, *Cousin Randolph*, p. 11.

60 If Clementine made: Ibid., p. 12; Soames, *Clementine Churchill*, p. 270.

61 'Randolph would pick: Soames, *Clementine Churchill*, p. 452; RDCH 10/19.

61 It was one of the first: RDCH 10/21; Lees-Milne, *Mingled Measure*, p. 134; Purnell, *First Lady*, p. 181; Manchester and Reid, *Last Lion: Defender of the Realm*, pp. 609–10; Brian Roberts, *Randolph*, p. 79.

62 'To me she was': MCHL 5/1/306.

62 Randolph's cousin Anita Leslie: Leslie, *Cousin Randolph*, pp. 36–7, 161; De Courcy, *Diana Mitford*, p. 24.

62 Knowing that she loved: RDCH 10/19; MCHL 5/1/306.

62 Later in life, whenever: KH 2/1 Box 48.

63 From time to time over: MCHL 5/1/69; MCHL 5/175.

63 But although their relationship: RDCH 10/1/9.

63 He was too busy: Randolph S. Churchill, *Twenty-One Years*, p. 48.

64 Clementine felt an almost: Soames, *Clementine Churchill*, p. 240.

64 One day when Winston: RDCH 10/1/9.

64 On another occasion, when Randolph: Leslie, *Cousin Randolph*, pp. 11–12.

65 He laughed at his: Lockhart, *Diaries*, vol. 1, p. 281.

65 Diana Cooper said that: Halle, *Young Unpretender*, pp. 2, 5, 290; Leslie, *Cousin Randolph*, pp. 11, 16; Randolph S. Churchill, *Twenty-One Years*, p. 36.

66 Randolph claimed in his: Randolph S. Churchill, *Twenty-One Years*, pp. 63, 64, 65, 68, 69, 86, 107; Brian Roberts, *Randolph*, pp. 39, 40; CHAR 1/205/8; Green, *Children of the Sun*, p. 270; Leslie, *Cousin Randolph*, p. 15; Lees-Milne, *Holy Dread*, p. 47; Halle, *Young Unpretender*, pp. 40, 55, 57, 271; Brian Roberts, *Randolph*, pp. 41–2.

68 Randolph had always regarded: Sarah Churchill, *Thread in the Tapestry*, p. 36; Cowles, *Winston Churchill*, p. 135; Moran, *Struggle for Survival*, p. 746; Asquith, *Great War Diary*, p. 246; Colville, *The Churchillians*, p. 9.

69 Weekends at Charlton followed: Green, *Children of the Sun*, pp. 80–4; Frederick Smith, *F. E.*, pp. 459, 461, 475, 476, 478, 543, 552.

70 It was here, Randolph's: Brian Roberts, *Randolph*, p. 32; Winston S. Churchill, *Memories and Adventures*, p. 245; RDCH 10/19.

70 F. E. would occasionally arrange: Frederick Smith, *F. E.*, p. 459.

71 'he more than defended': Soames, *Speaking for Themselves*, pp. 320–1.

71 'Politics is like prostitution': Pearson, *Citadel of the Heart*, p. 4; Randolph S. Churchill, *Twenty-One Years*, pp. 28, 117; Brian Roberts, *Randolph*, pp. 3, 35, 46, 48; RDCH 1/3/1; MCHL 5/1/66; Winston S. Churchill, *His Father's Son*, p. 48.

73 His star was plainly: Manchester, *Last Lion: Visions of Glory*, pp. 809–10, 812; Gilbert, *Churchill*, vol. 5, *Prophet of Truth*, pp. 236, 245–6.

74 Randolph made a precocious: Robin Birkenhead, *Churchill 1924–1940*, p. 36; Winston S. Churchill, *His Father's Son*, p. 54; Gilbert, *Churchill*, vol. 5, *Prophet of Truth*, p. 327.

75 Winston spent the evening: Jones, *Whitehall Diary*, p. 183; Gilbert, *Churchill*, vol. 5, *Prophet of Truth*, p. 329.

Chapter 5: I Love Him Vy Much

76 Those close to him: KH 2/1 Box 48; Gilbert, *Churchill Documents*, vol. 13, *Coming of War*, p. 557.

77 Writing to his old friend: Lough, *No More Champagne*, p. 182.

77 They left on the: RDCH 10/24; RDCH 1/2/38; Gilbert, *Churchill Documents*, vol. 12, *Wilderness Years*, pp. 16, 22, 31, 32, 33, 40, 44, 46, 50, 52–3, 54, 59, 61–2, 78, 82, 84, 86, 87, 88, 95, 96, 185; Brian Roberts, *Randolph*, pp. 50–8.

77 He regarded the other: RDCH 1/2/40.

78 An amused Winston liked: Halle, *Young Unpretender*, p. 58.

79 A moment would always: RDCH 10/19.

83 Although Randolph liked to: Brian Roberts, *Randolph*, p. 57; Leslie, *Cousin Randolph*, pp. 17, 18.

84 'It is rather awful to': RDCH 1/2/37.

84 Johnny remembered that: RDCH 10/19.

84 When one of the: Gilbert, *Churchill*, vol. 5, *Prophet of Truth*, p. 350.

84 The next day, Winston: Winston S. Churchill, *If I Lived My Life Again*, p. 140.

Chapter 6: But Words Are Useless

86 Randolph returned to university: Brian Roberts, *Randolph*, p. 60.

86 Winston still saw India: Boothby, *Recollections of a Rebel*, p. 53.

86 There were two strands: Gilbert, *Churchill Documents*, vol. 12, *Wilderness Years*, pp. 129, 185, 186.

87 In January 1931, Baldwin: Manchester, *Last Lion: Visions of Glory*, p. 852.

87 And he was sure: Ibid., p. 753.

87 He also found that: Gilbert, *Churchill*, vol. 5, *Prophet of Truth*, p. 387.

88 'My late colleagues': Boothby, *Recollections of a Rebel*, p. 54.

88 'Winston Churchill slouched in': Nicolson, *Diaries and Letters 1930–1939*, p. 38.

88 In September 1930 a: Gilbert, *Churchill Documents*, vol. 12, *Wilderness Years*, p. 215; RDCH 10/27.

88 After F. E. died, Winston: Lovell, *The Churchills*, p. 365.

89 Randolph, however, revealed: Lockhart, *Diaries*, vol. 1, p. 307.

89 Right through the rest: Gilbert, *Churchill*, vol. 5, *Prophet of Truth*, p. 374.

89 Although he wrote Winston: Gilbert, *Churchill Documents*, vol. 12, *Wilderness Years*, pp. 140, 143; CHAR 1/214/1.

89 'Your idle & lazy': RDCH 1/3/1.

90 'I wasted time until': Winston S. Churchill, *If I Lived My Life Again*, p. 180.

90 As Randolph reported excitedly: CHAR 1/214/1; Brian Roberts, *Randolph*, pp. 43, 64–6; Randolph S. Churchill, *Twenty-One Years*, pp. 98, 104, 106, 107.

91 Randolph was, his tutor: Halle, *Young Unpretender*, pp. 31–3; Bonham-Carter, *Churchill as I Knew Him*, p. 22; Robert Boothby, *I Fight to Live*, p. 45.

93 In the New World: Halle, *Young Unpretender*, pp. 2, 67; Leslie, *Cousin Randolph*, pp. 19–20; Brian Roberts, *Randolph*, p. 72.

93 'Do you realise what': RDCH 1/2/42.

93 'Of course, they publish': RDCH 1/3/3.

94 'On his return, Randolph': Hardwick, *Clementine Churchill*, p. 199.

94 Randolph opted instead to: Randolph S. Churchill, *Twenty-One Years*, pp. 86, 108.

94 It was all very: Brian Roberts, *Randolph*, p. 84; Leslie, *Cousin Randolph*, pp. 21, 24, 27, 34; Halle, *Young Unpretender*, p. 52; Waugh, *Diaries*, pp. 315–20; Hastings, *Evelyn Waugh*, p. 464.

95 He was amusing, keen: Lockhart, *Diaries*, vol. 1, pp. 117–18, 191.

95 The political situation was: RDCH 1/3/1.

96 When, in 1931, Gandhi: Brian Roberts, *Randolph*, p. 86.

96 Over lunch at the: Nicolson, *Diaries and Letters 1930–1939*, p. 38; Nicholas Mosley, *Rules of the Game*, p. 203; Taylor et al., *Churchill: Four Faces and the Man*, p. 65.

97 'Winston is very weak': Lockhart, *Diaries*, vol. 1, p. 186.

97 'I do not drink': McGinty, *Churchill's Cigar*, p. 91.

97 It was important: Howells, *Simply Churchill*, p. 153.

97 The 1929 crash had: Lough, *No More Champagne*, pp. 193–4, 199.

98 'It may never happen': Soames, *Clementine Churchill*, p. 107.

98 Winston always based his: Lough, *No More Champagne*, pp. 206, 207, 209, 258; Purnell, *First Lady*, p. 173.

98 None of this was enough: Lough, *No More Champagne*, p. 205.

98 On 22 August, for: Gilbert, *Churchill Documents*, vol. 12, *Wilderness Years*, p. 350.

99 He arranged a lavish: Gilbert, *Churchill*, vol. 5, *Prophet of Truth*, p. 579.

99 'What are you doing?': Lockhart, *Diaries*, vol. 1, p. 229.

99 'Randolph's contact was Ernst': RDCH 1/2/13.

100 'Then, in October 1931: Lough, *No More Champagne*, p. 208; RDCH 1/3/1; Winston S. Churchill, *His Father's Son*, p. 80; Gilbert, *Churchill Documents*, vol. 12, *Wilderness Years*, pp. 369–71.

100 'I am ready to pay': CHAR 1/226/74.

101 'I have been up': CHAR 1/222/18.

101 When, on 28 May: Gilbert, *Churchill*, vol. 5, *Prophet of Truth*, pp. 434–5; Randolph S. Churchill, *Twenty-One Years*, pp. 108–12; RDCH 10/21; RDCH 8/1/1; RDCH 8/1/2; RDCH 10/19; MCHL 5/8/52; Lockhart, *Diaries*, vol. 1, p. 219.

Chapter 7: They Fight Like Cats

105 Some evenings might find: Channon, *Chips*, p. 21; Boothby, *Recollections of a Rebel*, p. 71.

105 Even now, his burning: Taylor et al., *Churchill: Four Faces and the Man*, pp. 56, 84; Pearson, *Citadel of the Heart*, p. 83; Manchester, *Last Lion: Visions of Glory*, pp. 753, 812.

106 Randolph was not a cruel: Halle, *Young Unpretender*, p. 59; RDCH 2/2; Lockhart, *Diaries*, vol. 1, pp. 203, 219.

106 Winston seemed entertained by: Lockhart, *Diaries*, vol. 2, p. 760; Gilbert, *Churchill Documents*, vol. 12, *Wilderness Years*, p. 1113; McGowan, *My Years with Churchill*, p. 153; Manchester and Reid, *Last Lion: Defender of the Realm*, p. 16.

107 'a large sherry': Lockhart, *Diaries*, vol. 1, p. 281.

107 He also did: KH 2/1 Box 48.

107 'They both use a': RDCH 8/1/4.

107 Winston, Randolph later recorded: RDCH 10/27.

108 In the summer they: Gilbert, *Churchill Documents*, vol. 12, *Wilderness Years*, pp. 847–8, 853, 862; Gilbert, *Churchill*, vol. 5, *Prophet of Truth*, p. 559; Soames, *Clementine Churchill*, pp. 287–9; Purnell, *First Lady*, p. 156; Gilbert, *Churchill*, vol. 7, *Road to Victory*, p. 37.

108 What Winston omitted to: Lough, *No More Champagne*, pp. 141, 231, 244; RDCH 2/1; Brian Roberts, *Randolph*, p. 114; CHAR 1/285/113.

109 His archives contain: RDCH 2/16.

109 Especially since he was: Sulzberger, *Last of the Giants*, p. 108.

109 Before long, both: Winston S. Churchill, *His Father's Son*, p. 104.

110 They made money together: Gilbert, *Churchill Documents*, vol. 12, *Wilderness Years*, pp. 869, 876; Gilbert, *Churchill*, vol. 5, *Prophet of Truth*, p. 561.

110 'I thought it would': Gilbert, *Churchill Documents*, vol. 12, *Wilderness Years*, p. 448.

111 When Winston gave speeches: Brian Roberts, *Randolph*, p. 91; RDCH 8/1/4.

111 'As to Winston, he': Gilbert, *Churchill Documents*, vol. 12, *Wilderness Years*, pp. 448, 480–1.

111 In 1934, Winston tried: Brian Roberts, *Randolph*, pp. 124–6; Gilbert, *Churchill*, vol. 5, *Prophet of Truth*, p. 532.

112 'I do not know which': Robin Birkenhead, *Churchill 1924–1940*, p. 50.

113 'clarity of thought, command': Winston S. Churchill, *His Father's Son*, p. 86.

113 Randolph appeared with his: Gilbert, *Churchill Documents*, vol. 12, *Wilderness Years*, pp. 825–8.

114 'Johnny, I'm going to': Pearson, *Citadel of the Heart*, p. 241.

114 'I think Winston Churchill': Pearson, *Citadel of the Heart*, p. 285; Gilbert, *Churchill Documents*, vol. 12, *Wilderness Years*, p. 700; Halle, *Young Unpretender*, p. 173.

114 Winston was haunted by: Gilbert, *Churchill Documents*, vol. 12, *Wilderness Years*, p. 704.

115 Randolph's frustration at: Randolph S. Churchill, *Twenty-One Years*, p. 117.

115 And yet perhaps most: Channon, *Chips*, p. 46; Manchester, *Last Lion: Visions of Glory*, p. 14.

116 Randolph believed that Baldwin: Randolph S. Churchill, *Twenty-One Years*, pp. 118, 122.

116 This meant that: Randolph S. Churchill, *Rise and Fall*, pp. 73–4.

Chapter 8: My Brother, the Bastard

117 Randolph revered Winston: Randolph S. Churchill, *Twenty-One Years*, p. 123.

117 He might have deliberately: RDCH 8/1/1; RDCH 8/1/2.

117 Sarah was confronted by: Hardwick, *Clementine Churchill*, p. 215.

117 Decades later, far away: Leslie, *Cousin Randolph*, p. 118.

117 The only option Randolph: Randolph S. Churchill, *Twenty-One Years*, p. 123.

118 'He is very ambitious': Lockhart, *Diaries*, vol. 1, p. 191.

118 He was not a man for: Colville, *The Churchillians*, p. 2; Taylor et al., *Churchill: Four Faces and the Man*, pp. 55–6.

118 'This is a pushing': Pearson, *Citadel of the Heart*, p. 65.

118 More than one man: Lees-Milne, *Ancestral Voices*, p. 50.

118 Reflecting on this time: Randolph S. Churchill, *Twenty-One Years*, p. 123.

119 In July 1929: Gilbert, *Churchill Documents*, vol. 12, *Wilderness Years*, p. 23.

119 Winston's archives are full: Ibid., pp. 971, 974–5.

120 As time went on, both: Colville, *The Churchillians*, p. 23.

120 They also shared: RDCH 1/3/1.

121 Winston was sensitive: RDCH 10/19.

121 'You are not on': Bonham-Carter, *Churchill as I Knew Him*, p. 132.

121 'the mention of gallantry': Manchester, *Last Lion: Visions of Glory*, p. 36.

121 'we don't register when': RDCH 10/19.

121 'prone to fits of': Colville, *The Churchillians*, p. 5.

121 When Randolph got angry: Leslie, *Cousin Randolph*, pp. 49, 114.

122 After one of their rows: Lockhart, *Diaries*, vol. 1, p. 229.

122 'He was so badly': Norwich, 'The Jekyll and Hyde Nature of Randolph Churchill'.

122 It was different for: Purnell, *First Lady*, p. 183.

122 'She didn't come into': RDCH 10/19.

122 These years were: Purnell, *First Lady*, pp. 174, 176, 177.

123 'You always seem to': MCHL 5/1/306.

123 Winston, so easily and: Soames, *Clementine Churchill*, p. 285.

123 'queer ideas about what': Manchester, *Last Lion: Visions of Glory*, p. 701.

123 Mary witnessed acrimonious rows: Soames, *A Daughter's Tale*, p. 98.

123 At one point in: Lovell, *The Churchills*, p. 360.

123 'She was very frightened': RDCH 10/21.

124 But what Clementine could: Taylor et al., *Churchill: Four Faces and the Man*, pp. 124, 241.

124 'Some take drugs.': Pearson, *Citadel of the Heart*, p. 206.

124 'Contact with you is': Gilbert, *Churchill*, vol. 3, *Challenge of War*, p. 145.

125 Witness the crackling, almost: Morris, *Fisher's Face*, pp. 184–6.

125 Violet Asquith recognised the curious: Bonham-Carter, *Churchill as I Knew Him*, p. 392.

125 'Clementine felt differently.': Asquith, *Great War Diary*, p. 246.

125 Randolph's sisters knew this: MCHL 1/1/8.

126 On a morning in: Boyle, *Poor, Dear Brendan*, pp. 7, 12, 15, 32, 37, 42, 77, 78, 79, 81, 100, 104, 109–10, 169, 195; Brian Roberts, *Randolph*, p. 17; Randolph S. Churchill, *Twenty-One Years*, p. 48; Soames, *Clementine Churchill*, p. 279; Purnell, *First Lady*, pp. 159, 177–8, 286; KH 2/1 Box 48.

128 'Mummy won't call him': Diana Mosley, *Life of Contrasts*, p. 40.

128 In one version Bracken: Brian Roberts, *Randolph*, pp. 18–19.

129 But by 1929: Soames, *Clementine Churchill*, pp. 279, 281.

129 An impudent coiner: Colville, *The Churchillians*, pp. 43, 45.

130 Randolph was, Christopher Sykes: Sykes, *Evelyn Waugh*, p. 253.

130 Randolph loved Bracken's company: Diana Mosley, *Life of Contrasts*, p. 40.

130 As Randolph grew older: Boyle, *Poor, Dear Brendan*, pp. 117, 167.

131 Randolph and Bracken's trip: Randolph S. Churchill, *Twenty-One Years*, pp. 95–7; Boyle, *Poor, Dear Brendan*, pp. 180–2, 222; Boothby, *Recollections of a Rebel*, p. 70; Brian Roberts, *Randolph*, p. 109; KH 2/1 Box 48.

Chapter 9: This is a Most Rash and Unconsidered Plunge

133 Two significant things happened: Gilbert, *Churchill Documents*, vol. 12, *Wilderness Years*, pp. 1031–3, 1034, 1035, 1037, 1042, 1044, 1045, 1046, 1048, 1049, 1052, 1063, 1064, 1071, 1072, 1078, 1081; Brian Roberts, *Randolph*, pp. 130–9; Winston S. Churchill, *His Father's Son*, pp. 104–13, 120; RDCH 8/1/4, RDCH 8/1/5; Sarah Churchill, *Keep on Dancing*, pp. 20–1; MCHL 5/1/80.

133 Randolph was the only member: RDCH 10/19.

135 Sarah rather resented: Sarah Churchill, *Keep on Dancing*, p. 19.

138 Winston's black moods: *The Churchills* (Television).

138 'when he does the': MCHL 5/1/83.

139 'The Churchill campaign': Channon, *Chips*, p. 23.

139 On Monday, 21 January: Sarah Churchill, *Keep on Dancing*, p. 23.

143 Sarah was struck by: Ibid., p. 19.

143 As the evening of: Channon, *Chips*, pp. 25, 26.

145 'that little brute Randolph': Robin Birkenhead, *Churchill 1924–1940*, p. 52.

146 'He had nothing': RDCH 10/19; Randolph S. Churchill, *Twenty-One Years*, p. 122.

Chapter 10: Everything is Black, Very Black

147 Randolph saw the thirties: Halle, *Young Unpretender*, p. 242; KH 2/1 Box 48; RDCH 10/19; Leslie, *Cousin Randolph*, p. 35.

147 Randolph had been quick: Winston S. Churchill, *His Father's Son*, pp. 91, 97.

147 In July 1932, shortly: Randolph S. Churchill, *Twenty-One Years*, p. 112.

147 There was an ambiguous: Manchester, *Last Lion: Alone*, p. 66.

148 Winston liked to say: Gilbert, *Churchill Documents*, vol. 12, *Wilderness Years*, p. 557; Cowles, *Looking for Trouble*, p. 119.

148 One grisly estimate warned: Gilbert, *Churchill*, vol. 5, *Prophet of Truth*, pp. 573–4.

148 'They can't seem to': Cowles, *Looking for Trouble*, p. 114.

149 'the deadly years of': Gilbert, *Churchill*, vol. 5, *Prophet of Truth*, p. 886.

149 'Apparently Mr Baldwin's idea': RDCH 2/2.

149 The phrase 'wilderness years': Gilbert, *Churchill*, vol. 5, *Prophet of Truth*, pp. xxi, 729–30, 866; Gilbert, *Churchill Documents*, vol. 12, *Wilderness Years*, pp. 6, 7, 12, 420, 422, 423, 901, 906, 949; Channon, *Chips*, p. 122.

151 Another source was: RDCH 1/2/17.

151 Winston took more persuading: Gilbert, *Churchill Documents*, vol. 12, *Wilderness Years*, pp. 52–3.

152 Most pertinent to: Halle, *Young Unpretender*, p. 189.

152 He could draw on: RDCH 1/2/40; Leslie, *Cousin Randolph*, pp. 35–7.

152 Randolph travelled pursued by: CHAR 1/271/76; CHAR 1/271/83; CHAR 1/285/91; CHAR 1/285/129.

152 The American journalist: Winston S. Churchill, *His Father's Son*, p. 143; Halle, *Young Unpretender*, pp. 108–11.

153 Closer to home, Randolph: Maisky, *Diaries*, pp. 107, 121, 157, 162; Nicolson, *Diaries and Letters 1930–1939*, pp. 249, 325, 332.

154 Those who warned against: Duff Cooper, *Old Men Forget*, pp. 252, 255.

154 In London, it was: Lockhart, *Diaries*, vol. 1, p. 271.

154 MPs carried on drinking: Channon, *Chips*, p. 131.

155 'the narrowest, most ignorant': Colville, *Fringes of Power*, p. 352.

155 'There is too deep': Gilbert, *Churchill*, vol. 5, *Prophet of Truth*, pp. 297, 860.

155 'There's no plan of': Gilbert, *Churchill Documents*, vol. 12, *Wilderness Years*, p. 1111.

155 As the situation in: Taylor et al., *Churchill: Four Faces and the Man*, pp. 105–6.

155 Winston could still hush: Cowles, *Looking for Trouble*, p. 121.

156 Winston took no offence: Randolph S. Churchill, *Twenty-One Years*, p. 124; Winston S. Churchill, *His Father's Son*, p. 155; Channon, *Chips*, p. 60; Gilbert, *Churchill Documents*, vol. 12, *Wilderness Years*, pp. 179, 693, 695.

157 'It would in my belief': RDCH 1/3/1.

157 'You can't say that!': RDCH 10/19.

157 On one night: Halle, *Young Unpretender*, p. 35.

158 On those occasions when Randolph: Gilbert, *Churchill Documents*, vol. 12, *Wilderness Years*, pp. 1083, 1111.

158 There was, Bob Boothby: Boothby, *Recollections of a Rebel*, p. 44.

158 In December 1937: RDCH 4/12.

159 A few months later: Gilbert, *Churchill Documents*, vol. 13, *Coming of War*, pp. 908–12, 920–1, 970.

160 Randolph went to see: Leslie, *Cousin Randolph*, p. 35.

161 The truth was: KH 2/1 Box 47.

161 'probably the only subject': RDCH 1/3/3.

161 Anyone listening carefully to: Eden, *Memoir*, pp. 4, 5.

162 The same was true of: Hardwick, *Clementine Churchill*, p. 216; Winston S. Churchill, *His Father's Son*, pp. 120–1; CHAR 2/235/1.

162 When his patron: Leslie, *Cousin Randolph*, pp. 30–1, 33, 34.

162 With war looming: Gilbert, *Churchill Documents*, vol. 13, *Coming of War*, p. 1090.

163 'I'm just off to': Ibid., p. 1159.

163 Before he left, Randolph: Winston S. Churchill, *His Father's Son*, pp. 159–60.

164 Winston told friends that: Gilbert, *Churchill Documents*, vol. 13, *Coming of War*, pp. 1162, 1171.

164 Harold Nicolson wrote: Nicolson, *Diaries and Letters 1930–1939*, p. 355.

164 And yet men like: Channon, *Chips*, p. 166.

164 Both father and son: Gilbert, *Churchill*, vol. 5, *Prophet of Truth*, pp. 1008, 1031.

164 Randolph's reaction was: Winston S. Churchill, *Memories and Adventures*, p. 36.

165 'Shits like you': Gilbert, *In Search of Churchill*, pp. 36–7.

165 But, for the moment: Halle, *Young Unpretender*, p. 290.

165 In a debate on: Gilbert, *Churchill*, vol. 5, *Prophet of Truth*, p. xx; Winston S. Churchill, *His Father's Son*, p. 164.

166 On 10 March 1939: Boothby, *Recollections of a Rebel*, p. 126.

166 As the news broke: Lees-Milne, *Diaries 1942–1954*, p. 171.

166 Perhaps wary of past: Gilbert, *Churchill*, vol. 5, *Prophet of Truth*, p. 1083.

166 Randolph's *Evening Standard* diary: RDCH 8/1/8; RDCH 8/1/9.

167 In July 1939: Cowles, *Looking for Trouble*, p. 251.

Chapter 11: Winston is Back

169 The war, when it: MCHL 1/1.

169 On the day war: Hickman, *Churchill's Bodyguard*, p. 82.

169 'A darkened emaciated face': Maisky, *Diaries*, pp. 223–4.

170 Clementine, who had come: Hickman, *Churchill's Bodyguard*, p. 83.

170 When he walked back: Gilbert, *Churchill*, vol. 6, *Finest Hour*, p. 4.

170 Winston seemed to know: Lovell, *The Churchills*, p. 410.

170 Sitting at his desk: Colville, *Fringes of Power*, p. 104; Gilbert, *Churchill*, vol. 6, *Finest Hour*, p. 156.

171 And while Randolph had: Green, *Children of the Sun*, p. 397; Leslie, *Cousin Randolph*, p. 47; RDCH 4/16.

171 Although he was sleeping: Brian Roberts, *Randolph*, pp. 175–6; Leslie, *Cousin Randolph*, p. 46.

172 The Honourable Pamela Digby: Sally Bedell Smith, *Reflected Glory*, pp. 19, 29, 30, 33, 34, 36, 50, 51, 53, 54, 55, 59, 60, 61, 62; Ogden, *Life of the Party*, pp. 26, 45, 56, 69, 75–6, 84; RDCH 10/21; Winston S. Churchill, *Memories and Adventures*, pp. 5–6; *Churchill's Girl* (Television).

173 'Don't marry someone because': MCHL 1/1/3.

175 She did not really: RDCH 1/3/6; MCHL 1/1/7.

176 Most people came away: RDCH 10/21.

176 Writing to her sister: MCHL 5/1/84.

176 Clementine's doubts were less: Hardwick, *Clementine Churchill*, p. 238.

177 Because Lady Digby had: MCHL 1/1.

177 'We must eat': RDCH 4/16.

178 When the Fourth Hussars: RDCH 10/21; Sally Bedell Smith, *Reflected Glory*, pp. 63, 65, 66–7; Ogden, *Life of the Party*, pp. 91, 92.

178 'I am sure yr': Winston S. Churchill, *His Father's Son*, p. 175.

178 Down in London: MCHL 1/1/7.

179 The worst of his: Fleming, *Letters*, p. 40.

179 'don't be enchanted by': Manchester, *Last Lion: Alone*, pp. 310–11.

179 Don't worry about bills: RDCH 10/21.

180 And yet the letters: RDCH 1/3/5.

181 'Are you having a': RDCH 10/21.

181 'his eyes lit up': RDCH 1/3/5.

Chapter 12: I Could Discipline the Bloody Business at Last

182 On the night of: Lockhart, *Diaries*, vol. 2, p. 564; Leslie, *Cousin Randolph*, p. 48; Gilbert, *Churchill*, vol. 6, *Finest Hour*, pp. 286–7, 305–6, 313–14; Gilbert, *Continue to Pester*, p. 32.

183 'I could discipline the': Moran, *Winston Churchill*, p. 324.

183 The next morning, Winston swept: Sally Bedell Smith, *Reflected Glory*, p. 69.

184 Wilson had arrived that: Maisky, *Diaries*, p. 280.

184 It was a time: Green, *Children of the Sun*, p. 363.

185 But when he became: Gilbert, *Continue to Pester*, pp. 5–7.

185 Randolph, suddenly, found he: Colville, *Fringes of Power*, p. 54.

185 'Bless you for your': Winston S. Churchill, *His Father's Son*, p. 177.

186 These trips still had: Gilbert, *Churchill*, vol. 6, *Finest Hour*, p. 460.

186 'that supreme combination of': Pearson, *Citadel of the Heart*, p. 192.

186 'It took Armageddon to': Boothby, *Recollections of a Rebel*, p. 145.

186 Giddy with the new: Manchester and Reid, *Last Lion: Defender of the Realm*, p. 25; Lovell, *The Churchills*, p. 453; Montague Browne, *Long Sunset*, p. 318.

187 'Have you done justice': Manchester, *Last Lion: Visions of Glory*, p. 253.

187 He could do this: Ibid., p. 27.

187 His secretaries and ministers: CHOH 3 CLVL.

187 There were some weeks: Nicolson, *Diaries and Letters 1939–1945*, p. 103.

187 (it was a shame: Manchester, *Last Lion: Visions of Glory*, p. 10.

188 It is difficult to imagine: Manchester and Reid, *Last Lion: Defender of the Realm*, p. 4.

189 He was as happy: Winston S. Churchill, *If I Lived My Life Again*, p. 305; Moran, *Struggle for Survival*, p. 324; Montague Browne, *Long Sunset*, p. 177.

189 There were bleak moments: Eden, *Memoir*, p. 52.

189 Alive as always: MCHL 5/8/137.

189 But although many of: Channon, *Chips*, p. 254.

189 Days later, at a: Moran, *Struggle for Survival*, p. 324.

189 Looking back years later: RDCH 10/21.

189 'I began gradually': Manchester and Reid, *Last Lion: Defender of the Realm*, pp. 609–10.

190 Nevertheless, she was quick: PH Papers 30; *Churchill's Girl* (Television); RDCH 1/3/5; Purnell, *First Lady*, pp. 211, 212, 331; Hardwick, *Clementine Churchill*, p. 246.

191 Diana and Sarah had a: Sally Bedell Smith, *Reflected Glory*, pp. 67, 68; MCHL 1/1/9.

191 Mary found herself thinking: MCHL 1/1/3.

191 His post came with: Pearson, *Citadel of the Heart*, p. 297; Soames, *A Daughter's Tale*, p. 251.

192 'Everywhere he had an': Alanbrooke, *War Diaries*, pp. 173–4.

192 Chequers compensated for Chartwell's: Maisky, *Diaries*, p. 372; Lough, *No More Champagne*, p. 292; Manchester and Reid, *Last Lion: Defender of the Realm*, pp. 26, 187–8, 195; Colville, *Fringes of Power*, pp. 128–9, 242–3, 265, 378; Alanbrooke, *War Diaries*, pp. 145, 194, 314.

193 The visit he made: Gilbert, *Churchill*, vol. 6, *Finest Hour*, pp. 609, 619, 622, 649.

194 It was this issue that: Leslie, *Cousin Randolph*, pp. 35, 43, 48; De Courcy, *Diana Mitford*, p. 35.

194 Winston's private secretaries did: Colville, *Fringes of Power*, pp. 146–7; Colville, *The Churchillians*, p. 23.

195 On one occasion during: KH 2/1 Box 51; Halle, *Young Unpretender*, pp. 52, 60.

196 Mary, perhaps more used: MCHL 1/1/2.

196 Winston's ascension: RDCH 10/21.

196 Kathleen Harriman, the daughter: WA Papers 4.

197 Clementine was alive to: Soames, *Clementine Churchill*, p. 330; MCHL 1/1/5; Purnell, *First Lady*, pp. 235–6.

198 One morning in August: RDCH 10/21; Purnell, *First Lady*, pp. 237–8.

199 Then, suddenly, it appeared: Brian Roberts, *Randolph*, pp. 193–5; Colville, *Fringes of Power*, p. 218; Sally Bedell Smith, *Reflected Glory*, p. 72; Leslie, *Cousin Randolph*, p. 49; Winston S. Churchill, *His Father's Son*, p. 183; Winston S. Churchill, *Memories and Adventures*, p. 1; Manchester and Reid, *Last Lion: Defender of the* Realm, p. 186; RDCH 8/1/11; RDCH 10/21; MCHL 1/1/3; PH Papers 30.

Chapter 13: My Favourite American

201 The year 1941 was difficult: Soames, *Clementine Churchill*, p. 342.

201 As soon as he heard that: Hastings, *Evelyn Waugh*, pp. 413–16; Waugh, *Diaries*, pp. 488, 491, 493; Green, *Children of the Sun*, p. 396; Winston S. Churchill, *Memories and Adventures*, pp. 14, 16, 17.

202 Randolph, carrying enough luggage: Hastings, *Evelyn Waugh*, pp. 417–18; Waugh, *Letters*, pp. 149–50, 154; Artemis Cooper, *Cairo in the War*, pp. 87, 89; Ogden, *Life of the Party*, p. 104.

203 Pamela had never been even: RDCH 10/21; Winston S. Churchill, *His Father's Son*, pp. 186–7; Sally Bedell Smith, *Reflected Glory*, pp. 18, 74, 85, 86; Winston S. Churchill, *Memories and Adventures*, p. 17; Purnell, *First Lady*, p. 254; PH Papers 26.

204 When she visited Mary's: MCHL 1/1/9.

205 'I went up to': Gilbert, *Churchill*, vol. 6, *Finest Hour*, p. 358.

205 American support was always: Harriman and Abel, *Special Envoy*, pp. 21, 22; Manchester and Reid, *Last Lion: Defender of the Realm*, pp. 315, 317, 318; Soames, *A Daughter's Tale*, p. 189; Sally Bedell Smith, *Reflected Glory*, pp. 87–8, 91–2, 106; Ogden, *Life of the Party*, pp. 122–4, 127, 128

207 Harriman seemed intent on: WA Papers 3; MCHL 1/1/3.

207 And it was at Chequers: *Churchill's Girl* (Television); Pearson, *Citadel of the Heart*, p. 300.

208 People woke the next: Colville, *Fringes of Power*, pp. 323–4.

210 Bob Boothby, who despite: Boothby, *Recollections of a Rebel*, pp. 54–6.

211 Talking to an old: Lockhart, *Diaries*, vol. 2, p. 227.

211 Randolph, two thousand miles: Leslie, *Cousin Randolph*, pp. 56, 57; Artemis Cooper, *Cairo in the War*, pp. 4, 5, 37, 109, 114, 121, 122, 123; Hastings, *Evelyn Waugh*, p. 420.

212 One of these was Maud: Brian, *Randolph*, p. 211; Artemis Cooper, *Cairo in the War*, pp. 88, 183.

212 When he was not with: Halle, *Young Unpretender*, p. 46; Leslie, *Cousin Randolph*, pp. 57–8, 60; Artemis Cooper, *Cairo in the War*, pp. 219–21.

213 A constant stream of messages: Leslie, *Cousin Randolph*, p. 56; Brian Roberts, *Randolph*, p. 208; CHAR 1/362/12–15; CHAR 1/362/28–32; CHAR 1/362/18–25; CHAR 20/62/96–103.

214 In addition to this, Randolph: Gilbert, *Churchill Documents*, vol. 17, *Testing Times*, p. 220.

215 Promoted to major: Artemis Cooper, *Cairo in the War*, pp. 111, 126–7; Brian Roberts, *Randolph*, p. 207.

215 In June 1941: Leslie, *Cousin Randolph*, p. 56; WA Papers 4; CHAR 20/33/23–27; CHAR 20/33/37–44; Winston S. Churchill, *Memories and Adventures*, p. 247.

Chapter 14: R is His Blind Spot

217 Six months later: Sally Bedell Smith, *Reflected Glory*, p. 97; Gilbert, *Churchill Documents*, vol. 17, *Testing Times*, p. 37.

217 As Pamela cabled to: WA Papers 4.

218 By the time Winston: Montague Browne, *Long Sunset*, p. 116.

218 The first day of the confidence: Manchester and Reid, *Last Lion: Defender of the Realm*, pp. 476–8; Channon, *Chips*, pp. 318–19; Nicolson, *Diaries and Letters 1939–1945*, pp. 208–10; WA Papers 4.

221 On 15 February, Singapore: Manchester and Reid, *Last Lion: Defender of the Realm*, pp. 484–5; Nicolson, *Diaries and Letters 1939–1945*, pp. 211–13, 221.

221 Winston had suffered a: Gilbert, *Churchill*, vol. 7, *Road to Victory*, pp. 30–3; Manchester and Reid, *Last Lion: Defender of the Realm*, p. 469.

221 Mary's diary became: MCHL 1/1/5.

223 He was almost entirely: DIAC 1/1/23.

224 News of the cleavage: Lees-Milne, *Ancestral Voices*, p. 36; Waugh, *Letters*, p. 160.

225 Continuing the sly theme: Gilbert, *Churchill Documents*, vol. 17, *Testing Times*, pp. 433–4.

226 On 23 March: MCHL 1/1/5; MCHL 1/1/3; MCHL 1/1/7.

228 Randolph returned to Egypt: CHAR 1/369/3–4.

228 Clementine was appalled: Gilbert, *Churchill Documents*, vol. 17, *Testing Times*, p. 511; MCHL 1/1/6.

229 Winston, who had started: Gilbert, *Churchill*, vol. 7, *Road to Victory*, p. 95.

229 One witness remembers seeing: KH 2/1 Box 48.

229 'Of course I do': Gilbert, *Churchill Documents*, vol. 17, *Testing Times*, pp. 618–20; CHAR 1/369/5–8.

230 In May 1942: Maclean, *Eastern Approaches*, p. 202; Halle, *Young Unpretender*, pp. 89–90, 98, 113.

231 Winston pronounced himself 'thrilled': CHAR 20/65/33–78; CHAR 20/65/88–98.

231 'I lunched with Papa': RDCH 1/3/5.

231 In April 1942: Sally Bedell Smith, *Reflected Glory*, pp. 98, 99–101, 106, 108; Ogden, *Life of the Party*, p. 136; Lockhart, *Diaries*, vol. 2, p. 227; Leslie, *Cousin Randolph*, p. 71; Waugh, *Diaries*, pp. 524–5; RDCH 1/2/46; Randolph S. Churchill, *Twenty-One Years*, p. 37; Taylor et al., *Churchill: Four Faces and the Man*, p. 12.

233 In a letter to her father: Gilbert, *Churchill Documents*, vol. 17, *Testing Times*, p. 1331.

Chapter 15: Every Day I Think of You

234 'Randolph may see his': MCHL 5/1/87.

234 Laura's spring 1943 letter: RDCH 1/2/45.

235 On 26 February 1944: CHAR 20/158/2; CHAR 20/158/63.

235 Winston also continued to: Halle, *Young Unpretender*, p. 287.

235 He would telephone Randolph's: RDCH 10/21.

235 The first request had: Brian Roberts, *Randolph*, p. 188.

235 He liked the fact that: Gilbert and Arnn, *Churchill Documents*, vol. 18, *One Continent Redeemed*, pp. 15–17, 208.

236 'After the fascinating &': CHAR 1/375/17–18.

236 'humble affairs of the': MCHL 1/1/14.

236 Even Jock Colville admitted: Colville, *The Churchillians*, p. 22.

236 He was a gifted: KH 2/1 Box 51.

237 More than anything, though: Bonham-Carter, *Churchill as I Knew Him*, p. 392; Manchester and Reid, *Last Lion: Defender of the Realm*, p. 3; Halle, *Young Unpretender*, p. 125.

237 Winston tried his staff's: Gilbert, *Churchill*, vol. 7, *Road to Victory*, pp. 306, 358, 634.

237 'I am so happy': MCHL 5/1/109.

238 They sat with heads inches: Gilbert and Arnn, *Churchill Documents*, vol. 18, *One Continent Redeemed*, p. 327.

238 The sight of Randolph and: Moran, *Struggle for Survival*, p. 125.

238 But just as often: Colville, *Fringes of Power*, pp. 438–9, 445; Macmillan, *War Diaries*, pp. 163, 327, 331–3, 338; Gilbert, *Churchill*, vol. 7, *Road to Victory*, p. 608.

239 Winston still confided in: Pearson, *Citadel of the Heart*, p. 319.

239 Anthony Eden, who had: KH 2/1 Box 48.

239 An account by the: Halle, *Young Unpretender*, pp. 135–7.

240 After the 1942 landings: Brian Roberts, *Randolph*, p. 245; RDCH 10/20.

240 When Randolph wrote to: CHAR 20/102/8.

241 A solution came from: Halle, *Young Unpretender*, pp. 90, 96; Maclean, *Eastern Approaches*, p. 407.

241 Randolph landed by parachute: Winston S. Churchill, *Memories and Adventures*, p. 28.

241 With the invasion of: Gilbert, *Churchill*, vol. 7, *Road to Victory*, p. 775.

242 Over the course of the last: Hickman, *Churchill's Bodyguard*, p. 201; Gilbert and Arnn, *Churchill Documents*, vol. 18, *One Continent Redeemed*, p. 117; Channon, *Chips*, p. 351; Alanbrooke, *War Diaries*, p. 535; Gilbert, *Churchill*, vol. 7, *Road to Victory*, pp. 703, 753, 759.

242 Mary noted in early: MCHL 1/1/10.

243 Winston found time amid: CHAR 1/38.

244 Randolph was also on: RDCH 1/3/4; MCHL 5/1/109.

244 The partisan camp was: Brian Roberts, *Randolph*, pp. 253–62.

245 And then, as so: Gilbert, *Churchill*, vol. 7, *Road to Victory*, pp. 779–80.

Chapter 16: A Sorrow & a Mortification

247 In late June 1944: Halle, *Young Unpretender*, p. 46; Green, *Children of the Sun*, p. 397; RDCH 1/2/22; Waugh, *Letters*, p. 166; Brian Roberts, *Randolph*, p. 264; Hastings, *Evelyn Waugh*, p. 463; Nicolson, *Diaries and Letters 1939–1945*, p. 384.

248 Winston was also engaged: Gilbert, *Churchill*, vol. 7, *Road to Victory*, pp. 832–4.

248 Pamela wrote to Averell: PH Papers 22.

249 On 25 June, Winston: Macmillan, *War Diaries*, p. 474.

249 A brief attempt the: Gilbert and Arnn, *Churchill Documents*, vol. 18, *One Continent Redeemed*, p. 1311; CHAR 1/381/35–37.

250 His fundamentally uncomplex emotional: Charmley, *End of Glory*, p. 300; Pearson, *Citadel of the Heart*, pp. 321, 348; Soames, *Clementine Churchill*, p. 454.

250 Winston adored Randolph's son: Winston S. Churchill, *Memories and Adventures*, p. 31.

251 On 26 June, Harold: Macmillan, *War Diaries*, pp. 474–5.

251 That night, Randolph arrived: Lockhart, *Diaries*, vol. 2, p. 352; Sally Bedell Smith, *Reflected Glory*, pp. 117, 121; Buczacki, *My Darling Mr Asquith*, p. 356; PH Papers 22.

251 News crept out: Lockhart, *Diaries*, vol. 2, p. 354.

252 Randolph's sisters had all: MCHL 1/1/1; MCHL 5/1/110; MCHL 1/1/12.

252 On 27 June, Winston: CHAR 1/381/39–41.

253 They had agreed that: PH Papers 22; RDCH 1/3/4.

254 Twelve days later: Macmillan, *War Diaries*, p. 481; Hastings, *Evelyn Waugh*, p. 467; Waugh, *Diaries*, p. 573; Brian Roberts, *Randolph*, pp. 268–70; CHAR 20/150/48–49.

255 'On this day of': DIAC 1/1/23.

255 Clementine was unsure whether: MCHL 5/1/110.

255 She was, she recorded: MCHL 1/1/12.

255 Winston arrived on the: Brian Roberts, *Randolph*, pp. 270–1; Gilbert, *Churchill*, vol. 7, *Road to Victory*, p. 888.

255 Father and son started: MCHL 5/1/110.

256 Randolph's brush with death: Leslie, *Cousin Randolph*, p. 93.

257 With others he was: Brian Roberts, *Randolph*, p. 271; Halle, *Young Unpretender*, p. 87.

257 Randolph and Evelyn eventually: Hastings, *Evelyn Waugh*, pp. 468–74; Waugh, *Diaries*, pp. 578–81; Waugh, *Letters*, pp. 187–8; Brian Roberts, *Randolph*, pp. 272–6; Leslie, *Cousin Randolph*, pp. 93–4, 96, 101.

257 In theory their responsibilities: Winston S. Churchill, *His Father's Son*, p. 256.

258 Quite why Randolph thought: Hastings, *Evelyn Waugh*, p. 1.

259 Robert Bruce Lockhart came: Nicolson, *Diaries and Letters 1939–1945*, p. 397.

259 Randolph was delighted by: Waugh, *Diaries*, pp. 582–5; Waugh, *Letters*, p. 189; Hastings, *Evelyn Waugh*, p. 466.

260 Once again, its trigger: Sykes, *Evelyn Waugh*, p. 267; Leslie, *Cousin Randolph*, pp. 96–7; RDCH 1/2/22.

261 Pamela had kept at: PH Papers 22.

262 On 12 December: PH Papers 2; PH Papers 22; MCHL 1/1/9.

Chapter 17: Finis

263 On 8 May 1945: Manchester and Reid, *Last Lion: Defender of the Realm*, pp. 926–7; Gilbert, *Churchill*, vol. 7, *Road to Victory*, p. 1345; Pearson, *Citadel of the Heart*, p. 341.

263 The next day, though: MCHL 1/1/14.

263 During the last months: Nicolson, *Diaries and Letters 1939–1945*, p. 406; Hastings, *Evelyn Waugh*, p. 478; Halle, *Young Unpretender*, pp. 121–2; Leslie, *Cousin Randolph*, pp. 103–4.

264 The letters he wrote were: MCHL 5/1/118.

264 With the war in: PH Papers 22.

265 Pamela thought she knew: Sulzberger, *Last of the Giants*, p. 455.

265 Mary was pleasantly surprised: MCHL 1/1/14.

265 Staying once more in: RDCH 1/2/14; Colville, *Fringes of Power*, p. 567.

265 At the end of May: Winston S. Churchill, *Memories and Adventures*, p. 33.

265 Mostly, however, the two: Taylor et al., *Churchill: Four Faces and the Man*, pp. 12, 14, 39; Manchester, *Last Lion: Visions of Glory*, p. 26; Manchester and Reid, *Last Lion: Defender of the Realm*, pp. 619, 940–1.

267 Randolph was one of: Brian Roberts, *Randolph*, p. 283.

267 'You know I have': Nicolson, *Diaries and Letters 1939–1945*, p. 472.

267 'He is very low': MCHL 5/1/117.

267 By contrast, Randolph arrived: Brian Roberts, *Randolph*, pp. 281–6; Leslie, *Cousin Randolph*, p. 106.

268 This bullishness was shared: Manchester and Reid, *Last Lion: Defender of the Realm*, p. 943.

268 'He was very confident': MCHL 1/1/15.

268 That night, Winston too: MCHL 1/1/15; Soames, *Clementine Churchill*, pp. 425–6; Soames, *A Daughter's Tale*, pp. 356–7; Purnell, *First Lady*, p. 322; Cowles, *Winston Churchill*, p. 355; Charmley, *End of Glory*, p. 647.

270 There was time for: Sarah Churchill, *Thread in the Tapestry*, p. 86; Soames, *A Daughter's Tale*, pp. 361–2; Soames, *Clementine Churchill*, p. 426; MCHL 1/1/15; Manchester and Reid, *Last Lion: Defender of the Realm*, pp. 952–3.

272 'perching in film-starry': MCHL 1/1/15.

272 It was only after Mary: MCHL 5/1/117.

272 Winston had slept soundly: Pearson, *Citadel of the Heart*, p. 344.

272 His friends urged him: Cowles, *Winston Churchill*, p. 56.

272 Randolph was rudderless too: Winston S. Churchill, *Memories and Adventures*, p. 35; Waugh, *Diaries*, pp. 629–30; Waugh, *Letters*, p. 210; Brian Roberts, *Randolph*, pp. 287, 289.

274 'My Darling please ask': MCHL 1/1/117.

274 A few weeks later: Soames, *A Daughter's Tale*, p. 362; Soames, *Clementine Churchill*, p. 254; KH 2/1 Box 48; Winston S. Churchill, *His Father's Son*, p. 472.

Chapter 18: A Walking Volcano

275 'We'd all sort of': RDCH 10/19.

275 Sir Colin Coote remembered: KH 2/1 Box 47.

275 'I wish I knew': RDCH 1/3/1.

276 By 1947, Winston was: Manchester and Reid, *Last Lion: Defender of the Realm*, pp. 968–70; Manchester, *Last Lion: Alone*, p. 4; Lough, *No More Champagne*, pp. 317, 321, 328–9, 339, 340, 341.

277 'I hope that one': CHUR/1/42.

277 Chips Channon remembered: Channon, *Chips*, p. 440.

277 But he could no: Soames, *Clementine Churchill*, p. 453; CHUR 1/51.

278 Sarah, who in between making: CHUR/1/42.

278 Randolph was still bitter: Purnell, *First Lady*, p. 331.

278 These in turn led: Moran, *Struggle for Survival*, p. 314.

278 'Every time we meet': Lovell, *The Churchills*, p. 496.

278 It was hard for Winston: Purnell, *First Lady*, p. 330; Lough, *No More Champagne*, pp. 341, 357; Pearson, *Citadel of the Heart*, pp. 352, 396; Colville, *Fringes of Power*, p. 627; Montague Browne, *Long Sunset*, pp. 151–2.

280 Randolph's divorce had finally come: PH Papers 33.

280 Randolph, who had always: Leslie, *Cousin Randolph*, p. 115.

281 Even those, like Beaverbrook : Lockhart, *Diaries*, vol. 2, p. 703.

281 Although pursued by a: Winston S. Churchill, *His Father's Son*, p. 278; Winston S. Churchill, *Memories and Adventures*, p. 49; Waugh, *Diaries*, p. 676; Pearson, *Citadel of the Heart*, p. 350.

281 And although Randolph was: Leslie, *Cousin Randolph*, p. 44.

281 As always, Randolph was: RDCH 1/2/2.

282 His cousin Nancy Mitford: Hastings, *Nancy Mitford*, pp. 164–5.

282 In the years after the war: RDCH 1/3/6.

282 When invited to make: Leslie, *Cousin Randolph*, p. 112.

282 An altercation with an: Brian Roberts, *Randolph*, p. 292.

282 On a visit to the: Winston S. Churchill, *His Father's Son*, p. 373.

283 Isaiah Berlin, whose fondness: Halle, *Young Unpretender*, p. 278.

283 'exactly 3 times as fat': Waugh, *Letters*, p. 276.

283 Nevertheless, the new world: Pearson, *Citadel of the Heart*, p. 350.

283 In February 1947, alone: CHUR 1/42.

285 Randolph swapped his unhappy: Brian Roberts, *Randolph*, pp. 297–8; Hardwick, *Clementine Churchill*, p. 299; Pearson, *Citadel of the Heart*, p. 360.

285 'I do not know the': RDCH 1/2/22.

286 By the time he: Pearson, *Citadel of the Heart*, p. 346.

286 Before long, Winston was: Moran, *Struggle for Survival*, p. 313.

Chapter 19: I Love You More Than Any
Man or Woman I Have Ever Met

287 In the days leading up to Winston's: CHUR 1/51.

287 Randolph's efforts were, however: Winston S. Churchill, *Memories and Adventures*, pp. 71–3; RDCH 10/20; KH 2/1 Box 48; Waugh, *Letters*, p. 358.

288 'It's a big job': Moran, *Struggle for Survival*, p. 342.

289 Slowly, the seventy-seven-year-old: Manchester and Reid, *Last Lion: Defender of the Realm*, p. 1016.

290 Randolph wrote to congratulate: CHUR 1/51.

290 He did discover some: KH 2/1 Box 51.

290 His marriage was in: RDCH 1/3/10.

290 More and more often: Sulzberger, *Last of the Giants*, p. 115.

291 Randolph did not think: CHUR 1/51.

291 As time went on, Winston: Montague Browne, *Long Sunset*, p. 148; Colville, *The Churchillians*, p. 24.

291 Winston preferred to take: MCHL 1/1/24.

291 Winston was no longer: Colville, *The Churchillians*, p. 24; CHUR 1/51.

292 Winston's personal secretary: Montague Browne, *Long Sunset*, pp. 147–9.

292 On three different occasions: Taylor et al., *Churchill: Four Faces and the Man*, pp. 214–15.

293 During one of Randolph's: RDCH 10/19.

293 His happiness did not: CHUR 1/51.

295 There were some days: MCHL 5/1/160; RDCH 1/3/14; RDCH 1/3/17; MCHL 1/1/24.

295 Randolph routinely sent: RDCH 1/3/16; Moran, *Struggle for Survival*, p. 340.

295 The psychoanalyst Rupert Strong: KH 2/1 Box 49.

296 James Lees-Milne noted: Lees-Milne, *Diaries 1942–1954*, p. 475.

297 'Very, very old, tragically': Nicolson, *Diaries and Letters 1945–1962*, p. 212; Pearson, *Citadel of the Heart*, p. 362.

297 A combination of age: Moran, *Struggle for Survival*, p. 418.

297 'the vast dullness of': Boothby, *Recollections of a Rebel*, p. 243; Moran, *Struggle for Survival*, p. 517.

297 It was not just that he was: Moran, *Struggle for Survival*, pp. 498, 499, 518; Colville, *Fringes of Power*, pp. 596, 612.

297 What he still enjoyed: Moran, *Struggle for Survival*, pp. 328, 355, 357; Green, *Children of the Sun*, p. 410.

298 'I don't think we've': Moran, *Struggle for Survival*, p. 526.

298 Winston had talked often: Lockhart, *Diaries*, vol. 2, p. 730; Cowles, *Winston Churchill*, p. 360; Colville, *The Churchillians*, p. 170; Eden, *Memoir*, pp. 116, 169; MCHL 5/1/168; RDCH 1/3/13; RDCH 8/1/2; RDCH 10/20.

300 Clementine had been ground: Soames, *Clementine Churchill*, pp. 482–3.

300 His last weeks in: MCHL 1/1/27; Moran, *Struggle for Survival*, p. 649.

301 On the night before the handover: Hardwick, *Clementine Churchill*, p. 315; Eden, *Memoir*, p. 199.

301 The next morning, Winston woke: Moran, *Struggle for Survival*, p. 649; MCHL 5/1/168.

302 Randolph went, as usual: RDCH 1/3/13.

302 The ebullience Winston displayed: Soames, *Clementine Churchill*, p. 496; MCHL 1/1/27.

302 He was unsettled: Moran, *Struggle for Survival*, pp. 656, 665, 679.

302 Even the adulation: Howells, *Simply Churchill*, p. 46.

302 Randolph stayed with Winston: Winston S. Churchill, *His Father's Son*, p. 331.

303 Winston's resignation was not: Winston S. Churchill, *Memories and Adventures*, pp. 83–4, 237–8; Waugh, *Diaries*, p. 796; Halle, *Young Unpretender*, pp. 14, 272; Leslie, *Cousin Randolph*, p. 128; KH 2/1 Box 48.

304 In the end, Winston: RDCH 10/20.

304 Then came the evening: Waugh, *Letters*, p. 445; Waugh, *Diaries*, p. 731.

305 They had quarrelled hideously: Leslie, *Cousin Randolph*, p. 133; Brian Roberts, *Randolph*, pp. 315–16; MCHL 1/1/24.

305 'If you knew Randolph': KH 2/1 Box 50; KH 2/1 Box 51; RDCH 10/20; Brian Roberts, *Randolph*, p. 292; Halle, *Young Unpretender*, pp. 123, 155.

306 He burned through one hundred: Winston S. Churchill, *His Father's Son*, p. 389; Fleming, *Letters*, pp. 170, 207, 216, 251; KH 2/1 Box 48.

307 This was in large: Brian Roberts, *Randolph*, p. 356; Leslie, *Cousin Randolph*, pp. 150–2, 154; Winston S. Churchill, *His Father's Son*, p. 394; Pearson, *Citadel of the Heart*, p. 410.

308 On 12 September 1958: Howells, *Simply Churchill*, p. 29; RDCH 2/7; RDCH 1/3/17.

Chapter 20: He's Asked Me. He's Asked Me at Last

310 In February 1932: Randolph S. Churchill, *Churchill: Youth*, p. xix.

310 Bill Deakin absorbed: KH 2/1 Box 49; Pearson, *Citadel of the Heart*, p. 411.

311 Summoning as much delicacy: Montague Browne, *Long Sunset*, pp. 316–17; Leslie, *Cousin Randolph*, p. 131.

311 Norman McGowan, who started: McGowan, *My Years with Churchill*, pp. 41–2.

312 The first sign that: Lough, *No More Champagne*, p. 397; KH 2/1 Box 48.

312 'My dear Randolph': Winston S. Churchill, *His Father's Son*, p. 392.

313 On the day Randolph: Leslie, *Cousin Randolph*, p. 150.

313 Randolph had by now: KH 2/1 Box 48.

314 the sight of Randolph plotting: Eden, *Memoir*, p. 222.

314 It also made him: Lough, *No More Champagne*, p. 397; Winston S. Churchill, *His Father's Son*, pp. 405, 446.

315 Randolph's plan for the: WLFF 2/7; Brian Roberts, *Randolph*, pp. 344–5; Winston S. Churchill, *His Father's Son*, pp. 395–7, 414; KH 2/1 Box 47; KH 2/1 Box 48; RDCH 10/24; Halle, *Young Unpretender*, p. 170; Leslie, *Cousin Randolph*, pp. 156–7, 187, 189; Author interview with Jonathan Aitken, 6 July 2018; Aitken, *Heroes and Contemporaries*, p. 37.

317 At Stour, Randolph had: Author interview with Jonathan Aitken; Aitken, *Heroes and Contemporaries*, p. 34; Winston S. Churchill, *Memories and Adventures*, p. 53; MCHL 5/1/179; KH 2/1 Box 48.

319 Perhaps it was this: Montague Browne, *Long Sunset*, pp. 243, 245; Lough, *No More Champagne*, p. 385; McGowan, *My Years with Churchill*, p. 32.

320 Onassis treated the man: Moran, *Winston Churchill*, p. 767; McGowan, *My Years with Churchill*, p. 47; McGinty, *Churchill's Cigar*, p. 155; Lovell, *The Churchills*, p. 546; Howells, *Simply Churchill*, pp. 80–1; Nicolson, *Diaries and Letters 1945–1962*, p. 304; Montague Browne, *Long Sunset*, pp. 145, 256, 284, 312; Pearson, *Citadel of the Heart*, pp. 406–7.

321 The last decade had: Montague Browne, *Long Sunset*, p. xii; McGowan, *My Years with Churchill*, p. 32.

321 Instead he could be: Lees-Milne, *Mingled Measure*, p. 65; Howells, *Simply Churchill*, p. 144.

321 His skin had lost: Sulzberger, *Last of the Giants*, pp. 300–6, 541–2.

322 Sometimes he would try: Howells, *Simply Churchill*, pp. 151–2; Moran, *Struggle for Survival*, pp. 753–4.

322 To some people: Lees-Milne, *Mingled Measure*, p. 66; Montague Browne, *Long Sunset*, p. 220.

323 His trips on the: Howells, *Simply Churchill*, p. 46; Author interview with Jonathan Aitken.

323 Winston's son had come: Winston S. Churchill, *His Father's Son*, p. 436.

323 The trip had begun: Howells, *Simply Churchill*, p. 31; Manchester, *Last Lion: Visions of Glory*, p. 13.

324 Even at eighty-five: Howells, *Simply Churchill*, p. 47.

324 During the first few: Montague Browne, *Long Sunset*, pp. 298–301; Purnell, *First Lady*, pp. 347–8; Winston S. Churchill, *His Father's Son*, pp. 438–9.

325 Randolph told friends that: Sulzberger, *Last of the Giants*, p. 472.

325 In the summer of: Pearson, *Citadel of the Heart*, p. 421.

326 Sarah would sit with: Sarah Churchill, *Thread in the Tapestry*, p. 19; Soames, *Clementine Churchill*, p. 521.

326 On 11 January 1965: WLFF 2/5; Soames, *Clementine Churchill*, pp. 535–9; Moran, *Struggle for Survival*, p. 789; Leslie, *Cousin Randolph*, p. 179; Pearson, *Citadel of the Heart*, pp. 422–3; Brian Roberts, *Randolph*, p. 355.

328 He wanted desperately to: Winston S. Churchill, *His Father's Son*, pp. 479, 483; Jonathan Aitken interview; Leslie, *Cousin Randolph*, pp. 201, 204; Brian Roberts, *Randolph*, p. 363; KH 2/1 Box 48.

329 'That is the most': KH 2/1 Box 49.

330 One document in particular: Gilbert, *Churchill*, vol. 3, *Challenge of War*, p. 512.

330 'It's a monument to': KH 2/1 Box 48.

330 All of Franklin Roosevelt's: Collier and Horowitz, *The Roosevelts*, pp. 361–3; Roosevelt, *My Parents*, p. ix.

331 Stalin's children were even: Montefiore, *Stalin*, pp. 394–6; Sullivan, *Stalin's Daughter*, pp. 27, 60, 96, 99, 222, 230, 534.

331 'Demons seem to whisper': Montague Browne, *Long Sunset*, p. 302.

331 'strange capacity for making': Pearson, *Citadel of the Heart*, p. 93.

331 Winston was one of: McGowan, *My Years with Churchill*, pp. 40, 77.

332 'Towards the end': Winston S. Churchill, *His Father's Son*, pp. 86–7.

333 'grinning and dangling his watch': Channon, *Chips*, p. 459.

333 One thing remained true: Pearson, *Citadel of the Heart*, p. 389.

Select Bibliography

Archives

Churchill College, Cambridge

The Papers of Julian Amery
AMEJ 2/1/3

Churchill Archives
CHAR 1/172
CHAR 1/178
CHAR 1/199
CHAR 1/205
CHAR 1/214
CHAR 1/222
CHAR 1/226
CHAR 1/271
CHAR 1/285
CHAR 1/362
CHAR 1/369
CHAR 1/375
CHAR 1/381
CHAR 2/235
CHAR 20/33
CHAR 20/62
CHAR 20/65
CHAR 20/102
CHAR 20/150
CHAR 20/158
CHUR1/42
CHUR 1/51

The Papers of Sir John Colville
CHOH CLVL

The Papers of Lady Diana Cooper
DIAC 1/4/11
DIAC 1/1/23

The Papers of Lady Soames
CSCT 3/2
MCHL 1/1
MCHL 1/1/2
MCHL 1/1/3
MCHL 1/1/5
MCHL 1/1/6
MCHL 1/1/7
MCHL 1/1/8
MCHL 1/1/9
MCHL 1/1/10
MCHL 1/1/12
MCHL 1/1/14
MCHL 1/1/15
MCHL 1/1/24
MCHL 1/1/27
MCHL 1/59
MCHL 5/1/17
MCHL 5/1/66
MCHL 5/1/69
MCHL 5/1/80
MCHL 5/1/83
MCHL 5/1/84
MCHL 5/1/87
MCHL 5/1/109
MCHL 5/1/110
MCHL 5/1/117
MCHL 5/1/118
MCHL 5/1/160
MCHL 5/1/168
MCHL 5/1/179
MCHL 5/1/306
MCHL 5/175
MCHL 5/178
MCHL 5/8/52
MCHL 5/8/137

The Papers of Randolph Churchill
RDCH 1/2/13
RDCH 1/2/22
RDCH 1/2/37
RDCH 1/2/40
RDCH 1/2/42
RDCH 1/2/45
RDCH 1/2/46
RDCH 1/3/1
RDCH 1/3/2
RDCH 1/3/3
RDCH 1/3/4
RDCH 1/3/5
RDCH 1/3/6
RDCH 1/3/10
RDCH 1/3/13
RDCH 1/3/14
RDCH 1/3/16
RDCH 1/3/17
RDCH 2/1
RDCH 2/2
RDCH 2/7
RDCH 2/16
RDCH 4/12
RDCH 4/16
RDCH 8/1/1
RDCH 8/1/2
RDCH 8/1/4
RDCH 8/1/5
RDCH 8/1/11
RDCH 10/2
RDCH 10/4
RDCH 10/14/1
RDCH 10/19
RDCH 10/20
RDCH 10/21
RDCH 10/24
RDCH 10/25
RDCH 10/27
RDCH 10/28
RDCH 10/37
WLFF 2/5
WLFF 2/6
WLFF 2/7

John F. Kennedy Presidential Library, Boston, MA

Kay Halle Archives
KH 2/1 Box 47
KH 2/1 Box 48
KH 2/1 Box 50
KH 2/1 Box 51

Library of Congress, Washington, DC

Pamela Digby Churchill Hayward Harriman Papers
PH Papers 2
PH Papers 22
PH Papers 26
PH Papers 30
PH Papers 33

W. Averell Harriman Papers
WA Papers 3
WA Papers 4

Television Programmes and Websites

The Churchills, 1999
Churchill's Girl, 2006
Norwich, John Julius, 'The Jekyll and Hyde Nature of Randolph Churchill', Web of Stories, YouTube, 3 October 2018

Books

Aitken, Jonathan, *Heroes and Contemporaries*, Bloomsbury Continuum, 2007

Alanbrooke, Field Marshal Lord (ed. Alex Danche and Daniel Todman), *War Diaries, 1939–1945*, Weidenfeld & Nicolson, 2001

Asquith, Margot (ed. Eleanor and Michael Brock), *Margot Asquith's Great War Diary 1914–1916: The View from Downing Street*, Oxford University Press, 2014

Attenborough, Wilfred, *Churchill and the 'Black Dog' of Depression: Reassessing the Biographical Evidence of Psychological Disorder*, Palgrave Macmillan, 2014

Beaton, Cecil (ed. Richard Buckle), *Self Portrait with Friends: The Selected Diaries of Cecil Beaton*, Pimlico, 1991

Berlin, Isaiah, *Mr Churchill in 1940*, John Murray, 1964

Birkenhead, Frederick, *The Prof in Two Worlds: The Official Life of Professor F. A. Lindemann, Viscount Cherwell*, Collins, 1961

Birkenhead, Robin, *Churchill 1924–1940*, privately published, 1989

Bloch, Michael, *James Lees-Milne: The Life*, John Murray, 2009

Bonham-Carter, Violet, *Churchill as I Knew Him*, Eyre & Spottiswoode/Collins, 1965

Boothby, Robert, *I Fight to Live*, Gollancz, 1947

——, *Recollections of a Rebel*, Hutchinson, 1978

Boyle, Andrew, *Poor, Dear Brendan: The Quest for Brendan Bracken*, Hutchinson, 1974

Bracken, Brendan (ed. Richard Cockett), *My Dear Max: The Letters of Brendan Bracken to Lord Beaverbrook, 1925–1958*, Historians' Press, 1990

Buczacki, Stefan, *My Darling Mr Asquith: The Extraordinary Life and Times of Venetia Stanley*, Cato & Clarke, 2016

Chamberlain, Neville (ed. Robert Self), *The Neville Chamberlain Diary Letters*, Vol. 4, *The Downing Street Years, 1934–1940*, Ashgate, 2000

Channon, Henry (ed. Robert Rhodes James), *Chips: The Diaries of Sir Henry Channon*, Weidenfeld & Nicolson, 1967

Charmley, John, *Churchill: The End of Glory, A Political Biography*, Hodder & Stoughton, 1993

Churchill, Randolph S., *The Rise and Fall of Sir Anthony Eden*, MacGibbon & Kee, 1959

——, *Twenty-One Years*, Weidenfeld & Nicolson, 1965

——, *Winston S. Churchill: Youth 1874–1900*, Heinemann, 1966 (First volume of official biography; see Martin Gilbert for volumes 3–8)

——, *Winston S. Churchill: Young Statesman 1901–1914*, Heinemann, 1967 (Second volume of official biography)

Churchill, Sarah, *A Thread in the Tapestry*, André Deutsch, 1967

——, *Keep on Dancing: An Autobiography*, Weidenfeld & Nicolson, 1981

Churchill, Winston S., *Lord Randolph Churchill*, Macmillan, 1906

——, *A Roving Commission: My Early Life*, T. Butterworth, 1930

—— (ed. Jack Fishman), *If I Lived My Life Again*, W. H. Allen, 1974

——, *Memories and Adventures*, Weidenfeld & Nicolson, 1989

—— (ed. Emery Reves and Martin Gilbert), *Correspondence 1937–1964*, University of Texas Press, 1997

Churchill, Winston S., II, *His Father's Son: The Life of Randolph Churchill*, Weidenfeld & Nicolson, 1996

Collier, Peter, and Horowitz, David, *The Roosevelts: An American Saga*, André Deutsch, 1995

Colville, John, *The Churchillians*, Weidenfeld & Nicolson, 1981

——, *The Fringes of Power: Downing Street Diaries 1939–1955*, Weidenfeld & Nicolson, 2004

Cooper, Artemis, *Cairo in the War 1939–1940*, Hamish Hamilton, 1989

Cooper, Diana, *Trumpets from the Steep*, Rupert Hart-Davis, 1960

Cooper, Duff, *Old Men Forget: The Autobiography of Duff Cooper, Viscount Norwich*, Rupert Hart-Davis, 1954

Coward, Noël (ed. Graham Payn and Sheridan Morley), *The Noël Coward Diaries*, Weidenfeld & Nicolson, 1982

Cowles, Virginia, *Looking for Trouble*, Hamish Hamilton, 1941

——, *Winston Churchill: The Era and the Man*, Hamish Hamilton, 1953

De Courcy, Anne, *Diana Mitford*, Chatto & Windus, 2003

Eden, Clarissa (ed. Cate Haste), *A Memoir: From Churchill to Eden*, Weidenfeld & Nicolson, 2007

Fleming, Ann (ed. Mark Amory), *The Letters of Ann Fleming*, Collins Harvill, 1985

Gilbert, Martin, *Winston S. Churchill*, Vol. 3, *The Challenge of War, 1914–1916*, Heinemann, 1971

——, *Winston S. Churchill*, Vol. 4, *The Stricken World, 1917–1922*, Heinemann, 1975

——, *Winston S. Churchill*, Vol. 5, *Prophet of Truth, 1922–1939*, Heinemann, 1979

——, *Winston S. Churchill*, Vol. 6, *Finest Hour, 1939–1941*, Heinemann, 1983

——, *Winston S. Churchill*, Vol. 7, *Road to Victory, 1941–1945*, Heinemann, 1986

——, *Winston S. Churchill*, Vol. 8, *Never Despair, 1945–1965*, Heinemann, 1988

——, *In Search of Churchill: A Historian's Journey*, HarperCollins, 1994

——, *Continue to Pester, Nag and Bite: Churchill's War Leadership*, Pimlico, 2004

Gilbert, Martin (ed.), *The Churchill Documents*, Vol. 11, *The Exchequer Years, 1922–1929*, Heinemann, 1979

——, *The Churchill Documents*, Vol. 12, *The Wilderness Years, 1929–1935*, Heinemann, 1981

——, *The Churchill Documents*, Vol. 13, *The Coming of War, 1936–1939*, Heinemann, 1982

——, *The Churchill Documents*, Vol. 17, *Testing Times, 1942*, Hillsdale College Press, 2014

——, *The Churchill War Papers*, Vol. 1, *At the Admiralty, September 1939–May 1940*, Heinemann, 1993

——, *The Churchill War Papers*, Vol. 2, *Never Surrender, May 1940–December 1940*, Heinemann, 1994

——, *The Churchill War Papers*, Vol. 3, *The Ever-Widening War, 1941*, Heinemann, 2000

Gilbert, Martin, and Arnn, Larry P. (ed.), *The Churchill Documents*, Vol. 18, *One Continent Redeemed, January–August 1943*, Hillsdale College Press, 2015

——, *The Churchill Documents*, Vol. 19, *Fateful Questions, September 1943–April 1944*, Hillsdale College Press, 2017

——, *The Churchill Documents*, Vol. 20, *Normandy and Beyond, May–December 1944*, Hillsdale College Press, 2018

——, *The Churchill Documents*, Vol. 21, *The Shadows of Victory, January–July 1945*, Hillsdale College Press, 2019

Green, Martin, *Children of the Sun: A Narrative of 'Decadence' in England after 1918*, Constable, 1977

Halle, Kay (ed.), *Randolph Churchill, the Young Unpretender: Essays by His Friends*, Heinemann, 1971

Hardwick, Joan, *Clementine Churchill: The Private Life of a Public Figure*, John Murray, 1997

Harriman, W. Averell, and Abel, Elie, *Special Envoy to Churchill and Stalin, 1941–1946*, Random House, 1975

Hastings, Selina, *Nancy Mitford: A Biography*, Hamish Hamilton, 1985

——, *Evelyn Waugh: A Biography*, Sinclair-Stevenson, 1994

Hickman, Tom, *Churchill's Bodyguard*, Headline, 2006

Hough, Richard, *Winston and Clementine: The Triumph of the Churchills*, Bantam Press, 1990

Howells, Roy, *Simply Churchill*, Robert Hale, 1965

James, Edward (ed. George Melly), *Swans Reflecting Elephants: My Early Years*, Weidenfeld & Nicolson, 1982

Jenkins, Roy, *Churchill*, Macmillan, 2001

Jones, Thomas (ed. Keith Middlemas), *Whitehall Diary*, 3 vols, Oxford University Press, 1969

Kennedy, Kate, and Lee, Hermione (ed.), *Lives of Houses*, Princeton University Press, 2020

Lees-Milne, James, *A Mingled Measure: Diaries 1953–1972*, John Murray, 1994

——, *Ancestral Voices: Diaries 1942–1945*, John Murray, 1998

——, *Another Self*, John Murray, 1998

——, *Through Wood and Dale: Diaries 1975–1978*, John Murray, 1998

—— (ed. Michael Bloch), *Holy Dread: Diaries 1982–1984*, John Murray, 2001

——, *Beneath a Waning Moon: Diaries 1985–1987*, John Murray, 2003

——, *Diaries 1942–1954*, John Murray, 2006

Leslie, Anita, *Cousin Randolph*, Hutchinson, 1985

Lloyd George, Robert, *David & Winston: How a Friendship Changed History*, John Murray, 2005

Lockhart, Robert Bruce (ed. Kenneth Young), *The Diaries of Sir Robert Bruce Lockhart*, Vol. 1, *1915–1938*, Macmillan, 1973

——, *The Diaries of Sir Robert Bruce Lockhart*, Vol. 2, *1939–1965*, 1980

Lough, David A., *No More Champagne: Churchill and His Money*, Head of Zeus, 2015

Lovell, Mary S., *The Churchills: A Family at the Heart of History*, Little, Brown, 2011

McGinty, Stephen, *Churchill's Cigar*, Macmillan, 2007

McGowan, Norman, *My Years with Churchill*, Souvenir Press, 1958

Macintyre, Ben, *SAS: Rogue Heroes – The Authorized Wartime History from the Secret SAS Archives*, Viking, 2016

Maclean, Fitzroy, *Eastern Approaches*, Jonathan Cape, 1949

Macmillan, Harold, *War Diaries: Politics and War in the Mediterranean, January 1943– May 1945*, Macmillan, 1984

Maisky, Ivan, *Memoirs of a Soviet Ambassador: The War, 1939–1943*, Hutchinson, 1967

—— (ed. Gabriel Gorodetsky, trans. Tatiana Sorokina and Oliver Ready), *The*

Maisky Diaries: Red Ambassador to the Court of St James's, 1932–1943, Yale University Press, 2015

Manchester, William, *The Last Lion, William Spencer Churchill: Visions of Glory, 1874–1932*, Michael Joseph, 1983

——, *The Last Lion, William Spencer Churchill: Alone, 1932–1940*, Michael Joseph, 1988

——, and Reid, Paul, *The Last Lion, William Spencer Churchill: Defender of the Realm, 1940–1965*, Little, Brown, 2012

Montague Browne, Anthony, *Long Sunset: Memoirs of Winston Churchill's Last Private Secretary*, Cassell, 1995

Montefiore, Simon Sebag, *Stalin: The Court of the Red Tsar*, Weidenfeld & Nicolson, 2003

Moran, Lord, *Winston Churchill: The Struggle for Survival, 1940–1965*, Constable, 1966

Morris, Jan, *Fisher's Face*, Viking, 1995

Mosley, Charlotte (ed.), *The Mitfords: Letters Between Six Sisters*, Fourth Estate, 2007

Mosley, Diana, *A Life of Contrasts: The Autobiography of Diana Mosley*, Hamish Hamilton, 1977

Mosley, Nicholas, *Rules of the Game: Sir Oswald and Cynthia Mosley, 1896–1933*, Secker & Warburg, 1982

——, *Beyond the Pale: Sir Oswald Mosley and Family, 1933–1980*, Secker & Warburg, 1983

Mosley, Oswald, *My Life*, Nelson, 1968

Nicolson, Harold (ed. Nigel Nicolson), *Diaries and Letters 1930–1939*, Collins, 1967

——, *Diaries and Letters 1939–1945*, Collins, 1967

——, *Diaries and Letters 1945–1962*, Collins, 1968

Ogden, Christopher, *Life of the Party: The Biography of Pamela Digby Churchill Hayward Harriman*, Little, Brown, 1994

Pearson, John, *Citadel of the Heart: Winston and the Churchill Dynasty*, Macmillan, 1991

Profumo, David, *Bringing the House Down: A Family Memoir*, John Murray, 2006

Purnell, Sonia, *First Lady: The Life and Wars of Clementine Churchill*, Aurum Press, 2015

Rhodes James, Robert, *Bob Boothby: A Portrait*, Hodder & Stoughton, 1991

Roberts, Andrew, *Churchill: Walking with Destiny*, Allen Lane, 2018

Roberts, Brian, *Randolph: A Study of Churchill's Son*, Hamish Hamilton, 1984

Roosevelt, James, *My Parents: A Differing View*, W. H. Allen, 1977

Skidelsky, Robert, *Oswald Mosley*, Macmillan, 1975

Smith, Frederick, *F. E.: The Life of F. E. Smith, First Earl of Birkenhead*, Eyre & Spottiswoode, 1960

Smith, Sally Bedell, *Reflected Glory: The Life of Pamela Churchill Harriman*, Simon & Schuster, 1996

Soames, Mary, *Clementine Churchill: The Biography of a Marriage*, Doubleday, 2002

——, *A Daughter's Tale: The Memoir of Winston and Clementine Churchill's Youngest Daughter*, Doubleday, 2011

—— (ed.), *Speaking for Themselves: The Personal Letters of Winston and Clementine Churchill*, Doubleday, 1998

Stelzer, Cita, *Dinner with Churchill: Policy-Making at the Dinner Table*, Short Books, 2011

Stevenson, Frances (ed. A. J. P. Taylor), *Lloyd George: A Diary*, Hutchinson, 1971

Sullivan, Rosemary, *Stalin's Daughter: The Extraordinary and Tumultuous Life of Svetlana Alliluyeva*, Fourth Estate, 2015

Sulzberger, C. L., *Last of the Giants*, Weidenfeld & Nicolson, 1972

Sykes, Christopher, *Evelyn Waugh: A Biography*, Collins, 1975

Taylor, A. J. P., Rhodes James, Robert, Plumb, J. H., Storr, Anthony, and Liddell Hart, B. H., *Churchill: Four Faces and the Man*, Allen Lane, 1969

Thompson, Laura, *Life in a Cold Climate: Nancy Mitford, The Biography*, Review, 2003

Waugh, Evelyn (ed. Michael Davie), *The Diaries of Evelyn Waugh*, Weidenfeld & Nicolson, 1976

—— (ed. Mark Amory), *The Letters of Evelyn Waugh*, Weidenfeld & Nicolson, 1980

——, and Cooper, Diana (ed. Artemis Cooper), *Mr Wu and Mrs Stitch: The Letters of Evelyn Waugh and Diana Cooper*, Hodder & Stoughton, 1991

Index

RSC refers to Randolph Churchill; WSC refers to Winston Churchill.
Page numbers in italics denote illustrations.

014391688 X